ATHENS FROM ALEXANDER TO ANTONY

ATHENS
FROM
ALEXANDER
TO
ANTONY

———

Christian Habicht

TRANSLATED BY
DEBORAH LUCAS SCHNEIDER

HARVARD UNIVERSITY PRESS
Cambridge, Massachusetts
London, England
1997

Originally published in 1995 as *Athen. Die Geschichte der Stadt in hellenistischer Zeit,*
Verlag C. H. Beck, Munich

Publication of this volume was assisted by a grant from Inter Nationes.

Library of Congress Cataloging-in-Publication Data

Habicht, Christian.
[Athen. English]
Athens from Alexander to Antony / Christian Habicht ; translated
by Deborah Lucas Schneider.
p. cm.
Includes bibliographical references and index.
ISBN 0-674-05111-4
1. Athens (Greece)—History. 2. Hellenism. I. Title.
DF285.H313 1997
938′.5—dc21 97-5180
CIP

PREFACE

This book is a synthesis of the author's earlier and more specialized studies. It was written with the aim of making those studies accessible to a wider audience without compromising scholarly standards. Since the surviving narrative sources for the Hellenistic era are quite inadequate, no coherent account of events can be presented. On the other hand, the evidence from inscriptions and coins is much richer than for earlier periods and illuminates important developments and areas of public life in unprecedented ways. With Athens as its model, the book aims to show how, after the death of Alexander the Great, the Greek cities strugggled to keep their own in a world drastically changed by the appearance of major powers. Successes and setbacks followed one another, as did times of independence and times of foreign domination. Some cities, such as Corinth, were razed by one of the great powers, while others, Athens among them, succeeded in surviving as vital social organisms, despite considerable loss of political clout. The epigraph from Horace expresses what Athens meant to the best of her conquerors.

The book contains only minor changes from the German edition of 1995; most noteworthy of these are revisions of calendar dates provided by Professor John D. Morgan of the University of Delaware, to whom I am grateful. More importantly, his work on the Athenian calendar and on the chronology of archons of the period will result in numerous changes of accepted archon-years. Dr. Morgan kept me informed and even authorized me to make his findings known. But since he has not yet published his study, I find that difficult to do. A short note in the *American Journal of Archaeology* 100 (1996) 395 reveals his most important result, in accordance with the rule mentioned by Plato, *Laws* 767C, that the new year began with the new moon after the summer solstice, there was a nineteen-year cycle of twelve ordinary and seven intercalary years, following each other in fixed order. If rigorously observed (as seems to have been the case), the character of every single year, whether ordinary or intercalary, is determined a priori. This, in turn, requires the shift of a number of accepted archon dates, for instance, downdating most of the archons from around 240 to 200 by one year. As a consequence, a number of dates in this book will have to be revised, and while these revisions will rarely seriously affect the sequence of events as told, I would have preferred, had circumstances allowed, to have made full use of Dr. Morgan's work.

I am very grateful to Julia Bernheim, who typed and proofread the manuscript and contributed much to the final version. I am also deeply obliged to Deborah Lucas Schneider, who ably translated the book from the German and made me aware of a number of errors. To work with both was always pleasant and stimulating. Harvard University Press did everything in its power to make this book conform to its high standards. I am also grateful to all the people, too numerous to mention here, who have helped this project along in many discussions and by sending me copies of their own work. Any imperfections that remain are my responsibility alone.

CONTENTS

Romae nutriri mihi contigit atque doceri . . .
adiecere bonae paulo plus artis Athenae

I had the good luck to be educated at Rome . . .
Amiable Athens carried me further along.

Horace, *Epistles* 2.2.41 and 43,
translated by Smith Palmer Bovie

Introduction

More than eighty years have passed since William Scott Ferguson published the last account of Athens in the postclassical period, in his excellent book *Hellenistic Athens*. Since then many new sources have been discovered and new insights gained, creating the need for a new account. The reasons why such a history has nonetheless remained lacking are not difficult to discover, however. The interest of scholars has always been drawn first and foremost to the events of the fifth and fourth centuries B.C., the period when Athenian power and civilization were at their height: the city's defense against Persian attack, the creation of an Athenian empire, competition with Sparta for hegemony over the rest of Greece, the blossoming of Athenian culture in the age of Pericles, and the rise of democracy. In studying the period after the catastrophe of 404, historians have been fascinated by Athens' resurgence, the founding of the second Naval Confederacy, the further development of democracy, and finally the struggle against domination by King Philip of Macedon.

The second reason for the neglect of the postclassical era lies in the nature of the source material: it is not only much scantier than for the classical age, but also so fragmented that it is extremely difficult to gain an overview of the entire corpus of texts. Longer texts by individual authors are lacking almost entirely; the available sources tend to be limited to inscriptions in varying states of preservation. Fortunately far more of them have survived from the postclassical period than from earlier epochs, but their publication has been scattered in countless different works. Such inscriptions also require scholars to take a different approach; they cannot be read and interpreted in the same way as

1

the complete, coherent text of an ancient historian who intended his work for future generations as well as his own. A student of the postclassical period must spend years acquiring familiarity with the sources, and the learning process is never complete: new inscriptions are discovered almost daily, requiring us constantly to round out and adjust our picture of the age.

The gaps in the sources and the fortuitous nature of their preservation make it impossible to frame a connected narrative history of Athens in the 300 years from Alexander the Great to Antony and Octavian, even in bare outline. Yet the inscriptions that have survived can often provide detailed insights into the workings of the state. Many aspects of public life in which every adult male citizen actively participated are better documented than for earlier times, such as the membership and actions of the Council and its committees, the celebration of great festivals with their literary and athletic contests, the activities of the ephebes, or life in Attic garrisons. The most lasting impression produced by a study of the inscriptions is that of a community regulating its affairs in exemplary fashion. Even if Athens was not always a sovereign power, and often had to follow the dictates of Macedonia, and later Rome, in foreign policy, the Athenians never relinquished control of their own internal affairs. They kept them in admirably good order, and the institutional framework within which they did so remained remarkably stable. Thus, for example, the very detailed records of resolutions passed by each Assembly looked in Augustus' time precisely as they had 300 years earlier; only the names and dates varied.[1] Such continuity over a period that, in American terms, would reach far back into colonial times is no mere matter of form; it reflects a general will to preserve procedural norms that had proven effective, such as the daily rotation of the president of the Assembly, the monthly rotation of the executive committee of the Council, the annual rotation of the secretary, the responsibility of the introducer of a motion for his bill, and the responsibility of the nine *proedroi* (presiding officers) for the motions they brought to a vote.

Evidence of this orderly administration of affairs, which the citizenry of Athens took pains to preserve, has survived in a variety of forms. Among them are lists, chiseled in stone, of the 500 councillors of a

---

1. The wording of the prescript of *IG* VII.4253, from 331, corresponds exactly to that of *SEG* 30.93, from 20 B.C.

given year[2] and lists containing the names of all 50 councillors of the tribe that took its turn as the Council's executive committee for a month every year.[3] Evidence exists in the form of hundreds of inscribed lead tablets from the Council's annual inspection of the cavalry corps and valuation of individual horses.[4] For a span of 120 years we possess the whole series of "new style" silver coins issued annually, inscribed with the symbol of the year, the names of the two magistrates in charge of the mint, and the month of issue.[5] Further signs of this continuity can be found in the fact that for more than 150 years the office of public herald was filled by members of one family,[6] and that the two highest priesthoods of the Eleusinian Mysteries, the *hierophantes* and the *daduchos,* remained within two clans for centuries (the Eumolpidae and the Kerykes respectively).[7] Whereas foreign states frequently called upon Athenian citizens to act as judges or arbitrators, the Athenian judicial system itself never needed outsiders to guarantee impartial decisions; in this respect Athens and Rhodes, the other large republic with an exemplary administration, contrasted favorably with almost all the remaining Greek states.[8] These two states were sufficiently confident of their own power to be able to dispense with asking important Romans to advance their interests in the Senate and the higher ranks of Roman society.[9]

But as competently as the city may have regulated its internal affairs, its position in the larger world was usually precarious. With his superior military forces, Philip II of Macedon subdued the majority of Greek states and deprived them of their independence. When new monarchies arose to replace Alexander's former empire, the situation did not fundamentally change, except that occasionally, under favorable circumstances, some states were able to play the rival empires against one another and regain their freedom. Athens managed it in 287 and again

2. For the roster of the year 336/5 (*Agora* XV.42), almost all 250 names of the 5 tribes that have been preserved are still legible, and for other lists, extensive portions of all 10 tribes (or all 12 from the year 307 on; *Agora* XV.43, 61, 62, 72).

3. They are *Agora* XV.44, 85, 86, 89, 130, 137, 194, 206, 212, 214.

4. See Chapter 6 at note 41.

5. See Chapter 9 following note 79.

6. B. D. Meritt and J. S. Traill, *Agora* XV.14–15 (where certain data are now in need of correction).

7. Clinton, *Officials.*

8. L. Robert, "Xenion," *Festschrift P. I. Zepos* (Athens 1973) 778 (= *OMS* 5.140).

9. J.-L. Ferrary, *Rapports préliminaires (10th International Conference on Greek and Latin Epigraphy)* (Nîmes 1992) 80.

in 229. The only Greek states to remain permanently independent after Alexander's death, however, were Rhodes and the Aetolian League. Athens repeatedly received support from the Ptolemaic empire until the closing years of the third century, but this was not always sufficient to guarantee the city's independence from Macedonia.

The decline of the Ptolemaic dynasty's power and a renewed threat from Macedonia led Athens to call upon Rome for help in the year 200. This was a fateful step, for even though the Senate had already decided to go to war against Macedonia for its own separate reasons and the Romans did not send their army to Greece on Athens' account, they could later point out that the Athenians had invited them. In the following period Athens adopted Rome's political line so readily that the city was soon allied with Rome against other Greeks.[10]

Thus from the late third century on Athens' policies were opportunistic and based entirely upon self-interest. Not long before, sometime between 270 and 260, the city had led a coalition in a war against the Macedonian king Antigonus, thereby serving the interests of other Greek states as well as its own. The unfavorable outcome of this war made a change of policy seem advisable. Thirty years later, when the liberation of 229 made an independent policy possible once again, its adherence to pure self-interest became obvious and was deplored by Polybius.[11]

Such a course may have brought little recognition to the citizens of Athens, but it was realistic, and furthered peace both at home and abroad. Avoidance of major wars lengthened the life expectancy of citizens and improved the quality of life for the entire population of Attica.

Nothing justifies the occasional claim that political participation by Athenian citizens declined in the Hellenistic age. The history of Athens did not end with its military defeats by the armies of Macedonia. Even after these defeats the administration of justice and official cults, the provision of food supplies, the regulation of finances and all the other areas of government administration remained the exclusive responsibility of the citizens of Athens. When in times of independence foreign affairs were added to these tasks, there was certainly enough business

---

10. Nabis of Sparta, the Aetolian League, the Greek allies of King Perseus, the Achaean League.

11. Polybius 5.106.6–8.

at hand to require that the citizenry continue to participate actively in the running of the state. The Assembly met at least thirty-six times a year, and the Council met daily except on important holidays. The list of jurymen, revised annually, continued to carry the names of 6,000 citizens; from this list juries were chosen by lot for duty in the various courts, as needed for each trial, and sometimes consisted of more than 1,500 members. For the Assembly to pass certain resolutions, such as the relatively frequent grants of Athenian citizenship to foreigners, the law required 6,000 voting members to be present, and the evidence makes it virtually certain that this quorum was reached without difficulty at most sessions. The number 6,000 symbolizes the entire body of citizens. When the case demanded a quorum, it was not settled by the usual show of hands, but by secret balloting in which citizens recorded their votes on potsherds.[12]

Throughout the three centuries of the Hellenistic age the city retained its role as a leader in intellectual life and the arts. There was only one area in which Athenian achievements were surpassed by the community of scholars assembled at the Museum in Alexandria by the Ptolemaic rulers of Egypt: the Alexandrians dominated the new field of philology—the study, criticism, and interpretation of classical texts—until the king banished all intellectuals from Egypt in 145 B.C. After the two schools of Epicurus and Zeno, both founded toward the end of the fourth century, began to rival the older schools of Plato and Aristotle, Athenian cultivation of philosophy was unparalleled in the ancient world, in both its attainments and its scope.

12. P. Gauthier, *Cahiers du Centre Glotz* 1 (1990) 77–84.

O N E

In the Shadow of Macedonian Expansion
(338–323)

1. Political Leaders

The defeat which Philip II of Macedonia, through his effective generalship and strong Macedonian phalanx, inflicted on the Athenians and their Theban allies in the summer of 338 at Chaeronea in Boeotia left both Greek powers severely weakened and in a state of shock. Their ensuing fate, however, was quite different. Only a few years later the Thebans reacted with a spontaneous uprising to the false news that Alexander, the young Macedonian king, had died; they attempted to shake off the foreign occupation that had been imposed on them, and paid a terrible price when their city was sacked and utterly destroyed in the late summer of 335. The leading politicians in Athens, by contrast, managed to reconcile their differences and agree on a more prudent policy. They refrained—if only by the slimmest of margins—from joining the Thebans in their rash venture, and abstained as well from the rebellion led four years later by Agis of Sparta, which collapsed when Agis was defeated at Megalopolis in Arcadia in the spring of 330 by Antipater, Alexander's viceroy in Europe.

Athens also profited during these fifteen years from the fact that even during Philip's lifetime the focus of political and military activity began to shift away from the Greek mainland, first to Asia Minor in 336 and then further eastward beginning in 332. After the catastrophe of Thebes, Greece entered a period of relative calm that lasted until Alexander's return from India in 324. Alexander's sudden death in June 323 only fanned the flames of renewed conflict.

In the meantime, however, despite occasional tensions with Alexander, Antipater, or the queen mother, Olympias, Athens experienced a respite of peace in which most of its energies could go toward rebuilding the city and restoring morale. As luck would have it, four exceptionally capable men, all at the height of their powers, chose to devote themselves to this task. All born between 390 and 385, they were about fifty years old at the time of the battle of Chaeronea. Besides participating actively in politics, Lycurgus, Demosthenes, Demades, and Hypereides were also gifted orators. And despite their differences in character, temperament, and political views, they were all first and foremost Athenian citizens, patriots with their city's best interests at heart. No matter how much their opinions might diverge on important political questions, no matter how hard they fought one another to win a majority in the Assembly, they were still capable of close cooperation until 324, when Alexander's threats from his army headquarters, the flight of his treasurer Harpalus, and the death of Lycurgus brought this period of relative peace and harmony among the four leaders to an abrupt end. Of the four, only Lycurgus died a natural death; the others became victims of politics. On Antipater's demand, Demades pushed a death sentence against Demosthenes and Hypereides through the Assembly in 322. In turn Demades was condemned to death by Antipater three years later, for although he owed his control of Athens to Antipater, Demades had conspired against his protector.

Demosthenes, the best known of the four men, is famous both as the implacable enemy of King Philip and as the greatest Greek orator in the view of ancient and modern critics alike. Several times in his political career he sought the support of the distant king of Persia against Athens' powerful neighbor Macedonia, and Persian gold, intended to finance Greek resistance to the Macedonians, passed through his hands more than once. Some of it went into his own pocket. It was Demosthenes who at the last minute persuaded Athens' longtime enemy Thebes to join the alliance against Philip in 338, a venture for which he also risked his own life at the battle of Chaeronea. Even after the Athenians' defeat there, the citizens remained loyal and chose him—over considerable opposition—to deliver the funeral oration for the fallen.[1] The remaining critics of his policies were silenced eight years later, when Demosthenes defended himself vehemently in his speech

1. N. Loraux emphasizes the pessimistic tone of the speech that has been preserved, noting that it offers no hopeful perspective for the future; *The Invention of Athens*, trans. Alan Sheridan (Cambridge, Mass., 1981) 125–127. Whether the speech is actually Demosthenes' is a matter of controversy.

On the Crown. Demosthenes not only won the case against Aeschines, his accuser, but also humiliated him so that Aeschines was forced to go into exile. After Chaeronea Demosthenes continued to be held in high esteem but no longer played the leading role that had enabled him to forge the coalition against Philip. He had to cede part of his influence to Demades, who had earned credit for achieving peace with the Macedonian king. Demosthenes' chief successor, however, was Lycurgus. The latter rose to such preeminence that the period from 338 to 324 has been called "the Age of Lycurgus."

Lycurgus was a conservative, deeply religious man from a prominent family who had married into the wealthy family of Callias of Bate.[2] Not long after the battle of Chaeronea he was placed in charge of the public treasury, a position he held for twelve years, most likely from 336 to 324 (rather than from 338 to 326). He oversaw the finances of the city directly for a term of four years; after that, since an additional term was not allowed, he placed front men in office and exerted indirect control. Lycurgus was an administrative and financial genius. He increased state revenues many times over and determined their use, spending one-third on improvement of the city's defenses on land and sea, one-third on imposing architecture to improve its appearance, and saving one-third to build up its monetary reserves. He envisioned a state strong enough economically, militarily, and morally to break the bonds restricting its independence. He prosecuted relentlessly all those who failed to meet his standards, including profiteers, defeatists, and those with unpaid debts to the state, and confiscated their property if they were found guilty. As a politician he acquired a reputation for inflexibility and harshness but also for complete integrity. During these years he created the conditions that would make it possible, after Alexander's death, for Athens to challenge Macedonia's military might with some prospect of success.

In a number of fundamental respects Demades was Lycurgus' polar opposite. Though from a poor family, Demades possessed such gifts as an orator that he was able to acquire considerable wealth as an attorney and, later, influence in politics. He understood better than anyone, including Demosthenes, how to turn such influence into material profit; he maintained his own racing stable and sent a winning team of horses to the games at Olympia. Because Demades always delivered his

2. The recently discovered grave mound of the family near the state cemetery *(demosion sema)* provides new inscriptions on the genealogy of the family; *Horos* 5 (1987) 31–44.

speeches extemporaneously, no written versions have survived, but he may well have been the most talented of the famous orators; in any case he was the most flexible. His conscience allowed him a wider field of activity than Lycurgus' or Hypereides' did, and Demades was never at a loss when rapid adjustment to a new situation was called for. No one could equal him in summing up an unexpected turn of events in pithy, accurate language that at the same time conveyed a powerful image. Demades has been severely criticized by earlier scholars, who could discern few if any virtues in him. Yet even if he deserves reproach more frequently than the others, his shortcomings should be weighed against his great achievements. He was no friend of the Macedonians, nor the opportunistic turncoat he has often been called. He was certainly more willing than the others to come to terms with and accept foreign domination when superior strength was on the other side, but he fought in the ranks at Chaeronea and as a politician always put Athenian interests first. More than once he helped bring peace to his country (in 338, as a prisoner of Philip, and again in 322) or preserved the peace (335 and 331). Demades acquired his bad reputation in part because he was the one to propose the (inevitable) motion to ostracize Demosthenes and Hypereides.

Hypereides, the son of a wealthy family, was a man of the world and devoted to all the good things in life. It was no accident that he acted as defense counsel for Phryne, the most famous courtesan of ancient times after Aspasia, when she faced the death penalty for alleged crimes of sacrilege. (It is said that he sealed the verdict of "not guilty" by granting the jury a glimpse of a part of her exquisitely beautiful body that was normally clothed; Greeks throughout the ages have regarded extraordinary beauty as a sign of divinity.) Although Hypereides was the equal in oratory of his three previously named contemporaries, he held virtually no public offices. In 338, however, he belonged to the Council and was therefore unable to take part in the battle of Chaeronea. But the citizens entrusted difficult diplomatic missions to him again and again, and his success always justified their confidence. His personal integrity matched that of Lycurgus. He once sued Demades for introducing a resolution to award honors to a man who had betrayed his city of Olynthus to Philip. Hypereides maintained close political and personal ties to Demosthenes for many years, until the scandal over Alexander's disloyal treasurer Harpalus shattered the friendship. Hypereides then acted as one of Demosthenes' accusers, charging that he had accepted twenty talents from Harpalus. Demosthenes was convicted and went into exile. The two were not reconciled until Alexander's death brought Demosthenes back to Athens. And just as Demosthenes had delivered the funeral oration for the dead after the battle of Chaeronea in 338, Hypereides was chosen by the people in 323 to speak the epitaph for the general Leosthenes and the soldiers who had fallen in the first months of the Lamian War. The major part of this speech, a swan song of Athenian greatness, has survived.

Another important figure half a generation older than these four men was Phocion, a man of conservative stamp who had been a pupil of Plato at the Academy. In contrast to the others, Phocion spent most of his long career as a military leader. He had learned his skills from Chabrias, one of the great *strategoi,* and the Athenians chose him as their commander no fewer than fifty times. As a general, Phocion tended toward caution and avoidance of losses whenever possible. He gained fame above all in three campaigns on the island of Euboea in the years 349, 348, and 341 and in defending Byzantium against Philip in 340. This successful military career gave him some influence in the political sphere, which, as his character would lead one to expect, he used to combat nationalist fervor and to further peace with the great power of Macedonia in particular. Thus he took Aeschines' side in the latter's debate with Demosthenes over the "false embassy" in 343/2. Alexander the Great held Phocion in high esteem, and Plutarch considered him worthy of a biography. Phocion was incorruptible, a man who never hesitated to speak the truth, however harsh, to his fellow citizens and to offer unwelcome advice. He was called to take charge of the government at the age of eighty, and soon afterward sealed his own doom by acting against the declared will of the people during the tumultuous period of the *diadochoi* (Successors).

2. Endangered Peace

As darkness fell that summer night in 338, 1,000 Athenians lay dead on the battlefield of Chaeronea.[3] Another 2,000 had fallen into Philip's hands as prisoners of war, heavy losses for a state whose total adult male population numbered at most 30,000, the old and unfit included. Yet

---

3. They were buried in a single mass grave in the common burial-place *(polyandreion)* (Pausanias 1.29.13). A contemporary epigram written in their honor is partially preserved as an inscription (Peek, *GVI,* no. 27); the full text is in *AP* 7, no. 245. An epigram honoring an individual citizen killed at Chaeronea was discovered recently; *Horos* 3 (1985) 132–133.

even though the losses were great and the impression of defeat over-whelming, Athens set to work at once on energetic preparations to defend itself. The city's fortifications needed strengthening, and even the private tombs in the Cerameicus were plundered for materials.[4] Each of the ten tribes was assigned responsibility for a section of the city walls and received the sum of ten talents to spend on improving them; Demosthenes served as one of the ten commissioners for his tribe, Pandionis. Work on these fortifications continued on a consider-able scale in the following years.[5] In the Council Hypereides intro-duced a motion to grant citizenship to foreigners, and freedom to those slaves willing and able to bear arms; he also proposed arming the 500 members of the Council itself.[6] These motions all failed to pass when it was pointed out that they were contrary to law. In keeping with tradition, Athens took in citizens from allied states seeking safety, in this case mostly refugees from Thebes, Acarnania, and the island of Euboea. The Athenian fleet had suffered no damage and remained a potent weapon.

Confronted with such determination, Philip was wise enough not to seek further hostilities, and showed himself willing to make peace with Athens. The negotiator in this process was Demades, who, like Dem-osthenes, had taken part in the battle but unlike him had been taken prisoner. When the king, celebrating his victory, strutted drunkenly before his captives, Demades caught his attention by speaking out boldly (saying that although fate had given him the role of Agamem-non, Philip was acting more like Thersites). Struck by this, Philip freed Demades immediately and later sent him to negotiate the peace.

The terms acknowledged Athens' full autonomy in internal affairs but required the city to dissolve its naval alliance and to join the Hellenic League Philip was planning, thereby depriving it of inde-pendence in foreign affairs. The Athenians lost their possessions in the northern Aegean but in return acquired Oropus on the Attic-Boeotian border, when Philip took this city away from the Boeotians and gave it to Athens, along with its surrounding territory and the shrine of Amphiaraus.[7] Athens retained control of the islands of Salamis, Delos,

---

4. Lycurgus *Leoc.* 43; D. Ohly, *AA* 80 (1965) 341–343.

5. F. G. Maier, *Griechische Mauerbauinschriften*, 2 vols. (Heidelberg 1959 and 1961) 1: 36–48.

6. Lycurgus *Leoc.* 36–37.

7. [Demades], *On the Twelve Years,* ed. F. Blass, in *Dinarchi Orationes* (Leipzig 1888) 9, says it was done at Philip's behest. D. Knoepfler argues that Athens did not acquire Oropus

and Samos (where Athenian citizens had first settled in 365/4), as well as Lemnos,[8] Imbros, and Skyros.[9] Philip demanded no ransom for his prisoners and returned them to Athens under the charge of his son, Alexander. The Athenians responded by bestowing honors on the king, his son, and several prominent officials.

In the following winter (338/7) delegates from all the Greek states met in Corinth, where Philip had summoned them, and negotiated a general peace. Only Sparta, which had ignored the invitation, was absent. Following on the peace agreement came the founding of a Hellenic League. All the member states sent representatives to the union's legislative body, the *synedrion*. Philip, through his rank as *hegemon*, or commander-in-chief, of the armed forces, had the power to call the assembly into session and to introduce bills. Fragments of the union's constitution have been found in Athens.[10] The *synedrion* passed a bill introduced by Philip containing a joint declaration of war against Persia, making it appear as if such a war, which was in fact Isocrates' idea and solely in Philip's interest, were a common goal of all the member states. Many Greeks would have preferred to join a pact with the king of Persia against Philip. The Persian empire had long before ceased to pose any threat to Greece, since it was held together less by its own strength than by the presence of large numbers of Greek mercenaries, who found in the service of the Great King the employment they could not find at home. To the general population in Greece the war was presented as revenge for Xerxes' campaign against the Greeks in the year 480. Soon an advance force commanded by Attalus and Parmenion set out, landed in Asia Minor, and began hostilities. Philip intended to direct the campaign himself, but before he could carry out this plan he was murdered in Aegae (Vergina), where the wedding of his daughter Cleopatra and King Alexander of Epirus was taking place. Whatever the real motives behind the assassination, they were limited to Macedonian circles at Philip's court.

As a result of the war in Asia begun by Philip and continued by Alexander in 334, Athens lay outside the focus of political events for

---

until 335, after the catastrophe of Thebes, and that it was therefore granted by Alexander; "Adolf Wilhelm et les Amphiaraia d'Oropos," *in Aristote et Athènes,* ed. M. Piérart (Paris 1993) 295–296.

8. *Hesperia* 9 (1940) 325, no. 35.

9. *Ath. pol.* 62.2.

10. *StV,* no. 403; all the evidence from literary sources has also been assembled and is discussed there.

the next twelve years. This is not to say that the city played no role in the war; it had to contribute twenty triremes to Alexander's fleet and probably cavalrymen to the army as well, and in 333 many citizens of Athens fighting on Darius' side as mercenaries were taken captive by the Macedonians at Issus. Concern for the safety of all these citizens— the men in the ships' crews were simultaneously Alexander's hostages—dictated the city's difficult relationship with the king for many years to come. On the other hand it must be said that both Philip in his later years and Alexander, except for the last year of his life, refrained from all interference in Athenian affairs.[11] The story that after the conquest of Susa Alexander restored to Athens the sculptures of the tyrant-slayers seized by Xerxes in 480 is a legend.[12]

It is not possible to explain in unambiguous terms all the political activities of Athenian citizens during this period. One of the most puzzling events occurred in the spring of 336, a few months before Philip was assassinated, when Eucrates introduced the bill whose text was found in the Agora in Athens in 1952.[13] Passed by the board of lawgivers, this law was intended to protect the democracy from possible overthrow by a tyrant or oligarchs; it guaranteed immunity from prosecution to anyone who killed another person attempting to lead or participating in a coup against the government. To this extent it merely repeated existing provisions. The next section of the bill, however, contained threats addressed to the members of the Council of the Areopagus about what would happen should they, in case of an attempt to overthrow democracy, not refrain from all political activity. Up to now no satisfactory explanation has been found for why the citizenry thought it desirable to renew the old protective legislation, that is to say, why they felt concern for the continued existence of democracy at that particular moment. Nor is there any explanation for why suspicion fell specifically on the group of former archons who made up the Areopagus, for the Council could not be considered either overly friendly toward Macedonia or undemocratic and unpatriotic in

11. The claim that Macedonian troops occupied Athens during Alexander's reign and kept the city quiet is as false as the claim that Antipater was "the real ruler of Athens" at that time and that Aristotle, who was living in the city, enjoyed protection through Antipater's friendship; I. Düring, "Aristoteles," *RE Suppl.* 11 (1968) 180.

12. M. Moggi provides a detailed discussion of the story, ascribed to different kings by various ancient authors; *ASNP* (1973) 1–42.

13. B. D. Meritt, *Hesperia* 21 (1952) 335–359, no. 5; M. Ostwald, *TAPhA* 86 (1955) 103–28. See also R. W. Wallace, *The Areopagus Council to 307* B.C. (Baltimore 1989) 179–184; and M. Faraguna, *Atene nell'età di Alessandro* (Rome 1992) 270–272.

spirit; some few years thereafter, in 330, Lycurgus praised it publicly.[14] Eucrates, who introduced the motion, later died as an enemy of Macedonia along with Demosthenes and Hypereides in 322, and only this much seems certain: that this law forms a part of the democratic ideology that was finding visible and official expression at that time in the creation of a cult of democracy.[15]

The news of Philip's murder was received in Athens with rejoicing. On Demosthenes' motion the Council voted to offer a sacrifice of thanksgiving, and the populace awarded posthumous honors to the assassin, who had been killed following the attack. The Athenians did not content themselves with ceremonies and oratory, however; they also sought contact with other Greek states, with representatives of Persia, and with Attalus, one of the two Macedonian generals in Asia Minor, who may have entertained hopes of occupying the now vacant throne himself. All these activities violated the terms of the Hellenic League.[16] Hypereides expressed the reigning anti-Macedonian sentiment with his charges against Philippides, whose case was heard shortly after the assassination of Philip.[17] This mood sobered very rapidly, however, when it became clear that Alexander not only stood unopposed as successor to his father but also had at once taken the necessary steps to safeguard his position as *hegemon* of the Greeks. The Athenians counted themselves fortunate when a delegation led by Demades received confirmation from Alexander of his continued peaceful intentions toward them.

But less than a year later the city made a very daring move that almost led to catastrophe, when the rumor reached it that Alexander had been killed fighting the Illyrians. At that time a rebellion against Macedonian rule was under way in Thebes, and the king of Persia had sent considerable funds to Greece to support the enemies of Macedonia. In Athens officials refused to take any money from Persia, but Demosthenes, acting as a private citizen, accepted quite a large sum and joined a group that was sending arms and supplies to Thebes. The rebellion had been planned in Athens by Theban fugitives to whom the Athenians had granted refuge. The Athenian Assembly expressed its support for

14. Lycurgus *Leoc.* 12 and 52.
15. A. E. Raubitschek, "Demokratia," *Hesperia* 31 (1962) 238–243.
16. A. B. Bosworth, *Conquest and Empire* (Cambridge 1988) 188.
17. Hypereides' mention of Philippides' belief that Philip was immortal (4.7) indicates that the king was in fact no longer alive.

the rebels by joining a mutual pact with Thebes, which under the circumstances could only have been directed against Macedonia. It must have been about then that Iphicrates, son of a famous Athenian general, left for the court of the new Great King of Persia, Darius III.[18] Believing that the *hegemon* of the Hellenic League to whom they had sworn an oath of loyalty was dead, Demosthenes and Lycurgus were now determined to do their utmost to shake off the Macedonian yoke. A corps of Athenians was raised to go to the Thebans' aid, but before they had crossed the borders of Attica, the first reports arrived that Alexander was alive and encamped with his army before Thebes.

News of the city's conquest and utter destruction reached Athens around early October 335, while the Great Mysteries were being celebrated. Shortly thereafter the Athenians, who had placed themselves in a most compromising position, received Alexander's ultimatum: they were to hand over to him eight of their citizens most suspected of complicity in the uprising, and all Thebans who had fled to Athens after the fall of their city. It is to the credit of Athens that, ignoring the threats at the end of Alexander's message, it refused to comply with his demands and sent emissaries to negotiate instead. And it is to Alexander's credit that he listened to these ambassadors—Demades and Phocion—and accepted their proposals. His decision may have been influenced by a preoccupation with Persia; the war there had bogged down, and Alexander intended to inject new vigor into the campaign by taking charge himself.

And so Athens escaped, by a hair's breadth, the catastrophe that had threatened to engulf it. Thereafter Demosthenes, Lycurgus, and their faction acted with considerably more caution, while Demades and Phocion, who had succeeded in maintaining the peace, had a direct interest in seeing their policy continued. All participants in the debate realized that they would have to live with Macedonian hegemony, at least for the time being. Only a minority of citizens was willing to accept it as a permanent measure. Yet if they wanted to win back their freedom one day, they would first have to make sweeping reforms and build up their country again, both materially and morally. It was Lycurgus who developed the overall concept for this project and had the opportunity to put it into practice as public treasurer.

18. Arrian *Anab.* 2.15.2–4; A. B. Bosworth, *A Historical Commentary on Arrian's History of Alexander,* vol. 1 (Oxford 1980), 233–234.

Nothing else is so characteristic of the spirit of this renaissance as the reform of the training of young citizens (ephebes) as established by the law of Epicrates. The new regulation almost certainly dates from 336/5, since it first appears in four inscriptions of 335/4 and is referred to in numerous inscriptions from the years immediately following. Aristotle describes it in detail in chapter 42 of his work on the Athenian state, which he wrote between 335 and 324. Although the institution of *ephebia* had been in existence for a long time, very little is known about how it functioned originally; the new law transformed it into a two-year period of introductory military training for all citizens who had reached the age of eighteen and were physically fit. The ephebes, young men from eighteen to twenty, made up the first two of the forty-two annual cohorts required to provide military service and lived communally during this term of active duty. In the first year of their service they were assigned to guard duty in Acte and the fortress of Munychia in Piraeus. Officially they served under the two commanders-in-chief there, but the ephebic corps also had its own commander, elected by popular vote and known as the *kosmetes*. He was assisted by one *sophronist* (superintendent) from each of the ten tribes. The ephebes of each tribe had meals in their barracks, paid for out of a sum which their *sophronist* received from the public treasury. Instructors trained the young men in the use of hoplite weapons, as well as the bow, javelin, and catapult. At the beginning of the second year the ephebes gave a public demonstration in the theater of their ability to maneuver in formation; after this ceremony each received a shield and spear at the state's expense. Thus equipped, the ephebes were posted to one of the Attic fortresses (Eleusis, Panakton, Phyle, Rhamnus, Sunium) and spent their second year patrolling the rural areas. The oath they took upon entering the corps of ephebes was known from the works of Greek authors even before the actual text, containing only a few minor variants, was discovered on an inscription at Acharnae in 1938. The ephebes swore to defend their homeland and its possessions, never to desert their rank or the man next to them, to obey their commanders and the laws, and to defend the government.[19]

The goals of the reform can easily be deduced from the known

---

19. For a discussion of Epicrates' reform see Rhodes, *Commentary* 493–510, summarizing the views of earlier scholars. The inscriptions of the first decade are in O. Reinmuth, *The Ephebic Inscriptions of the Fourth Century B.C.* (Leiden 1971), nos. 1 (334/3) to 15. Texts discovered since are in *AE* (1988) 19–30 (class of 333/2 of Kekropis); *ABSA* 84 (1989)

dctails and the text of the ephebic oath. It aimed at increasing the size of the group from which hoplites were recruited by including members of the poorer classes, and thereby improving the hoplites' ability to defend Attic soil and the democratic constitution. At a time when a foreign power with a monarchical form of government was imposing limits on the sovereignty of the demos, requiring an avowal of loyalty to the principles of democracy amounted to a proclamation that the Athenian demos was not willing to accept these limits forever. But the reform also reflects the realization of civic leaders that they could not attempt to rid themselves of this outside control unless the body of citizens was better equipped, both mentally and physically, for the inevitable struggle. In the decade following the reform of the *ephebia*, Athenian politics concentrated above all on achieving the level of preparedness that this would require. There are no indications that differences of opinion existed among political leaders on this funda-mental goal, although they certainly had diverging views on the best means for reaching it. Despite the existence of ideological and political differences, Lycurgus and Demades worked hand in hand in adminis-tering public finances and as members of commissions,[20] and several times both of them won votes in the Assembly on the same day for motions they had introduced.[21] When a motion to erect a statue in

---

333–344 (class of 333/2 of Erechtheis); and possibly J. S. Traill, *Demos and Trittys* (Toronto 1986) 3–5 (Kekropis, ca. 332/1); however, see K. Clinton, *AE* 127 (1988) 30. Two other texts from Panakton (Kavasala) dating from the late 330s are still unpublished; one is announced in *SEG* 38.67, and one is a dedication from the ephebes of the tribe Oineis from 332/1, found at Rhamnus in 1993 (B. C. Petrakos, *Ergon* [1993] 7). The ephebic oath, the text of which antedates the reform of 336/5 in any case, is in *GHI* 204. Controversy continues over whether all young citizens were required to serve as ephebes, as the testimony of Aristotle and Lycurgus indicates (most recently accepted by N. V. Sekunda, *ABSA* 87 [1992] 329; and Faraguna, *Atene* 277), or only the three highest classes, i.e., only the sons of citizens of the hoplite census class, excluding the *thetes* (so Rhodes, *Commentary* 503).

20. Between 334 and 330 Demades oversaw the military treasury, while Lycurgus—or his surrogate—was in charge of state revenues. Evidence of direct cooperation between them exists for 334/3 (Bosworth, *Conquest* 206). For Lycurgus and Demades serving on the same commissions as representatives of their tribes, see *FD* III.1.511 from 330, *IG* VII.4259 from 329/8.

21. On the success of both in winning majority votes in the same session of the Assembly, see C. Schwenk, *Athens in the Age of Alexander* (Chicago 1985), nos. 23–25 for 334/3, nos. 36–37 for 332/1, and no. 53 and *IG* II^2.399 for 328/7; on the dating see C. Habicht, *Chiron* 19 (1989) 1–5. These are cases for which there is direct evidence; presumably many more occurred.

honor of Demades was introduced in 335, after the destruction of Thebes, to express the citizens' gratitude for protecting them from the rashness of several other politicians, Lycurgus spoke against it but failed to win a majority for his opposition. Here the tensions between leading politicians, smoldering below the surface, become evident. Yet while such rivalries may occasionally have erupted into the public arena, they did not prevent old political enemies from pulling together when it was a question of liberating Athens from its role as a vassal state.

For a long time they nourished the hope that Persian resistance to Alexander would help bring them closer to their goal. Athenian mercenaries who fought with the Persian forces contributed actively to such resistance, and some of them were taken prisoner at the battle of the Granicus in 334, in Alexander's first major victory over the Persians. In principle Alexander could not hold against them the fact that they (and other Greeks) had fought for the Persian cause, since most of them must have been serving in the Persian army long before the Greek members of the League of Corinth voted to join the war on Alexander's side. Nevertheless, after their capture he sent them in chains to Macedonia to do forced labor. The eight male skeletons with shackled feet found recently in a grave from the Hellenistic era in Acanthus in Macedonia may well be the remains of some of these prisoners.[22] Athens repeatedly petitioned the king to free them, a request not granted until the spring of 331. The reason for this harsh treatment probably lay in the mercenaries' espousal of the Persian cause, since it ran directly counter to Alexander's declared aim of a war of national revenge against Persia. This contradiction was all the more striking because the Athenians had been the main victims of the Persian attack in 480 and had suffered the most from the Persians' devastations. Alexander did not fail to remind them of this at the time, by sending them 300 captured Persian weapons as an offering to the goddess Athena, with an inscription "Alexander and the Greeks, with the exception of the Spartans, from the barbarians who inhabit Asia." However, since at the same time he refused to return the Athenian citizens he was holding prisoner, most Athenians undoubtedly found this dedication offensive.[23]

22. *AAA* 19 (1986 [1990]) 178–184.
23. For Alexander's Athenian prisoners see Arrian *Anab.* 1.16.6; 29.5; 3.6.2. For Alexander's dedicatory inscription, Arrian *Anab.* 1.16.7 with F. W. Mitchel's assessment, *Lykourgan Athens* (Cincinnati 1970) 8. There was a long tradition of dedicating armor to Athena;

Alexander had other grounds for dissatisfaction with Athens, for in the first winter of the war the Persian fleet put in at Samos, where it was allowed to take on food and water. Samos was governed by Athenian settlers and had been in Athenian hands for thirty years; one of the generals elected annually, with the title *"strategos* for Samos," was in charge of defending the island. It cannot have escaped Alexander's notice that he permitted such support to be given to the Persians, either willingly or because his forces were too weak to resist. The incident, a violation of Athens' obligations as a member of the Hellenic League, may have played a role ten years later in Alexander's decision to take Samos away from the Athenians.[24]

With his victory at Issus in the autumn of 333, Alexander captured not only King Darius' camp but also a delegation sent to the Persian ruler from Athens. Among this group was Iphicrates, son of the famous general of the same name. The date of the delegation's departure from Athens is not documented, but presumably it took place before the storming of Thebes in 335. Alexander treated the son well out of respect for the father and sent his remains home to Athens after the younger Iphicrates succumbed to an illness.[25]

The citizens of Athens also had other problems besides Alexander to occupy them during those years. One of these, involving an athlete named Callippus, caused a considerable stir in the summer of 332. Callippus had won the pentathlon for Athens at the Olympic Games but was later accused of having bribed the other competitors. They were all fined by the officials. But just as victories at the games were considered to enhance the reputation of the victor's home city, Callippus' offense brought discredit on the entire city of Athens. The affair became a matter of civic pride. Convinced that Callippus had been the victim of an intrigue, the citizens chose Hypereides to defend his cause and gave him the task of persuading the Elean officials to revoke the judgment. When they refused, the conflict escalated. Athens refused to pay the fine, whereupon Athenian citizens were barred from participat-

the Ionian colonies of Athens, joined by members of the Naval Confederacy in the fifth century, did so every four years at the Great Panathenaea, celebrated around the beginning of August. It seems likely that Alexander had this tradition in mind and planned for the dedication to be made public at the Great Panathenaea of 334.

24. Arrian *Anab.* 1.19.8 with Bosworth, *Commentary* 141 n. 18.
25. Arrian *Anab.* 2.15.3.

ing in future games. It took an announcement from the officials at Delphi that the Pythian oracle would give no pronouncements to them as long as the fine was not paid to make the Athenians yield. The money from the fines was used for monuments (as had been done after a similar case of fraud in 388); six bronze images of Zeus, called *zanes,* were inscribed with exhortations to honesty and fair play and placed in the sanctuary at Olympia.[26]

This incident may have some connection with the fact that in 331 the Athenians began turning their attention to a different oracle, that of Dodona in Epirus. The newfound interest in this oracle led in turn to a further diplomatic wrangle, in which Hypereides again defended the city's actions. In response to a pronouncement from the oracle, the Athenians had added lavish ornamentation to the image of the goddess Dione at Dodona, thereby offending Alexander's mother, Olympias, a member of the Epirote royal family and regent there at the time in the name of her brother and son-in-law, Alexander of Epirus (then absent in Italy). Olympias sent a delegation to Athens with a letter of protest setting out her claim to the territory of the Molossians in Epirus, where Dodona was situated. The protest was discussed in the Assembly, where Hypereides presented the city's case. Among other things he pointed out that only a short time before Olympias had herself made an offering to Hygieia, the goddess of health, at the Acropolis in Athens, in gratitude for the recovery of her son from a severe illness. Hypereides argued that Athenians should have the same rights in Dodona. When not long thereafter the news reached Athens that the king of Epirus had died in Italy, the Athenians sent delegations to express their con-dolences to Olympias as well as to her daughter Cleopatra, the king's widow.[27]

These delegations undertook their mission at a time of renewed tensions, for in the summer of 331 King Agis led the Spartans and several allied Greek states into war against Macedonia, and Athens came very close to joining them. A motion was passed to send a contingent of the fleet to support Agis but was never carried out, thanks to a clever tactical maneuver by Demades, who had responsibil-

26. Pausanias 5.21.2–7; Hypereides frs. 111–112 Jensen; [Plut.] *mor.* 850B; H.-V. Herrmann, "Zanes," *RE Suppl.* 14 (1974) 977–981. Apollo of Delphi had helped his divine father, Zeus of Olympia, to obtain satisfaction through the intervention of his servants.

27. Hypereides 3.19–26; J. Engels, *Studien zur politischen Biographie des Hypereides* (Munich 1989) 189–191.

ity for the finances of such an operation.[28] While even Demosthenes advised against such involvement, other politicians declared themselves in favor of joining the war. The speech of an unknown orator preserved in the corpus of Demosthenes' texts, *On the Treaties with Alexander*, probably belongs in the context of this debate. In it the speaker addressed the Assembly to rebut the arguments of a previous speaker, who had advised the Athenians to observe scrupulously the provisions of the treaties with Alexander and the general peace. The author of the rebuttal pointed out various ways in which Alexander and the Macedonians had broken the treaties and the peace, above all by setting up tyrants in the Peloponnesian cities of Messene, Pellene, and Sicyon, and further by seizing grain ships in the Black Sea headed for Athens. A Macedonian trireme had also entered the harbor of Piraeus without authorization. Now, the speaker argued, the time had come to take a stand, and if he could find a majority to back him, he would move to declare war on those who had broken the peace.[29]

Similar complaints are to be found at about this time in a speech by Hypereides. This speech is far milder in tone, however; Hypereides mentions no specific details, charging Alexander and Olympias only with occasionally making unlawful and excessive demands. The *synedrion* of the League of Corinth would be the proper place to oppose these tactics, according to Hypereides, but the Athenian delegate Polyeuctus had been lacking in determination.[30]

In the meantime Antipater, Alexander's viceroy in Europe, had defeated King Agis and his allies in a great battle at Megalopolis in Arcadia (probably in the spring of 330). Agis was killed in the encounter, which also brought a violent end to the Greek states' uprising. Alexander's great victory over King Darius at Gaugamela on 1 October 331 dashed the last hopes the Athenians had placed in the Persian forces.[31] They

28. [Plut.] *mor.* 818E.

29. [Demosth.] 17. I follow the generally accepted dating. W. Will has argued for dating the speech in September or October 333, shortly before the battle of Issus; *RhM* 125 (1982) 202–213. Faraguna has adopted Will's view; *Atene* 254 and 332 n. 32.

30. Hypereides 3.20 and 24, dating from 330 at the earliest and thus almost certainly from after Agis' campaign.

31. The date of the battle of Megalopolis has not been precisely determined; estimates range between the autumn of 331 and the spring of 330. We know the exact date of the battle of Gaugamela, however, thanks to the astronomical diaries of Babylon (A. Sachs and H. Hunger, *Astronomical Diaries and Related Texts from Babylonia*, vol. 1 [Vienna 1988] 179: the 24th of the month of Ululu), which corroborate the date given by Plutarch (*Camillus* 19.5; *Alexander* 31.8). See also P. Bernard, *BCH* 114 (1990) 515–517.

fortified ring of walls erected under Themistocles, which Conon had repaired with the aid of Persian funds at the beginning of the fourth century. A moat was added in front of the walls, and Cephisophon successfully introduced a measure to fortify Piraeus.[41] Even earlier, during the archonship of a younger Themistocles, the construction of new docks in Piraeus had begun, which were finally finished some twenty-four years later, in 323/2. The number of warships, both the traditional triremes and the increasingly popular larger quadriremes, was growing year by year.[42] And after passage of Epicrates' reform of the ephebic corps, the military training provided to the young men of Athens improved in scope and thoroughness.[43] The estimated cost of maintaining the corps (approximately 1,000 men strong, with 500 in each cohort) was at least forty talents annually, and to this sum must be added the cost of the arms supplied to each ephebe by the state.[44]

Not since the days of Pericles, a century earlier, had there been a building program on the scale undertaken during Lycurgus' administration. It was also the last time Athens itself had the means to pay for public architecture in the grand style. Later phases of comparable large-scale building were financed by foreign rulers, chiefly the rulers of the Attalid and Seleucid dynasties in the second century B.C., and the emperor Hadrian in the second century A.D. In the late fourth century it is as if the citizenry wanted to demonstrate that although Philip had defeated them, their vitality remained unimpaired.[45] At once the walls were reinforced, the docks enlarged, and an arsenal built.[46] As part of these defense measures Lycurgus and Aristonicus jointly

41. Aeschines 3.27–31; Maier, *Mauerbauinschriften* 1: 36–48.
42. N. G. Ashton, *ABSA* 72 (1977) 1–11; J. Tréheux, *RPh* 63 (1989) 284.
43. See note 19 above.
44. Bosworth, *Conquest* 209–210.
45. For more on Lycurgus and the construction during his administration see the biography of Lycurgus, [Plut.] *mor.* 841D and the decree in his honor, *IG* II^2.457b.5–9 and [Plut.] *mor.* 852C. See further Mitchel, *Lykourgan Athens* 33–48; and R. E. Wycherley, *The Stones of Athens* (Princeton 1978) 19–20 (the walls), 60–62 (Pnyx), 66–67 (Apollo Patroos), 181–183 (Sanctuary of Asclepius), 207–211 (theater), 215 (stadium), 226 (Lyceum). For more on the construction of the stadium, see *IG* II^2.624 (Schwenk, *Athens,* no. 48); Faraguna, *Atene* 257–269.
46. For the arsenal of Philo see Vitruvius *De architectura, praef.* 7.12, and the description of the building in *IG* II^2.1668. The foundations were discovered in 1988 and have determined the location: G. Steinhauer, in *Haus und Stadt im klassischen Griechenland*^{2}, ed. W. Hoepfner and E.-L. Schwandner (Munich 1994) 44–50.

introduced a proposal in 335/4 for combatting piracy. A squadron of fast sailing ships was sent out under the command of Diotimus, and they must have succeeded in their mission, for Lycurgus proposed honors for Diotimus the next year.[47]

During the celebration of the Great Panathenaea in the summer of 330, the dedication took place of a stadium Lycurgus had built on land donated by Deinias. The new stadium provided the Athenians with a suitably imposing setting for the athletic contests, artistic competitions, and races held until then in the Agora. A law introduced by Aristonicus of Marathon has survived in part from this same period containing regulations on the annual, or lesser, Panathenaea.[48] To the venerable theater of Dionysus at the foot of the Acropolis Lycurgus added new seats of hewn stone and an elaborate *prohedria,* the privileged seats for official dignitaries.[49] He also commissioned the building of the Lyceum with its palaestra, one of the city's famous gymnasia. Work had been going on for some time on the Pnyx, the hill where the *ekklesia* (Assembly) met, as it needed to be enlarged; these renovations, resulting in the so-called Pnyx III, must have begun in the 340s and were completed in about 325.[50] A temple of Apollo Patroos was built in the Agora, and a columned hall more than 160 feet long was added to the sanctuary of Asclepius.[51] The well-preserved and architecturally innovative monument of Lysicrates at the foot of the Acropolis also dates from this period. It was dedicated by Lysicrates in 335/4 after the boys' chorus of which he was patron won a choral competition during the Great Dionysia.[52]

There were also two sites outside the city where construction on a large scale was undertaken during this period: at the sanctuary of Demeter and Kore in Eleusis and at the sanctuary of Amphiaraus in

47. *IG* II^2.1623.276–308; [Plut.] *mor.* 844A with *IG* II^2.414 (Schwenk, *Athens,* no. 25).

48. *IG* II^2.334 (Schwenk, *Athens,* no. 17); see further L. Robert, *Hellenica* 11–12 (1960) 189–203.

49. M. Maass, *Die Prohedrie des Dionysostheaters in Athen* (Munich 1972).

50. The most recent discussion is in H. A. Thompson, *Hesperia Suppl.* 19 (1982) 133–147, which cites the older literature. On the period of construction of the Pnyx III, see 144–145.

51. H. A. Thompson, *Hesperia* 6 (1937) 77–115; for a partial rebuttal, C. W. Hedrick, *AJA* 92 (1988) 185–210.

52. For the inscription on the monument see *IG* II^2.3042; Hans Riemann, "Lysikrates-monument," *RE Suppl.* 8 (1956) 266–347; H. Bauer, *AM* 92 (1977) 197–227.

Oropus. A long inscription from 329/8 is the primary source for details on the work at Eleusis.[53] Processions and pilgrims made their way from Athens to Eleusis along the Sacred Way. A few years after Lycurgus' death his colleague Xenocles of Sphettos had a stone bridge built across the Cephisus to make the journey safer for the pilgrims.[54] Athens had acquired the shrine of Amphiaraus, the hero and healer, along with the city of Oropus on the border between Boeotia and Attica after the battle of Chaeronea. The Athenians immediately placed Pytheas, their superintendent of wells, in charge of improving drainage and sanitary conditions there;[55] in honor of the hero they also instituted a new festival with gymnastic and equestrian contests, which took place every five years and was celebrated for the first time in 329/8.[56]

In the first half of the 320s Athens experienced a serious grain shortage that made itself felt throughout Greece and the Aegean between 331 and 324. Several authors and numerous inscriptions bear witness to the gravity of the situation.[57] Demosthenes' speech against Phormio in 327/6 reveals that the price of wheat had risen from five drachmas a bushel to sixteen, and emergency measures were taken to ensure that everyone received a share of the available supplies.[58] Numerous decrees were passed to honor merchants who contributed to the relief efforts. A unique document from Cyrene was discovered in 1925.[59] It is a list from one of the years of the shortage headed "Those to whom the city gave grain when it was scarce in Greece," containing the names of almost fifty states.[60] The list also notes the amount provided to each in descending order, from 100,000 bushels for Ath-

---

53. *IG* II^2.1672. See further 1673–75 and 1933; Mitchel, *Lykourgan Athens* 45.

54. *IG* II^2.1191; *AP* 9, no. 147, with the literature cited in note 35 above.

55. *IG* II^2.338. See C. Habicht, *ZPE* 77 (1989) 83–87; and C. Veligianni, *Hellenica* 40 (1989) 245–247.

56. L. Deubner, *Attische Feste* (Berlin 1932) 229; D. Knoepfler, "Les Amphiaraia d'Oropos" 279–302.

57. *IG* II^2.360.8–9; [Plut.] *mor.* 851B; P. Garnsey, *Famine and Food Supply in the Graeco-Roman World* (Cambridge 1988) 154–166; Faraguna, *Atene* 225–230 and 330–331.

58. Demosth. 34.37 ff.; see also [42].20 and 31. *IG* II^2.360.30 and 68 confirms that the normal price for a bushel of wheat was 5 drachmas.

59. *Abh. Akad. Berlin* 5 (1925) 24–26 no. 3 (*SEG* 9.2). Text revised with commentary by A. Laronde, *Cyrène et la Libye hellénistique* (Paris 1987) 30–34; a map shows where grain was distributed, and the amounts in each case (34). P. Brun, *ZPE* 99 (1993) 185–196. See the general discussion in G. Marasco, *Athenaeum* 62 (1984) 286–294.

60. Olympias is mentioned for Macedonia, and her daughter Cleopatra for Epirus. Cleopatra had only recently exported grain to Greece between 334 and 331 (Lycurgus *Leoc.* 26).

ens to 900 for Knossos in Crete (after an earlier shipment of 10,000 bushels). Seventy-two thousand bushels were shipped to Macedonia and 50,000 to Epirus, but it is Athens that heads the list of needy states. The decision of the Assembly in 325/4 to create a military base on the Adriatic Sea was related to the food shortage of those years. The measure aimed at protecting grain shipments from Etruscan pirates. A fleet was equipped for this purpose and deployed under the command of Miltiades of Lakiadai, but nothing is known about the results of the expedition.[61]

During these years of intensive activity, Athenians who displayed signs of weakness or cowardice were called to account by their fellow citizens. Here Lycurgus played a particularly active role. Very soon after the battle of 338 he sued Autolycus, a former archon, for having evacuated his wife and children from the city when it was threatened by Philip. Eight years later he took to court another citizen, Leocrates, because after Chaeronea he had departed for Rhodes, taking his money and family with him, and eventually moving on to Megara. The people of Athens had threatened to punish with death any more attempts to flee. Leocrates, correctly assessing the drift of public opinion, stayed away for many years and conducted his business affairs from Megara. Finally, however, he risked a return in 330, expecting that interest in his case would have died down. Lycurgus wished to make an example of him, however, and brought a charge of treason, based on the law that had been passed after Leocrates' own flight. In his speech to the court (which has been preserved), Lycurgus argued in favor of applying the law retroactively to Leocrates. Despite the fact that the proposal lacked all legal basis, Lycurgus came very close to winning, thanks to his eloquent appeals to the jurors' patriotic feelings: the vote ended in a tie, with the result that Leocrates was acquitted and spared from the death penalty.[62]

Even more representative of the dominant public mood was the celebrated trial over Demosthenes' crown, which also took place in 330, not long after the trial of Leocrates. Officially Demosthenes

---

Cleopatra also represents the crown of the Molossians of Epirus in the list of hosts to *theoroi* from Argos (ca. 330); *BCH* 90 (1966) 156 ff., col. I.11, with commentary by P. Charneux, 177–182.

61. *IG* II².1629.145–271 (*GHI* 200). See also Engels, *Biographie des Hypereides* 247–251.

62. Lycurgus *Leoc.* For the case of Autolycus, see *PA* no. 2746.

appeared in court to speak on behalf of the defendant, Ctesiphon of Anaphlystus. In fact Ctesiphon is barely mentioned, and Demosthenes dwelled instead on his own past actions. He delivered a stirring defense of his earlier policies, which had led to the war against Philip and the defeat at Chaeronea. The nominal defendant Ctesiphon had proposed awarding a crown to Demosthenes at the Great Dionysia for his services to the state, particularly his work on the city walls. Aeschines thereupon brought suit against Ctesiphon, charging that such an award would be illegal, because Demosthenes had not yet submitted the required account of his activities as commissioner for the repairs. The real aim of the lawsuit was thus to humiliate Demosthenes publicly. The great majority of the jury found in his favor, however; Aeschines, the plaintiff, received less than one-fifth of the votes. The verdict ended Aeschines' political career and sent him into permanent exile. Why the case was not heard until six years after the fact is unclear. Aeschines may have been tempted to dredge up the old charge after Agis was defeated by Antipater, Alexander's viceroy for Europe, calculating perhaps that this recent show of Macedonian strength would discredit Demosthenes and his anti-Macedonian policy in the eyes of the jury. The outcome of the trial represented a political triumph for Demosthenes; it also indicated clearly that popular opposition to Macedonia was still widespread, and that Macedonia was indeed the prime target of Athenian national sentiment.[63] The unambiguous response of the jury appears almost like defiance, all the more notable because at that point Athens could no longer hope for military support from either Persia or Sparta.

This strongly nationalistic mood was matched by an equally strong emphasis on democracy in the political thought of the time. It found expression not long after Chaeronea in Eucrates' law to protect democracy from any attempt to overthrow it. It can also be seen in the decision of the departing Council in June 332 to erect a bronze statue of a figure representing Democracy as one of the last acts of their year in office.[64]

---

63. The main speeches for the opposing sides at the trial have survived: 3 by Aeschines (*Against Ctesiphon*) and 18 by Demosthenes (*On the Crown*). For an exhaustive commentary see H. Wankel, *Demosthenes' Rede für Ktesiphon über den Kranz* (Heidelberg 1976). In contrast to the prevailing view, E. Harris argues that Demosthenes (not Aeschines) had the law on his side; *Persuasion: Greek Rhetoric in Action*, ed. I. Worthington (London 1994) 140–150.

64. A. E. Raubitschek, "Demokratia," *Hesperia* 31 (1962) 238–243. He cites a considerable amount of further evidence for the existence of a cult of Democracy in Athens at that time.

It was during Lycurgus' administration, not long after Alexander's razing of Thebes, that Aristotle returned to Athens after an absence of more than twelve years. Among the works he produced in the following years is the *Athenaion Politeia,* an account of the Athenian state preserved almost complete in a London papyrus published in 1891. This is the sole surviving work from the series of 158 such essays on individual Greek states produced by Aristotle and his circle in that period. It was written between 335 and 330, perhaps by Aristotle himself.[65] The first and longer section (chapters 1–41) describes the development of the Athenian constitution up to the opening years of the fourth century; the second section (chapters 42–69) provides a systematic review of existing constitutional institutions and their functioning at the time of writing.[66] It is not known with certainty whether Lycurgus actually invited Aristotle to settle in Athens again.[67] The commission for a statue of Socrates awarded to the sculptor Lysippus[68] can hardly have come from anyone but Lycurgus, and placing it in the Pompeion was tantamount to official rehabilitation. Lycurgus also initiated an official review that would result in accurate texts of the works of the three great tragedians Aeschylus, Sophocles, and Euripides, to protect them from unauthorized interpolations of the kind that actors occasionally inserted.[69] While a philological undertaking of this nature resembles some of the work being done at the time by Aristotle and his pupils, the inspiration for it need not have come from that source.

Lycurgus still participated in the debate that took place in Athens in 324 over granting Alexander the status of a god,[70] but he must have died shortly thereafter and played no part in the uproar over Harpalus.

---

65. Rhodes, *Commentary* 51–58; the mention of the archon of 329/8 in 54.7 is considered a later interpolation.

66. A detailed discussion is in ibid.; see also the collection by M. Piérart, *Aristote et Athènes.*

67. See Mitchel, *Lykourgan Athens* 38.

68. Diog. Laert. 2.43.

69. Galen *Corpus Medic. Graecor.* V.10.2.1, p. 79 Wenkebach; R. Pfeiffer, *History of Classical Scholarship from the Beginnings to the End of the Hellenistic Age* (Oxford 1968) 82 and 192. Lycurgus had statues of these three dramatists placed in the Theater of Dionysus as part of his renovation and improvements. Statues of other poets were added later: the Athenians Menander and Philippides, Phanes of Chios, and Diodorus of Sinope (Habicht, *Untersuchungen* 14–15); for more on the general topic see Pausanias 1.21.1. The base of the statue of Menander, sculpted by Cephisodotus and Timarchos, sons of Praxiteles, is in *IG* II^2.3777.

70. [Plut.] *mor.* 842D.

In general, critics have taken a positive view of Lycurgus' achievements on Athens' behalf, although recently Sally Humphreys reached a very different conclusion. She argues that Athens isolated itself from its surroundings and failed to develop "a constructive foreign policy" as a result of Lycurgus' "lack of political insight and imagination."[71] Such criticism seems unjustified in light of the political situation that existed after the defeat at Chaeronea and the destruction of Thebes. The events following Lycurgus' death demonstrated swiftly enough that Athens had by no means departed from the political arena for good.

4. The Crisis

Alexander's return from India to Persia and Mesopotamia put an end to the respite Athens had enjoyed during the years of his expedition to the East.[72] Relations deteriorated so swiftly and seriously that war appeared imminent. Alexander's sudden death on 10 June 323 did not prevent its outbreak but rather hastened its coming. The two events precipitating the war were the flight of Alexander's treasurer Harpalus to Athens[73] and the king's proclamation that he intended to take Samos away from the Athenians, whose settlers had occupied it for forty years, and return it to the Samians, now living scattered throughout the ancient world.[74] Additional tensions arose from the king's wish to

71. Humphreys, "Lycurgus" 220. She also observes for this period an "increasing tendency of the city to act out a representation of polis life for her contemporaries in the Hellenistic World rather than seek a role in the new configuration of power. And this, surely, is the most significant criticism to be made of his [Lycurgus'] politics," the "absence of any constructive foreign policy . . . a lack of political insight and imagination" (219).

72. The most important recent works on the period are S. Jaschinski, *Alexander und Griechenland unter dem Eindruck der Flucht des Harpalos* (Bonn 1981); W. Will, *Athen und Alexander* (Munich 1983); Bosworth, *Conquest* 215–228 and 278–290; and R. Sealey, *Demosthenes and His Time* (New York 1993) chap. 8.

73. For more on Harpalus and the involvement of Athens in his fate, see H. Berve, *Das Alexanderreich auf prosopographischer Grundlage,* vol. 2 (Munich 1926) 75–80; E. Badian, *JHS* 81 (1961) 16–43; Jaschinski, *Alexander und Griechenland;* I. Worthington, *SO* 61 (1986) 63–76; R. Lane Fox, *Chios: A Conference at the Homereion in Chios 1984* (Oxford 1986) 117–120.

74. For more on developments concerning Samos, see C. Habicht, *AM* 72 (1957) 156–169 and *Chiron* 5 (1975) 45–50; R. M. Errington, *Chiron* 5 (1975) 51–57; E. Badian, *ZPE* 23 (1976) 289–294; K. Rosen, *Historia* 27 (1978) 20–39; W. Transier, *Samiaka: Epigraphische Studien zur Geschichte von Samos in hellenistischer und römischer Zeit* (Mannheim 1985) 19–26 and 163–164; G. Shipley, *A History of Samos, 800–188 B.C.* (Oxford 1989) 161–168.

receive the kind of honors from the Greek states traditionally reserved for the gods.

Whether the Athenians had earned Alexander's wrath by permitting the Persian fleet to take on supplies in Samos on one occasion is not certain. But around March 324 or shortly thereafter Alexander made a public announcement, either in Susa or in his camp, of his intention to return Samos to the Samians.[75] The news must have reached Athens before the summer, just when the Athenians were beginning the debate over whether or not to award Alexander divine honors.[76] The situation was exacerbated by the unexpected arrival of Harpalus in late spring of that year. Fearing, presumably with good reason, that Alexander would punish him for his misdeeds, Harpalus had absconded with a large amount of treasure from Babylon and set out for Athens by way of Tarsus, with a large fleet of warships and an army of mercenaries. When they arrived in June, however, Philocles, the general in command of Piraeus, refused them entry to the harbor. Harpalus thereupon sailed on to Taenarum in Laconia, which had long been a gathering place for mercenaries looking for employment. There he disposed of his ships and their crews and returned to Athens as a supplicant, with only three ships and 700 talents of silver. He received permission to enter the city about the middle of June. A few years before Harpalus had been awarded Athenian citizenship in gratitude for his help in keeping the city supplied with grain.[77] He could thus claim some right to be taken in, no matter how difficult his request might prove for the Athenian state.

At about this time Nicanor, Aristotle's adopted son and son-in-law, arrived in Greece as ambassador to attend the Olympic Games (which took place in late July 324) and to proclaim Alexander's new "exiles' decree": the Greek states must readmit all citizens whom they had previously sent into exile. The contents of this decree were in fact

75. See the decree issued by the Samians only a short time later for Gorgos of Iasos, Alexander's guardian of arms, who put their case to Alexander; *Syll.* 312, reprinted with detailed commentary by A. J. Heisserer, *Alexander the Great and the Greeks: The Epigraphic Evidence* (Norman 1980) 169–203. There it is further stated that other Greeks congratulated Alexander on his decision. At least one more officer intervened on behalf of the Samians and was honored by them not long afterward (*AM* 44 [1919] 6, no. 5G). A little later, in the fall of 324, Gorgos urged Alexander to wage war against the Athenians (Ephippos, *FGrHist* 126 F 5).

76. Habicht, *Gottmenschentum* 28–36 and 246–250; Bosworth, *Conquest* 288–290.

77. Python, *TGrF* 1, no. 91, F 1.16.

already known, since Alexander had read it to his army that spring. In expectation of its enforcement, countless Greek exiles had streamed into Olympia, and they greeted the announcement with enthusiastic applause. Demosthenes, who was present at the games as official leader of the Athenian delegation, seized the opportunity to negotiate on behalf of the city with Nicanor. The situation had become critical. Alexander had ordered the Athenians both to vacate Samos,[78] a colony they were unwilling to give up, and to hand over Harpalus.[79]

Demosthenes was apparently able to negotiate a delay on the question of Samos, enabling a delegation from Athens to negotiate with the king; in any event the royal decree was not enforced immediately. The Athenians avoided having to extradite Harpalus by allowing him to escape. (Soon afterward he was murdered by one of his own lieutenants in Crete.) Demosthenes yielded on the question of Alexander's divinity; he had previously opposed every such proposal, but now he was clearly hoping to win a concession from the king regarding Samos. The citizens of Athens duly approved a motion introduced by Demades to worship Alexander as a god. It was then discovered that half of Harpalus' 700 talents—deposited at Demosthenes' suggestion on the Acropolis for safekeeping after Harpalus' arrest—was missing. The disappearance of the money caused a tremendous scandal, and the populace, already stirred up by the demand to give up Samos, was in an uproar. The city buzzed with rumors, and suspicion fell on a number of politicians, especially Demosthenes. In September responsibility for investigating the matter was given to the Areopagus Council made up of former archons. The investigation ran on for six months, until March 323. About this time the delegation sent to Alexander returned with the news that he was unwilling to bargain in the matter of Samos. It may have been this decision which prompted the Areopagus to hand down indictments in the case of the missing funds. Those named had to stand trial, chief among them Demosthenes, accused of having accepted 20 talents of Harpalus' money, and Demades. Among Demosthenes' accusers at his trial were Hypereides, who had been his

78. It remains an open question whether this demand arose from applying the provisions of the decree on the return of exiles or—as seems more probable—was a separate action along the same lines.

79. No fewer than three people demanded Harpalus' extradition: Alexander's representative Philoxenus, Antipater, and Olympias; Hypereides 1.8.10–24; Diodorus 17.108.7; Pausanias 2.33.4.

close associate for so long, and Deinarch; their speeches have survived complete or nearly complete. Demades had gone into exile without waiting for trial. Demosthenes received a large fine and, proving unable to pay it, was thrown into prison. He soon managed to escape, however, and fled to Aegina or Troizen. There the news of Alexander's death in Babylon must have reached him.

In the meantime the conflict over Samos had intensified. Two resolutions of the Samian popular assembly from the years 321–319, discovered not long ago, have provided some unexpected details. The first is a decree honoring Antileon of Chalcis for the following services.[80] A number of Samians returned to the island from Anaia, the Samian territory on the mainland of Asia Minor (near present-day Kuşadaşi). The Athenian Assembly thereupon passed a decree ordering the Athenian *strategos* for Samos to arrest them all, including the children, and send them to Athens. These orders were sent by the fast government sailing ship *Paralos*. When the Samian captives reached Athens, they were imprisoned and sentenced to death. As soon as he heard, Antileon intervened, out of the long-standing friendship existing between his city of Chalcis and Samos. He sent a sum of his own money to the Council of 500 and "the Eleven," the officials responsible for executions, thereby saving the captives' lives. Antileon then arranged for their transport back to Chalcis. After their return, the Samians honored him with a bronze statue in the sanctuary of Hera and a gold crown at the games held in honor of the kings.

The Samian resolution must date from 321–319, since this was the only period in which the festival of the kings Philip Arrhidaeus and Alexander IV took place in Samos. In 321 Perdiccas, then regent for the kings, carried out Alexander's intention of returning the island to its original inhabitants; this must have been the occasion for instituting the games in the kings' names. Only two years later, however, the new regent Polyperchon reversed the decision and returned Samos to the Athenians. As it transpired, the new decision was never enforced: the Athenians did not reclaim the island, and the Samians kept their territory. Nonetheless the cult of the two kings and the games can hardly have continued under the new circumstances.

The Samian returnees' arrest and sentencing took place before Per-

80. C. Habicht, *AM* 72 (1957) 156–164, no. 1; A. Bielman, *Retour à la liberté* (Athens 1994) 22–31, no. 7.

diccas' decision, however, when there was still an Athenian general for Samos and the island was still in the hands of Athenian cleruchs—in other words, before 321, and also before the end of the Lamian War.[81] The Samians taken captive by the Athenian commander must have decided to return home after hearing of Alexander's intention to restore their island to them, which he announced in the summer of 324. They may even have arrived while Alexander was still alive, before June 323; in any event, they came early enough to fall into the Athenian general's hands.[82]

The second resolution, passed at approximately the same time, honors Nausinicus of Sestus on the Hellespont for having helped the Samians return to their island by sending two warships.[83] Gaps in the surviving text of the inscription leave unclear whether he only helped transport them from the mainland to the island[84] or also supported them in a war against the remaining Athenian cleruchs.[85]

Both the order sent by the Athenian people to the commander at Samos to place returning Samians under arrest and the death sentence passed against them (though never carried out) demonstrate unmistakably that Athens had no intention of accepting Alexander's decision and was determined to fight to keep the island.[86] Thus as soon as Alexander's intention became known in the summer of 324, the city began reckoning with the possibility of war and secretly started preparing for it. The Athenians sought allies among those states which had suffered most from Alexander's policies. The Aetolian League was an obvious choice, since Alexander had threatened to take revenge personally on the Aetolians for destroying the Acarnanian city of Oeniadae.[87]

The Athenians made contact with the Aetolians through Leosthenes, an Athenian citizen who does not appear to have held public office before this period.[88] Leosthenes proved an able organizer and diplomat

---

81. R. M. Errington was the first to recognize this correctly; *Chiron* 5 (1975) 51–57.
82. Whether this occurred shortly before or after Alexander's death is immaterial.
83. C. Habicht, *AM* 72 (1957) 164–169, no. 2.
84. For the restoration of lines 8–9 see J. and L. Robert, *Bulletin épigraphique* (1960) 318.
85. E. Badian, *ZPE* 23 (1976) 289–294, suggests π[όλεμον].
86. Diodorus 18.8.7.
87. Diodorus 17.111.3 and 18.8.6; Plut. *Alexander* 49.
88. Both Jaschinski (*Alexander und Griechenland* 51–54) and Bosworth (*Conquest* 293–294) have made a strong case that this Leosthenes is not the territorial commander for Attica

in the ensuing months and emerged as a military leader. His rise to prominence is linked with the problem of mercenaries. In 324 Alexander had ordered all satraps to disband their mercenary armies. Leosthenes gathered together a large number of these rootless, unemployed men and transported them to Taenarum, already known as an assembling point for mercenaries looking for work. The soldiers at Taenarum chose Leosthenes as their new leader, and Leosthenes in turn placed himself at the disposal of the Athenian government. The Council secretly approved his request for aid, sending him fifty talents and a shipment of weapons. With the approval of the Council, but still acting as a private citizen, Leosthenes approached the Aetolians.[89] At the time of Alexander's death he headed an army of 8,000 battle-trained mercenaries. This must have been when he was chosen hoplite general of his home city for 323/2. The Athenians had funds at their disposal from the treasure Harpalus had left behind, and they had already sent out secret diplomatic feelers to various Greek states. The Athenian navy numbered several hundred ships. When the news of the king's death in Babylon reached the city, it was prepared for war. Now that Alexander was no more, however, the aims of the impending war would be different: the Athenians would be fighting not only to maintain possession of Samos but to rid themselves and their Greek allies of Macedonian domination altogether. In the fall of 323 what was then called the Hellenic War broke out, which has since come to be known as the Lamian War.

in the much-discussed inscription of Oropus, *AE* (1918) 73–100, no. 95–97 (Reinmuth, *Inscriptions,* no. 15). It has also been demonstrated that this inscription belongs not to 324/3 but rather to between 329/8 and 326/5; see A. W. Gomme, *The Population of Athens in the Fifth and Fourth Centuries B.C.* (Oxford 1933) 67–69; H.-J. Gehrke, *Phokion. Studien zur Erfassung seiner historischen Gestalt* (Munich 1976) 78–79; Bosworth, *Conquest* 294.

89. Diodorus 17.111.3 and 18.8.7–9.4.

Under Foreign Rule
(323–307)

1. The Hellenic War

As soon as the reports of Alexander the Great's death were confirmed, most Greek states felt the time had come to put an end to Macedonian domination; new tension had arisen when Alexander ordered them to readmit all the citizens they had exiled.[1] A few states felt differently, such as Sparta, still suffering from the effects of King Agis' war, and Boeotia, where the neighbors of the razed city of Thebes had carved up Theban territory and shared it among themselves. The Boeotians had no interest in disturbing the status quo. But most cities were in ferment. In Rhodes the inhabitants drove out the Macedonian forces of occupation; in Athens Leosthenes came out in the open and, with the support of Hypereides among others, persuaded a majority of the Assembly to vote for war. The warnings of Demades and Phocion, now almost eighty years old, fell on deaf ears. Athens entered into alliances with the Aetolians, the Phocians, and the Locrians in central Greece, with the city of Sicyon in Achaea, and with others on the Peloponnese. The Aetolians were especially important, for their population was large and they controlled Thermopylae, the strategic narrow pass between Macedonia and Greece. Demosthenes lobbied the Peloponnesians to join a coalition against Macedonia and, as an exile from Athens, found a hearing where official delegations had failed. After this success his kinsman Demon introduced a motion to rehabilitate him; Demos-

---

1. See in general for this chapter Will, *Histoire* 1: 27–74; J. M. Williams, *Athens without Democracy: The Oligarchy of Phocion and the Tyranny of Demetrius of Phalerum, 322–307 B.C.* (Ann Arbor 1985); H.-J. Gehrke, *Phokion. Studien zur Erfassung seiner historischen Gestalt* (Munich 1976); L. A. Tritle, *Phocion the Good* (London 1988).

thenes returned to Athens and made peace with Hypereides, a political comeback reminiscent of Alcibiades' return from banishment in 408. The Assembly voted to mobilize the fleet and the army and declared war to liberate Greece from Macedonian occupation.[2] Citizens up to the age of forty were called up, that is, half of the forty-two year-classes (ages eighteen to fifty-nine) expected to bear arms. The members of three tribes received orders to defend Attica; the other seven tribes were to hold themselves in readiness for an offensive.[3]

The public mood turned against all who had maintained close ties with Macedonian leaders. Because he had sponsored the bill to grant Alexander divine status, Demades was fined ten talents for the crime of "introducing a new god." When he proved unable to pay, he was deprived of the rights to vote and to hold public office. Other compromised politicians, such as Pytheas and Callimedon "the Crab," left Athens and joined Antipater in the Macedonian camp. Aristotle, widely known to be on friendly terms with Antipater, left the city toward the end of 323 to live at his mother's house in Chalcis, on the island of Euboea. (All Euboea except the city of Carystus remained loyal to Macedonia.) A charge of impiety was entered against him, related to a poem he had written some twenty years earlier in honor of his father-in-law, the tyrant Hermeias of Atarneus; allegedly it bore a suspicious resemblance to a religious hymn of worship. Before his death in Chalcis in 322, Aristotle learned that he had been further punished by revocation of the honors granted to him by the Amphictionic Council at Delphi. He wrote to Antipater that this caused him no great distress, although naturally he resented the insult.[4]

2. The most important sources for the Lamian War are Diodorus 18.8–18; Plut. *Phocion* 23–29, *Demosthenes* 27–31; and Hypereides' *Funeral Oration* (6). Numerous passages of various authors and several Attic inscriptions from 323/2 mention alliances with the Aetolians, Phocians, Sicyon (*StV,* no. 413), and the Locrians (*Hesperia* 2 [1933] 397, no. 17). Still valuable is A. Schaefer, *Demosthenes und seine Zeit*[2], vol. 3 (Leipzig 1887) 351–398; see also F. Stähelin, "Lamischer Krieg," *RE* (1924) 562–564; G. A. Lehmann, *ZPE* 73 (1988) 121–149.

3. Diodorus 18.10.2. For the strength of the Athenian navy, see N. G. Ashton, *ABSA* 72 (1977) 1–11; J. S. Morrison, *JHS* 107 (1987) 88–97; N. V. Sekunda, *ABSA* 87 (1992) 348–354. Although 417 warships are registered for the year 323, many of them did not see action.

4. Aelian *Var. hist.* 14.1 and further I. Düring, *Aristotle in the Ancient Biographical Tradition* (Göteborg 1957) 339–340 and 401, T 67 c. Düring notes that the statement is consistent with a passage in the *Nicomachean Ethics* and that the letter might thus well be genuine. Aristotle named none other than Antipater as executor of his will (Diog. Laert.

The Greek allies formed their own *synedrion* (council), which consisted of one delegate from each member state, and met at army headquarters.[5] Leosthenes was elected commander-in-chief. He immediately attacked and defeated the Boeotians, occupied Thermopylae, and joined forces with the troops of the Aetolian League. Antipater, hoping to prevent Thessaly from entering the war on the Greek side, moved south from Macedonia. With his forces badly outnumbered, he lost a battle to Leosthenes and withdrew to Lamia, a city that now endured a long siege and gave the war the name by which it would later be known. Antipater had hopes that two of Alexander's generals, Craterus and Leonnatus, would come to his aid with reinforcements. Shortly before his death Alexander had appointed Craterus to succeed Antipater as "general for Europe," and at the time of the Lamian War Craterus was in Asia Minor at the head of an army of 11,000 veterans. Leonnatus, a relative of the Macedonian royal family and satrap of the territory near the Hellespont, had been a member of Alexander's bodyguard and was said to have ambitions to the throne.

For the time being, however, Antipater had to hold out alone. He repulsed Greek attacks on the city of Lamia but was in danger of being starved out. The situation became so precarious that finally he agreed to negotiate. Leosthenes demanded unconditional surrender, but Antipater refused. With the early Greek victories still being celebrated in Athens and the allied states, the war of attrition around Lamia continued. Leosthenes was killed in one of the skirmishes. The Athenian Antiphilus succeeded him as commander-in-chief but was no match for his predecessor in energy or prestige; Leosthenes' death proved a severe blow to the Greek cause.

Leosthenes and the others killed in the early months of the war were buried in the winter in a ceremony in the Cerameicus. Hypereides delivered the funeral oration in their honor, just as Pericles had done for the Athenian soldiers killed in the first year of the Peloponnesian War, and as Demosthenes had done after the battle of Chaeronea. Large portions of Hypereides' speech, which achieved fame in its own time, have been preserved on papyrus. He praised Leosthenes for initiating the war and serving as its commander, and praised Athens as

---

5.11). On the honors from Delphi see W. Spoerri, in *Comptes et inventaires dans la cité grecque*, ed. D. Knoepfler (Geneva 1988) 111–140, esp. 129–130.

5. *IG* II².467.8–10.

the champion of Greek liberty, a cause for which Leosthenes and the other citizens had given their lives. Hypereides placed the fundamental opposition between monarchy and republican government at the core of his speech, equating them with despotism on the one hand and with the rule of law on the other. Defeat, he said, would mean the triumph throughout Greece of Macedonian arrogance over the power of law.[6]

This funeral oration is the last surviving great speech from Athens, the swan song of Greek freedom. At the battlefront the balance of power was beginning to shift. The allies were finding it difficult to keep an army in the field for such a long siege, and the Aetolians withdrew. The remaining allied troops appeared strong enough to overcome Antipater's last resistance. But in the spring of 322 Leonnatus and his forces arrived. The Greeks attacked early to prevent them from reaching Antipater in Lamia, and the Thessalian cavalry under Menon of Pharsalus won a splendid victory, forcing Leonnatus back onto a hill. By the end of the battle Leonnatus was dead. Nevertheless on the following day his infantry, which had not participated in the first day's fighting, entered Lamia, and Antipater was saved. The Greek forces had prevailed on the battlefield, but they were unable to block Antipater's withdrawal to the north.

In the meantime the war had spread to the sea. The Athenian admiral Euetion set out with 170 ships to find and destroy Antipater's fleet at the Hellespont. However, Perdiccas, the regent, sent Alexander's fleet out from Phoenicia under the capable command of the Macedonian admiral Cleitus, and Antipater's fleet was soon enlarged. Cleitus was in time, and in two naval battles around the first of July 322, at Abydos on the Hellespont and then off the island of Amorgos in the Cyclades, their combined forces destroyed the Athenian armada.[7] The decisive land battle took place not long afterward. Craterus and his army had joined forces with Antipater under the latter's command. A total of 40,000 Macedonian hoplites thus faced only 25,000 Greeks in a battle near Crannon in Thessaly in early August 322. Once again the Thes-

6. Hypereides 6.3; 5; 16; and 20. At the start of the war he encountered a delegation from Antipater in Rhodes whose members praised Antipater as a just and honorable man. Hypereides responded, "Yes, we know, but we do not want a despot, even if he is a just one"; [Plut.] *mor.* 805A.

7. The naval battles, especially the first one at the Hellespont, are mentioned in several resolutions of the Athenian Assembly from the next few years: *IG* II^2.398, 492(?), 493, 505, 506; *Hesperia* 8 (1939) 30, no. 8.18–21(?); 40 (1971) 174, no. 25. See also A. Wilhelm, *Attische Urkunden*, vol. 5 (1942) 175–181 (= *Akademieschriften* 1: 791–799).

salian cavalry held its own, but the Macedonian phalanx defeated the Greek footsoldiers. The Greeks managed to retreat without a rout, but the war was lost. When they asked for terms, Antipater insisted on negotiating with each Greek state separately, thus dissolving the alliance and forcing the allies to compete with one another for the most favorable terms. Very soon the Athenians and Aetolians were left isolated.

For their own negotiations with Antipater and Craterus, the Athenians sent a delegation led by Demades and Phocion, the very men who had advised against the war in the first place, joined by Xenocrates of Chalcedon, a philosopher who had become the third warden of Plato's Academy.[8] It was now Antipater's turn to demand unconditional surrender. When the Athenian delegation agreed, Antipater stipulated his own conditions for peace: Athens would have to permit stationing of Macedonian troops in the harbor fortress of Munychia and extradite the chief Athenian politicians responsible for the war. He also demanded an amendment to the city's constitution providing that only citizens with assets worth 2,000 drachmas or more would enjoy political rights, although democracy would continue to exist in name. This census class, most likely proposed by the Athenian representatives themselves,[9] reduced the number of citizens with full rights from 21,000 to 9,000. Athens once again lost the city of Oropus and the sanctuary of Amphiaraus. Officially Antipater left the fate of Samos to be decided by the two kings, but in actual fact by the regent, Perdiccas, as neither of the two kings was capable of independent action. Antipater cleverly avoided taking sides on an unpopular question by declaring Samos to be Asian territory; as *strategos* for Europe only, he had no authority in the matter.

Phocion and Demades now assumed leadership of the government in Athens. Demades lent his name to the inevitable motion to condemn to death those Athenians who had opposed Antipater. Prominent among those condemned were Demosthenes, Hypereides, and Eucrates, who had initiated one of the reforms of 336. Antipater's hench-

---

8. Demades' privileges as a citizen, which he had lost for proposing to honor Alexander as a god, were hastily restored to him to enable him to participate in the mission. Despite his opposition to the war, Phocion had served Athens loyally as a general, defeating a Macedonian force that landed near Rhamnus in Attica.

9. Gehrke, *Phokion* 91; see also R. W. Wallace, *The Areopagus Council to 307 B.C.* (Baltimore 1989) 201.

men pursued them to the Peloponnese, and Hypereides and Demosthenes met their deaths in October within a week of each other: Hypereides on the ninth of Pyanopsion according to the Athenian calendar and Demosthenes, by his own hand, on the sixteenth. Euphron of Sicyon and the surviving leaders of other Greek states met the same fate.[10] However, Antipater appears to have avoided excesses. In the rest of Greece he arranged political matters to suit himself, and only the Aetolians remained independent. With Craterus, who had married his daughter Phila, he began a war against them, but they soon broke it off to devote all their attention to Asia, where developments were moving swiftly after Perdiccas, who had mounted an unsuccessful attempt to invade Egypt, was murdered in 321.

In mid-September 322 Macedonian troops took over the fortress in Piraeus.[11] At once they became the despised symbol of foreign control, not only renewed but now exerted much more directly than before. Simultaneously, however, the occupying troops guaranteed the stability of the Athenian regime. In Caesar's time the historian Diodorus saw Athens' subjugation as a late but deserved punishment for its part in the sacrilege committed by the Phocians at Delphi a generation earlier.[12] The philosopher Xenocrates, offered Athenian citizenship in recognition of his service as a member of the delegation that had negotiated peace with Antipater, refused it, saying that he did not want to become an Athenian citizen through the provision of a constitution he had labored to avert.[13]

A few months later, near the end of 322, news about the fate of Samos reached Athens from the kings' court; Demades and his delegation had failed to win their case. Alexander's order was upheld: the Athenian cleruchs had to leave the island, and the Samians regained possession after forty-three years in exile.[14] Among those forced to return to Athens were the family of the philosopher Epicurus, who was

10. *IG* II[2].448.52–56.

11. This event occurred on the 20th of Boedromion, 13 years to the day after news of the destruction of Thebes had reached Athens.

12. Diodorus 16.64.1.

13. Plut. *Phocion* 29.6; D. Whitehead, *RhM* 124 (1981) 238–241.

14. Diodorus 18.18.9; Diog. Laert. 10.1; and the "Demades Papyrus" (*Berliner Klassikertexte* 7 [1923], lines 188 ff. and 213–214), with commentary by H. von Arnim, *WS* 43 (1922–23) 87–88. Approximately 35 decrees from the next two decades are known in which the Samians thanked citizens of various states throughout the Greek world for the assistance they had rendered to Samian refugees during their exile. The Samians also asked for loans to

born on Samos and twenty years old at the time of the family's resettlement.[15]

Athens was hit far harder by its defeat in 322 than in 338. Its fleet had been destroyed, and Athens never regained its status as a major sea power.[16] In addition the city suffered the loss of its outposts Oropus and Samos[17] and, most humiliating of all, was forced to accept the presence of foreign troops in Piraeus. Nonetheless the Athenians did not have to hang their heads in shame; they had led a courageous rebellion to liberate their city and all of Greece, and had fought bravely. Their achievement has never been so misunderstood as by the classicist Ulrich von Wilamowitz-Moellendorff, who wrote at the age of thirty-two that "the Athenians completely lost their heads after Alexander's death, imagining that because it was possible for the king to die, they could scream their long-lost freedom back to life"[18] The opposite, and in my view correct, conclusion is that of A. B. Bosworth, who recently wrote, "Once Alexander's death was known, the people rose to the call of liberty and . . . to the sacrifices war demanded of them in an effort not unworthy of their greatest days."[19]

2. Unsettled Postwar Years

During the war significant political changes had taken place in Asia that would powerfully affect Athens and the rest of Greece.[20] Alexander's field marshals had met in Babylon to choose the king's successor and

---

cover the costs associated with their return and the foundation of a new government; among those who contributed were the state of Sparta ([Aristotle] *Oeconomica* 2.2.9) and the respected Milesian citizen Sosistratus (*AM* 87 [1972] 199, no. 4); C. Habicht, *Chiron* 5 (1975) 45–50.

15. Diog. Laert. 10.1. He had joined the corps of ephebes in the city in 325/4, together with his contemporary Menander.

16. Beloch, *GG* 4.1: 73. M. Amit's *Athens and the Sea* (Brussels 1965) ends with the year 322. In a curse tablet from the period A. Wilhelm, recognizing the names of ten *trierarchs* and others involved in the administration of the fleet, realized that it was occasioned by a lawsuit of 323/2 involving the fleet; *JÖAI* 7 (1904) 122–126. The unknown author's curses on his opponents were all too effective.

17. Thus when Demades observed that he was at the helm of the wreck of Athens, his remark had some truth to it.

18. *Antigonos von Karystos* (Berlin 1881) 182.

19. *Conquest* 211.

20. For more on the subject of this section see Beloch, *GG* 4.1: 61–133; Will, *Histoire* 1: 19–65; and Hammond, *History* 95–150. For the dual monarchy see C. Habicht, *Vestigia* 17

divide up the most important offices of the empire among themselves. They decided to have two kings rule jointly: Alexander's half-brother Philip Arrhidaeus and the son, also named Alexander, born to the late king's Iranian wife Roxane several months after the father's death. But as Philip was feeble-minded and Alexander still an infant, the Macedonian Perdiccas took command of the empire as regent. The other chief posts were shared among Craterus, then on his way to relieve Antipater in Macedonia and Europe; Ptolemy, who received the satrapy of Egypt; and Lysimachus, who got Thrace. Leonnatus received Hellespontine Phrygia, and Antigonus the satrapy of central Phrygia. Antigonus became the first to rebel against Perdiccas' autocratic ambitions. Too weak to oppose Perdiccas alone, he enlisted the help of Antipater and Craterus, who, having defeated the Greek alliance at Crannon, were now involved in a war against the Aetolians. They agreed to drop the Aetolian campaign immediately and come to his support in the fight against Perdiccas, and their alliance was soon strengthened by Ptolemy and Lysimachus. In the following years this pattern would prove typical of the struggles among Alexander's successors: when one of them (first Perdiccas and later Antigonus) achieved a position of primacy, all the others banded together against him. Some of the Successors, such as Antigonus and probably Craterus, harbored their own ambitions to achieve sole dominance, whereas others like Ptolemy and Lysimachus simply wanted to prevent any one leader from gaining the upper hand.

Perdiccas attacked Ptolemy in Egypt before Antipater and Craterus

---

(1973) 367–377. The chronology of events from 321 to 312 is extremely controversial. The foundation was laid by Beloch; the most important recent contributions are R. M. Errington, *JHS* 90 (1970) 49–77 and *Hermes* 105 (1977) 478–504; B. Gullath and L. Schober, in *Festschrift S. Lauffer* (n.p. 1986) 329–378; and A. B. Bosworth, *Chiron* 22 (1992) 55–81. Errington and Gullath/Schober reject Beloch's chronology, arguing that the conference at Triparadeisos took place not in the summer of 321 but a year later, and that the naval battle at the Bosporus in which Antigonus defeated Cleitus took place in the summer of 317 rather than 318. However, Bosworth supports Beloch's conclusions. Scholars agree that Philip Arrhidaeus and Eurydice died in the fall of 317. For the events of this period in Athens, Errington's "low" chronology has been corrected: The restoration of democracy and Phocion's execution took place in the spring of 318 (J. M. Williams, *Hermes* 112 [1984] 300–305; Gullath and Schober 338–349; Bosworth 68–69). According to Beloch and Bosworth, Cassander began rebuilding Thebes in the summer of 316; Errington and Gullath/Schober argue for the summer of 315. Cassander's campaign against Lemnos, in which Athenian forces participated, is assigned by Errington to the fall of 313 (*Hermes* 398).

could arrive with reinforcements from Europe. However, Ptolemy managed to defeat Perdiccas on his own, inflicting such great losses that two of Perdiccas' officers murdered him; one of them was Seleucus, who later founded what was to become the greatest of the "successor" kingdoms. After the mutiny the army offered Ptolemy the regency in Perdiccas' place, but Ptolemy refused. At the time of Perdiccas' disastrous attack, his ally Eumenes opened hostilities on another front. Eumenes, a Greek by birth who had once served as Alexander the Great's secretary, won a resounding victory in Asia Minor at a battle in which Craterus, the third of Alexander's outstanding generals after Leonnatus and Perdiccas, was killed. Meanwhile Antipater had taken his forces to Syria to meet Perdiccas' army on its return from Egypt, which had elected him regent in his absence. The leaders of both armies conferred at Triparadeisos in central Syria in the summer of 320; the election of the now seventy-eight-year-old Antipater as regent was confirmed, and he also took over Perdiccas' files containing all the murdered regent's correspondence. Among the documents were letters from Demades in Athens that would prove fatal once their contents were discovered. The army leadership passed death sentences against Eumenes and the leaders of Perdiccas' party and delegated Antigonus to campaign against them. Antipater dispatched his son Cassander to assist and no doubt also to keep a watchful eye on him. Antipater himself then returned to Macedonia with the two kings.

In the interim Athens' defeat in the Lamian War had resulted in major political changes at home. The new leaders called the basis of their regime "the constitution of the fathers" *(patrios politeia)*, but their democratic opponents soon decried it as a virtual oligarchy.[21] The most significant innovation was the creation of two classes of citizenship, one with full rights and the other with restricted rights. Members of the second class could neither vote nor hold elective office. They were thus placed in effect on a level with the *atimoi,* the "dishonored." These were citizens who had been found guilty of committing an offense and deprived of their political rights. Antipater offered land in Thrace to the disfranchised Athenians, and although many must have accepted, the claim that Athens lost a third of its population at this time

21. *IG* II^2.448.60–62 of 318. According to Gehrke, *Phokion* 95, this was a "modified oligarchy." For details of the constitution see Ferguson, *HA* 22–27; F. W. Mitchel, *Hesperia* 33 (1964) 346–347; Gehrke 90–97; Williams, *Athens* 113–129; and Wallace, *Areopagus Council* 201–204.

seems greatly exaggerated.[22] We do not know whether payments were continued for jury duty or attendance at Assembly meetings (to reimburse citizens for the time lost from their regular employments). If the corps of ephebes continued to exist at all, it must have lost members and potential recruits in the same proportion as the citizenry lost citizens with full rights, namely about four-sevenths. The chief alteration to the structure of government was the replacement of the secretary of the Council (*grammateus*) by a registrar (*anagrapheus*), who took up his duties at the beginning of the next term, in July 321, about eleven months after the new leaders assumed office. In the records of the years 321/0 and 320/19, this official is usually named before the eponymous archon; this fact, together with the known activities of the registrars, suggests that the office was filled by powerful members of the new regime, elected rather than chosen by lot. Another new office, that of the "guardians of the laws" (*nomophylakes*), was created at this time (or shortly afterward under Demetrius of Phalerum). The authority of the ten city magistrates, whose responsibilities included streets and public thoroughfares, was transferred to another ten-member board in charge of the city's markets.[23]

The leaders of the new regime were Demades and the now aging Phocion, who had been elected *strategos* almost every year since he first reached the minimum age of thirty in 371/0, or forty-five times in all. Demades' forum was the Assembly, where his name appears in the records of the next few years primarily as the sponsor of decrees. On his motion the most active opponents of Macedonian rule had been outlawed; their burial on Attic soil was forbidden. (Hypereides' relatives managed to circumvent this prohibition and hold a secret funeral in Attica.) The new regime dealt with Euphron of Sicyon as well. The first Peloponnesian leader to join the Greek alliance in 323, he was granted citizenship by the people of Athens as a mark of gratitude that same year. His honors were now revoked and the tablets on which they were inscribed destroyed. But the Athenians did not shun all those who had fought at their side. In 321/0, upholding one of the city's most laudable traditions, they took in some fifty Thessalians expelled by Antipater at the end of the war and gave asylum to a number of Dolopians who had suffered the same fate, probably in the same

22. Williams, *Athens* 112.
23. *IG* II^2.380.

year.[24] An exception to the general rule was made to permit the refugees to purchase land in Athens if they wished; their names were appended to the Assembly resolution. Stephen Tracy has shown that *IG* II^2.2406 contains nine names from the list of Thessalians given asylum, one of them definitely from the city of Pherae.[25] A fragment of another Assembly decree dating from the early summer of 321 is notable because it was found in Oropus, a city the Athenians had lost almost a year earlier. Presumably it is a copy, sent to Oropus, of a law related in some way to the transfer of power.[26] Hegemon, the sponsor of the resolution, belonged to the circle around Phocion and was among the politicians prepared to negotiate with Macedonia as early as 338.[27]

In the few years of its existence the moderate oligarchy of Athens was quite generous toward foreigners: six decrees involving awards of citizenship have survived in full or in part, and evidence from other periods suggests that this constitutes only a fraction of the total number.[28] Honors were also given to several foreigners who had aided the Athenians after the recent naval battles by rescuing shipwrecked sailors or assisting prisoners of war with supplies, ransom money, or transport home.[29] The general public began to find the presence of the Macedonian soldiers in Piraeus more and more disagreeable and pressed civic leaders harder to try to make Antipater withdraw them. Phocion refused to associate himself with any such initiative, but Demades, relying apparently on previous assurances from Antipater, bowed to the general will; he and his son Demeas were elected as ambassadors to Antipater, who had returned from Asia in the spring. But when they reached Antipater's court at Pella in the summer of 319, they had no opportunity to plead their case; they were at once accused of high treason and thrown into prison. Deinarch of Corinth presented the charges against them to a tribunal presided over by Cassander, Anti-

---

24. *IG* II^2.545 as reconstructed by A. Wilhelm (1939) 20–21 in *Akademieschriften* 3: 32–33. For the dating see also J. Pecírka, *The Formula for the Grant of Enktesis in Attic Inscriptions* (Prague 1966) 83–84. For the Dolopians: *IG* II^2.546.

25. S. V. Tracy, *Athenian Democracy in Transition: Attic Letter Cutters of 340 to 290 B.C.* (Berkeley 1995) 84 and 87–90.

26. *IG* II^2.375.

27. Gehrke, *Phokion* 100–101. Hegemon was executed at the same time as Phocion.

28. Osborne, *Naturalization* 1: 88 ff., D 29–34, and perhaps also *Hesperia* 62 (1993) 249.

29. *Hesperia* 40 (1971) 174, no. 25, dating from sometime around June 319 and, from about the same period, *IG* II^2.398.

pater's son. Cassander had been summoned back from Asia Minor because his father was near death. The charges against Demades were not unfounded, for among the papers in Perdiccas' files were letters he had written to Perdiccas urging him to come to Greece and rid the country of "the old despot" (meaning Antipater). All the prisoners' appeals to respect their diplomatic status were of no avail: Cassander had them both executed.

Antipater died not long afterward, and his demise further altered the political landscape. In choosing his successor he had passed over his son Cassander and named as regent an aging Macedonian general named Polyperchon. Cassander, unwilling to accept the role of second-in-command, secretly left the court at Pella to set up new headquarters. From there he sent demands to all Antipater's commanders in Greece to place their forces at his disposal. The man he dispatched to carry this order to Athens was Nicanor, who may have been his nephew. Nicanor's mission succeeded, and Menyllos, the commander of the Macedonian garrison in Piraeus, did in fact step down and hand over his troops.[30] Cassander also sent appeals to Ptolemy and other satraps of the empire, seeking their support.

In the fall of 319 Polyperchon issued a proclamation in the name of the two kings, hoping both to prevent his allies from shifting their loyalty to Cassander and to win the Greeks over to his side.[31] In it he blamed Antipater for the disasters that had befallen Greece in 322, and urged the Greeks to reopen their battle for freedom, promising that all Greeks who had been banished from their homelands by Macedonian commanders since 334 would be allowed to return and reclaim their property. The Greek states were ordered to readmit them by mid-April (the thirtieth of Xandikos according to the Macedonian calendar). Samos was also promised to Athens again, since King Philip had "given" it to them (that is, had not taken it away). All Greeks were called upon to live in peace with one another, and Polyperchon was ordered to implement the royal edict (actually his own).

The proclamation created a sensation in Athens, for it held out the

---

30. Until recently it was agreed that Nicanor was Aristotle's son-in-law who had announced Alexander's order concerning the exiled Greeks at Olympia. A. B. Bosworth, however, has made the attractive suggestion that he should instead be identified as a son of the Macedonian Balakros and Phila, i.e., a nephew of Cassander; *CQ* 44 (1994) 57–65.

31. Diodorus 18.56.1–8 (where 56.3 should read as suggested by L. Robert (*RPh* 50 [1926] 66).

prospect that they might regain not only their freedom but also Samos.[32] Phocion's public support declined immediately, and over his opposition the citizens sent a delegation to Pella to ask for help in achieving the goals of the proclamation. The Athenians also debated how they could rid themselves of Nicanor and the troops in Munychia without outside intervention. The Council held a meeting in Piraeus that Nicanor attended after Phocion promised him safe conduct. Dercylus, the *strategos* in charge of the harbor, urged the Council to arrest him, but Phocion refused to break his word; under the circumstances, Nicanor was his most important source of support. The Assembly then directed Phocion, as commanding general, to expel Nicanor from the fortress, but again Phocion refused to act, and Nicanor, instead of withdrawing, quickly summoned reinforcements and brought all of Piraeus under his control. A further resolution now instructed Phocion and others to meet with Nicanor and insist that he carry out the royal orders. This time Nicanor replied that he had been sent by Cassander to take over the fortress and could do nothing without further instructions from him. (Cassander had already departed for Asia Minor.) When an order to vacate the Piraeus arrived from Olympias, however, Nicanor began to waver; he agreed to go, then stalled for time.

At this point Polyperchon's son Alexander appeared with an army, raising hopes in the population that he would help them regain Munychia and Piraeus. Instead, Phocion persuaded Alexander to negotiate with Nicanor, and the two commanders began talks that excluded the Athenians. Phocion was acting in obvious defiance of the public will. In March or April 318 he and the members of his government were removed from office and indicted. Phocion could flee to either Nicanor or Alexander and chose the latter, who passed him on to his father with a letter of recommendation. At the same time the new masters in Athens sent a delegation to Polyperchon under the leadership of Hagnonides. At a meeting with both sides in Phocis, Polyperchon demonstrated both a lack of political skill and the extent of his perfidy: he dropped all pretense of support for Phocion and his party, handing them over to their opponents to deal with as they saw fit. He wrote to the Athenians that in his eyes Phocion was a traitor, but they were a

32. For more on the events related here, see Gehrke, *Phokion* 108–120. The main sources are Diodorus; Plut. *Phocion* 30–38; and Nepos *Phocion*. On the chronology of events in Athens see note 20 above. F. W. Mitchel has argued convincingly for placing the decree from Eleusis in honor of Derkylos (*IG* II^2.1287) in the year 319/8; *Hesperia* 33 (1964) 337–351.

free and independent people and should decide for themselves. "A victim of his own policies, he dropped Phocion in order not to lose face with the Greeks."[33] In Athens affairs were now in the hands of Hagnonides and a circle of radical democrats who had returned from exile. The Assembly met in a tumultuous session and illegally passed Hagnonides' motion condemning Phocion and his followers to death; the condemned men were led away to prison immediately. In early May 318 (the tenth of Munychion in the Attic calendar) Phocion drank the cup of hemlock to which he had been sentenced and died at the age of eighty-three.[34]

Such were the circumstances under which Athens returned to democracy in the spring of 318. The new public officials created by the oligarchs remained in office until the year ended at the beginning of July (a reference to the *anagrapheus* occurs on the last day of the year),[35] but with reduced responsibilities; as soon as the new term began they were replaced by traditional officials. In the fall Hagnonides introduced a motion officially to award once more to Euphron of Sicyon the honors earlier revoked by the oligarchy. A new monument containing both the old and the new decrees was erected in Euphron's honor; the text of the original decree had to be copied from the Assembly archives, as the old stele had been destroyed.[36] Shortly before this, at the Great Panathenaea about the beginning of August, Polyperchon's son Alexander dedicated a set of hoplite arms to the goddess, as Alexander the Great had done in 334 on a grander scale. At the same celebration Conon, a descendant of the famous admiral of the same name who had lived around the turn of the century, received a crown from the people; the honor is notable in view of the fact that in the year just past he had been a member of Phocion's political circle.[37]

All in all Polyperchon and Alexander failed to fulfill the hopes placed in them by the Athenians. They succeeded in holding the city and rural

33. Gehrke, *Phokion* 118.

34. Characteristically, Demophilos, one of the leaders in Phocion's prosecution, also appeared as one of Aristotle's prosecutors in 323 (Athen. 15.696B; Diog. Laert. 5.5), and Hagnonides introduced charges against Theophrastus in 318/7 (Diog. Laert. 5.37). After the Lamian War, Hagnonides was allowed to stay on the Peloponnese during his exile thanks to Phocion (Plut. *Phocion* 29.4; *AM* 67 [1942] 41, no. 49).

35. *Hesperia* 10 (1941) 268, no. 69.

36. See *IG* II^2.448.1–34 for the earlier and 35–87 for the later decrees.

37. *IG* II^2.1473, col. I.6–8 (Alexander); 1479 A 18–21 (Conon). For Conon's role before the democratic coup, see Diodorus 18.64.5.

areas of Attica, and protected its democratic government.[38] But Polyperchon's attempt to besiege Piraeus and drive Nicanor out was unsuccessful; Nicanor retained control of the harbor and was prepared to hand it over to Cassander, who would soon return to Athens with Antigonus' troops after his campaign in Asia Minor. Asia Minor was also the scene of strife over the succession, and, as usual, events in one part of the empire swiftly influenced developments elsewhere as a leader's star rose or fell. At the Triparadeisos conference, Antigonus had received the new title of "general of Asia" and with it orders to make war on the supporters of Perdiccas. He waged a highly successful campaign and began to expand his authority at the expense of other satraps. In the spring of 318 he expelled Arrhidaeus from all but a small enclave of his satrapy on the Hellespont and forced Cleitus, satrap of Lydia, to flee to Macedonia. Cleitus, who had won the sea battles of the Lamian War, allied himself with Polyperchon; he was present in Athens for the verdict against Phocion. Meanwhile their opponent Cassander approached Antigonus with a request for support; Antigonus acceded, as his own best interests lay in weakening the central authority of the old empire now controlled by Polyperchon. He supplied Cassander with an army and ships, and Ptolemy also promised to send help from Egypt.

Polyperchon countered by inviting Alexander's mother, Olympias, to come from Epirus and take over the education of her royal grandchild, hoping that some of the great respect she enjoyed in Macedonia would accrue to him and his cause. Olympias agreed, since she hated Cassander as much as she had hated his father, Antipater. Polyperchon and Olympias also attempted to reassert their control over Asia, where Antigonus was more and more openly flouting their authority. His disloyalty was becoming apparent in such actions as his seizure at Ephesus of a shipment of gold intended for the two kings, which he used to pay his own mercenaries. Polyperchon and Olympias appointed Eumenes as their representative in Asia, giving him instructions to start a campaign against Antigonus. Eumenes was just recovering from a loss to Antigonus, who had subjected him to a long siege in a Cappadocian fortress. With great ingenuity and boldness (and a measure of luck)

---

38. In May or June 318 Polyperchon wrote to Athenian officials asking that two of his aides be awarded Athenian citizenship; the Assembly resolution granting this request is *IG* II^2.387; cf. Gullath and Schober, in *Festschrift S. Lauffer* 343 n. 44.

Eumenes escaped from what had seemed a hopeless situation, only to see the outcome of the Triparadeisos conference turned on its head: in a flash he had been transformed from an enemy of the kings into their guardian and protector. It was then that Eumenes achieved his greatest coup: armed with authority from Polyperchon and Olympias, he won over the corps of 3,000 elite veteran troops in Cilicia known as the "silver shields" *(argyraspides)* and, with them, control of the large treasury of silver they guarded in the kings' names. With this money Eumenes recruited an army of mercenaries strong enough to withstand Antigonus.

Thus as the year 317 opened, two great opposing factions had formed: Polyperchon, as regent of the two kings, headed one coalition with Olympias and their allies Cleitus and Eumenes; Antigonus, Cassander, and Lysimachus, satrap of Thrace, composed the other. Polyperchon held Athens, and Cassander Piraeus. February saw the commencement of skirmishes in which elite Athenian soldiers *(epilektoi)* played a praiseworthy role.[39] While Polyperchon tried to win over to his own coalition Cassander's allies among the Greek states on the Peloponnese, Antigonus began preparations to cross the straits and attack Macedonia. To support this effort Cassander, now in Piraeus, sent Nicanor to the Bosporus with the ships he had received from Antigonus. Polyperchon sent Cleitus out to intercept him. Cleitus reached the Bosporus and joined forces with Arrhidaeus, who was holding out in the remaining portion of his Hellespontine satrapy. In July or August 317 two naval battles ensued at the Bosporus: Cleitus defeated Nicanor, but that night after his troops went to sleep, Antigonus fell on them in a surprise attack; assisted by the rulers of Byzantium, he had managed to sneak his army across the strait. While Antigonus struck at Cleitus' army taken unawares, Nicanor returned with his remaining ships and sank Cleitus' fleet at anchor. Utterly routed, Cleitus tried to flee but was killed by Lysimachus' soldiers.

The defeat was a heavy blow for the regent's cause. His prestige fell throughout Greece, while Cassander's supporters grew bolder and more vocal. Antigonus now decided to let Cassander pursue the war in Greece, and Cassander at once mounted an attack against Athens. His first attempt to take the island of Salamis failed, but he took Aegina,

39. *Hesperia* 4 (1935) 35, no. 5, with commentary by P. Roussel, *RA* (1941) II.220–222; cf. *IG* II^2.1209.

then Salamis[40] and the fortress of Panakton on the Attic-Boeotian border. When Polyperchon suffered a major defeat at Megalopolis, his coalition began to lose support at an even faster pace. In Athens the democratic regime came under attack; citizens demanded in the Assembly that the city negotiate with Cassander.[41] Talks began with residents of Piraeus, particularly with supporters of Phocion, who had fled to Nicanor in order to escape trial and condemnation, and also with Cassander's officers. A leading role in these talks fell to Demetrius of Phalerum, an Athenian educated in the philosophical school of Aristotle and Theophrastus and a man of the world who had been sentenced to death in absentia after Phocion's overthrow. They reached a settlement with Cassander in 317.[42] Athens allied itself with him, a step that reunited the city and its harbor under one government and allowed Cassander to maintain troops in Piraeus for the duration of the war. Otherwise Athens was guaranteed full sovereignty in all its internal affairs. A few of the most heavily compromised political leaders were executed, foremost among them Hagnonides, who had introduced the resolution sentencing Phocion to death. Phocion's remains were brought back to Attica and reburied in a state ceremony. The city retained a democratic form of government, at least in name; poorer citizens were again excluded from full political rights, but the census was not as rigorous as the measure of 322. The new minimum property qualification for full citizenship was set at 1,000 drachmas, or half the previous requirement. Cassander appointed Demetrius of Phalerum to head the new government, a position he would retain for the next ten years.[43] Soon afterward a conflict erupted between Nicanor, vainglorious after his recent victories, and Cassander. It ended with Cassander's

40. Pausanias 1.35.2; Polyaenus 4.11.13.

41. Diodorus 18.74. Fragments of two decrees from Samos date from the first decade after the Samians returned to their island in 321; though incomplete, they reveal that the Athenians mounted a lightning attack against the island. The Samians repelled it with the support of one of the rulers' generals (*AM* 72 [1957] 182–186, nos. 18–19). This probably happened after publication of Polyperchon's edict, which returned the island to the Athenians, and after Phocion's overthrow but before the fall of the democratic regime; that would place the attack between the spring of 318 and the summer of 317, the other possibility being during 315–311 (see below, text following note 73).

42. *IG* II^2.1201; Diodorus 18.74.

43. In *Stadt und Herrscher des Hellenismus* (Leipzig 1937) 53, A. Heuss has misinterpreted Diodorus' text, which appears to mention an election. Heuss concludes that the people participated in selecting a regent. In fact the text says merely that Demetrius of Phalerum was selected by Cassander.

army trying Nicanor, who was found guilty and executed. Cassander returned control of the harbor to the city, although he still controlled the fortress of Munychia overlooking it. He then returned to Macedonia, where new developments were demanding his attention.

3. Demetrius of Phalerum

Demetrius, whom Cassander placed at the head of the Athenian government in the summer of 317, was born around 360.[44] The son of Phanostratus from the demos of Phalerum, he may have been related by marriage to the family of the famous generals Conon and Timotheus. Demetrius is reported to have been a pupil of Aristotle and his successor Theophrastus in the Peripatetic school, where he received an education both broad and thorough. He emerged as a skilled and active writer interested in a wide variety of subjects, and even during the years he ruled Athens he continued to write. His surviving works include texts on philosophy, philology, rhetoric, history, politics and political theory, as well as a list of Athenian archons, an essay on the interpretation of dreams, and numerous speeches. Later generations have differed in their judgments of his political role, but for centuries Demetrius of Phalerum the author was read and admired. Cicero, who shared his conservative outlook and intellectual and literary interests, regarded him as the only Greek who excelled at both politics and scholarship.[45] Throughout his life Demetrius remained loyal to the Aristotelian school and to his teacher Theophrastus, who came from Eresus on the island of Lesbos; when during Demetrius' rule Theophrastus was unable to buy land in Attica because he was a foreigner, Demetrius helped him find a piece of property and thereby assisted him in keeping the school open. Since the time of Aristotle's service as tutor to Alexander at the Macedonian court, he and his pupils had been considered loyal royalists and supporters of Antipater and Cassander. In times of intense nationalism Aristotle and his pupils found them-

44. The texts relating to the biography of Demetrius of Phalerum and the surviving fragments of his writings are collected by F. Wehrli in *Die Schule des Aristoteles*, vol. 4[2]: *Demetrios von Phaleron* (Basle 1968). The historical fragments are also in *FGrHist* 228 F 1–52, with Jacoby's commentary. For more on the life of Demetrius, see Davies, *APF* 107–110; and H.-J. Gehrke, *Chiron* 8 (1978) 149–193 (with bibliography 192–193); cf. note 61 below.

45. Cicero *De leg.* 2.66; 3.14. Positive opinions of Demetrius are also expressed by Cicero in frs. 16, 62, 73, and 135. Strabo mentions him favorably in 9.398.

selves in some danger; after Alexander's death in 323, Aristotle found it advisable to leave for Chalcis; a similarly tense period occurred after Demetrius' overthrow in 307/6. However, sympathetic Athenians, just as good patriots as the nationalists, always came forward to protect them.

It is thus hardly surprising that Cassander chose a member of Aristotle's circle to rule Athens. Demetrius himself had served as a member of the delegation that had gone to negotiate peace with Antipater in 322. Demetrius' brother Himeraeus, however, was an ardent nationalist and one of the politicians whose extradition Antipater had demanded as part of the settlement; the Athenians yielded, delivered up their compatriots as prisoners, and Antipater had them executed. When the rebellion against Demetrius' close political associate Phocion came to a head, Demetrius took refuge with Nicanor, commander of the Macedonian troops in Piraeus. Cassander's conquest of the city deprived Athens of all independent initiative in foreign affairs; such policy was now dictated by Cassander. Demetrius' willingness to relinquish the city's independence was vehemently opposed by those (such as Demosthenes' nephew Demochares) who clung to Athens' past as a great imperial power, yet it brought the city a decade of quiet and almost continuous peace.[46]

The official title Demetrius bore as ruler of Athens is not known; in old texts he is variously styled as *epimeletes* (governor, commissar), *epistates,* or *prostates* (president or superintendent), while in the scholarly literature the title *nomothetes* (lawgiver) also has been proposed.[47] In 309/8, in addition to his other functions, he served as eponymous archon of Athens. Whether he ever filled the office of *strategos* is uncertain, however; the text always cited in support of this claim actually refers to his grandson of the same name, placed in charge of the city by King Antigonus Gonatas after the Chremonidean War.[48]

As foreign policy was closed to him, Demetrius focused his attention

---

46. Two long decrees of the deme of Acharnae from 315/4 contain no indication of unruly times; *AE* 131 (1992 [1993]) 179–193.

47. The references are in G. Marasco, *Democare di Leuconoe* (Florence 1984) 184–185.

48. *IG* II².2971. S. V. Tracy, *Boiotia antiqua*, vol. 4 (Montreal 1994) 151–161. It is questionable how much credence should be given to Polyaenus' report (4.7.6) that the elder Demetrius served as *strategos* in 308/7. But in the decree of the deme of Aixone in honor of Demetrius (*IG* II².1201), [στρατηγός] should perhaps be restored in line 11 (in agreement with De Sanctis, Ferguson, Heuss, and Gehrke). Whether the inscription on the base of the statue erected by the deme of Sphettos refers to the elder or the younger Demetrius

on internal affairs, and in this field he made a name for himself as lawgiver, reformer, and administrator. He began with legal reforms, some of which aimed to secure his tenure in office.[49] He himself served as archon, so we may presume that the other archonships, at the very least the office of the eponymous archon, were filled by election rather than by lot during his rule. He either created or greatly strengthened the board of seven "guardians of the law," also elected to a one-year term. Their duties included supervising other officials to ensure they conformed to existing laws (which under the democracy had been a function of the Council) and intervening in the Council or the Assembly if a proposed resolution appeared to them either contrary to law or detrimental to the city. Before that time objections to illegal actions or proposals could be raised only by lodging a formal complaint, which could no more than postpone the matter in question until a verdict was reached.[50]

Demetrius' laws imposing curbs on extravagance have always received particular attention, seeming as they do to combine two opposing tendencies, namely the democratic idea of equality, which finds excessive displays of wealth abhorrent, and a thoroughly undemocratic desire to regulate citizens' private lives. In fact, however, the dislike of flaunted wealth and excessive consumption sprang not from a democratic ideology but from an aristocratic outlook preferring that no individual should appear superior to other members of his class. Because the authorities' opportunities to introduce regimentation were essentially limited to two spheres, religious ceremonies and burial practices, private households were affected mainly on occasions such as weddings, funerals, and feasts. All excessive expenditure was prohibited. The maximum number of guests for any one feast was set at thirty, for example, and newly created officials ensured that this and similar laws were obeyed. Though known in Athens and elsewhere as *gynaik-onomoi*, "supervisors of the women," their authority extended to the

---

of Phalerum remains an open question (*BCH* 93 [1969] 56–71). The sculptor Antignotos is otherwise unknown.

49. In the marble chronicle of Paros for the year 317/6, *FGrHist* 239 B 13.

50. H.-J. Gehrke, *Chiron* 8 (1978) 151–162. Formal complaints against illegal or detrimental resolutions began to be passed again in 307, with the return of democracy; the law of Sophocles (see Chapter 3) was objected to on the former grounds in 306. The office of *nomophylax* was presumably abolished in 307.

activities of men.[51] Funerals were henceforth to take place before dawn, and the law imposed limits on the number and cost of shrouds. In one of the most radical provisions of the new decree, only gravestones of a plain and modest kind were allowed; elaborate monuments with statues or reliefs disappeared at once.[52] Gone forever were the large marble vases crowned with palmetto finials, the superb reliefs with scenes of leavetaking, and the impressive grave steles. A single funerary relief has survived from the third century along with a small number of grave steles, but without exception the monuments are for foreigners, revealing that the restrictions applied only to citizens.[53] The rich funerary art of Attica vanished, for there was no other demand for sculpture from private citizens. Many artists who made a living from cemetery commissions must have emigrated, and in fact a notable example of Attic funerary art from a slightly later date has been found in Demetrias in Thessaly.[54] Since the law remained in force for centuries, it must have had the approval of a majority of citizens unwilling to permit a small number of very rich Athenians to flaunt their wealth in such a manner.

While the moneyed class thus lost one favorite avenue of display and self-advertisement, another of Demetrius' reforms removed a burden under which they had long suffered. From the middle of the fourth century on, numerous critics—including Isocrates, Lycurgus, Aristotle, and Theophrastus—had spoken out against the institution of liturgy, the state's requisition of private funds from citizens for one of its activities. *Choregia*—the practice of requiring the most affluent citizens to sponsor a chorus and to pay for the members' room, board, and rehearsals during the annual dramatic festivals—was one of its most unpopular forms, and complaints about it had abounded.[55] Demetrius himself remarked that many a lavish tripod was a monument only to the ruin of the family that had overspent its resources in commissioning

51. Philochorus, *FGrHist* 328 F 65; C. Wehrli, *MH* 19 (1962) 33–38; B. J. Garland, "Gynaikonomoi: An Investigation of Greek Censors of Women" (Diss. Johns Hopkins 1981).

52. Cicero *De leg.* 2.64–66; A. Brueckner, *Der Friedhof am Eridanos* (Berlin 1909) 25–26; J. Kirchner, *Die Antike* 15 (1939) 93–97; H. Möbius, *Die Ornamente der griechischen Grabstelen klassischer und nachklassischer Zeit*[2] (Munich 1968) 44–45; J. Twele, *AJA* 74 (1970) 204; R. Stichel, *AA* 107 (1992) 433–440 and the literature cited on 433 n. 1.

53. J. Kirchner, *AE* (1937) 338–340.

54. A. Conze, *Die attischen Grabreliefs*, vol. 3 (Berlin 1906) no. 1563; Möbius, *Ornamente* 60; C. Wolters, *La Thessalie*, ed. B. Helly (Lyon 1979) 86–87.

55. U. Koehler, *AM* 3 (1878) 229–241.

it.[56] The reform provided for the annual election of a director of the competition, the *agonothetes,* whose expenses were reimbursed by the state, although he was allowed (and possibly often expected) to fund special touches, such as more elaborate decorations or an additional contest, from his private purse.

Presumably the other onerous forms of liturgy were abolished at the same time, such as trierarchy, which required one wealthy citizen or a small group to equip a trireme and keep it seaworthy. The role of the Athenian navy had shrunk considerably after 322, and even if trierarchy persisted in name (or was reintroduced),[57] the burden for the rich certainly ceased to exist in the old form. To this extent it is correct to say that the constitution of the Hellenistic period, including that of the reestablished democracy, was modified in the interests of the wealthier classes.

The powers of the Areopagus, the "aristocratic" Council consisting of former archons, had been severely limited during the radical democracy, but several of its reported activities during this period indicate that Demetrius endowed it with renewed authority and prestige. The philosophers Theodorus, nicknamed "the Godless," and Stilpon of Megara had to appear before the Areopagus to answer to charges of sacrilege; the regent himself is said to have intervened in favor of Theodorus. Whether the Council had any authority to punish is uncertain, but it is known to have been responsible, along with the *gynaikonomoi,* for enforcing the laws against extravagance.[58]

Noting that the years of archons in office frequently appear on *horoi* (stones marking mortgaged property) from 315/4 on, some scholars have conjectured that a law was passed in 316/5 requiring mortgage contracts and similar legal documents to be dated and deposited with third parties.[59] Later critics have generally rejected this suggestion, pointing out, among other things, that many undated *horoi* exist from later periods.[60] A recently discovered *horos* from 319/8 has now undermined the very foundation of the theory.

---

56. Wehrli fr. 136; *FGrHist* 228 F 25. The duty of *choregia* fell to 28 citizens annually.
57. *IG* II^2.1491.26 and 30 from 305/4; *ISE* 29 from 225/4.
58. Wallace, *Areopagus Council* 204–205; S. Said, in *Aristote et Athènes,* ed. M. Piérart (Paris 1993) 179–181.
59. W. S. Ferguson, *Klio* 11 (1911) 265–276; S. Dow and A. H. Travis, *Hesperia* 12 (1943) 159–165.
60. M. I. Finley, *Studies in Land and Credit in Ancient Athens, 500–200 B.C.* (New Brunswick, N.J., 1952) 177–181; H.-J. Gehrke, *Chiron* 8 (1978) 176–177.

Most historians have long been agreed that Demetrius' legal reforms were directly derived from the philosophical doctrines of Plato, Aristotle, and Theophrastus, but opinions vary widely about which particular philosopher or doctrine may have inspired a given law. However, H.-J. Gehrke has discovered so many discrepancies between these teachings and Demetrius' reforms that it becomes difficult to accept the notion of any immediate influence beyond the most general kind. On the other hand, he notes the many similarities between the Athenian reforms and the laws of other Greek states, and concludes that some of the new laws may have arisen quite naturally out of the situation in which Demetrius and the city found themselves. Other scholars, occupying the middle ground between Gehrke's standpoint and that of earlier scholars, stress that although there is no evidence of specific borrowings from Aristotle, Theophrastus, or other philosophers, the general tendency of Demetrius' innovations conforms to the doctrines of various philosophers and Greek reformers of the fourth century.[61]

One of Demetrius' most important administrative measures was the introduction of a general census. The census he carried out resulted in a count for all Attica of 21,000 citizens, 10,000 resident foreigners, and 400,000 slaves. (The last figure is certainly corrupt.)[62] Scholars agree that the census of citizens included only males age eighteen and older. This figure plays a key role in studies on the population of Attica in the late fourth century. Historians who accept the number 21,000 as accurate estimate the total population to have been about 150,000 (including citizens, foreigners, and slaves of both sexes).[63] Others believe the adult male population to have been much higher—around 31,000—and reach a figure for the total population closer to 250,000.[64]

Although Demetrius is known to have criticized the amount of money Pericles spent on the construction of the Propylaea, he carried on at least part of the building program begun under Lycurgus. The

61. Gehrke, *Chiron* 8 (1978) 176–177; J. M. Williams, *AncW* 15 (1987) 87–98.

62. Ctesicles, *FGrHist* 245 F 1.

63. In the recent lively discussion of this issue, one of the main proponents of the smaller number has been E. Ruschenbusch; see *ZPE* 54 (1984) 253–269; 72 (1988) 139–140; 75 (1988) 194–196; Williams, *Athens* 226–240; and Sekunda, *ASBA* 87 (1992) 311–355.

64. The most active proponent of the larger numbers is M. H. Hansen, particularly in *Demography and Democracy* (Herning 1986), *Historisk-Filosofiske Meddelelser* 56 (1988) 7–13, and *ZPE* 75 (1988) 189–193.

portico in front of the temple of Demeter and Kore in Eleusis was completed during Demetrius' time in office by Philo of Eleusis, the architect of the arsenal in Piraeus.[65]

Demetrius possessed outstanding ability as a financial administrator, as even his political opponents grudgingly conceded. During his administration he reduced the state budget by ending payments to citizens for attending meetings of the Assembly and jury sessions, and he also abolished the custom of paying *theorika*, subsidies that enabled poorer citizens to attend the theater. Demetrius is further said to have increased state revenues to 1,200 talents annually, exactly the sum mentioned for Lycurgus' administration. The source of this information, Duris of Samos, also reports that while he spent little on the administration and defense of the city, and through his laws imposed limits on others' extravagance, Demetrius himself lived a life of great luxury. Duris' testimony, however, may be biased: though a former schoolmate of Demetrius, he was also a political opponent. Demochares, another political opponent, mentions that Demetrius boasted about how many goods had been available at moderate prices during his rule. Demochares wrote a rebuttal after Demetrius' fall, accusing him of thinking like a peddler or customs clerk, who had forgotten all the great Greek ideals and served a foreign master without any sense of shame.[66] The rebuttal was written after Demetrius' fall, since Demochares refers to the regent's defense of his administration titled "On the Ten Years."

In fact Demetrius must have looked back on his achievements with some satisfaction, for despite his unpopularity later governments with a very different political outlook retained most of his important reforms. After his overthrow Demetrius found asylum and protection with Cassander for ten years, until Cassander himself died; thereafter he lived at the court of Ptolemy I of Egypt, where he once again played an important political role as one of the king's influential advisers. He is credited with having persuaded the ruler to found both the famous Library at Alexandria and the Museum, the royal academy of scholars and poets supported by the king.[67] Demetrius also urged Ptolemy to

---

65. Vitruvius *De architectura* 7, praef. 17; K. Clinton, Φίλια ἔπη: *Festschrift G. Mylonas*, vol. 2 (Athens 1987) 260.

66. See Wehrli fr. 132 (Demochares, *FGrHist* 75 F 4) and Marasco's commentary, *Democare* 181–190.

67. The documentation for this is late and weak but not necessarily untrustworthy; see

choose as his successor his son by Antipater's daughter Eurydice, Ptolemy "Keraunos" ("the Thunderbolt"). The king ignored this advice and chose his younger son by Berenice, also named Ptolemy, instead. When the younger Ptolemy became sole ruler in 283, he is said to have remembered this slight and to have kept Demetrius under arrest in the countryside, where he died from a snakebite. Further evidence suggests that Demetrius may have played a role in framing the laws of Alexandria, which are supposed to have resembled those of Athens.[68]

Demetrius devoted one of his writings to Tyche, the goddess of fortune, whose influence on human affairs is profound but utterly unpredictable. Polybius preserved an excerpt from this work in which the author expresses amazement at how quickly the all-powerful Persian empire was eclipsed by the formerly insignificant Macedonia. He goes on to prophesy that one day Tyche will put an end to the reign of the Macedonians as well.[69] It would be interesting to know when Demetrius wrote this observation, which one is tempted to read as a reflection of his own experience.

Under Demetrius' government, Athens long avoided becoming involved in the fierce battles among several of the *diadochoi* in Asia Minor, Syria, Mesopotamia, and Iran; the city was spared as long as Cassander retained control of the Balkans and Greece. Cassander soon defeated Polyperchon and his son Alexander, but the victory was not achieved without great upheaval in the Macedonian royal family.[70] After Cleitus' defeat at the Bosporus and about the time Cassander conquered Athens, Eurydice, the wife of Philip Arrhidaeus, changed sides in the conflict, a shift with dire consequences. She persuaded her

R. Pfeiffer, *History of Classical Scholarship from the Beginnings to the End of the Hellenistic Age* (Oxford 1968) 96–104.

68. P. Hibeh no. 196, with commentary by E. G. Turner; further J. Bingen, *CE* 32 (1957) 337–339; and P. M. Fraser, *Ptolemaic Alexandria*, vol. 2 (Oxford 1972) 179 n. 27. For more on the correspondence between the laws of Athens and Alexandria, see *P.Oxy.* 2177; for Demetrius as lawgiver to Ptolemy I, see Aelian *Var. hist.* 8.17.

69. Wehrli fr. 81 from Polybius 29.11.1–6. The conclusion is reminiscent of Scipio Aemilianus' prophecy on seeing the smoking ruins of Carthage, that Rome too would one day be reduced to ashes.

70. For the difficulties in establishing the chronology of the events reported in this section, cf. Gullath and Schober, in *Festschrift S. Lauffer* 363–377.

husband to name Cassander regent in Polyperchon's place. Refusing to accept his demotion, Polyperchon joined forces with the queen mother Olympias, and the two seized a moment when Cassander was absent from Macedonia to attack with an Epirote army. In the fall of 317 Philip Arrhidaeus and Eurydice mounted a defense, but their Macedonian soldiers deserted to the other side out of loyalty to Olympias. When Olympias captured king and queen, she had them brutally executed and began a bloodbath against their followers and those of Cassander. She had Cassander's brother Nicanor killed and desecrated the grave of his brother Iolaus, rumored to have brought, on his father Antipater's orders, the poison that killed Alexander the Great in Babylon. These excesses cost her a great deal of support; as soon as Cassander returned to Macedonia from the Peloponnese the following spring (316), he defeated Polyperchon's troops and trapped Olympias in the city of Pydna. After a long siege the threat of starvation forced the queen to surrender in the spring of 315. Breaking his promise to spare her life, Cassander had her sentenced to death by his army and executed. He had now also acquired custody of the younger king Alexander and his mother, Roxane. After arranging for the bodies of Philip Arrhidaeus and Eurydice to receive proper burial in the old Macedonian capital of Aegae (Vergina),[71] Cassander himself married Thessalonike, a daughter of Philip II of Macedon and half-sister of Alexander the Great. He then set to rebuilding Thebes, the city Alexander had destroyed twenty years earlier.

The Athenians followed the reconstruction process with great sympathy, not just because they were now members of Cassander's coalition. The Thebans had been their allies against Philip and the Macedonians at Chaeronea in 338, and in 335 Athens had been on the verge of coming to Thebes's assistance when news of the city's annihilation reached them. Now, hearing that Cassander intended to rebuild it and had summoned the scattered Thebans to return home, the Athenians put on garlands, their customary acknowledgment of good news. In the following years they participated actively in the rebuilding and reportedly constructed most of the new city wall, while other states,

71. They are the probable occupants of the large tomb excavated in 1977, but this remains a matter of controversy. See R. M. Errington, *A History of Macedonia* (Berkeley 1990) 281 n. 5, which cites the relevant literature; and E. Borza, *In the Shadow of Olympus: The Emergence of Macedon* (Princeton 1990) 260–266.

including some as far away as Italy and Sicily, contributed money.[72] The Thebans' loss of their homeland had aroused as much sympathy throughout the Greek world as the Samians' had earlier when the Athenians expelled them from their island.

While Cassander was besieging Olympias in Pydna, the successors' wars continued in the East. Antigonus defeated Eumenes in Iran after long and heavy fighting and subjugated all the satraps of the eastern empire except Seleucus of Babylonia, who escaped and was given asylum by Ptolemy in Egypt. Antigonus' ascendancy led to the formation of a new coalition against him in 315, consisting of Ptolemy, Lysimachus, Cassander, and Asander, the satrap of Caria. Antigonus responded by forming his own coalition with Polyperchon and Alexander, who continued to hold part of the Peloponnese. Antigonus attempted to undermine his opponents' position in Greece by issuing the famous decree of Tyre and giving it as much publicity as possible; it declared that all Greek states should be independent, autonomous, and free from foreign occupation.[73] A small Athenian fleet took part in the battles between the two coalitions. In 315/4 an Athenian naval squadron was operating in the Cyclades; commanded by Thymochares of Sphettos (father of the two brothers Callias and Phaedrus, who would later become famous), it took the island of Cythnos and captured the pirate Glaucetes.[74] The following year Cassander wrote to Demetrius of Phalerum and to Dionysius, his own commander of the occupation forces at Munychia, demanding twenty warships for an attack on Lemnos. This island, long an Athenian possession, had obviously been captured by Antigonus in 318. Lemnos was an important base for voyages between the Bosporus and the Aegean. Cassander's campaign to recover it was backed by a fleet of Ptolemy's under the command of Seleucus, the expelled satrap of Babylon, and by Athenian ships under the command of the admiral Aristotle. When the garrison on Lemnos remained loyal to Antigonus, Cassander's allies laid waste the countryside and began a siege of one of the island's two cities.

72. Diodorus 19.53–54 and 63.4; [Plut.] *mor.* 814B. For a catalogue of the cities and rulers that contributed to the rebuilding of the city, see M. Holleaux, *REG* 8 (1895) 7–48 (= *Etudes* 1: 1–40).

73. Diodorus 19.61.3–4; A. Heuss, *Hermes* 73 (1938) 113–194.

74. *IG* II^2 682.9–13; H. Hauben, *ZPE* 13 (1974) 62; L. Robert, *RN* (1974) 23–24 (= *OMS* 6.185–186). If the Athenian attack on Samos (above, note 41) was part of this war, then one can wonder whether the same squadron led by Thymochares tried to take the island and failed.

Seleucus sailed on to Cos, leaving only the Athenian force behind; Dioscurides, one of Antigonus' naval commanders, easily captured most of the Athenians' ships and crews and drove the rest from the island.[75] The same Dioscurides put an end to Athenian rule on Delos, probably in September 314, and, in accordance with Antigonus' proclamation, declared the island's independence, which Delos was to maintain for almost 150 years.[76]

One of the very few surviving Assembly decrees from the time of Demetrius of Phalerum dates from January or February 313; it honored Asander, satrap of Caria, apparently in gratitude for his support of Athenian naval operations. As a member of the opposing coalition in Asia Minor, Asander proved unable to withstand strong pressure from Antigonus. He was forced to sign a treaty dictating that he would surrender control of his military forces, administer the satrapy as a virtual fief for Antigonus, and declare the Greek cities in it autonomous. As a warrant that he would honor the treaty provisions, Asander sent his brother Agathon as hostage. A few days later, however, he changed his mind, reclaimed his brother, and appealed to Seleucus and Ptolemy to send help quickly. Antigonus reacted immediately, dispatching an army under the command of his generals Medeius of Larissa and Docimus. They made short work of capturing Miletus and declared it free in accord with Antigonus' policy.[77]

A parley at the Hellespont between Antigonus and Cassander on possible peace terms ended in failure. As the war continued, the Athenians participated in Cassander's campaign, ultimately unsuccessful, to take the city of Oreos on Euboea. But Antigonus was equally unsuc-

75. Diodorus 19.68.3–4. There is much in the chronology of events in 315–312 on which scholars remain divided. R. M. Errington (*Hermes* 105 [1977] 496–500) places many events a year later than I do here, e.g., Antigonus' proclamation of Greek freedom in 314, the battle for Lemnos sometime around October 313, and the siege of Oreos in 312. There are some good reasons for doing so, but problems remain, such as the liberation of Miletus in 313/2. Cf. Will, *Histoire* 1: 40. J. Tréheux, *RA* 31–32 (1948) II.1031, also dates Dioscurides' voyage to the islands (Diodorus 19.62.9) in September 314, whereas Errington assigns it to 313.

76. J. Tréheux, *RA* 31–32 (1948) II.1008–32, esp. 1031.

77. The decree honoring Asander, introduced by the *anagrapheus* for the year 321/0, is *IG* II².450; the honors awarded him far exceeded the norm and included an equestrian statue in the Agora and the right to dine in the *prytaneion*. For the further events see Diodorus 19.68.2, 5–7; and 75.1–6. With its liberation, a new era began for Miletus; in the list of their annual eponyms the following remark is appended to the name of the *stephanephoros* of 313/2: "Under him the city received its freedom and autonomy from Antigonus and democracy was reinstated" (*Milet* I.3, no. 123.2–4).

cessful in his attempt to cross the straits and attack Cassander in Macedonia, for the city of Byzantium, whose cooperation was necessary for the crossing, refused assistance on the urging of Lysimachus. Nonetheless Antigonus increased the pressure on Cassander by sending his nephew Polemy with a fleet of 150 ships. Polemy conquered or won over Chalcis, Eretria, and Carystus on Euboea, as well as the city of Oropus on the Attic frontier, which could then serve as the base for an attack on Attica itself.[78] Diodorus reports at this point that the Athenians had already sent a secret appeal to Antigonus to liberate them (a step that can only have been the private initiative of a group of Athenian citizens, and not an official embassy voted by the Assembly). With Polemy now poised on their borders, the citizens forced Demetrius to agree to a truce and to send negotiators to discuss the possibility of their forming an alliance with Antigonus. The city was thus on the point of changing sides in the conflict, a move that would easily have caused Demetrius to fall from power.[79]

Demetrius' overthrow was staved off by the truce and by a great battle in distant Syria, where in 312 Ptolemy of Egypt won a momentous victory at Gaza over Antigonus' inexperienced son Demetrius. The defeat was a major setback for Antigonus and forced him to come to terms with the opposing coalition. After protracted negotiations they reached a peace agreement in 311, whereby Cassander was to be *strategos* for Europe (like his father Antipater before him) until King Alexander came of age. Lysimachus would retain possession of Thrace; Ptolemy would keep Egypt and Cyrenaica. Antigonus was to be ruler of all Asia, and Seleucus was left empty-handed.[80]

The coming of peace reduced the pressure on Cassander and also on the government of Demetrius of Phalerum. The very next year (310) Cassander rid himself and the other *diadochoi* of a final encumbrance by putting to death the young King Alexander and his mother, Roxane. In response Polyperchon sent to Pergamum for Heracles, the seventeen-year-old illegitimate son of Alexander the Great by an Iranian

78. Diodorus 19.75.6–8, 77.2–7, and 78.2–3. For Athenian support in the attempt to seize Oreos, see *IG* II².682.13–18.

79. Diodorus 19.78.4.

80. Diodorus 19.69.1; 80.1–86.5 (Gaza); and 105.1–4. See further C. B. Welles, *RC* 1 (on the peace); and *StV*, no. 428. As a result of the battle of Gaza, Seleucus succeeded with Ptolemy's help in winning back his old satrapy in battles against Antigonus' generals. He thereby laid the foundation for the largest empire to grow out of the old monarchy of Alexander the Great over the next 30 years.

woman named Barsine, and proclaimed him the new king of Macedonia. Cassander, however, talked him into having Heracles and Barsine executed in 309.

In 310/9 a distant war between Syracuse, led by its tyrant, Agathocles, and Carthage had repercussions in Athens. Agathocles had enlisted the Macedonian Ophellas, a veteran of Alexander the Great's wars, as an ally for a joint campaign in North Africa. Ophellas, then serving as Ptolemy's governor of Cyrenaica, had an Athenian wife, Euthydice, from the family of Miltiades, the victor at Marathon. As a result of this connection he was able to recruit a large number of Athenian citizens as mercenaries for the war against Carthage, particularly from the group that had lost its political rights in 317. But after Ophellas joined forces with Agathocles, the tyrant had him murdered and appropriated his army.[81]

In 309/8 Demetrius of Phalerum held the office of eponymous archon. He organized the festival of the Dionysia with particular splendor in the spring of 308; poems in his honor were recited during the great procession, in which he was celebrated as *heliomorphos,* "sunlike."[82] During his term as archon Athens faced new dangers. Ptolemy had come to terms with Antigonus and now attacked Greece, perhaps in response to Cassander's alliance with Polyperchon. In the spring of 308 he captured the island of Andros and soon thereafter was given control of Corinth, on the isthmus, and Sicyon, on the Peloponnese, by Cratesipolis, the widow of Polyperchon's son Alexander. Next Ptolemy drove out Cassander's forces and seized Megara, even closer to Athens. As the occupier of Andros and Megara he represented a threat to Athens until he negotiated a new peace with Cassander in the summer of 308.[83]

But Cassander's loss of Athens and its harbor, and his appointed

81. Diodorus 20.40.1–42.5; Plut. *Demetrius* 14; *StV,* no. 432. The statement that Ophellas sent a delegation to Athens "concerning an alliance" (Diodorus 20.40.5) can be understood only as explained in the text. The presence in Athens of a delegation from Carthage (*IG* II^2.418) could be connected with Ophellas' activities there, for the inscription mentioning it (assigned by Koehler to the period 330–300) is the work of a stone cutter active between 320 and 298; see Tracy, *Athenian Democracy in Transition* 138. Theophrastus may have learned from Athenian mercenaries in Ophellas' employ that his army had to live for several days on the fruit of the *lotos* during its march through the African desert (*Historia plantarum* 4.3.2). For more on Ophellas' campaign, see E. Will, *REA* 66 (1964) 320–333; and A. Laronde, *Cyrène et la Libye hellénistique* (Paris 1987) 203, 206–207, and 357–358.

82. Duris, *FGrHist* 76 F 10.

83. Diodorus 20.37.1–2.

governor's fall from power, were less than a year away. Antigonus sent his son Demetrius to liberate first Athens and then the rest of Greece, as called for in his proclamation of 315, and in June 307, mistaking Demetrius' ships for Ptolemy's (with whom they had made peace the year before), the Athenians admitted the enemy fleet into their harbor. The attackers stormed Piraeus, and at once Demetrius of Phalerum's regime crumbled. The Athenian ruler was escorted safely to exile in Thebes with all due honors, and Cassander's garrison in the fortress of Munychia was encircled. At this time Antigonus' son Demetrius received the epithet "Poliorcetes," "the Besieger." Only after conquering the city of Megara did he attempt to storm Munychia. The fortress fell in August 307, in the year of the new archon Anaxicrates, and was razed at once.[84]

Thus ended Demetrius of Phalerum's ten-year rule over his home city. He had headed a peaceful and mild government and later claimed he had not only preserved democracy but also "corrected" it.[85] Nevertheless it was rule by one man, placed in command by a foreign potentate and maintained there by foreign troops. In those circumstances it made no great difference that many citizens lost their political rights as a result of the new census classes, for the citizens who retained theirs were unable to exercise them freely. "They had an oligarchical constitution in name, but in reality it was a monarchy."[86] Demetrius Poliorcetes' immediate proclamation of freedom and a return to democracy was thus received with great rejoicing; the Athenians expressed their gratitude to the conqueror and his father, Antigonus, by awarding them honors the city had never before granted to mortals. After fifteen years of servitude to Macedonia, a new era was about to begin.

84. Diodorus 20.35.1–46.3; Plut. *Demetrius* 8–10; *FGrHist* 239 B 20–21.
85. Diodorus 18.74.3: ἦρχεν εἰρηνικῶς καὶ πρὸς τοὺς πολίτας φιλανθρώπως; Strabo 9, p. 398: οὐ μόνον οὐ κατέλυσε τὴν δημοκρατίαν ἀλλὰ καὶ ἐπηνώρθωσε.

THREE

Between Freedom and Dependency
(307–287)

1. Democracy without Full Freedom

In an assembly of Athenian citizens called at the start of the Attic new year in July 307, Prince Demetrius Poliorcetes declared the city's independence and announced that city and harbor would remain free of a garrison. At the same time, speaking on behalf of his father, Antigonus, he promised the Athenians a large donation of grain and a supply of lumber for shipbuilding. The democratic constitution abolished in the spring of 317 was restored, and the innovations introduced by Demetrius of Phalerum that were incompatible with it, such as the new census classes and the board of *nomophylakes,* were revoked, while some of his other reforms, such as the abolition of *choregia* and the laws limiting extravagance, remained in force. The new government declared the deposed governor a nonperson, tore down all statues of him, and began proceedings against his supporters, accusing them of participation in the overthrow of democratic rule (literally, "the dissolution of the people"). The shift of power occurred without violence, for the most incriminated members of the old regime took advantage of the opportunity offered them to go into exile rather than stand trial. The smaller fry who remained in Athens and had their cases tried all won acquittal. Pro forma death sentences were handed down against the leaders, including the former governor, after they had left the country. Among those who went into exile was Deinarch of Corinth, a wealthy attorney famous for his oratory, but he was allowed to sell his property first. Some others who had been on friendly terms with Demetrius of Phalerum fell under suspicion, including the poet

Menander, who, however, was spared through the intervention of influential associates.[1]

Lycurgus, who had died in 324, was now awarded posthumous honors on a motion introduced by Stratocles of Diomeia. The text of the resolution elevates him to a symbol of Athenian democracy and national aspirations[2] and ends with the tribute "As an officeholder in a free and democratic city he frequently had to submit reports on his activities; every audit showed his conduct to have been above reproach, with no hint of corruption." While Lycurgus was thus belatedly awarded the recognition he deserved, the two men who had restored freedom and democracy received lavish honors of a kind never before voluntarily granted by the city to mortals.[3] The Athenians made offerings to them as "saviors" or "savior gods," instituted games, and appointed a priest for the cult of their worship. Two new tribes, Antigonis and Demetrias, were added to the existing ten and placed at the head of the list. At the same time the total membership of the Council, to which each tribe sent 50 representatives annually, increased from 500 to 600. In the Agora, statues of Antigonus and Demetrius were added to the group of founders who had given their names to the other tribes; the pedestal had to be specially enlarged to make room for them.[4] The city also erected statues of them next to those of the tyrant-slayers Harmodius and Aristogeiton, regarded not only as liberators of Athens from the tyranny of the Pisistratids, but also in popular tradition as early champions of democracy. Finally, in addition to many lesser honors and awards proposed but not ratified, two new

1. Demetrius of Phalerum, frs. 52–57. For the identity of Menander's advocate, see D. Potter, *Historia* 36 (1987) 491–495.

2. *IG* II².457 contains the fragmentary inscribed version; [Plut.] *mor.* 852A–E, the text handed down in the literary tradition, is more complete but differs slightly. The stele is decorated with 12 inscribed crowns, a reference to the crowns awarded to Lycurgus during his public career (A. Wilhelm (1925) 1–4 in *Akademieschriften* 1: 463–466). A portion of the base of the statue dedicated to Lycurgus has survived (*IG* II².3776). Lycurgus' son Habron served as chief administrator of the city's finances in 307/6 (*IG* II².463.36) and as military treasurer in 306/5 (*IG* II².1492 B 123), and was thus a leading member of the government in the first few years after the city's liberation.

3. For more on the subject covered in this section see the full discussion in Habicht, *Gottmenschentum* 44–55. At Alexander's behest an official cult of worship was introduced for him in 324, but the city was under pressure to pass the decree. The Athenians revoked it immediately after the king's death and punished its initiator, Demades.

4. T. L. Shear Jr., *Hesperia* 39 (1970) 171–176 and 196–198.

ships named after Antigonus and Demetrius were built to join the "sacred triremes" *Paralos* and *Ammonias*.[5]

The Spartan admiral Lysander had received comparable honors in Samos in 404 after restoring to power the oligarchs previously driven out by the Athenians, and several Greek cities in Asia Minor had paid similar homage to Alexander the Great for liberating them from Persian domination; but nothing like this had ever occurred in the mother country itself. Athens' reaction to the liberation of 307 set a new standard: truly exceptional achievements, such as ending a period of foreign domination or rescuing the city from great peril, could henceforth be rewarded with honors formerly reserved for the gods. The feats of such men ranked with those of the immortals. Only three years later the inhabitants of Rhodes approved honors of this kind for King Ptolemy, after his aid in preventing their subjugation by Demetrius Poliorcetes, the very man the Athenians saw as their "divine savior."[6]

The Athenians' shift of allegiance—from Cassander's Macedonian-Greek realm to that of Antigonus in Syria, Asia Minor, and the Aegean—renewed old connections, in particular with the communities in Ionia that had traditionally regarded Athens as their mother city. These communities had followed the events of 307 closely and were highly pleased with the outcome; many Ionian cities expressed their sense of solidarity with the new democratic regime in Athens by sending delegations with crowns and honors for its leaders. Between 307 and 301, inscriptions document such demonstrations of goodwill from Miletus, Ephesus, Priene, Colophon, and the Ionian communities of Chalcis and Tenos.[7] At the same time Athenian merchants gained access to the territories ruled by Antigonus, so that in 305/4, for example, importation of grain "from Asia" is documented.[8]

5. Philochorus, *FGrHist* 328 F 48.

6. See below after note 32.

7. Miletus: *IG* II^2.1129 and 1485 A 24. Ephesus: *IG* II^2.1485 A 9. For Colophon there are numerous inscriptions discussed by A. Wilhelm in *Anatolian Studies W. H. Buckler* (Manchester 1939) 345–352. For Priene see the texts discussed by Wilhelm in *Attische Urkunden*, vol. 5 (1942) 166–175 (= *Akademieschriften* 1: 782–791). Chalcis: *IG* II^2.563 and *Hesperia* 6 (1937) 323, no. 4. Tenos: *IG* II^2.466. The interpretation of this text by G. Reger greatly overstates the case (*CQ* 42 [1992] 366–368); the citizens of Tenos certainly did not actively participate in the liberation of Athens.

8. *Hesperia* 5 (1936) 201. Sicily, then ruled by Agathocles, was another region where the Athenians bought grain; *IG* II^2.499 from 302/1.

To create even stronger ties, Antigonus gave back to the city the islands of Lemnos and Imbros, which he had seized when Athens was allied with Cassander.[9] Demetrius, speaking in Antigonus' name, had promised the Athenians 150,000 bushels of grain and timber for 100 warships; Antigonus presented these gifts to a delegation from Athens, adding to them a large sum of money.[10] The new Athenian government, anticipating an attempt by Cassander to regain control of the city and harbor, regarded as one of its most urgent tasks the repair and reinforcement of the walls in the city and Piraeus, as well as the Long Walls connecting the two. An Assembly resolution introduced at once in 307/6 by Demosthenes' nephew Demochares ordered the necessary measures and even specified which jobs were to be awarded to which contractors. As in 338, the program was divided into ten segments; the retention of this number, reflecting the original number of tribes, may indicate that administrative reorganization connected with the founding of the two new tribes Antigonis and Demetrias was still in progress, or it may have been kept for other unknown reasons. It was estimated that the work would take five years to complete, and each of the contractors received a schedule.[11]

Characteristic of the new spirit prevailing at the time, the decree required the names of the contractors chosen and the amount of money each would receive in payment to be made public, "so that any Athenian citizen who wants to know what work is being carried out on the walls can go and see for himself."[12] This approach reflects two priorities of radical democracies: the wish to keep the public well informed and the importance of the oversight function performed by ordinary citizens. The same attitude revealed itself again a few years later in 304/3, when the entire code of laws was published.[13]

9. Lemnos: *IG* II^2.1492 B 133 (305/4) and 550; *ISE* 8.8–9 (303/2); Imbros: *IG* II^2.1492 B 133 (305/4) and Diodorus 20.46.4.

10. *IG* II^2.1492 B 97–99 and 119–121 with the observations of R. Meiggs, *Trees and Timber in the Ancient Mediterranean World* (Oxford 1982) 494 n. 87. See also Diodorus 20.46.4 and Plut. *Demetrius* 10.1.

11. *IG* II^2.463, with detailed commentary by F. G. Maier, *Griechische Mauerbauin-schriften*, 2 vols. (Heidelberg 1959 and 1961) 1: 48–67. For the estimated time span of the project, see lines 106–107. Cf. also *IG* II^2.550 and, from the year 306/5, *IG* II^2.505.30–36 and 554.14–16. The Council of 500 is still mentioned in *IG* II^2.466.45 (probably from 307/6).

12. *IG* II^2.463.29–31.

13. *IG* II^2.487.6–10.

But perhaps the most striking evidence of change under the new leadership was the almost excessive zeal with which the Assembly recorded and publicized its activities. Whereas there is only one major Assembly resolution from the decade of Demetrius of Phalerum's rule extant, namely the decree awarding honors to Asander, satrap of Caria, the following six years of democracy are represented by well over a hundred resolutions in more or less complete form, still only a fraction of the total number passed by the citizenry; all were copied onto wooden tablets for the archives, but only a few were inscribed on marble steles for public display. All the former and many of the latter perished. Yet the discrepancy between the surviving evidence from the two regimes cannot be attributed solely to chance; it proves that different circumstances prevailed. In the period from 317 to 307 the *ekklesia* had both somewhat circumscribed possibilities for action and a strong disinclination to publish its decrees in lasting form. Between 307 and 301, however, the democratic Assembly was almost frenetically active, and eager to exhibit the results of its work in a highly visible manner. One—though by no means the only—reason for this change in behavior lies in the nature of the resolutions typically passed: the great majority of them honored individuals or foreign states for the support and assistance they had rendered to Athens. Often the individuals named were in the service of Prince Demetrius (soon to become King Demetrius), and all the honorees had an interest in seeing their awards publicized.

One man in particular stands out for the number of motions he introduced to award honors to men in Demetrius Poliorcetes' service: Stratocles of Diomeia, who also proposed the award of posthumous honors for Lycurgus. Of the surviving decrees from this period, no less than twenty-six stem from him (only two of them after 301), and these must represent only a small part of the actual total.[14] Evidence of such intense activity by the *ekklesia* exists for no earlier or later period. A further indication of the activity can be seen in how many resolutions came to a vote during a single meeting of the Assembly: from two to four of the surviving decrees from each of the years

14. A list is in W. B. Dinsmoor, *The Archons of Athens in the Hellenistic Age* (Cambridge, Mass., 1931) 13–14, with additions by C. Habicht, *AJAH* 2 (1977) 39 n. 15; a new decree has been published in *Horos* 4 (1986) 11 ff.

307/6, 306/5, 304/3, and 303/2 passed the Assembly on the same day.[15]

Some resolutions were drawn up after Demetrius informed the Athenians that one or another of his retainers had done something to benefit the city.[16] Stratocles' assiduity in introducing the corresponding resolutions and proposing honors for Antigonus, Demetrius, and their confederates quickly earned him a reputation for servility toward the new regime. His career revealed with particular clarity that Athens was now neither entirely free nor entirely dependent; the city's freedom was relative, and limited to matters to which its new masters were indifferent. When their wishes or interests were at stake, the city had to submit, as it had submitted to Cassander's wishes during the administration of Demetrius of Phalerum. The Athenians had served in Cassander's military operations whenever ordered, and now they had to provide troops for Demetrius on demand.

These circumstances left the political leaders of Athens little room to maneuver, but all the same the alacrity with which Stratocles accommodated the city's new masters caused offense. It provoked a conflict with Demochares of Leukonoe, who had urged the strengthening of the city's fortifications in 307/6 and who shared political leadership with Stratocles in the first three years of Demetrius Poliorcetes' rule. During the winter of 304/3 Demochares castigated an especially servile action of Stratocles with such cutting irony that he was banished, to return only in 286/5, after the city had liberated itself for a second time from Demetrius' rule.[17] By the time Demochares and Stratocles clashed, however, Athens' political climate had shifted, and Demetrius Poliorcetes was no longer celebrated as the liberator and restorer of democracy. After taking up residence in Athens, he acted in such a

---

15. For 307/6: *IG* II².460, 461. For 306/5: *IG* II².471, 472. For 304/3: *IG* II².486, 597; *Hesperia* 7 (1938) 297, no. 22; and *Horos* 4 (1986) 11 ff. For 303/2: *IG* II².493, 494, 495, 496 (+ 503), and 497.

16. This is the case for 3, and perhaps all 4, of the decrees from the end of the year 304/3 mentioned in the preceding note. Polyperchon had procured honors for two of his retainers from Athens in this manner in 319/8 (*IG* II².387).

17. Plut. *Demetrius* 24; [Plut.] *mor.* 851E in the proposal of Demochares' son Laches for posthumous honors for his father from the year 270. In it Stratocles, the man responsible for Demochares' banishment, is referred to as one of the "destroyers of democracy" *(katalysantes ton demon)*, i.e., accused of the same crime for which he had brought proceedings against the supporters of Demetrius of Phalerum in 307/6.

high-handed and autocratic manner that many citizens grew disillusioned and resentful.

At first, though, the two Athenian politicians worked in harmony. Demochares, who devoted much effort to improving the city's defenses, also made a name for himself in another, less praiseworthy connection by backing Sophocles' resolution of 307 or 306 to place the philosopher schools under state control. The bill required schools to obtain licensing from the Council and the citizenry in order to operate. The Assembly passed it, no doubt in part because it appeared harmless, and in part because a faction actively opposed to the schools did exist. This group mistrusted the philosophers' doctrines and suspected them of exercising a subversive influence on their pupils—of "corrupting the youth," the charge leveled against Socrates. The poet Alexis presented the view of this party in a contemporary comedy in which he praised Prince Demetrius and the lawgivers for the law that drove the philosophers out of Attica and into the desert ("to the crows").[18] The philosophers, led by Theophrastus, had indeed left Athens right after passage of Sophocles' bill, for the idea of giving the voting majority control over their activities was abhorrent to them.

Their forced departure created a scandal that threatened to do as much damage to the city's reputation and prestige as the trial and execution of Socrates had. Philo, a former pupil of Aristotle, sued Sophocles on the grounds that his law was unconstitutional. At the ensuing trial Demochares (who may have been using Sophocles as a front) spoke on behalf of the defendant, severely attacking Aristotle and other philosophers.[19] Nonetheless a large majority found Sophocles guilty as charged and fined him; the law was revoked. The philosophers returned to Athens, and the state never again interfered with their freedom.[20]

Although Sophocles' bill applied to all existing (and future) schools,

18. *PCG* 2.73, fr. 99. Alexis' satire, however, is aimed not at Aristotle's school but at Plato's Academy and its head, Xenocrates. A. Meineke characterized these verses as "the words of an old man angry at the philosophers because they had corrupted his son"; *Fragmenta Comicorum Graecorum*, vol. 3 (1840) 421.

19. G. Marasco, *Democare di Leuconoe* (Florence 1984) 140, fr. 2.

20. Diog. Laert. 5.38.79; Pollux *Onomastikon* 9.42; Athen. 13.610F. See J. P. Lynch, *Aristotle's School* (Berkeley 1972) 103–104 and 117–118; C. Habicht, "Hellenistic Athens and Her Philosophers" David Magie Lecture, Princeton 1988 7–10, reprinted in Habicht, *Athen in hellenistischer Zeit. Gesammelte Aufsätze* (Munich 1994) 231–247 and 357–358.

there was little doubt in Athenians' minds that the principal target of his resolution was the school of Aristotle and Theophrastus. It had been under attack for some time, since its heads were suspected—not without reason—of opposition to radical democracy and friendly feelings first toward the royal house of Macedonia and then toward Antipater, Cassander, and Demetrius of Phalerum. It is easy to see why the radical democrats and nationalist politicians attempted to gain control over it right after Cassander's puppet regime was overthrown. In Alexis' play, however, the first political figure to be mentioned in connection with Sophocles' resolution is Prince Demetrius. This fact suggests that Demetrius was associated with the group behind the motion or at least favored its passage. In these circumstances the outcome of the vote does great credit to the citizens of Athens, who refused to accept the power over the philosophers that Sophocles' law proposed to give them. A few months later Epicurus, an Athenian citizen, returned home from Colophon and opened his own school in Athens, which became the third of its kind after the Academy and the *Peripatos*.[21]

As was to be expected, Cassander did not give up Athens without a fight. He attempted to retake it more than once during the conflict known as the Four Years' War (307–304). Surviving records show that he attacked Attica in 306. The Athenians repelled this attack, in part because of their own strength, but also because of military support from the Aetolians.[22] The city was exposed to even greater danger in 304, when Cassander's troops first besieged and then assailed it. They laid waste to Attica and conquered the two Attic fortresses Phyle and Panakton, in addition to the island of Salamis. They surrounded the city, and Athens might well have fallen had King Demetrius not returned from Rhodes with reinforcements in the summer or fall. He landed at Aulis and forced Cassander to retreat beyond Thermopylae.[23]

21. Diog. Laert. 10.2; 15 (Apollodorus, *FGrHist* 244 F 42).

22. The hostilities of that year are documented in *IG* II^2.467.22, 470.11–14, 469.8–10. The credit for gaining the support of the Aetolians belongs to the Athenian general and statesman Olympiodorus, and the year in which they came to the aid of Athens is more likely to have been 306/5 than 304 (Pausanias 1.26.3); according to Pausanias their assistance was a crucial factor in saving the city. *IG* II^2.503.11–13 can refer to hostilities in either 304 or 306. A surviving dedication of Athenian citizen soldiers from 306/5 exists as well (*IG* II^2.1954).

23. Plut. *Demetrius* 23; Diodorus 20.105–106; *IG* II^2.492.8–9; *Horos* 4 (1986) 11, lines 13–15, 19 ff.; *Hesperia* 6 (1937) 323, no. 4; *Ancient Macedonian Studies in Honor of C. F.*

This was no doubt the occasion on which Cassander's brother Pleistarchos led an enemy charge that breached the walls; it was beaten back by the Athenian cavalry, whose achievement was later commemorated by a memorial at the site.[24] The arrival of Demetrius compelled Cassander to abandon all the territory he had conquered in Attica. A year later, in 303, Demetrius and a force of Athenians headed by an elite corps of volunteers known as the *epilektoi* defeated Cassander and his ally of the moment, Polyperchon, in the Peloponnese.[25] During this period an encounter mentioned by Pausanias took place (although no specific date can be assigned to it), in which the Macedonians may have penetrated Attica by land via Eleusis, attacked Piraeus and the fortress of Munychia, and been driven off by the Athenian Olympiodorus. The meaning of this much-discussed passage is obscure, however, and its interpretation open to doubt.[26]

Indeed, much about the course of this war is unknown, but the details are less significant than the interpretation given it in Athens. According to Athenian documents from these years, Cassander represented pure evil, and the aim of his offensive was the "enslavement" of Greece.[27] The Athenians, on the other hand, under the leadership of King Demetrius and his allies, saw themselves as fighting for deliverance, freedom, and democracy—for their own city and for the rest of Greece.[28] In the wording of such defiant claims the Athenians adopted

---

Edson (Thessaloniki 1981) 359–360 and the ensuing discussion in *Hesperia* 58 (1989) 297–301 and 59 (1990) 463–466. See further *ISE* 7, a decree of Athenian volunteers in honor of Demetrius Poliorcetes; *IG* II^2.499.20. Cf. H. Hauben, *ZPE* 14 (1974) 10.

24. Pausanias 1.15.1 and the curse tablet found nearby with the names of Pleistarchos, Eupolemos, Cassander, and Demetrius of Phalerum. The foundations of the gates on which the trophy was placed were found in 1982 (T. L. Shear Jr., *Hesperia* 53 [1984] 19–24). Cf. C. Habicht, *Pausanias' Guide to Greece* (Berkeley 1985) 81–82.

25. The inscriptions cited above in note 23, esp. *ISE* 7, refer to the hostilities of this year. The Athenians killed in the war against Cassander received a state funeral on the Cerameicus; Pausanias 1.29.7.

26. This interpretation of Pausanias 1.26.3 is offered in Habicht, *Untersuchungen* 95–112; it has been challenged by U. Bultrighini, *RFIC* 112 (1984) 54–62, but supported by E. Lanciers, *RBPh* 65 (1987) 63.

27. The expression used is [ἐ]πὶ δουλείαι, in lines 7–8 of the decree published in *Ancient Macedonian Studies* 359–360. *IG* II^2.469.9–10: [ἐπὶ δουλείαι τ]ῆς πόλεως.

28. For "deliverance" *(soteria)*: *Hesperia* 10 (1941) 55, no. 19.7; *Horos* 4 (1986) 11, line 17 (as restored). For "freedom" *(eleutheria)*: *IG* II^2.558.14 and 559.9 (of the Greeks); *Horos* 4 (1986) 11, line 14 (of the Athenians). For "democracy" *(demokratia)*: *IG* II^2.559.10; *RFIC* 70 (1942) 12; *Horos* 4 (1986) 11, line 15.

phrases used by Demetrius upon his entry into the city in 307: he had his herald proclaim that he had come in his father's name to drive out the foreign garrison, liberate the Athenians, and restore to them their laws and traditional constitution.[29]

Such were the official pronouncements, at any rate, and immediately after the liberation of 307 most Athenians would probably have accepted them as close to the truth. As the years went by, however, a large proportion of citizens became disillusioned as a result of the complicated and problematic nature of their relationship with the king. This shift in public opinion was caused by a variety of events, both within and outside Attica. Demetrius' extended stays in the city during the winters of 304/3 and 303/2 revealed the more repellent sides of his character and the servility of his Athenian supporters. Antigonus' ceaseless attempts to wrest control of the empire from his rivals also affected the city. The first of these encounters after the liberation of Athens took place in 306 near Salamis on Cyprus, where Demetrius won a great naval victory over Ptolemy.[30] After this battle Antigonus assumed the title of king and granted it to his son as well.[31]

Next came a joint attack on Egypt by both kings toward the end of 306, which Ptolemy succeeded in repelling.[32] Because the Rhodians had refused to participate in this campaign, Demetrius made Rhodes his next target and laid siege to the island from the spring of 305 to the spring of 304. During this year Ptolemy, Lysimachus, and Cassander renewed their earlier alliance and came to the threatened island's aid.[33] Within a short time all three assumed the title of king, as did Seleucus. The last significant event of these years occurred in 302, when Demetrius went to Corinth to create a second league, in an attempt to revive the tradition of Philip's Hellenic League, founded in

---

29. Plut. *Demetrius* 8.7.

30. Diodorus 20.47–52; Plut. *Demetrius* 15–17.

31. The precise dates when this battle occurred and when, not long afterward, Antigonus assumed the title of king are not known. In an Athenian document from the 22nd day of the 10th prytany of 306/5, approximately April 305, he is named without the title (*IG* II^2.1492 B 97–99), but on the last day of this prytany, at most 8 days later, his name occurs with it (*IG* II^2.471). The verses by Alexis in celebration of the victory refer to Antigonus as king; *PCG* 2.85, fr. 116.

32. Diodorus 20.73–76; Plut. *Demetrius* 19.

33. Diodorus 20.81–88 and 91–100; Plut. *Demetrius* 21–22; Marmor Parium, *FGrHist* 239 B 23; Pap. Berol. 11632, ed. F. Hiller von Gaertringen, *SB Berlin* (1918) 752–762.

338/7. In the new league Antigonus and Demetrius united the regions of Greece they had wrested from Cassander's control.[34]

The Athenians contributed thirty triremes to the victorious naval fleet at Salamis, which fought on the left wing under the aristocratic Aleuad Medeius of Larissa. Twenty years earlier Medeius had been an admiral of Alexander the Great in India and host at the last meal the king shared with his companions. He had accompanied Demetrius to Athens and was awarded honors by the Athenians in 303/2.[35] Demetrius recognized the city's contribution by sending 1,200 hoplite arms from the immense spoils of victory, in a grand gesture far exceeding the 300 arms Alexander had sent after the battle of the Granicus.[36] The numerous Greek delegations that attempted to negotiate an end to the hostilities on Rhodes in the winter of 305/4 included one from Athens.[37] Although their efforts failed, the warring parties did reach an agreement in the spring of 304—fortunately for Athens, as the city was in desperate straits and needed Demetrius' help. His arrival freed them from Cassander's stranglehold, and thanks to his military successes he returned to the Athenians not only the fortresses of Panakton and Phyle but also Oropus and the sanctuary of Amphiaraus.[38]

The Athenians thus had good cause to be content with Demetrius. But his long periods of residence in the city revealed the dark sides to his rule. Plutarch makes the shrewd comment that becoming a king altered something in a ruler's nature. More than merely adding a title

34. A considerable portion of the decree creating the League has been edited along with other related materials and published by H. H. Schmitt, *StV,* no. 46. Antigonus had announced his intention to found such a league in 307 (Diodorus 20.46.5).

35. For more on Medeius' career under Alexander, see H. Berve, *Das Alexanderreich auf prosopographischer Grundlage,* vol. 2 (Munich 1926) 261–262, no. 521. For the latter part of his life see C. Habicht, *Ancient Macedonia,* vol. 1 (Thessaloniki 1970) 265–269. The Athenian honors are in *IG* II^2.498. His nephew Oxythemis was also employed in the service of the kings and also received honors in Athens; see the decree *IG* II^2.558 and the acts cited below in note 45.

36. Plut. *Demetrius* 17.1. For Alexander's dedication see Chapter 1, note 23.

37. Diodorus 20.98.2–3; Plut. *Demetrius* 22.8.

38. *ISE* 8.14. The philosopher Menedemus' intervention with Demetrius on behalf of Oropus belongs to a later era, however; see D. Knoepfler, *La vie de Ménédème d'Erétrie de Diogène Laërce* (Basle 1991) 197 n. 74. An unpublished inscription from Rhamnus reveals that Demetrius himself appointed an Athenian to a two-year term as *strategos* for the defense of Attica at that time (*Ergon* [1993] 7). He was the namesake of another Adeimantus, one of the king's closest associates, and had held the position previously, undoubtedly chosen by the citizens. In the meantime Demetrius had usurped this function of the Assembly.

before his name, it confused his judgment and puffed up his vanity, and he became pompous and arrogant in both speech and manner.[39] The Athenians were shocked by Demetrius' licentiousness and unusual fondness for women and courtesans; one of them, for a long time his favorite who bore him a daughter, was an Athenian-born woman named Lamia who had been captured at Salamis. Like most courtesans she was well educated and a witty conversationalist. But she was by no means the only woman in Athens to enjoy the king's favor: other women mentioned as his courtesans were Leaina, Mania, and Myrrhine. He squandered lavish sums of money on them, which on at least a few occasions came from the city treasury; he allowed Lamia and Leaina to be celebrated as personifications of Aphrodite and worshipped as goddesses. Lamia's influence with the king was said to be a source of great annoyance to his closest advisers.[40] Although Demetrius had been married for some time to Antipatros' daughter Phila and made no attempt to conceal his concubines from the Athenians, he took another wife at about this time, Euthydike, an Athenian woman of noble birth who had accompanied her first husband, Ophellas, to Africa and returned to Athens after his death.[41]

Among contemporary authors, only Philippides accused Demetrius of turning the Parthenon and the Acropolis into a brothel. This statement must be accepted with caution, however, for Philippides was the king's sworn enemy and a resident at the court of Lysimachus. Plutarch reports that of all the rival rulers Lysimachus hated Demetrius most bitterly. Alluding to Lamia, Lysimachus remarked that it was the first appearance of a prostitute on the tragic stage, prompting Demetrius to retort that his prostitute had more sense than Lysimachus' Penelope.[42] Philippides may well have exaggerated, but there can be little doubt that the king's behavior was gross enough to cause offense. Other reports claim that one particularly beautiful boy, seen by the king while

39. Plut. *Demetrius* 18.5.

40. The king's Athenian hetaerae are mentioned by the contemporary authors Demochares (*FGrHist* 75 F 1), Philippides (*PCG* 7: 347, fr. 25), and Lynceus of Samos (Athen. 3.101E.4, 128A) and by the slightly later authors Machon (frs. 12, 13, 15, ed. Gow) and Phylarch (*FGrHist* 81 F 12). Most of the material is contained in Athenaeus 3, 4, 6, 13, and 14 and can be easily found in the index of Kaibel's edition under the names of the individual courtesans.

41. Plut. *Demetrius* 14.1.

42. Philippides, *PCG* 7.347, fr. 25; the exchange between Lysimachus and Demetrius is reported in Plut. *Demetrius* 25.9.

bathing, could escape Demetrius' pursuit only by committing suicide. Another boy from a prominent family is supposed to have used the king's favor by persuading him to write to city officials and order them to cancel a large fine owed by the boy's father.[43]

Nothing reveals more clearly than this last incident the illusory nature of the city's independence when Demetrius' own interests were concerned. But this was not the end of the episode. Ashamed of its own weakness in yielding to the royal will in the matter of the fine, the Assembly passed a resolution forbidding any citizen accused or convicted of wrongdoing to present a letter from the king in connection with his case. This defiance so incensed Demetrius that the decree was repealed and its authors punished. This was the controversy in which Demochares clashed with Stratocles and was afterward sent into exile. Stratocles continued to spare no effort in his service to the king. When Demetrius returned to Athens in the spring of 302 from Corinth, where he had founded the second Hellenic League, he wished to be initiated into the Eleusinian Mysteries in a single ceremony. Normally this occurred in three stages: candidates were admitted to the Lesser Mysteries in the eighth month (Anthesterion) and to the Greater Mysteries in the third month (Boëdromion) of the following year; after this they were required to wait another year before being admitted to full membership in the cult. Pythodorus, chief priest of the Mysteries, refused to allow these steps to be compressed into a single act, but the ever-resourceful Stratocles hit on a scheme to fulfill the king's wishes: he introduced a resolution that temporarily renamed the current (tenth) month of the year 302—which happened to be Munychion (April)—Anthesterion, thereby making it the appropriate time for Demetrius' initiation into the lesser rites; as soon as this had been done, it was immediately declared to be the month of Boëdromion, and the king was admitted to the Greater Mysteries.[44] This travesty of their religious ceremonies must have deeply offended many Athenians, and Philippides expressed their anger in caustic language. Demochares condemned just as sharply the exceptional honors awarded to the courtesans Lamia and Leaina, and criticized the Assembly for extravagantly exceeding the customary limits in honoring influential agents of

43. Plut. *Demetrius* 24.6–12. The boy was Cleaenetus, son of Cleomedon of Cydathen, a descendant of the famous demagogue Cleon.

44. Philochorus, *FGrHist* 328 F 69–70; Plut. *Demetrius* 26.1–5; Diodorus 20.110.1; Clinton, *Officials* 50.

the king such as Adeimantus of Lampsacus, Oxythemis of Larissa, and Burichos.[45] The impression given by these authors that Stratocles was responsible for most of these resolutions is confirmed by the epigraphic evidence.

In the early summer of 302, soon after his return from Corinth, Demetrius reopened the campaign against Cassander, which he had waged so successfully in the Peloponnese the preceding year. As Cassander had blocked the route through Thermopylae, Demetrius embarked at Chalcis and sailed north to Thessaly, where he first seized Larissa Cremaste and then the more important city of Pherae. There messengers from his father, Antigonus, reached him with a request for help: Lysimachus, Seleucus, and Ptolemy had joined forces to attack Antigonus, and he needed the support of Demetrius' troops. Demetrius negotiated a provisional peace with Cassander and set out for Asia Minor at once; in 301 he took part in the battle of Ipsus at his father's side, against the coalition of the other kings, which in the end did not include Ptolemy (who had turned around on hearing the false rumor of a great victory by Antigonus) but did include some of Cassander's forces. It is reported that the battle was lost when Demetrius, pursuing the opposing cavalry too rashly, left the flank of his father's phalanx exposed. Antigonus, who had delayed the battle until his son's return, numbered among the slain.[46]

As a result of this victory, Seleucus gained the territory of northern Syria and, with it, access to the Mediterranean; Lysimachus emerged as ruler of the Asia Minor. Many Athenian prisoners, fighting with Demetrius' forces, had fallen into his hands. The decree of 283 awarding honors to Philippides reveals some details of what happened. Philippides, held in high esteem by Lysimachus, interceded with the king on the prisoners' behalf. He was granted permission to bury the dead, and successfully arranged for the prisoners' release. Those who wished were allowed to join Lysimachus' army, while those who wanted to return home received money and supplies for the passage

45. *FGrHist* 75 F 1. I have discussed the subject in greater detail in *Gottmenschentum* 55–58. Their characterization as "lackeys" (*kolakes*, flatterers) is unjust, as L. Robert in particular has shown in the case of Adeimantus, a celebrated citizen of Lampsacus and a close friend of Theophrastus, who served as Demetrius' representative to the council of the League of Corinth and was honored in Eretria and Athens; *Hellenica* 2 (1946) 15–33. Oxythemis and Burichos were also prominent men assisting Demetrius.

46. The main sources for the war fought by this new coalition are Diodorus 20.106–113 and Plut. *Demetrius* 28–29.

from Philippides. Since this last group is said to have numbered 300 men, it seems a reasonable estimate that at least 1,000 Athenians must have taken part in the battle. Philippides' final achievement was to persuade Lysimachus to release the Athenians whom Antigonus and Demetrius had been holding prisoner in Asia Minor (for reasons unknown).[47] Antigonus had also founded a city in northern Syria named after himself, Antigoneia, and settled it, among others, with a large number of Athenians. In 300 Seleucus destroyed the city and founded his new capital, Antiocheia, nearby on the Orontes River. The Athenian settlers were moved to the king's new residence.[48]

The defeat at Ipsus marked the end of the first phase of Demetrius Poliorcetes' rule over Athens.

2. Tyranny

The news of the battle of Ipsus cannot have reached Athens before September 301, for evidence has survived showing that Stratocles could still command a majority in the Assembly on the twenty-third of Metageitnion (the second month of the Athenian year, which began in July).[49] As Diodorus' work on the period after the autumn of 301 is lost, the general history of the following decades is known only in the barest outlines; the same holds true for the history of Athens, for which very little information is available apart from Plutarch's biography of Demetrius. Obviously, Stratocles' influence must have ended the moment the Athenians received a reliable account of the outcome of the battle in Asia Minor. The Assembly convened and voted never again to accept a king within the city walls,[50] an unceremonious dismissal of Demetrius. The king had left one of his wives behind in Athens, the Epirote Princess Deidameia, a sister of Pyrrhus, as well as part of his fleet and a sizable amount of money. As it seemed clear that he would return for them, the Athenians sent a delegation to inform him of their resolution and provided Deidameia with an escort as far as Megara.

The king, who had stopped in Ephesus to gather several thousand troops and whose fleet was still intact, was indeed on his way back to

47. *IG* II^2.657.16–29.

48. Pausanias of Damascus, *FGrHist* 854 F 10.6. See also C. Habicht, *Chiron* 19 (1989) 9 with n. 8.

49. *IG* II^2.640.

50. Plut. *Demetrius* 30.4.

Athens when the representatives of the city caught up with him in the Cyclades. Their news came as a shock and a bitter disappointment to him, but he only mildly reproached the ambassadors; he asked only that his ships be returned to him, and the Athenians complied.[51] While most of the states Demetrius had previously controlled now drove out his forces and allied themselves with his enemies, the Athenians declared their intention to remain neutral in the same resolution that repudiated Demetrius. Of course this did not exclude contacts with other kings, and such dealings were no doubt necessary to ensure the city's continued food supplies.[52] The evidence shows that the Athenians were in contact with Demetrius' opponents Cassander and Lysimachus within two years of the battle of Ipsus. On the twenty-first of Metageitnion (about 4 September) of the year 299 (exactly two years after Stratocles' last documented appearance before the Athenian Assembly), a delegation returned from the court of "King Cassander" and delivered its report.[53] And in the same year a large donation of grain, procured from Lysimachus for the city by the poet Philippides,[54] was distributed among the citizenry. Thanks to this aid, there were sufficient supplies in the year of the Archon Euctemon, 299/8; a dedication to Eueteria, the goddess of prosperity, and a decree in honor of the "guardians of the grain"[55] also indicate the presence of enough food.

These facts are significant because a severe famine occurred at some point during this period, allowing a popular demagogue named Lachares to take control of the city.[56] At the time of the coup, Lachares commanded the mercenary corps; he made himself tyrant of Athens at Cassander's urging, and possibly with Cassander's assistance. Since Cassander died in the spring of 297, Lachares' rule can have begun no

---

51. Plut. *Demetrius* 30.1–31.2.

52. G. Marasco, *Athenaeum* 62 (1984) 288–289. Details on Athens' political orientation in these years are in E. Meyer, *Klio* 5 (1905) 180–183.

53. *IG* II^2.641. Athenian documents from 307–301 never give Cassander the royal title, since he was an enemy of the city.

54. The same Philippides who had buried the dead and generously assisted the Athenian prisoners after the battle of Ipsus, and who had sharply attacked Stratocles.

55. The documentary evidence is given in Habicht, *Untersuchungen* 19.

56. Until 1959 the name Lachares was documented only a few times in Attica for the period of the emperors; S. Dow, *CPh* 52 (1957) 106–107. Since then evidence has been discovered of an Athenian sculptor Attalos, son of Lachares, presumably the same Attalos named by Pausanias (2.19.3; see *AJA* 63 [1959] 280). In any event Attalos son of Lachares was active in Pheneus in Arcadia and in Argos.

later than 298/7, but a more probable date is the spring of 300, during the festival of the Dionysia in the month of Elaphebolion (March/April). According to tradition Menander wrote his comedy *The Imbrians* in the archonship of Nicocles, 302/1, for performance at the Dionysia. The performance was canceled, however, "because of the tyrant Lachares."[57] The Dionysia in question must have been that of the year 300, because Stratocles had still dominated the political life of the city during the festival of the previous year (and for another six months). The most natural interpretation of the text is that the unrest associated with Lachares' seizure of power prevented performance of the play (and perhaps celebration of the festival altogether).[58]

A few details about this time of unrest are contained in the fragment of a chronicle found on a papyrus from Oxyrhynchus.[59] According to this text an Athenian military campaign was followed by a vehement dispute among its leaders, the main antagonists being Lachares (commander of the mercenary forces) and the hoplite general Charias. Apparently, after being accused of failing to provide food for the starving population, Charias retreated to the Acropolis to seek refuge there, but he was defeated. An agreement for the release of his followers was negotiated, but the leaders—including Charias and three others, possibly also generals—fled into the Parthenon. After their capture they were led before the Assembly, condemned by a single resolution introduced by Apollodorus, and summarily executed—illegally, since the accused men should have been granted separate votes. The generals of the battle of Arginusae had suffered a similar fate in 406.[60]

---

57. On the text of this document see M. Gronewald, *ZPE* 93 (1992) 20–21; and W. Luppe, *ZPE* 96 (1993) 9–10.

58. The chronology is a matter of debate because only a few documents related to the matter have survived, and they are capable of different interpretations. The opinion given here was worked out in its essentials by W. S. Ferguson, *CP* 24 (1929) 1–31. I formerly opposed it (*Untersuchungen* 1–21) but have now been persuaded by the arguments of Osborne (*Naturalization* 2: 144–153) and H. Heinen (*GGA* 233 [1981] 177–184). It follows that Lachares' overthrow probably belongs in the spring of 295 (and not the spring of 294), even though the similarity of events connected with his overthrow (Plut. *Demetrius* 34) and the decree of the city for Herodorus from the spring of 294 (*IG* II^2.646) remains so striking that one is more inclined to view them as simultaneous rather than separated by a year.

59. *P.Oxy.* 2082 = *FGrHist.* 257a.

60. *FGrHist* 257a F 2: reading [μιᾶι] ψήφωι, clearly the proper emendation proposed by G. De Sanctis (as opposed to the meaningless [τῆι] ψήφωι, *RFIC* 64 [1936] 140). Cf. the phrase μιᾷ ψήφῳ in Xenophon's account of the Arginusae trial in *Hellenica* 1.7.34. See

It is significant that the *ekklesia* pronounced the verdict against these men, even if its action was illegal, for it shows that the tyrant had not suppressed Athens' most important democratic institution. He also left in place the law decreeing that the secretaryship of the Council would rotate annually among the twelve tribes in their official sequence. Under Lachares the *strategoi* continued to be chosen by popular election as well,[61] a further indication that he left unaltered the most important outward forms of democracy. If he actually came to power in the spring of 300, as it appears, then the delegation that visited Cassander and returned from Pella in the summer of 299 must have been sent by Lachares on a mission to his mentor. In this case both Lysimachus' donation of grain, motivated in all probability by the famine of the previous year, and the gifts he sent to Athens in the first half of 298 for the celebration of the Panathenaea would also fall in the period of Lachares' rule.[62] In view of the good relations that always existed between Cassander and Lysimachus,[63] these benefactions to a city in the latter's realm would not be surprising.

A decree of the cavalry in honor of the treasurers of Athena from the year of the archon Hegemachus (300/299) also dates from the time of Lachares, if the chronology assumed here is correct,[64] offering further corroboration of the continued existence of traditional democratic institutions. In the same year the Doric portico was built in the sanctuary of Asclepius at the foot of the Acropolis.[65] In addition a long list has survived from around 300, containing the names of about 150 men from some fifty different states, with a particularly large contingent from Thrace,[66] almost certainly a list of mercenary soldiers. The list

---

also J. H. Lipsius, *Das attische Recht und Rechtsverfahren*, vol. 1 (Leipzig 1905) 185–186. According to Osborne this conflict did not occur until 298/7 (*Naturalization* 2: 148). The Ameinias named as one of the condemned men is Ameinias of Xypete, who received honors after a campaign, in 301/0 at the earliest, and definitely in that year if he was executed in 300. He may have been another member of the board of generals; B. D. Meritt, *Hesperia* 11 (1942) 279.

61. *IG* II^2.682.21–24. For the cycle of the Council secretaries see Habicht, *Untersuchungen* 11 n. 43.

62. *IG* II^2.657.14–16.

63. Diodorus 20.106.3.

64. *IG* II^2.1264.

65. *IG* II^2.1685, newly edited with commentary by S. B. Aleshire, *Asklepios at Athens* (Amsterdam 1991) 13–32; for the name of the archon, see 29.

66. *IG* II^2.1956, with the Thracians named in lines 1–46.

must date from later than 315, since it mentions the city of Cassandreia, and Cassandreia was not founded until that year. Similarly, it cannot date from the years 307–301, when Lemnos was an Athenian possession, because it names Lemnos as an independent state. It is thus quite possible that the list contains the names of Lachares' men, for Lachares was commander of the mercenary troops at the time of his coup.[67] In this case the document would date from some time between 301 and 295.

During the time Lachares ruled Athens he lost control of Piraeus, for many of the Athenian troops and citizens opposed to his takeover withdrew to the harbor and occupied it, turning it into a base of operations for resistance. The secession occurred before Cassander's death in the spring of 297.[68] And when King Demetrius returned and attempted to take the city for the second time—a campaign that cannot have occurred later than the summer of 296—Piraeus was still in the hands of Lachares' opponents.[69] Demetrius' appearance on the scene presaged the end of the tyrant's days in power, even though he was able to hold out until the following spring. Pausanias suggests that a rebellion against Lachares, or possibly an attempt on his life, may have taken place about this time when he mentions the graves of "brave men" in the state cemetery, "on whom fortune did not smile when they rose up against the tyrant Lachares."[70]

In the end, his overthrow in the spring of 295 was accomplished from the outside, by King Demetrius and his forces. Although Demetrius had suffered a severe defeat at Ipsus, he had saved his fleet and retained control of a number of important coastal cities, including Corinth in Greece, Miletus and Ephesus in Asia Minor, and Tyre and Sidon in Phoenicia. He also held Cyprus and the communities of the League of Islanders (which Antigonus had founded in the Cyclades in 314). In addition, Demetrius profited from a conflict that broke out between Seleucus and Ptolemy over southern Syria and Palestine. Seleucus needed an ally and sought Demetrius' support. The two rulers met near Rhosos in Syria on the great ship that the Athenians had returned to Demetrius after the battle of Ipsus; Demetrius and his wife Phila received Seleucus on board, and celebrated Seleucus' marriage to

67. *FGrHist* 257 a F 1.
68. *FGrHist* 257 a F 2–3.
69. Polyaenus 4.7.5.
70. Pausanias 1.29.10.

their daughter Stratonice.[71] Soon afterward Demetrius made peace with Ptolemy. These maneuvers gave him greater freedom of movement in the eastern Mediterranean, and his hopes of what he might be able to achieve rose when Cassander's death in 297 preceded by only four months that of his son and successor, Philip. Philip's two half-grown younger brothers became absorbed in a battle over the throne of Macedonia, increasing Demetrius' prospects.

Demetrius' first target was Athens, where he could count on support from the separatists in Piraeus. On his way to Attica, however, a storm destroyed much of his fleet. He sent orders to Phoenicia to begin building replacements and, after a few unsuccessful skirmishes near Athens, turned his attention toward the Peloponnese. During a siege of the city of Messene he suffered a severe wound from a catapult shot.[72] In the spring of 295 Demetrius renewed his attack on Attica, conquering the fortresses Eleusis and Rhamnus and the islands of Salamis and Aegina, and laying waste to the countryside. He also cut off supply routes to the city with a naval blockade, provoking what may have been the worst famine Athens had ever experienced. It is reported by Plutarch that Epicurus counted out the daily ration of beans for himself and his pupils; a handful of capers became a valuable possession, and in one family a fight broke out between father and son over a dead mouse.

Though surrounded, Lachares mounted a stubborn and courageous defense. When his soldiers demanded their pay, he took the offerings from religious shrines and melted them down for the precious metals they contained. He also took the golden robe Phidias had made for the statue of Athena in the Parthenon, so that it was said Lachares had stripped even the goddess naked. A bronze head of Athena Nike from the Age of Pericles, found stripped of its gold leaf, further testifies to Lachares' acts of sacrilege. The Assembly, which had good reason to fear a return of Demetrius after its vote against him in 301, passed a resolution threatening the death penalty for anyone who advocated reconciliation with the king.[73]

71. Plut. *Demetrius* 31.5–32.3; *OGI* 10. For the ship with 13 banks of rowers see Plut. *Demetrius* 31.1 and 32.2.

72. The alliance between Messene and Lysimachus, documented by a treaty found in the city in 1990, probably belongs in this context; see P. Themelis, *Praktika* (1990 [1994]) 83–84; P. Gauthier, *REG* 108 (1995) 467–468.

73. The main source for this passage is Plut. *Demetrius* 33–34. For more on the king's conquests see Polyaenus 4.7.5; for the famine see Demetrius, *PCG* 5.11. For the theft of

The arrival of a fleet of 150 vessels sent by Ptolemy (who had once again allied himself with Seleucus and Lysimachus against Demetrius) raised hopes that the siege might be lifted. But the would-be rescuers retreated immediately when they sighted the approach of Demetrius' replacement fleet, numbering 300 ships. Lachares now gave up the cause as lost and fled to Thebes in disguise. By about April 295 the Athenians had no choice: facing imminent starvation, they opened their gates to Demetrius.

3. King Demetrius

As they opened the city gates, the Athenians sent out a delegation to Demetrius, which returned with his instructions for the people to assemble in the theater. When they had gathered there, Demetrius posted a guard around the building and, in a melodramatic gesture, entered from the rear and descended the entire length of the theater to the stage in silence. His appearance only increased the anxiety the Athenians felt. But against all expectation Demetrius' tone was mild, almost friendly, as he chided them gently for their behavior toward him. He immediately ordered the distribution of 100,000 bushels of grain and announced his intention of creating the public offices that "the people most desired." The citizens who spoke in response expressed their gratitude and proposed new honors for him; indeed the demagogue Dromocleides went so far as to propose that they should hand over Piraeus and Munychia to Demetrius, and no one dared to speak out in opposition. The king himself created a garrison on the Museum hill at the southern edge of the city.[74]

Various other documents supplement this account, for which Plutarch is the source. Almost exactly one year after the city's fall the Athenians voted to award high honors to Herodorus of Lampsakos (or Kyzikos), one of Demetrius' close associates who had previously served Antigonus. The delegation sent to sue for peace at the end of the siege reported that Herodorus had been most supportive of their cause and had used his influence to gain the king's approval for a pact of friend-

---

gold, see Pausanias 1.25.7 and 29.16; [Plut.] *mor.* 379C. For the head of Nike, see H. A. Thompson, *HSCP Suppl.* 1 (1940) 207–208. Lachares used some of the gold to mint coins; see J. N. Svoronos, *Journal international d'archéologie numismatique* 21 (1927) 159–168; cf. G. Philipp, *Gymnasium* 80 (1973) 501–502. For Lachares' flight, see Polyaenus 3.7.1.
   74. Plut. *Demetrius* 34.1–7.

ship and the continuation of democratic government. Herodorus was granted rare honors, including the right to take meals with the *prytaneis* at state expense for the rest of his life, a bronze statue in the Agora next to those of the tyrant-slayers and the city's "saviors" (Antigonus and Demetrius), and Athenian citizenship. The citizens considered these honors appropriate to his high rank and his extraordinary efforts on their behalf.[75] It was then necessary to award even greater honors to the king himself. Plutarch describes Demetrius' honors of 295 and 307 not in chronological sequence but in a separate summary of all honors awarded to the kings in Athens.[76] One day of the year and the month of Munychion were renamed in his honor, and a Demetrius Festival was added to the festival of Dionysus (for which an inscription has survived from the year 292).[77] None of these honors seems to have remained in force after the city rebelled a second time (in 287), although the religious cult of the "saviors" Antigonus and Demetrius and the tribes named after them continued to exist.

Possibly Dromocleides' resolution giving Piraeus to the king merely sanctioned the existing state of affairs, for Demetrius may already have taken it when the city fell.[78] (This is not necessarily true for Munychia, however.) After the siege a large part of the king's fleet was stationed there.[79] Conditions in the following period also indicate that Demetrius must have occupied the fortresses of Attica, even though no mention of it occurs in the (very incomplete) records. It is also difficult to interpret the vague statement "he instituted offices that were popular with the people." But as the resolution granting honors to Herodorus specifically mentioned democracy, there can be no doubt that Athens had a democratic constitution at the time. We do know that the Council of 600 was abolished and replaced by a newly elected council, because a decree of the Assembly dated the tenth of Munychion 296/5, that is, the tenth month of the year, shows that this date was also the first day of the fourth prytany. Accordingly the first prytany must have begun about the eleventh of Elaphebolion, that is, at about the time the city fell, and each of the remaining nine prytanies must have lasted approximately nine days.[80] It is equally certain that a new

75. *IG* II^2.646 (= Osborne, *Naturalization*, D 68).
76. Plut. *Demetrius* 12.1–2; I have analyzed this passage in *Gottmenschentum* 50–55.
77. *IG* II^2.649, with the new fragment edited by Dinsmoor, *Archons* 7–8.42.
78. Cf. Pausanias 1.25.7.
79. Plut. *Demetrius* 43.4.
80. *IG* II^2.644; Beloch, *GG* 4.2: 247. See, however, J. Tréheux, *RPh* 63 (1989) 285.

election for *strategoi* was held, as the records show that Phaedrus was twice elected *strategos* in charge of arms under the archon Nicias (296/5). Thus he was elected to this office during Lachares' rule, lost it after Lachares' overthrow, won the new election, and served out the remainder of the year.[81]

A further, unknown man was honored with citizenship and a bronze statue at about the same time as Herodorus, but his statue was placed in the theater instead of the Agora or the Acropolis. This fact indicates quite reliably that the honoree was a dramatist whose plays were produced in the city at that time, presumably Diodorus of Sinope, a well-regarded comic poet who is known to have become an Athenian citizen. The award may have been related to political activity on his part, perhaps in connection with the events of 295.[82]

After reconquering Attica, Demetrius returned to the Peloponnese and attempted to regain a footing there. He defeated King Archidamus of Sparta at Mantinea, and it looked as if Sparta would fall to an invader for the first time in history, when Demetrius, distracted by the possibility of bigger prey elsewhere, suddenly ceased his attack.

Opportunity beckoned in Macedonia, where the ongoing struggle for the throne between Cassander's two young sons offered a chance to intervene. The elder of the two, Antipater, accused his mother, Thessalonike, of favoring his younger brother and murdered her. The brother, named Alexander, first called on Demetrius for aid, without success, and then on Pyrrhus, the king of Epirus. With Pyrrhus behind him, Alexander seized a part of Macedonia. When Demetrius arrived in Macedonia, Alexander sent word that his help was no longer needed. Demetrius agreed to withdraw and invited the young ruler to a farewell banquet in Larissa; there he arranged to have Alexander and his whole retinue killed, and added Alexander's troops to his own army. Demetrius then drove out Antipater and took the title of king of Macedonia. Antipater sought refuge with Lysimachus but had no better luck than his younger brother: he was also soon killed by his supposed protector. As young Antipater was the last remaining descendant of his grandfather Antipater and father Cassander, his death brought an end to their line of succession. In 294 Demetrius made a pact with Lysimachus in which the latter recognized him as king of Macedonia in return for

---

81. *IG* II^2.682.21–23.
82. *IG* II^2.648 (= Osborne, *Naturalization*, D 69); for the identity of the two honorees see Habicht, *Untersuchungen* 13–15; cf. Osborne, *Naturalization* 2: 153.

Demetrius' renunciation of all claims to the territory Lysimachus had conquered in Asia Minor.[83] Control of Macedonia brought with it control of Thessaly, and there, on the Gulf of Pagasae, Demetrius began to build his new capital in 293. Named Demetrias after its founder, the city grew rapidly and remained the Greek residence of the Antigonids (whose capital in Macedonia was Pella) until the end of the dynasty in 168.[84]

Demetrius' success in making himself king of Macedonia had a profound effect on Athens. He did not reside there as he had in 304/3 and 303/2, to the relief of the citizens, who had no desire to see a repetition of the king's previous excesses. On the other hand, his absence from the scene forced Demetrius to assert his authority indirectly, through means incompatible with the democratic freedom he had proclaimed not long before. One indication is the tenure of Olympiodorus, an Athenian, as eponymous archon in 294/3 and again in 293/2, in violation of the law that forbade anyone's holding that office a second time. He must have obtained the office either by appointment or by a rigged election, since he could not possibly have been chosen by lot, and moreover twice in succession. Olympiodorus had served with great success under Demetrius in the Four Years' War and acquired considerable fame. It is thus virtually certain that he acted as the king's commissar or representative, entrusted with powers far exceeding those of the normal eponymous archon. When he took office in the summer of 294, the secretaries of the Council (*grammateis*) were again replaced by so-called registrars, a shift of terminology that had characterized the oligarchy of 321–318. For this reason the Athenians, after regaining their independence in 287, referred to the period as an oligarchy.[85] Another indication of the oligarchic nature of the government at this time is the fact that Demetrius acceded to Theophrastus' urging and recalled the political leaders of the oligarchy and their followers from exile, Deinarch of Corinth among them.[86] Officially the Athenian state may have called itself a democracy (much

---

83. Walbank, *Macedonia* 210–218.

84. Strabo 9.436; F. Stählin, E. Meyer, and A. Heidner, *Pagasai und Demetrias* (Berlin 1934) 178 ff.; Habicht, *Gottmenschentum* 75–76; P. Marzolff, in *Die Paläste der hellenistischen Könige*, ed. W. Hoepfner and G. Brands (Mainz 1996) 148–163.

85. In Laches' *psephisma* for his deceased father Demochares ([Plut.] *mor.* 851F) and in the resolution awarding honors to Callias, *Hesperia Suppl.* 17 (1978) 4, ll. 79–83. See also Habicht, *Untersuchungen* 22–33.

86. Philochoros, *FGrHist* 328 F 167; Dion. Hal. *De Dinarcho* 2–3; [Plut.] *mor.* 850D.

as the recent Communist states of Europe called themselves "democratic republics" and "people's republics"), but the actual features of the government led the radical democrats in Athens to use the term "oligarchy."

Such deviations from the democracy proclaimed only fifteen months earlier probably reflect Demetrius' preoccupations with Macedonia after acquiring the crown there. Evidence suggests he pursued the same policy in Boeotia. This state, an ally of Aetolia, lay between the kingdom of Macedonia to the north and Demetrius' possessions in Attica and the Peloponnese to the south. Its strategic position could not escape Demetrius' notice, and in 294 he mounted a surprise attack. The Boeotian League was defeated and forced into the king's alliance. In the following two years he put down two rebellions, and in 291 after a long siege he conquered Thebes. Demetrius installed the historian Hieronymus of Cardia as governor of Boeotia, giving him the title "commissar" *(epimeletes)*. Hieronymus had previously served under Eumenes, and then, after Antigonus defeated him, under Antigonus. Now he took office under Demetrius, and would later serve under Demetrius' son Antigonus Gonatas.[87] Although Hieronymus in Boeotia and Olympiodorus in Attica held offices with different names, their functions must have been quite similar.[88]

Olympiodorus' second archonship ended in the summer of 292. He is not heard of again until the spring of 287, when he led a rebellion against Demetrius. He may have had a falling out with the king; in any event politicians more willing to do Demetrius' bidding seem to have pushed him from prominence after 292. Dromocleides was one, and Stratocles, who had distinguished himself as one of the king's most obsequious servants from 307 to 301, was another. About May 292 Stratocles introduced a motion to award honors to Philippides of Paiania.[89] (The man so honored is not identical with the comic poet Philippides, whose deme was Kephale.) After a brilliant political career

---

87. Walbank, *Macedonia* 219–221; J. Hornblower, *Hieronymus of Cardia* (Oxford 1981) 5–17.

88. Their offices are also comparable to that held by the younger Demetrius of Phalerum, who was appointed *thesmothetes* of Athens after the Chremonidean War (see Chapter 6, Section 1).

89. Dinsmoor, *Archons* 7–9 (*IG* II^2.649, with the right side of the stele added). Two very fragmentary decrees of the same date, *IG* II^2.389 and *Hesperia* 7 (1938) 97, no. 17, may also have been introduced by Stratocles.

spanning more than fifty years, Philippides of Paiania received the kind of high honors typically bestowed on elder statesmen.[90]

Each time Demetrius visited Athens during this period, his subjects offered new proofs of their devotion. The most extreme case occurred after his return from Corfu in 291 or 290, where Lanassa, the wife of Pyrrhus and daughter of Agathocles, had conspired to help Demetrius seize power (allegedly to take revenge on her husband for neglecting her). When Demetrius returned to Athens, a hymn in ithyphallic meter was composed for the Eleusinian Mysteries and reportedly received both public and private performances. Demochares provides a paraphrase of the text in his history, and Duris of Samos (who, like Demochares, was an enemy of Demetrius) included the full text in his history, whence it was preserved by Athenaeus.[91] The hymn celebrates two of the city's most cherished divinities, Demeter and Demetrius, on the occasion that brings them together, the Great Mysteries. As befits a god, Demetrius appears radiantly beautiful and smiling, surrounded by friends like a sun encircled by stars. He is addressed as Poseidon (an allusion to his victory at Salamis) and as the son of Aphrodite (an allusion to the Athenian cult of his queen, Phila, as Aphrodite). The other gods are either far away, inattentive, or perhaps even nonexistent; in any event they pay no heed to the concerns of mortals.

> But you we see here in the flesh instead of wood or stone. To you we pray. We ask you first to bring peace, as it lies in your power. I am speaking of the Sphinx, which holds not only Thebes, but all Hellas in its grip; I mean the Aetolian, who sits on the rock of Delphi like the Sphinx of old and robs us of our people, and against whom I am helpless. The Aetolians have always robbed their neighbors, and now they prey on even more distant peoples. Punish them, we beseech you, or send an Oedipus to fling them down and reduce them to dust.

Duris sees in these verses an indication of how far the former victors at Marathon had sunk. Once, he says, the Athenians sentenced one of

---

90. For the career of Philippides see Davies, *APF* 549–550; for this type of decree honoring a deserving citizen's entire career, see Habicht, *Studien* 124–127; Gauthier, *Cités* 77–92.

91. For more on Demetrius and Lanassa see Plut. *Pyrrhus* 10.6–7. For the ithyphallic verse see Demochares, *FGrHist* 75 F 2; Duris, *FGrHist* 76 F 13; Athen. 6.253B–F; Habicht, *Gottmenschentum* 232–233, with the older literature; Marasco, *Democare* 199–203; M. Marcovich, *Studies in Graeco-Roman Religions and Gnosticism* (Leiden 1988) 8–19.

their ambassadors to death for falling to his knees in the customary ceremonial greeting to the Great King;[92] here his descendants display far greater servility toward Demetrius. Demochares offers similar criticism. However, the author of the hymn had more in mind than mere flattery; its core is an appeal to the king for help against the Aetolians, who held the shrine of Delphi and had formed an alliance with Thebes (represented in the text by the Sphinx). A motion introduced by Dromocleides and passed by the Assembly, the text of which is given by Plutarch, addressed the very same problem.[93] The decree instructed the Athenians to choose a representative from among themselves to make an offering to the gods under favorable auspices, and then to approach the "savior" of the city, King Demetrius, for an oracle about the best procedure for rededicating the shields: the shields in question were booty from the campaign against the Persians of 480/79, which the Athenians hung on the walls of the temple of Apollo at Delphi. The temple was destroyed in 373, possibly by fire, and afterward a group of Greek states joined together to rebuild it. Shortly before the dedication of the new temple in 340, the Athenians again placed shields on the walls (either old shields that had escaped destruction or others from the same battles). The accompanying inscription, "The Athenians from the Persians and Thebans, when they fought against the Greeks," recalled the former alliance of Thebans and barbarians, and in the altered situation of 340 the Thebans took offense. Considerable wrangling followed; the old quarrel was renewed at the beginning of the third century, when the Aetolians acquired control of Delphi and formed a coalition with Thebes. At this point the Thebans must have persuaded their Aetolian allies to remove the shields from the temple; Dromocleides' resolution aims at restoring them to their traditional place. The resolution appeals to Demetrius to create the conditions under which a rededication of the shields can take place—a goal that can be achieved only through armed conflict; the hymn makes the same point by urging the king to topple the Aetolian Sphinx from the rock and Delphi and then restore peace. Dromocleides' resolution must date from exactly the same period; he is indeed known as an influential

92. The reference is to Timagoras and the embassy of 367. The reasons for Timagoras' sentence were, however, not as Duris describes; see G. Reincke, "Timagoras," *RE* (1936) 1073.

93. Plut. *Demetrius* 13.1–3. For the following passage see Habicht, *Untersuchungen* 34–44.

politician of the king's party during these years. Both the hymn and the decree implore Demetrius as a benevolent god to take the field against the enemy in the north. It is significant that Dromocleides' motion specifically asks for an oracle: the traditional site for obtaining divine oracles, Delphi, is in the hands of the enemy, making Apollo inaccessible to the Athenians. Thus the god Demetrius, present in Athens in the flesh, must take his place.

The same situation led Demetrius to introduce new games in Athens in the summer of 290. They were called the Pythian festival and were intended as a substitute for the traditional Pythian Games in Delphi, now controlled by the Aetolians.[94] If a list of the victors at the Athenian Pythia were ever found, we would have a picture (or at least an impression) of the effect produced on the Greek world by the invitation to these rival games.

In 289 Demetrius began the campaign against the Aetolians that the Athenians had urged on him. After invading Aetolian territory he pushed on to Epirus to force a confrontation with Pyrrhus, who marched out to meet him. However, the two armies missed each other; on reaching Aetolia Pyrrhus found not Demetrius' army but a rear-guard of Macedonians whom Demetrius had left behind under the command of Pantauchus. A battle occurred in which Pyrrhus and Pantauchus wounded one another in single combat, but Pyrrhus carried the day and captured 5,000 prisoners. The victory brought him tremendous prestige, and he made sure his fame was widely published.[95] He acquired particular status in the eyes of the Macedonians, many of whom began to regard him as the only worthy successor of Alexander the Great.[96] The battle was a major setback for Demetrius, further weakened by a long and serious illness at this time. The ancient sources speak of a change in his character, noting that his appearances were staged with more pomp and bombast than ever, and his court life grew even more luxurious; he adopted oriental dress, and the ruler who once had been open and accessible now became a recluse. Witnesses of the few audiences he gave described him as prone to rudeness and violent outbursts of temper. He held an Athenian delegation at bay for two years, refusing to meet with them, although he was thought to be

94. Plut. *Demetrius* 40.7–8; Walbank, *Macedonia* 224.
95. Plut. *Demetrius* 41.1–5; *Pyrrhus* 7.4–8.5; D. Kienast, "Pyrrhus," *RE* (1963) 123.
96. Plut. *Demetrius* 41.5; *Pyrrhus* 8.2.

particularly well disposed toward the city. He aroused fierce resentment in Macedonia after he was seen to accept a bundle of petitions from his subjects and toss it into the river without a glance.[97] In Macedonia and the regions of Greece that he controlled his rule was increasingly viewed as oppressive and tyrannical. As soon as his power was challenged in Macedonia, a rebellion in Greece became inevitable.

Pyrrhus succeeded in advancing as far as Edessa, but Demetrius, who had recovered his health, was able to drive him out without difficulty. All the same, Demetrius' luck was beginning to turn. He had developed a grandiose plan to win back his father's Asian empire, and started arming on a grand scale for an attack on Lysimachus. He commissioned warships in Athens, Chalcis, and Corinth. The other rulers, alarmed by these preparations, formed another coalition to oppose him: Lysimachus, Ptolemy, Seleucus, and Pyrrhus first established a defensive front and then took the offensive themselves. Ptolemy sent a fleet to the Aegean and in 287 appears to have wrested control from Demetrius of the League of Islanders.[98] Lysimachus and Pyrrhus invaded Macedonia simultaneously from the east and west, and the forces Demetrius sent out or led to repel them deserted in large numbers to the enemy. Demetrius fled to Cassandreia, where in despair his queen, Phila, committed suicide. Lysimachus and Pyrrhus divided up Macedonia between them.

Demetrius still had his possessions in Greece, and he used them as a base to begin reassembling his troops and allies. Tradition has it that for the first time in his life he adopted the dress of a private citizen. His courage appeared unbroken when a new blow struck: In the spring of 287 the Athenians rebelled against his rule and overran his garrison. The setbacks Demetrius had suffered in Macedonia encouraged the freedom-loving citizens of Athens to attempt to shake off their foreign yoke and return to the policies of 301.[99]

Led by general Olympiodorus, a former ally of Demetrius who had

---

97. Plut. *Demetrius* 41.5–42.7.

98. Walbank, *Macedonia* 228.

99. The most important sources for these events are the decrees awarding honors to the brothers Callias and Phaedrus of Sphettos (from 270/69 and ca. 255 respectively). The former contains important new facts and was published by T. L. Shear Jr., *Hesperia Suppl.* 17 (1978); the latter is *IG* II^2.682. All other sources, inscriptions, and reports by ancient authors have been assembled by Shear 87–97. The most important literature since his article appeared: Habicht, *Untersuchungen* 45–67; M. J. Osborne, *ZPE* 35 (1979) 181–194; H. Heinen, *GGA* 233 (1981) 189–194; E. Lanciers, *RBPh* 65 (1987) 52–86; Walbank, *Macedonia* 228–233;

served as his righthand man as archon in the years 294–292, they stormed and took the Museum hill with very few losses. The first man over the wall was Leocritus, who died a hero's death and was honored by his fellow citizens accordingly; they dedicated his shield, accompanied by an inscription describing his deeds, to Zeus the Liberator (Zeus Eleutherios). He and the others killed in the fighting were buried with honors in the state cemetery.[100] Some of the soldiers of the Macedonian garrison, presumably mercenaries, gave assistance to the rebels; twenty years later a certain Strombichus was praised for his actions in support of their cause.[101] Piraeus, on the other hand, remained in Macedonian hands, and the king himself set out with his army from the Peloponnese to subdue the uprising.[102] This was about the time of the grain harvest (which began in mid-May), and the city leaders' first concern was to bring it in quickly and prevent it from falling into the enemy's hands. Outstanding service in this effort was performed by Callias of Sphettos, an Athenian from a wealthy and prominent family whose father, Thymochares, had held high military and political offices. Callias himself had voluntarily gone into exile during the years of the oligarchy, and all his property had been confiscated. In 287 he was in the service of Ptolemy I, who ordered him to attempt a landing in Athens with a force of 1,000 elite soldiers. Callias sailed from the island of Andros, which Ptolemy had probably just annexed along with the other Cyclades. Under the leadership of Callias and the hoplite *strategos,* Callias' own brother Phaedrus, the harvest was saved. The resolutions later passed in their honor give them a large part of the credit for saving the city.

Soon after Callias' landing there were skirmishes with the soldiers of Demetrius' garrison in Piraeus, in the course of which Callias received a minor wound. Then Demetrius himself arrived with his army and surrounded the city. Very soon, however, a peace treaty was negotiated

---

B. Dreyer, *ZPE* 111 (1996) 45–67. A general consensus exists that Shear's placing of the uprising in the spring of 286 should be corrected to the spring of 287 (Habicht, Osborne).

100. Pausanias 1.26.2 and 29.13.

101. *IG* II^2.666 and 667. On the head of a Roman copy of a statue of Olympiodorus, probably from an original made at the time of Demosthenes' portrait, see G. M. A. Richter, *The Portraits of the Greeks,* rev. R. R. R. Smith (Ithaca, N.Y., 1984) 169–170 and fig. 131.

102. Although W. S. Ferguson assumes that Demetrius came from the north, via Panakton and Phyle (*HA* 149), the decree in honor of Callias reveals that he approached instead from Corinth.

that preserved the independence the Athenians had just won by force of arms. In the *ekklesia* Phaedrus argued for accepting Demetrius' terms, and it must have taken a good deal of pleading to bring the members of the Assembly around to his point of view, for although the treaty granted the city free and independent status, it also stipulated that Macedonian troops of occupation would remain in Piraeus and the Attic fortresses. That Demetrius was willing to concede Athens' independence at all (or at least lift the siege) was owed to two special circumstances: his impatience to embark on the long-delayed offensive against Lysimachus in Asia Minor, and Ptolemy's intervention on behalf of the Athenians. Ptolemy had sent a high-ranking official to negotiate with Demetrius, a man named Sostratus of Knidos (best known as the donor or designer of the lighthouse at Alexandria). Although the Athenians were not officially represented at the talks, Sostratus heard their case. The Council and the generals, among whom was Callias' brother Phaedrus, appointed Callias to present it to him, for he was both one of Ptolemy's officers and an Athenian citizen. The peace was negotiated between Demetrius and Ptolemy, and the Egyptian king (in the person of his representative Sostratus) persuaded Demetrius to respect the freedom of Athens but was unable to obtain an agreement for the withdrawal of all occupying forces from Attica. The peace treaty preserved the city's independence but fell short of the Athenians' hopes. They particularly resented the continuing foreign control of their harbor; nonetheless they had to endure it for another fifty-eight years.[103] The hostilities ended during the archonship of Kimon, that is, not later than July 287. Demetrius sailed for Asia Minor immediately, leaving his son Antigonus as his deputy in Greece and the one with whom Athens would have to deal in future; Demetrius' second period as ruler of Athens had come to an end.

---

103. Phocion's son Phocus was especially hated for his servility toward the Macedonian commander at Munychia; see Athen. 3.168E.

FOUR

Culture in Public Life

A general history of Athens in the Hellenistic age cannot hope to cover adequately the era's achievements in the arts. This chapter aims rather at giving an impression of the role that culture played in Athenian public life, such as the uniquely local and broader influences on cultural life, the extent to which citizens and foreigners contributed to it, whether creative artists worked also abroad, beyond the borders of Attica, whether they were absorbed by their profession or did their share in running the city, the kinds of response Athenian writers and artists received both at home and abroad, and whether they found patrons to support them.

Any discussion of Athenian art and culture during this period suffers from the same problem as the more general discussion of Athens' political history, namely the extreme scarcity of primary sources. Almost all the writings of Athenian authors of the period have been lost, as have the works of their foreign contemporaries who wrote about Athens. No Athenian paintings and few works of sculpture from the era have survived. The existing evidence has been found widely scattered through the Greek world, so that any general conclusion must remain tentative. New archaeological, epigraphical, or numismatic evidence could alter the picture dramatically, requiring a new assessment.

No complete tragedy that could be compared with those from the classical era has survived from the Hellenistic age, and no complete philosophical dialogue is available for comparison with one of Plato's. Nonetheless we can be certain that cultural activity in Athens was as vigorous as ever and may even have increased in scale. We also know that Athenian culture spread abroad during this time, for in every part of the ancient Greek world, including the eastern regions opened up by Alexander the Great, we find evidence of Athenian creativity.

1. Drama

The extant Greek tragedies and comedies preserved in manuscript (because ancient philologists regarded them as masterpieces) all date from the classical period, the fifth century B.C. Of all the extant dramatists, only Aristophanes was still writing in the early fourth century. The corpus of surviving classical drama consists of seven tragedies by Aeschylus, seven by Sophocles, eighteen by Euripides, and seven comedies by Aristophanes. Only one playwright from a later era has achieved an equal measure of fame: the comedian Menander, born in 342, the same year as the philosopher Epicurus. Menander's comedy *Dyscolus* ("The Misanthrope") is the single extant complete work by a postclassical Greek dramatist, and it survived not on a parchment manuscript like the others, but on a papyrus discovered after the Second World War. Before this text became known, knowledge of Menander's work was limited to Latin adaptations of his plays by the Roman dramatists Plautus and Terence, shorter or longer parts of other comedies, and a collection of aphorisms made in ancient times (perhaps excerpted from other works). Goethe used one such maxim, in the original Greek, as a motto for his autobiography: "Spare the rod and spoil the child."

We thus have today only a small portion of Menander's large output, and even less of other Hellenistic dramatists, whose work has survived only in fragments of varying length. We should recall, however, that even the four classical authors are known only through a small proportion of their total work. If the number of surviving plays from the two eras remains grossly unequal, the reasons may have to do as much with later tastes as with intrinsic literary quality: later audiences came to prefer the works of the older authors, but it is by no means certain that the plays of Menander and his contemporaries were inherently inferior. Menander may have displayed less originality than Aristophanes, and the tragic dramatists of the Hellenistic era—of whom we know little more than their names—may not have equaled the achievements of their predecessors, but there is no proof; we have no way of comparing them. It would certainly be a mistake to assume that Athenians in the postclassical era took less interest in the theater than their forebears. In the third and second centuries both tragic and comic drama continued to flourish in Athens, written both by Athenians and by foreigners drawn there by the city's unique opportunities. Year after year the great festivals—the Dionysia in spring and the Lenaea in winter—were celebrated with dramatic competitions requiring nine new plays. In the early fourth century one old tragedy was added to the program, and late in the same century it became the custom to perform one old comedy as well.[1]

The Athenians began keeping records of the annual competitions on stone tablets in 279/8 and continued for the next 150 years. A large number of these inscriptions have survived and provide a wealth of information about the dramatic festivals of the period. They record all plays produced at a particular festival with the author's name, the titles of the prize-winning entries, the runners-up, and the name of the performer chosen best actor. Since the eponymous archon is named, the date of the festival can be established. In many years either no festivals took place or they were celebrated without dramatic competitions; in these years the inscription is limited to a brief announcement of the fact after the name of the eponymous archon. But when the complete dramatic program was presented, a list of the comedies alone may fill fifteen lines of text, informing us, for example, that an old comedy was produced along with six new comedies. Most of the revivals presented during the second century were plays by Menander, Philemon, Poseidippus, and Philippides, the most successful authors of the early Hellenistic age. These masters of "New Comedy" were already the most popular dramatists, surpassing those of the fifth century, Aristophanes or Eupolis, and even more those of the "Middle Comedy," playwrights such as Alexis, who belonged to the generation before Menander but whose careers overlapped with his. (For this reason it is difficult to draw a sharp line between Middle and New

---

1. The standard collection of Greek comedy is *PCG*. Currently the list of published authors extends from Agathenor to Xenophon (with the exception of Menander). For those not yet covered see T. Kock, *Comicorum Atticorum Fragmenta*, 3 vols. (Leipzig 1880–1888). For Menander see A. Koerte and A. Thierfelder, *Menandri quae supersunt*, 2 vols. (Leipzig 1955–1959); E. W. Handley, ed., *The Dyskolos of Menander* (London 1965); A. W. Gomme and F. H. Sandbach, *Menander: A Commentary* (Oxford 1973); S. Jäkel, *Menandri Sententiae* (Leipzig 1964). For the treatment of women in New Comedy, see E. Fantham, *Phoenix* 29 (1975) 44–74; for the social milieu of Menander's characters, see L. Casson, *TAPhA* 106 (1976) 29–59. A thorough discussion of how the plays were produced is A. Pickard-Cambridge, *The Dramatic Festivals of Athens*[2], rev. J. Gould and D. M. Lewis (Oxford 1968; reissued with supplements 1988). B. Le Guen stresses the continued importance of the theater in Hellenistic times; *REG* 108 (1995) 59–90.

Comedy.) The six new comedies of a given year are listed in the inscription in their order of ranking by the judges.[2]

New and Old Comedy are distinguished by their subject matter. Whereas references to contemporary politics dominate some of Aristophanes' plays, they are rare in Hellenistic drama and, when they occur, tend to be of marginal importance. However, some exceptions can be found, such as Philippides' attacks on Stratocles or Archedicus' satire on the democratic politician Demochares. Archedicus, a comic playwright who was also a member of the oligarchy of 322–319, was an ally of Antipater, the Macedonian regent who had installed the oligarchs in power. His dramatic thrusts at the nephew of Demosthenes would have been soon forgotten had not Timaeus of Tauromenium (modern Taormina) quoted them in his universal history. Timaeus' inclusion incited his successor Polybius to some polemics of his own on the subject, and thus Archedicus' lines on political ephemera have been preserved.[3] Other comic dramatists also included well-known local figures in their plays, including philosophers and even celebrated chefs as well as politicians. They almost never wrote political verse in the narrower sense, however, much less tried to influence the course of politics through their work. Although politics plays no role at all in Menander's comedies, he was in danger of having to stand trial after Demetrius of Phalerum's overthrow, merely because he had been on friendly terms with the deposed ruler.[4]

New Comedy differs further from Old Comedy in that it lacks the obscenity so frequently found in the plays of Aristophanes. Obviously the public's taste had changed, and the social classes represented in the theatergoing public may have changed as well: in the classical era the poorest Athenians and citizens living far from the theater received subsidies called *theorika* to enable them to attend performances, but by the end of the fourth century these payments had ceased. In consequence playwrights perhaps needed to make fewer concessions to

2. *IG* II².2319–2325; A. Wilhelm, *Urkunden dramatischer Aufführungen in Athen* (Vienna 1906); B. Snell, *Zu den Urkunden dramatischer Aufführungen*, Nachrichten von der Gesellschaft der Wissenschaften zu Göttingen (1966), no. 2; C. Ruck, *IG* II².2323: *The List of Victors in Comedies at the Dionysia* (Leiden 1967); H.-J. Mette, *Urkunden dramatischer Aufführungen in Griechenland* (Berlin 1977); H.-G. Nesselrath, *Die attische Mittlere Komödie* (Berlin 1990).

3. For more on Archedicus see C. Habicht, *Hesperia* 62 (1993) 253–256; for a more general discussion see G. Philipp, *Gymnasium* 80 (1973) 493–503.

4. Diog. Laert. 5.79; D. Potter, *Historia* 36 (1987) 491–495.

lower-class or rural tastes and were still successful.[5] On the other hand, one reason for avoiding both politics and obscenity in Hellenistic comedies may have been the fact that they were produced throughout the Greek world. Numerous lists of the winners from dramatic festivals in many different Greek cities and islands such as Delos and Samos reveal that these plays were widely performed outside Athens. Audiences outside Attica would have had little interest in Athenian politics, and here and there they may not have shared the Athenians' tolerance of extreme frankness in reference to sexual matters. Menander's plays are morally unobjectionable, a quality that undoubtedly contributed to his unique popularity over the centuries.[6] Their settings are not specifically Athenian, and they deal with the quirks and passions, the strengths and weaknesses of ordinary people. As spectators could identify with the plays' heroes, the works had broad appeal for audiences in different epochs. Menander encourages his audience to judge persons not by the station of life to which they were born, but by their character. By emphasizing the basic human traits of his characters, he contributed decisively to a new image of man; he is deservedly recognized as the "father" of a particularly human type of dramatic figure.[7] In 322/1, while still an ephebe, Menander entered his first dramatic contest at the Lenaea and won; in 316/5, during the rule of Demetrius of Phalerum, he won again with the *Dyscolus*. He died at the age of fifty (or fifty-two). During his lifetime he was less popular than some of his rivals, but his posthumous fame grew until he eclipsed them all. An anonymous epigram on Menander closes with the words "You are immortal, and the fame of the Athenians / rises above the clouds to the heavens—through you."[8]

During the Hellenistic age more than fifty citizens or residents of Athens were active as writers of comedies.[9] The citizens among them

5. J. Buchanan, *Theorika: A Study of Monetary Distributions to the Athenian Citizenry during the Fifth and Fourth Centuries B.C.* (Locust Valley, N.Y., 1962) 82. Whether women were permitted to attend theatrical performances in Athens remains a matter of dispute (Pickard-Cambridge, *Dramatic Festivals*, chap. 4); J. Henderson argues that they were; *TAPhA* 121 (1991) 133–147.

6. Gomme and Sandbach, *Menander* 26.

7. W. Schadewaldt, *Der Gott von Delphi und die Humanitätsidee: Rede zur Verleihung des Reuchlinpreises*, in idem, *Hellas und Hesperien*[2], vol. 1 (Zurich 1970) 673–674.

8. *AP* 9, no. 187. On the chronology of Menander see H. de Marcellus, *ZPE* 110 (1996) 69–76; S. Schröder, *ZPE* 113 (1996) 35–48.

9. Their names are listed in C. Austin, *ZPE* 14 (1974) 201–225.

performed normal civic duties in various offices; some served as archon, priest of a religious cult, master of the mint, or as a member of a special delegation. One author represented Athens in the Amphictionic Council, which administered the temple of Apollo at Delphi and the Pythian Games celebrated in the god's honor. When money was needed for a cause, poets also responded to appeals from the city by making a voluntary contribution.[10] As commonly occurred in the arts and crafts, a son often took up his father's profession; one family in Phalerum produced four successive generations of comic poets whose works enjoyed success both in Athens and beyond.[11]

Beginning in the early third century, comic poets and other artists in the fields of literature, music, dance, and theater formed guilds, calling themselves "craftsmen [*technitai*] for Dionysus" in honor of the god associated with these endeavors. The term "festival artists" may express their function most accurately. Professional associations of this kind existed in various places, but the Athenian guild was the oldest and most important, although it had a longtime rival in the guild of Isthmus. The religious festivals provided the stage for the guild members to compete, including actors and musicians of all kinds as well as the dramatic poets. The practice of their profession was thus associated with religious worship and ritual, and their appearances were a feature of all the larger festivals. In consequence the *technitai* spent most of their time traveling from one city, shrine, or theater to the next and needed special status affording them protection. They received privileges from the Amphictionic Council in Delphi, as well as from kings, cities, and political leagues, such as guarantees of safe conduct and personal immunity, and special dispensation from taxes and performance of normal civic duties.[12] When the *Pythais*, the Athenian procession to Delphi, was celebrated in 98/7, participants included 23 festival

10. For service as *thesmothetes*, see *IG* II^2.1714.10; as priest of Asclepius, *IG* II^2.2336.123; as master of the mint, *Chiron* 21 (1991) 10; as *gymnasiarch*, I *Délos* 1928. For the delegate to the Amphictionic Council, see *FD* III.2.69.3 and 277.2 (in this case the delegate in question was a writer of tragedies from Athens). For an example of *epidosis* see *IG* II^2.2332.206.

11. E. Preuner, *RhM* 49 (1894) 362–369. Timostratus had plays produced successfully in Athens, as did his son Ariston in Samos, his grandson Poses in Tanagra, and his great-grandson Ariston in Oropus (*PCG* 7.560, T 1 and T 5; 783, T 1–3 and 7.

12. F. Poland, "Technitai," *RE* 5 A (1934), cols. 2473–2558. A complete list of all known *technitai* is in I. E. Stefanis, ΔΙΟΝΥΣΙΑΚΟΙ ΤΕΧΝΙΤΑΙ (Heraklion 1988).

delegates, a number of knights, 66 ephebes, and more than 100 festival artists from the association of the "craftsmen for Dionysus."[13]

Although fewer authors of tragedies and satyr-plays are known by name than comic poets, more than half of the sixty identified for the Hellenistic period were Athenians.[14] Their works have been almost completely lost; only nine fragments comprising 22 verses in all have survived, most of them as single lines that became popular aphorisms. This is all that remains of several thousand plays, which perished not because of their inferior quality but because they fell out of fashion at a later time, when the classic "Attic" style was in vogue. The titles of some fifty Hellenistic tragedies are known and reveal that many of them dealt with new subject matter, and in their own time these works were as famous as the tragedies of the classical period. They were immediately imitated in other cultures: for example, when Roman tragedy came into existence around 240, at the end of the First Punic War, it did so as an offshoot of contemporary Greek drama. In the second century B.C. a Jewish playwright named Ezekiel wrote a tragedy in Greek called *Exagoge* ("Exodus"), retelling the story of Moses and the exodus from Egypt; 269 lines in trimeter have been preserved in the works of the early church father Eusebius of Caesarea.[15]

Like their colleagues who wrote comedies, the tragic playwrights saw their works produced throughout the Greek world and received numerous distinctions both at home and abroad, including honorary decrees, awards of citizenship, and monuments. Evidence of such honors for Attic tragic playwrights has survived from Delos, Oropus, Thebes, Thespiae, Tanagra, Orchomenus in Boeotia, and Delphi. The actors also traveled from place to place, usually with their artists' guild. One successful actor from Tegea in Arcadia won prizes for his roles in

13. See the list of *technitai* in *FD* III.2.48 and the additions in *Hesperia Suppl.* 15 (1975) 60–63, lines 14–52. Cf. P. Ghiron-Bistagne, *Recherches sur les acteurs dans la Grèce antique* (Paris 1976).

14. For more on this subject see K. Ziegler, "Tragoedia," *RE* (1937) 1899–2075, esp. cols. 1967–81. On pp. 1967–70 Ziegler rejects "the traditional low opinion of postclassical tragedy, and Hellenistic tragedy in particular, for which there is no real basis." He cites a particularly disparaging appraisal by J. Geffcken, who referred to the works as "hothouse plants that wilted quickly and gave off a strong odor of decay." See also A. Lesky, *Die tragische Dichtung der Hellenen*[2] (Göttingen 1964) 222–224; and G. M. Sifakis, *Studies in the History of Hellenistic Drama* (London 1967).

15. The text can be found in B. Snell, ed., *Tragicorum Graecorum Fragmenta*, vol. 1 (Göttingen 1971) 288–301. Ezechiel is known to have written other tragedies on themes from the Old Testament.

various plays by Euripides in Athens, Argos, Delphi, and Dodona.[16] The tragic playwrights were by no means ivory-tower literati, any more than their predecessor Sophocles, who served on the board of *strategoi* in the Age of Pericles. They performed the usual duties of citizens in various offices, including mint magistrate. One of them, Dionysius of Anaphlystus, occupied some of the highest offices in existence at his time, serving as Athenian governor of Delos in 111/0 and five years later as hoplite general. In the latter function he led the *Pythais* procession to Delphi in 106/5.[17]

As mentioned above, the custom of preceding the competition for new plays at great festivals with revivals of one old comedy and one old tragedy became established in the fourth century. The (long deceased) authors were naturally not in competition, although awards were given for the best acting in these productions. Occasionally, however, the great figures of the past were granted even more space in the festival program. A surviving inscription from the middle of the third century shows that in the year of the archon Alcibiades no fewer than nine old plays were performed, three comedies (by Diphilus, Menander, and Philemon), three tragedies, and three satyr-plays. Menander was represented by his *Phasma* ("Phantom"), which another inscription shows was also produced in 167. The custom of presenting old tragedies helped at least one actor win a prize; he was honored for his performance in a play by Sophocles, who, together with Euripides, was far more popular than Aeschylus during this period.[18]

2. The Schools of the Philosophers

Splendid festivals, such as the Great Panathenaea celebrated every four years, attracted Greeks to Athens from near and far at regular intervals. The city's attraction for intellectuals knew no season, however; it was a permanent magnet for those seeking an education or intellectual stimulation.[19] Athens owed its unrivaled reputation in this field to its

16. *Syll.* 1080.

17. C. Habicht, *Hermes* 119 (1991) 198, 204, 212, 216.

18. *Hesperia* 7 (1938) 116, no. 2; A. Körte, *Hermes* 73 (1938) 123–127; *IG* II^2.2323.206.

19. For more on what follows see C. Habicht, "Hellenistic Athens and Her Philosophers," David Magie Lecture, Princeton 1988, reprinted in Habicht, *Athen in hellenistischer Zeit. Gesammelte Aufsätze* (Munich 1994) 231–247. For a brief description of the chief

famous schools of philosophy: Plato's Academy; its offshoot, the *Peripatos* of Aristotle;[20] Zeno's Stoa;[21] and the *Kepos* ("Garden") of Epicurus.[22] Founded during the fourth century (in 387, 335, 306, and 301 respectively), the four schools flourished throughout the Hellenistic age, although by the late third century Aristotle's had begun to fall behind the others.

As in other Greek states, the education of young Athenians was left to private initiative. The state set no regulations or requirements and maintained no schools; it limited itself to protecting the right of individuals to found associations for educational purposes as long as their activities remained legal. Higher education in Athens meant chiefly training in rhetoric and philosophy. Since rhetorical skills were regarded as the best preparation for a successful career, schools of rhetoric flourished. Philosophy, on the other hand, was regarded less as a stepping-stone to professional advancement than as a hobby for those affluent enough to dispense with paid careers. Virtually everyone with a desire to study or teach philosophy came sooner or later to Athens, home not just to the best teachers of a single school but to the outstanding figures of every philosophical orientation. Centuries later, St. Augustine would still refer to Athens as "the mother or wet-nurse of all the liberal arts and so many important philosophers."[23]

Previously scholars tended to view the philosophical schools of Athens as primarily religious communities; today they are generally recognized as institutions of higher learning, devoted not to the service of a deity but rather to gaining and imparting knowledge. They operated

---

doctrines of the most important philosophers of the period, based strictly on the sources, see P. O. Kristeller, *Greek Philosophers of the Hellenistic Age* (New York 1993). The essential sources for the history of Hellenistic philosophy are the *Index Academicorum,* now available with commentary as T. Dorandi, *Filodemo. Storia dei filosofi. Platone e l'Academia (PHerc. 1021 e 164)* (Naples 1991); the *Index Stoicorum,* now in the edition by Dorandi, *Filodemo. Storia dei filosofi. La Stoa da Zenone a Panezio* (Leiden 1994); F. Wehrli, ed., *Die Schule des Aristoteles,* 10 vols. and 2 suppl. vols. (Basle 1944–1978); H. von Arnim, ed., *Stoicorum Veterum Fragmenta,* 3 vols. (Leipzig 1923–1938); Epicurus, *Opere*[2], ed. G. Arrighetti (Turin 1993); *Diogenes Laertius,* ed. H. Long, 2 vols. (Oxford 1964). See also A. A. Long and D. N. Sedley, *The Hellenistic Philosophers,* 2 vols. (Cambridge 1987); and Dorandi, *Ricerche.*

20. J. P. Lynch, *Aristotle's School* (Berkeley 1972).

21. A. Erskine, *The Hellenistic Stoa* (London 1990).

22. U. von Wilamowitz-Moellendorff offers an affectionate account of Epicurus and the achievements of the Epicurean school in *Der Glaube der Hellenen,* vol. 2 (Berlin 1932) 286–290.

23. *De civitate dei* 18.9.

as private associations, without interference from the state; their independence was seriously threatened only once, by Sophocles' law of 306, and this attempt to impose control was quickly repealed. The schools were thoroughly cosmopolitan, for the majority of both teachers and students came from other parts of the Greek world. Other nations were also represented in considerable numbers, including Phoenicians, Carthaginians, and in later years Romans, whose early training in the Greek language allowed them to study on an equal footing with the Greeks themselves. The Stoa was headed by foreigners for almost two centuries, and Aristotle's school never had an Athenian citizen as its head.

In general, no fee was required for attendance at lectures except in the early days at the Stoa. Students at one of the schools were also free to attend lectures at the others, and occasionally a student would shift his allegiance, although this occurred less among the Epicureans, who strongly discouraged the practice. The founder Epicurus prided himself on being self-taught and seems to have demanded unconditional loyalty from his pupils. Supposedly only one student—a certain Metrodorus (but not Epicurus' noted friend of the same name from Lampsacus)—ever deserted the Garden in favor of the Academy. There appears to have been considerable traffic in the other direction, however, with many students joining the Epicurean school after attending one of the rival institutions. The Epicureans maintained, among other things, that the wise man should strive to keep aloof from politics and lead as quiet and inconspicuous a life as possible. When Arcesilaus, as head of the Academy, was once asked if he could explain why so many students dropped out of their schools to attend the Garden of Epicurus, whereas none of Epicurus' students withdrew, he is supposed to have replied: "Because while it is possible to emasculate someone, the process cannot be reversed."

It was only natural that schools and individuals should see themselves as competitors. In personal dealings, however, relations among members of the different institutions seem to have been generally amicable.[24] Many citizens, of course, had no clear notion of what use there might be in studying philosophy, and not everyone grasped the finer points of the various doctrines or the differences between them. As a

---

24. "All these philosophers were gentlemen and hence able to be in earnest without being enemies"; Ferguson, *HA* 233.

result the philosophers and their doings became a popular subject of Athenian humor, and the surviving fragments of Hellenistic comedies are full of jokes, usually good-natured, at the philosophers' expense.[25] These are clear signs that the philosophers stood out from ordinary citizens, in the same way that modern humor frequently targets eccentrics, celebrities, or figures in public life. Despite the occasional witticism, however, the Athenian public took the philosophers seriously,[26] as the failure of Sophocles' law demonstrated. Still another indication of the respect the philosophers enjoyed is the frequency with which they were selected to serve in important missions, even if they were not Athenian citizens. This was a sensational departure from the principles of democracy. The philosophers representing Athens on diplomatic missions included Xenocrates, Crates, Arcesilaus, and Carneades from the Academy; Aristotle, Prytanis, and Critolaus from the Peripatetic school; and Diogenes from the Stoa. Of these, only Crates was a native-born Athenian, and Carneades the only one of the remaining seven who had taken Athenian citizenship. When the heads of these three schools appeared before the Roman senate in 155 to plead for the cancellation or reduction of a large fine imposed on the city, not one of them was an Athenian.[27]

They probably could have acquired Athenian citizenship had they wished to, since it was frequently offered to prominent philosophers at the city's schools. Chrysippus of the Stoa, Carneades of the Academy, and Philonides the Epicurean, among others, did accept it. Some refused, such as Xenocrates and the Stoics Zeno, Cleanthes, and Panaetius. The last-named rejected the offer with the observation that for sensible people, being a citizen of one place was enough.[28] Hellenistic kings and rulers vied with one another to attract the Athenian philosophers to their courts, showering them with gifts and attention. Aristotle accepted an offer from Philip II of Macedonia to become tutor to Alexander. Aristotle, his successor Theophrastus, and their pupil Dem-

---

25. For examples see Epicrates, *PCG* 5, F 10; Philemon, *PCG* 7, F 74 and F 88; Damoxenos, *PCG* 5, F 2; Anaxippus, *PCG* 2, F 4. Cf. A. Weiher, *Philosophen und Philosophenspott in der attischen Komödie* (Diss. Munich 1913).

26. It was as a personal tribute to the founder of the Academy and the nephew who succeeded him that an Athenian citizen named his sons Plato and Speusippus; Habicht, *Studien* 187–188.

27. All the documentary sources for this famous "philosophers' embassy" are in H.-J. Mette, *Lustrum* 27 (1895) 66–70.

28. Plut., fr. 86 ed. Sandbach.

etrius of Phalerum were all on good terms with the regent Antipater and his son Cassander; and it was Theophrastus who in 292, near the end of his life, persuaded Demetrius to allow his opponents, the Athenian supporters of Cassander who had been banished, to return home.[29] Long after his own overthrow as regent, Demetrius of Phalerum attained a position of considerable influence at the court of Ptolemy I. Antigonus Gonatas, a king of the Antigonid dynasty that followed the house of Antipater on the throne of Macedonia, tried to attract Zeno to his court but had to settle for his pupil Persaeus. And when the city of Megalopolis in Arcadia needed a set of laws, Antigonus Doson gave the task to the Peripatetic philosopher Prytanis.[30] The Attalid kings of Pergamum tried to win over Arcesilaus and Lacydes of the Academy with gifts, but the latter refused an invitation to the court of Attalus I with the comment "Monuments are best viewed from a distance." Chrysippus responded similarly to an offer from one of the Ptolemies to come to Alexandria.[31] These refusals to exchange their residence in Attica for the atmosphere of a royal court reveal the high value the philosophers placed on the liberties granted them in Athens (and they were undoubtedly also aware of Plato's unfortunate experiences at the court of Dionysius II of Syracuse). All these reasons contributed to Athens' attractiveness and renown as an "intellectual Mecca,"[32] not just for a brief span but for centuries.

The subjects taught in the schools included far more than what is usually understood today by "philosophy." In addition to epistemology, ethics, logic, and other topics still considered part of the field, Hellenistic philosophers studied and taught physics, mathematics, botany, zoology, and meteorology, as well as religion, music, poetics and rhetoric, politics, economy, and psychology. No doubt individual scholars, though well versed in many subjects, had areas of specialization, and the same holds true of the schools. In Plato's Academy, for example, epistemology came to dominate the curriculum, culminating in the second century in the radical skepticism of Carneades, who believed that human perception was based on probability but in the last analysis uncertain. The Epicureans devoted themselves less to increasingly so-

29. [Plut.] *mor.* 850CD.

30. *FGrHist* 584 F 4; Diog. Laert. 7.6; Timon, *Supplementum Hellenisticum,* ed. H. Lloyd-Jones and P. Parsons (Berlin 1983), no. 780; Polybius 5.93.8.

31. Arcesilaus: Diog. Laert. 4.48; Lacydes: ibid., 4.60; Chrysippus: ibid., 7.185.

32. A. A. Long, *Elenchos 7* (1986) 439.

phisticated theories of epistemology than to its practice, attempting to integrate some of their principles in the shared daily life of the school; this emphasis gave it something of the character of a sect.[33] The Stoa, like the Epicurean school, gave ethics a central position in its doctrines and curriculum. The school of Aristotle, which under its founder and his successors Theophrastus and Straton placed a strong emphasis on the natural sciences, later abandoned this direction almost entirely. Modern scholars have sometimes assumed that the general decline of the Peripatetic school was connected with the loss of Aristotle's and Theophrastus' library, but this is by no means certain. It may also be incorrect to assume that the later Peripatetics had no access to the works of the first two heads of the school.[34]

We do know with certainty that the schools were private organizations. We are less sure about ownership, whether a school was the property of its head at the time, or of a particular group of members, for instance. Nor is it always clear what school property consisted of, apart from the buildings in which the school was housed and the land on which they stood; it is not known whether a school owned the contents of its library. Probably the circumstances varied from school to school. Some answers to these questions are provided by the surviving wills of Plato, Epicurus, Aristotle, Theophrastus, Straton, and Lyco. Preserved in the writings of Diogenes Laertius, they reveal that as a rule the head of a school was chosen by election; only in exceptional cases did a director appoint his own successor.[35]

Although the schools of philosophy were private institutions, the Athenian state finally recognized that their activities were in the public interest by decreeing that all ephebes must regularly attend classes (with the exception of the Epicureans' lectures, whose doctrines were considered too abstruse and remote from practical concerns). Decrees passed to honor the graduating classes of ephebes regularly mention this instruction beginning with the year 123/2; it is not mentioned in the decree from the year 128/7. A few years later each year-class was required to donate 100 books to the public library.[36] By this time,

33. H. Dörrie, "Epikur," *Der kleine Pauly* (1967) 315.

34. H. B. Gottschalk, *Hermes* 100 (1972) 335–342.

35. Ibid., 314–342; H. Glucker, *Antiochus and the Late Academy* (Göttingen 1978) 226–255.

36. *IG* II^2.1006.19–20 and 62–65, and frequently since then; the reference is still missing in *Hesperia* 24 (1955) 220 ff. For the donation of books see *IG* II^2.1009.7–8 from 117/6 and later decrees.

however, *ephebia* had long since ceased to be the military training period for the sons of all Athenian citizens created by the reform of 335. It had been shortened to one year and become a period of voluntary training for the sons of the affluent, with an accompanying shift in the curriculum away from military matters and toward intellectual pursuits and athletics.

Only one generation after these requirements were introduced, however, the great days of Athens' philosophical schools almost came to an end. After Athens entered the war against the Romans on the side of Mithridates of Pontus in the year 88, many Athenian citizens fled the city, including prominent philosophers such as Philon of Larissa, then head of the Academy. Two years later the Roman general Sulla attacked the city, inflicting considerable damage before taking it. When the young Cicero visited it only a few years afterward, he found the site of the Academy deserted.[37] The *Peripatos* had closed its doors long before.[38] Only the Stoa and the Epicurean school continued in existence, exerting considerable influence on Rome in the last years of the republic and the early empire. The Stoic school influenced the world of politics by holding that the wise man could and should participate in political life.[39] By contrast, Epicurus' wise man lived quietly—not necessarily as a hermit, but shunning the public glare. This contrary model of the good life also attracted many adherents.

3. The Fine Arts

Time has treated the works of ancient sculptors more kindly than those of ancient painters. Apart from vase painting, which reached its peak much earlier, nearly all evidence of painters' work has been lost forever, but many pieces of sculpture have survived the centuries more or less intact. Though not a large proportion of the total output, the number of extant ancient sculptures is far from negligible, and more are being discovered all the time. Many date from the Hellenistic age, beginning with the transitional figure of Praxiteles' Hermes, and extending to the famous ruler in the National Museum of Rome from the second century and the late Hellenistic Laocoön group. In addition to the large sculptures in marble and bronze, terra cotta was an important medium for smaller works. Many works in all these materials were

---

37. Cicero *De finibus* 5.1–4.
38. Ulrich von Wilamowitz-Moellendorff, *Antigonos von Karystos* (Berlin 1881) 83.
39. Kristeller, *Greek Philosophers* 83.

produced by both citizen and foreign artists working in Athens, and by Athenian craftsmen abroad.

One genre familiar from the classical era is entirely absent from the collection of surviving works of Hellenistic art: funerary art. The period offers no counterparts to the marvelous reliefs of the fifth and fourth centuries, with their depictions, immediately accessible to the modern viewer, of the deceased surrounded by family members, household retinue and slaves, and sometimes even a pet; nor are there any free-standing figures such as the magnificent steer from the grave monument of Dionysius of Collytus in the Cerameicus,[40] or marble urns with elaborately decorated lids. The practice of this refined art form ceased abruptly in 317 after Demetrius of Phalerum introduced reforms permitting no more than the barest minimum of decoration on funerary monuments. The new legislation put an end to virtually all private commissions for works of sculpture.

Though prohibited from portraying the recently deceased, Athenian sculptors continued to create portraits of distinguished living contemporaries and statues of gods and goddesses. Important figures in the political or cultural life of the city and famous athletes were frequently honored by statues, and many statues of divinities have survived, along with large numbers of smaller, decorative figures. For a long time Athens remained preeminent in the field of sculpture.

Slightly over 100 Athenian sculptors who worked in marble or bronze in the Hellenistic age are known by name.[41] To the extent that the findings permit any conclusions, they suggest that many worked exclusively in Athens, but that even more worked exclusively abroad (although in many of these cases the identification of location depends on the accidental nature of surviving evidence). Some 15 sculptors are known to have worked both in Attica and abroad. They include the members of two famous families of sculptors, one from Cropidae (Eucheir, Eubulus, and Eubulides), the other from Thoricus (Polycles,

---

40. The occupant of this particularly imposing grave has recently been identified as a cousin of the orator Hypereides; C. Habicht, *AM* 106 (1991) 239–242.

41. A list of names and documentary evidence for the period from 320 to the time of Augustus has been compiled by A. Stewart in *Attika: Studies in Athenian Sculpture of the Hellenistic Age* (London 1979) 157–174. To this list should be added the names of several older masters who were still active in 338–320 and a few others whom Stewart overlooked. In addition there have been new discoveries of works by sculptors already known. For a recent discussion see B. S. Ridgway, *Hellenistic Sculpture,* vol. 1: *The Styles of ca. 331–200 B.C.* (Madison 1990).

Timarchides, Timocles, and Dionysius). There is particularly rich evidence that Athenian artists worked in the two most important Greek shrines outside Attica, Delphi and Delos. (The latter became Athenian territory in 167.) Numerous works have also been discovered in Rhodes, Boeotia, and Rome[42] (from about 180 on), but the fact that pedestals carved by Athenian craftsmen were found in these places does not necessarily mean the works were created there, for in many cases these pieces were either imported from Greece or seized as war booty. And finally we know that Athenian sculptors worked at the Attalid court in Pergamum.

The names of some of these craftsmen have been preserved in the writings of ancient authors, chiefly in the *Natural History* of Pliny the Elder, who devoted much of books 34 and 36 to the subject of marble and bronze sculpture; and in Pausanias' *Description of Greece,* where he discusses more than 200 statues of victors at the games in Olympia alone, usually adding the names of the sculptors who made them.[43] More often, however, we know the names of Athenian sculptors of this period only from inscriptions on the bases of their statues, a "signature" of the type "Timarchides, son of Polycles, an Athenian, made this." These pedestals are usually the only part of the work to have survived. On Delos approximately 50 works by sixteen Athenian sculptors of the Hellenistic age, before and after 167, are documented in this manner.[44] There are at least 15 similar inscriptions from Delphi and 13 from Rhodes. Athenian master craftsmen are documented in ten different cities of the Peloponnese, in Olbia on the Hypanis (Bug),[45] and in Apollonia in Cyrenaica.[46]

What we have seen in the case of writers and philosophers is true of artists: they participated actively in Athenian government, serving as members of the Council, as supervisors of the harbor in Piraeus, as mint magistrates, as priests and administrators of sacred rites, or as delegates to the Amphictionic Council in Delphi. Quite frequently they received honors from other governments in the form of decrees, statues, and the like; there is documentation for Eubulides, Eubulus, Polycles,

42. Stewart, *Attika* 41–47.

43. H.-V. Herrmann, *Nikephoros* 1 (1988) 119–183.

44. J. Marcadé, *Au musée de Délos* (Paris 1969) 56–61.

45. *Inscriptiones Ponti Euxini* I², no. 271; *Inscriptiones Olbiae* (1917–1965), ed. E. I. Levi (1968), no. 65.

46. *SEG* 20.708.

Praxiteles of Sybridae, and Telesinus.[47] Altogether the evidence creates the impression that most of these artists came from affluent families of some standing rather than from the poorer classes.

Among the famous surviving works of Athenian sculptors of the Hellenistic age are statues of contemporary or recently deceased political leaders and other notable figures. They include a statue of Demosthenes, made by Polyeuctus in 280 in connection with the award of posthumous honors to the orator;[48] another posthumous statue of Hypereides by Zeuxiades;[49] a statue of Menander by Cephisodotus, son of the great Praxiteles;[50] and one of the Stoic philosopher Chrysippus by Eubulides.[51] A head of Carneades, the philosopher of the Academy, was found in the Agora;[52] and a copy of a head of the Cynic philosopher Antisthenes by Phyromachus was preserved at Ostia.[53] An Attic artist of this name was best known, however, for the statue of Asclepius he made for the god's shrine at Pergamum. Prusias II of Bithynia, who looted and demolished the shrine in 155, took the figure but was forced through Roman intervention to make peace with Attalus II and pay reparations to him; most certainly he also had to return the stolen sculpture.[54] Another Athenian sculptor, an artist named Niceratus who worked in cast bronze, was active at the court in Pergamum in the third century, and his son Micion was employed by Hieron II of Syracuse at least for a time. Micion made statues and dedicatory offerings that Hieron sent to Olympia.[55]

The first Athenian sculptor known to have worked for an important Roman is Timarchus of Thoricus. Marcus Aemilius Lepidus (censor in

47. Stewart, *Attika* 106–109. A new piece of evidence for Timarchides as *hieropoios* in Athens about 150 B.C. is in *AM* 97 (1982) 178–180, where I discuss different attempts to reconstruct the family tree and reach the same conclusion as Johannes Kirchner many years ago. See note 58 below.

48. G. M. A. Richter, *The Portraits of the Greeks,* rev. R. R. R. Smith (Ithaca, N.Y., 1984) 108–113.

49. Ibid., 150–151.

50. Ibid., 159–164.

51. Ibid., 101–108.

52. Ibid., 152–155.

53. Ibid., 87–89. For more on various sculptors by the name of Phyromachus, presumably all Athenians, see the collection by B. Andreae, *Phyromachosprobleme, MDAI (R)* 1990, esp. the contributions by the editor, 7–11 and 45–100, and that by N. Himmelmann, 13–23. See further H. Müller, *Chiron* 22 (1992) 195–226; F. Queyrel, *RA* (1992) 367–380.

54. C. Habicht, *Hermes* 84 (1956) 101–110; and idem, *CAH* 8² (1989) 373–375.

55. For more on Niceratus see Stewart, *Attika* 7–8; for Micion see ibid., 8.

179) built a temple to Juno Regina and commissioned Timarchus to make a statue of the goddess.[56] Timarchus' sons Polycles and Dionysius made a statue of Jupiter for a temple to the god built by Metellus Macedonicus to celebrate his victory over Andriscus, pretender to the throne of Macedonia, in 148.[57] A little later, between 130 and 120, two other members of this family, the cousins Dionysius and Timarchides, carved a statue of the Roman Ofellius Ferus in Delos, which has survived in good condition except for the head.[58] Athenian art was about to conquer the Roman world.

Just as the sons of dramatic poets often entered their fathers' profession, Athenian sculptors frequently employed their sons as assistants in their workshops and taught them their craft; later the younger man would become the father's partner and finally his successor in the family business. In addition to the two families from Cropidae and Thoricus already mentioned, members of the family of Praxiteles are documented as sculptors over four centuries.[59]

Art historians distinguish two periods in Hellenistic sculpture, the first a kind of baroque era, and the second an era of increasingly sterile neoclassicism setting in around 160 and lasting, in the case of Athens, until the city's almost total collapse after it was conquered by Sulla and laid waste in 86. As time went by sculptors stopped creating statues of contemporaries and started to reproduce late classical and early Hellenistic works over and over again. A sharp decline in the quality of both large-scale sculptures and terra-cotta figurines can be observed with regard to choice of subject, taste, and execution; one can even speak of a sudden onset of "decadence."[60]

When Athenians wished to honor their fellow citizens for particularly notable achievements, they might commission a statue for a public place or, occasionally, a painted portrait to be dedicated to a god in a shrine or hung in a public building. Two leaders honored in this manner were Leosthenes, commander in the Lamian War; and Callippus of Eleusis, who led the Athenian contingent in the defense of

56. Pliny *Nat. hist.* 36.35.
57. Ibid.
58. I *Délos* 1688. See F. Queyrel, *BCH* 115 (1991) 389–464, whose reconstruction of the family tree agrees with the views of Kirchner and Habicht (see note 47 above).
59. Stewart, *Attika* 102.
60. D. B. Thompson, *Hesperia* 34 (1965) 34–71, esp. 47 and 68–69; Stewart, *Attika* 34–64.

Delphi when the Celts raided it in 279. Pausanias saw both portraits centuries later, that of Leosthenes and his sons as depicted by Arcesilaus in the shrine of Zeus in Piraeus, and that of Callippus by Olbiades in the *bouleuterion* (where the Council met) in the Agora.[61] In both cases the portraits were undoubtedly official commissions.

4. Prose: Historiography and the *Characters* of Theophrastus

Like so many products of the time, the historical writings of the Hellenistic age have disappeared almost entirely. Apart from several books by Polybius, the little that has survived exists mostly in the form of fragments quoted by later writers. However, in some cases enough of their work and reputation has survived to allow us to form an impression. Among these are three Athenian historians: two older authors, Philochorus and Timaeus, followed a century later by Apollodorus. Philochorus and Apollodorus were Athenian citizens; Timaeus was a Greek from Sicily who lived in Athens for fifty years. Philochorus and Timaeus wrote the definitive histories of their respective homelands, Attica in the case of Philochorus and the Greek west in the case of Timaeus. Apollodorus' work was more ambitious in scope; in his large and many-faceted output, his chronicle of world history occupies a central place.

Philochorus, born in Athens in 350 and put to death as a supporter of Ptolemy of Egypt in about 260 by Antigonus Gonatas of Macedonia, was the last and presumably most important of the writers of Athenian local history known as the Atthidographers.[62] Next to nothing is known about Philochorus' life, except that in the year 306/5, when Athens was enjoying the democracy just restored by Demetrius Poliorcetes, he served as Athens' official seer, assisting city officials in interpreting signs. In ancient times he was known as the author of a book on the art of prophecy and many other works on religious matters such as sacrifices and festival contests, most of them concerned solely with Attica. His greatest achievement, however, was *Atthis,* a work in sev-

---

61. Pausanias 1.1.3 and 1.1.5.

62. The fundamental study on Philochorus is F. Jacoby, *FGrHist* 328, with a 700-page commentary; cf. also idem, *Atthis: The Local Chronicles of Ancient Athens* (Oxford 1949). In what follows, single fragments are labeled with an F. A brief appreciation of Philochorus is in P. J. Rhodes, *Studia Hellenistica* 30 (1990) 79–81.

enteen books chronicling the history of Attica from its mythical dawn to the year 261. He dealt with recent history in great detail; the forty years following the battle of Ipsus in 301 took up eight books, nearly half the total work.

Philochorus' account of events in his own lifetime has perished almost entirely, but much of the earlier history has been preserved in numerous fragments, some of them quite informative. The latter books of *Atthis* "are all but completely lost to us because they dealt with a time that did not interest the scholars of Alexandria, who studied him (Philochorus) carefully for help in interpreting the great Attic orators."[63] The surviving parts reveal Philochorus as much more of a scholar and researcher than his predecessors, perhaps the first scholarly historian. The antiquarian interest so typical of most local historians is clearly discernible in the extant fragments. Philochorus, seemingly a man of conservative and religious views, does not appear to have participated actively in politics—a fact that makes the circumstances of his death shortly after the end of the Chremonidean War all the more puzzling.

A few references to Philochorus' own era can be gleaned from the surviving fragments of the later books. There is a mention of the *gynaikonomoi* in book 7, which probably commenced with the year 321/0.[64] Events during Demetrius Poliorcetes' first period in power, from 307 to 301, are described[65] with cautious but unmistakable criticism of the manipulation of procedures by servile politicians to enable the king to be initiated into the Eleusinian Mysteries without the usual waiting period.[66] And finally there is mention of Theophrastus' success in persuading Demetrius to allow his banished opponents to return to Athens in 292/1.[67]

Timaeus, Philochorus' exact contemporary, lived from about 350 to 254.[68] Both men lived in the same city for fifty years and must have known one another. Timaeus was born in Tauromenium, Sicily, the son

63. R. Laqueur, "Philochoros," *RE* (1938) 2436.
64. Jacoby, *FGrHist* 328 F 65.
65. Ibid., F 66, 67, 70, and 165–166.
66. Ibid., F 70; see Chapter 3, Section 1.
67. Ibid., F 167; cf. F 67; see Chapter 3, Section 3.
68. Jacoby is also the basic source for information on Timaeus, *FGrHist* 566, with commentary on 526–594 and notes on 311–347. There is also much of value in A. Momigliano, *Terzo contributo alla Storia degli Studi Classici e del Mondo Antico* (Rome 1966) 23–53 (*Rivista storica italiana* 71 [1959] 529–556), although Momigliano's assumption that

of its ruler Andromachus. He left home in 316, never to return, shortly before or after Agathocles, tyrant of Syracuse, conquered the city and put an end to whatever hopes Timaeus may have had of succeeding his father. Timaeus found refuge in Athens and settled there permanently, devoting his long life to writing the history of Sicily and the western-most regions of the Greek world. His great themes were the struggle between Greeks and Carthaginians over control of the islands and the role played by Greek tyrants, who often attained their leading positions in the course of these wars. The thirty-eight books of Timaeus' history of the west became the definitive work on the subject, and their loss is due solely to a later era's narrow-minded preference for the classical prose style. The last five books dealt with the rule of Timaeus' archen-emy Agathocles, who had made himself king of Syracuse and who died in 289.

In old age Timaeus produced a sequel to his history of the west, in which he described Rome's battles against King Pyrrhus of Epirus and carried the chronicle down to 264, the year the first war broke out between Rome and Carthage. It was Timaeus, writing in far-off Ath-ens, who first recognized the importance of Rome and sensed the role Romans would play on the world stage. "The Carthaginians and later the Romans . . . were more important to him than Alexander, the Eastern world, the struggles of the *diadochoi,* and the fate of the mother country," Jacoby observed.[69] Timaeus knew more about the Romans and conveyed more information about them to the Greeks than any of his predecessors. His world was one of cities, not the world of the Hellenistic monarchy.[70]

In the annals of historiography, Timaeus won recognition for first dating events by the Olympic year, beginning with 776/5, the first year of the first quadrennial Olympic Games. This system permitted the date of every event to be established without reference to lists of archons or consuls.[71] Pedant that he was, Timaeus often criticized his predecessors

---

Antigonus Gonatas ruled Athens after 277 is utopian, and his description of the opening of the Chremonidean War as an "Athenian rebellion" thus totally inaccurate (Habicht, *Unter-suchungen* 68–75). The passages on Timaeus in the text owe a great deal to both authors.

69. Jacoby, *FGrHist* 535. K. Hanell even refers to Timaeus as the "ancestor" of Roman historiography, *Entretiens sur l'antiquité classique,* vol. 4 (Geneva 1956) 152.

70. Momigliano, *Terzo contributo* 36.

71. Timaeus also wrote a work on Olympic victors.

quite sharply for their inaccuracy, a characteristic that earned him the nickname "Epitimaeus" ("the Faultfinder"). He in turn was the subject of lengthy and biting criticism by Polybius, often of a spiteful and biased nature. But Polybius' polemical style makes it clear that he was attacking a widely respected figure; indeed Polybius himself had some sense of Timaeus' importance, for in the preface to his own history he started where Timaeus had left off, at the beginning of the First Punic War in 264.

Apollodorus, a scholar of considerable versatility, is one of the figures most appealing to modern sensibilities from the Athens of the second century.[72] An Athenian citizen and the son of Asclepiades, he began his education as a pupil of the philosopher Diogenes of Babylon, then the head of the Stoa. Apollodorus went on to Egypt for a long period, perhaps when Diogenes left Athens for Rome as a member of the "philosophers' embassy" in 155, and continued his studies with the eminent Homer specialist Aristarchus. Forced to leave Egypt in 145 when Ptolemy VIII Euergetes II banished the scholars from Alexandria, Apollodorus found a new home in Pergamum at the court of Attalus II, to whom he dedicated the chronicle he completed in 144/3. After the king's death in 138 (or after the death of the last Pergamene king in 133), he returned to Athens, where he spent the rest of his life. There he maintained friendly relations with a number of scholars and philosophers, including Panaetius of Rhodes, a Stoic philosopher roughly his contemporary. It was probably during this last period of his life, when his chronicle made him famous and widely read, that Apollodorus was honored by the Amphictionic Council in Delphi.[73]

Apollodorus' works cover a broad spectrum of subjects, including Greek religion, Attic comedy, and—perhaps in connection with his study of theater—Athenian courtesans; he also wrote a commentary on

72. The fundamental work on Apollodorus is F. Jacoby, *Apollodors Chronik. Eine Sammlung der Fragmente* (Berlin 1902). There is a collection of fragments of works that can be considered historical in *FGrHist* 244, with commentary. A list of religious officials from the year of the archon Lysiades (around 150) contains the names of Apollodorus and Asclepiades, both of the deme Piraeus, right next to each other; they may have been relatives of Apollodorus the historian (almost certainly in Egypt at the time), but given the frequency of both names in the Athenian population, this is far from certain (*IG* II².1938.63–64).

73. Pliny *Nat. hist.* 7.123. Other luminaries of Athenian intellectual life so honored (several centuries earlier) were Aristotle and his nephew Callisthenes, a historian and victim of Alexander the Great; *FD* III.1.400; cf. W. Spoerri, in *Comptes et inventaires dans la cité grecque*, ed. D. Knoepfler (Neuchâtel 1988) 111–140.

Homer's catalogue of ships in book 2 of the *Iliad* on which Strabo drew heavily. However, his most important and influential work was the three-volume chronicle mentioned above, covering 1,040 years of Greek history from the destruction of Troy (which he placed in the year 1184, following Eratosthenes) down to 145/4. To this he later added a fourth book extending the chronicle to 120/19 (the year of the archon Eumachus) with a particularly detailed discussion of recent events. Not long afterward—almost certainly no later than 110—the writer long known as Pseudo-Scymnus (actually Pausanias of Damascus)[74] included a quotation from this addition. Apollodorus wrote his chronicle in iambic trimeter, the meter used in Greek drama, perhaps because its regularity made the text easier to memorize. Nevertheless, the content of the work places it in the tradition of prose historiography.

Apollodorus modeled his history on the chronicle of Eratosthenes of Cyrene, who had lived a century earlier and possessed a universality of learning reminiscent of Aristotle and Theophrastus. But although as a young man in Athens Eratosthenes had attended lectures of the philosophers and later wrote philosophical works of his own, he was not a philosopher in the narrower sense and cannot be considered a member of one of the Athenian schools. He saw his calling as new and invented a term for it: "philologist" *(philologos)*, a "lover of words" or "lover of learning."[75] After completing his studies in Athens he was invited to Alexandria by Ptolemy III Euergetes (sometime after 246) and named director of the royal library, succeeding Apollonius of Rhodes. A productive scholar who became a leading authority in many branches of knowledge such as mathematics, astronomy, geography, and grammar, Eratosthenes was also appreciated as a fine poet with an elegant style.[76] In addition, he founded chronography as a scholarly discipline, and in this respect had a decisive influence on Apollodorus. Eratosthenes began his chronicle with the fall of Troy and closed with the death of Alexander the Great in 323. Apollodorus began at the same point but ended 200 years later; Apollodorus' work became the

74. A. Diller, *TAPhA* 86 (1955) 276–279. For the time of composition see F. Gisinger, "Skymnos," *RE* (1927) 674–675.

75. Suetonius *De grammaticis* 10.

76. G. Knaack, "Eratosthenes," *RE* (1907) 358–388; J. Mau, "Eratosthenes," *Der kleine Pauly* (1979) 344–346; *FGrHist* 241. On his measurements of the earth, see Strabo 2.5.7 (p. 113C); O. Neugebauer, *A History of Ancient Mathematical Astronomy* (Berlin 1975) 1: 305 n. 27 and 2: 734–735.

more popular and eventually supplanted that of his predecessor and model.

In his history Apollodorus devoted some attention to politics and politicians but gave more space to writers, philosophers, and scholars. A disproportionate number of the surviving fragments deal with the latter figures, since most of them were preserved as citations in Philodemus' history of the Academy. Apollodorus rejected the system of dating introduced by Timaeus, preferring the older system based on the archons of Athens. This method forced readers to consult a table of archons but saved them the trouble of having to calculate the actual dates of events.

Apollodorus' chronicle became a standard work used down to the early Christian era; nothing reflects this popularity so well as a letter Cicero wrote to his friend Atticus in 45 B.C.[77] Cicero, working on the *Academica,* asks for information on the background of the "philosophers' embassy" in 155. He recalls (correctly) that it had something to do with a quarrel over Oropus on the Attic-Boeotian border, but wants to know who the Epicureans in Athens were at the time (although they did not participate in the embassy, as it happens), who was head of the Epicurean school, and who the city's most respected political leaders were. Cicero suggests that Atticus can look up the answers in Apollodorus if necessary.

The passages cited by Philodemus on the philosophers of the third and second centuries[78] give a good impression both of the wealth of information contained in Apollodorus' chronicle and its objectivity. The chronicle, of which modern scholars would dearly like to have more than the few surviving fragments, also conveys a sense of the high quality of the ancient scholarly tradition founded at the Peripatetic school in Athens and brought to Alexandria by Demetrius of Phalerum after his overthrow as regent. Scholars such as Apollodorus later carried this tradition back to Athens, completing the circle.

Very few prose works from Hellenistic Athens have survived in their entirety. One of the most interesting is *Characters,* a series of short sketches by Theophrastus.[79] Born in Eresus on Lesbos, he succeeded his teacher Aristotle as head of the Peripatetic school in 322 at the age of fifty, having demonstrated an ability almost equal to Aristotle's in his

77. Cicero *Ad Atticum* 12.23.2.
78. *FGrHist* 244 F 47 and 53–60.
79. The article on Theophrastus by O. Regenbogen provides good background on the philosopher; *RE Suppl.* 7 (1940) 1354–1562; for his discussion of *Characters* see 1500–11.

numerous, wide-ranging, impressive writings. As an expert on botany, a field that expanded rapidly after members of Alexander's expedition to the East brought back new information and specimens,[80] Theophrastus had no equal in the ancient world. Two major works of the six he wrote on botany have survived, the *Enquiry into Plants* in nine books and the later *De causis plantarum* in six books.[81] But although his fame as a scholar derives from his philosophical and scientific treatises, *Characters* has remained his most popular and influential work.

In the *Characters* Theophrastus presents thirty human personality types (or rather *male* types, a limitation then taken for granted) in brief sketches about a printed page long. As their titles suggest, he describes figures such as "the Superstitious Man," "the Miser," "the Flatterer," and "the Old Fool" in terms of a dominant character flaw. But none of them is presented as irredeemably evil or reprehensible; they are verbal caricatures drawn with light strokes, with echoes of Aristotle's *Nicomachean Ethics* and a resemblance to some of the figures of New Comedy.

In modern times this brief work came to light again piece by piece, with the first fifteen sketches published in the early fifteenth century, numbers sixteen through twenty-eight in the sixteenth century, and the last two in 1786. Readers can glimpse the Athenian background everywhere, for example, in the references to city officials such as the director of processions at the Dionysia (number 26), to the ceremonial religious activities of the ephebes (27), and to the parade of the cavalry (21). Theophrastus mentions liturgies, particularly the *choregia* and trierarchy, several times (22 and 23), suggesting they were either still in existence at the time of writing or at least recent and familiar phenomena. One reference to the great famine of the 320s applies not only to Athens but to much of the Greek world.

Scholars have carried on a lively debate regarding the work's date of composition, especially since Conrad Cichorius claimed in 1907 that he had established it definitively as 319.[82] More recent writers, noting

---

80. H. Bretzl, *Die botanischen Forschungen des Alexanderzuges* (Leipzig 1903).

81. There are 2-vol. editions of the *Historia* by A. Hort (1916) and by S. Amigues (books 1–4 completed to date) (1988–1989). The *Causae* have been edited by B. Einarson and G. Link in 3 vols. (1976–1990).

82. Conrad Cichorius in the *Philologische Gesellschaft* edition (Leipzig 1907) lvii–lxii. See also F. Rühl, *RhM* 53 (1898) 324–327; A. E. Boegehold, *TAPhA* 90 (1959) 15–19; R. Lane Fox, *PCPS* 42 (1996) 127–170.

that Theophrastus may well have composed the various pieces over several years, tend to be more cautious. There is some evidence for the latter assumption in the fact that several sketches seem to assume the existence of a democratic government with functioning people's courts (such as numbers 12 and 26), while others show the city in Cassander's hands. In number 8 in particular, the title figure "the Rumormonger" claims to have heard that Polyperchon and the king have won a battle and taken Cassander prisoner, to the great dismay of the current rulers of Athens. This sketch cannot have been written before 317, and it is unlikely that it was written much later. On the other hand, when "the Braggart" claims that Antipater, the regent, has written him three times inviting him to Macedonia, it is not necessarily an indication that the sketch was composed before Antipater's death in 319. "The Windbag" (7) mentions the trial in 330 over Demosthenes' crown with its accompanying oratory as a notable event of some years back. It is thus possible that parts of the work were written before 322 and others as late as 317. The years 324–315 should be accepted as reasonable boundaries.

The special charm of *Characters* lies in its evocation of atmosphere, its vivid depiction of everyday life and behavior in Athens at the time, the local color at the Assembly, at the marketplace, at court, or at a dinner party. Theophrastus conveys a sense of the norms of behavior by showing how his characters deviate from them in serious or trivial ways, thereby revealing themselves as representatives of a particular type.

Theophrastus died roughly at the time of the liberation of Athens from Demetrius in the spring of 287. Though a foreigner, he was taken to heart by the residents of his chosen city; the entire citizenry is said to have joined his funeral procession and accompanied him to his last resting place.[83]

---

83. Diog. Laert. 6.41.

F I V E

The Independent City
(287–262)

1. Policy amid Competing Forces

The independence Athens won back in the spring of 287 with some
assistance from Ptolemy I lasted twenty-five years (although the Athenians had to spend the last few at war, resisting the attempts of Antigonus Gonatas of Macedonia to subdue them). New findings have
established that the city remained independent throughout this period.
Attica did not become Macedonian territory, nor did Antigonus make
Athens into a second capital of his Greek possessions. Earlier views that
the Athenians regained control of Piraeus during this quarter century
have also proved false; it is now virtually certain that the Piraeus
remained in Macedonian hands without interruption until 229.[1]

Upon his hasty departure for Asia Minor Demetrius left his son
Antigonus in charge of his remaining Greek territories, which included,
besides Piraeus, Demetrias on the Gulf of Pagasae and Corinth with its
fortress Acrocorinth. After several indecisive battles against King Lysimachus that led him through all of Asia Minor and bled away his
troops, Demetrius was taken prisoner in Syria by King Seleucus and
died in 283 still in captivity. Even before Demetrius reached Syria the
Athenians attacked his remaining forces in an attempt to take back the
fortress of Munychia and Piraeus. They bribed the commander of the

---

1. For a more detailed account see Habicht, *Untersuchungen* 68–112, although several
errors there now require correction: Antigonus' meeting with the philosopher Arcesilaus took
place not before 287 but after 262 (D. Knoepfler, *MH* 44 [1987] 241 n. 36); the meeting
between Hierocles and Menedemus took place not in 273 or 272 but sometime after 268
(G. Reger, *CQ* 42 [1992] 373–377); and the Macedonians retained control over several Attic
fortresses in these years (*IG* II².657.34–36), including Eleusis.

mercenaries' garrison; he agreed to let them in, but betrayed their plans to his commanding officer, Heracleides, so that the Athenians walked into a trap. The 420 men who entered the garrison, hopelessly out-numbered, were all killed. They received burial in the state cemetery, and the names of two *strategoi* and seven officers are known.[2] A short time later the Assembly passed a decree that mentions the citizens' continuing determination to reunify the city and its harbor as their chief political goal.[3] Sometime around 280 a man named Mithres, treasurer to the recently slain Lysimachus, was detained by the Mace-donian commander of the Piraeus. Since Mithres was a follower of Epicurus' teachings and one of his patrons, Epicurus sent Metro-dorus, one of his closest associates, to Piraeus to negotiate Mithres' release.[4]

The continuing foreign occupation of Piraeus kept alive a spirit of opposition against the Macedonian rulers, first Demetrius and later his son Antigonus Gonatas. The Athenians knew they could count on the support of the Antigonid dynasty's other opponents. Pyrrhus of Epirus, who had driven Demetrius out of Macedonia with help from Lysi-machus, is reported to have come to Athens immediately after its liberation and offered a sacrifice to Athena on the Acropolis. The same source also reports that he advised the Athenians not to let any more kings into their city.[5] Lysimachus was a more important threat to Demetrius than Pyrrhus, and the Athenians approached him immedi-ately after Demetrius' departure from Greece. Toward the end of the winter in 286/5 they awarded honors to his deputy, Artemidorus of Perinth, and erected a statue of Lysimachus still standing when

2. Polyaenus 5.17.1; Pausanias 1.29.10; Beloch, *GG* 4.1: 238–239. Cf. also *ISE* 13. For Macedonian commanders of this period and "friends" of the king in the areas around Athens and Corinth, see Plut. *Demetrius* 51.1.

3. *Hesperia* 7 (1938) 102, no. 18.30–31. It is going too far to conclude from these words (which express no more than a hope) that an agreement had been reached with the occupying forces and that the Athenians could firmly expect to regain their harbor in the near future, as has been done by P. Gauthier, *REG* 92 (1979) 356–395; and by G. Reger, *CQ* 42 (1992) 372. Both Gauthier and Reger assume a peaceful but only temporary reunification of city and harbor in 281. But in the summer of 283 (and no doubt on other occasions) the *ekklesia* also expressed hope that the city would be rejoined with its harbor (*IG* II.657.34).

4. *P.Herc.* 1418, col. 32a; the sizable literature on the subject is listed in *Catalogo dei papiri Ercolani*, ed. M. Gigante (Naples 1979) 312–314; on the wording of the text see C. Militello, *CronErc* 20 (1990) 75 and 82. See also H. Streckel, "Epikuros," *RE Suppl.* 11 (1968) 591–592.

5. Plut. *Pyrrhus* 12.6–7.

Pausanias visited Athens many centuries later.[6] During this period they awarded citizenship to Artemidorus and also to Bithys, another high-ranking member of the king's court.[7] On several occasions Athens sent envoys to Lysimachus, hoping to persuade him to continue as bene-factor to the city, as he had in the early 290s, before the beginning of Demetrius' second regime. Demosthenes' nephew Demochares served twice on such missions once he came back, in 286, from the exile imposed on him in 303.[8] The Athenian poet Philippides of Kephale, a friend of the king who had interceded with him on the city's behalf in the past, was again able to obtain gifts of money and grain. In 284 Philippides served as director *(agonothetes)* of an especially splendid dramatic contest, and the following year, shortly before Lysimachus' death, Philippides was awarded honors by the assembly on the initiative of his fellow demesman Niceratus.[9]

After the city's liberation, Athens' transition from a satellite of the Antigonid dynasty to a member of the opposing camp led at once to resumption of normal relations with the Aetolian League, then grow-ing in importance. In the early 290s the League had seized control of the shrine of Delphi and its administrative Amphictionic Council, pro-voking the enmity of the Athenians. Olympiodorus, a statesman with a long history of friendship toward the Aetolians, probably played a role in the restoration of friendly relations. In the years 287–280 five awards of honors to Athenian citizens in Delphi are documented.[10] Not long afterward the Athenians again sent a representative to the Am-phictionic Council, to retake the seat to which Athens had traditionally been entitled. The Athenians had not attempted to use their vote and influence since the Aetolians had occupied Delphi, and perhaps not since the death of Alexander the Great. But the Athenians rejoined the

6. The decree honoring Artemidorus has survived in two different versions, *IG* II².662 (with the new fragment *Hesperia* 26 [1957] 29, no. 2) and 663. Artemidorus' nationality was determined by Habicht on the basis of the Ephesian decree in his honor (I *Ephesos* 1464); *Chiron* 2 (1972) 107–109. For the statue of Lysimachus see Pausanias 1.9.4. For recent work see H. S. Lund, *Lysimachos* (New York 1992); and C. Franco, *Il regno di Lisimaco* (Pisa 1993).

7. *IG* II².808. After long discussion the identity of the honoree and the date of the award have been decided in favor of Lysimachus' courtier, thanks to a new document of the king from the same period that also names him; M. Hatzopoulos, *Une donation du roi Lysimaque* (Athens and Paris 1988).

8. [Plut.] *mor.* 851E.

9. *IG* II².657, esp. lines 33–36 and 43–45.

10. R. Flacelière, *HSCP Suppl.* 1 (1940) 473 (Olympiodorus); *FD* III.2 71–72 and 198–200.

Pythian Games as participants as early as 286,[11] and it no longer mattered that only a few years earlier Demetrius had resorted to holding his own "Pythian" Games in Athens.

However, the city's closest and most useful ally remained the royal court at Alexandria.[12] Ptolemy I Soter ruled there alone until 285, and then for two more years jointly with his son by Berenice, Ptolemy II Philadelphus. Upon his father's death in 283, Ptolemy II became sole king. He founded a festival known as the Ptolemaea in honor of his father, the dynasty's founder; first conceived as a single day of commemoration and celebrated as such in 282, it later became a festival celebrated every four years, to which the entire Greek world was invited.

Both father and son supported Athens generously, especially with contributions of grain. As long as Demetrius governed the city, Macedonia had kept it supplied with food, but after the Athenian rebellion the situation became precarious.[13] In July 286 an officer in Ptolemy's service named Zeno was honored by the citizens for having safely delivered to Athens a shipment of grain from the king.[14] A delegation dispatched to Alexandria on the initiative of Demochares returned with fifty talents of silver from the king.[15] The admiral of Ptolemy's fleet, King Philocles of Sidon, made a dedicatory offering at Athens around this time and was honored as a benefactor of the city with Athenian citizenship and other awards.[16]

The decree of the year 270/69 in honor of Callias, published in 1978, reveals many new details about the relationship between Athens and the Ptolemaic dynasty. Callias, after participating in the struggles to liberate the city, accompanied a group of Athenian envoys to Alexandria and gave them strong support in their mission to the old king.

11. Habicht, *Untersuchungen* 73–75. For Athenian participation in the Pythian Games of 286, see A. Wilhelm (1936) 13 in *Akademieschriften* 2: 527. The fragment of an Athenian-Aetolian pact found in Delphi (*StV*, no. 470) probably dates from this period of renewed friendship. D. Knoepfler now puts it at the beginning of the Chremonidean War; *BCH* 119 (1995) 150–151.

12. For the following see C. Habicht, *CA* 11 (1992) 68–90.

13. G. Marasco, *Athenaeum* 62 (1984) 286–294.

14. *IG* II^2.650, with comments by Habicht, *Untersuchungen* 48–52; and M. J. Osborne, *ZPE* 35 (1979) 189–190.

15. [Plut.] *mor.* 851E.

16. *ISE* 17; *Hesperia* 9 (1940) 352, no. 48; I. Merker, *Historia* 19 (1970) 141–150. Cf. H. Hauben, *Orientalia Louvaniensia Analecta* 22 (1987) 413–427.

When the new king ascended the throne, Callias returned home, but he was soon being urged by the generals in Athens to go back and plead with him for immediate assistance in the form of desperately needed funds and grain. Callias agreed and set out to meet Ptolemy II, this time at his own expense. He caught up with him in Cyprus and obtained an additional fifty talents of silver and 20,000 bushels of wheat, which the Athenian delegation received from royal officials in Delos.[17] When Ptolemy II was preparing to celebrate the first Ptolemaea, the Athenian Assembly voted to send a state delegation to the games and elected Callias to lead it. He accepted the position but refused the accompanying stipend of fifty minas (almost one talent), choosing instead to finance the mission himself. Sometime later, most likely in the summer of 282, the first Great Panathenaea since the liberation was to be celebrated, and once again Callias was able to persuade the king to help out, this time with a donation toward the purchase of necessary ceremonial paraphernalia.[18] As it happened one of the two directors of the contests that year—perhaps the one responsible for the Panathenaea—was Callias' brother Phaedrus.[19]

Callias must have reentered the king's service at some point, for in 270/69, when the Athenian Assembly passed the decree honoring him, he was commanding a corps of Ptolemy's army at Halicarnassus on the west coast of Asia Minor; nonetheless he was in a position to assist Athenian envoys on their way to the king.[20]

The evidence reveals not only the level of activity but also the continuity of friendly relations between Athens and the Egyptian court over a period of seventeen years. By 270/69, the year of Callias' honors, the outbreak of the Chremonidean War was not far off, a conflict that would unite the two powers against Macedonia. Because essential evidence was still undiscovered in his day, Ferguson mistakenly concluded that Ptolemy's fleet refrained from intervening in the events of 287 and that after the city's liberation the Athenians' good relations

17. Lines 40–55 of the decree for Callias, *Hesperia Suppl.* 17 (1978) 2–4. Soon after the liberation of 287 Athens began minting coins again for the first time in about 10 years. The silver used was inferior to the ore mined at Laurium in Attica. An appealing theory has been advanced that the coins of this period may have been minted from the silver donated by Lysimachus and Ptolemy I and II; Kroll, *Coins* 10.

18. Lines 55–70 of the decree for Callias. B. Dreyer now proposes a different chronology; *ZPE* 111 (1996) 50–56.

19. *IG* II^2.682.63–64 for Phaedrus; *IG* II^2.3079 for Glaucon, brother of Chremonides.

20. Lines 70–78 of the decree for Callias.

with Lysimachus could have led them to expect only harm from Ptolemy.[21] In fact, however, the city never had stauncher supporters than the two first kings of the Ptolemaic dynasty, who at all times proved ready to supply what was needed.

It is more difficult to follow the course of Athens' relations with Boeotia, its neighbor to the north, after 287. In the mid-290s the Boeotians were allied with the Aetolians against Athens, then under Demetrius' rule. But in 291 Demetrius seized control of Boeotia and installed the historian Hieronymus of Cardia as his governor.[22] When Athens rebelled against Demetrius in 287, it again lost the city of Oropus and its surrounding territory to the Boeotian League,[23] which kept it for the next 115 years. After Antigonus Gonatas lost a naval battle to Ptolemy Keraunos (a half brother of Ptolemy II) in 280, he retreated to Boeotia.[24] Although this fact seems to indicate that he still had control over it, there is no doubt that the Boeotian League and Athens were on friendly terms in the summer of 281: an Athenian delegation made up of six infantry officers *(taxiarchoi)* took part in the Basileia, the League's festival in Lebadeia.[25] It is also unknown if or when the border fortresses of northern Attica, Panakton and Phyle, still occupied by Macedonian troops in 287, became Athenian territory again.

We do know that Athens regained Eleusis, the strongest fortress in northern Attica, sometime after the liberation. Credit for this is given to Demochares, who, finally returning from exile in 286/5, "[re]acquired Eleusis for the people by persuading the Assembly to capture it and then carrying out this resolve."[26] It used to be assumed, on the basis of a document from the archonship of Diotimus,[27] that this occurred before April 284, but this Diotimus has now been recognized to be the archon of 354, not his later successor of the same name.[28] Very little is known about the two coastal fortresses of Rhamnus and

21. Ferguson, *HA* 149 n. 2 and 153.

22. Plut. *Demetrius* 39.3–7; J. Hornblower, *Hieronymus of Cardia* (Oxford 1981) 13–14.

23. R. Etienne and P. Roesch, *BCH* 102 (1978) 374; B. Gullath, *Untersuchungen zur Geschichte Boiotiens in der Zeit Alexanders und der Diadochen* (Frankfurt 1982) 199.

24. Memnon, *FGrHist* 434 F 8.6.

25. *ISE* 15. For more on the festival of the Basileia see L. Moretti, *Iscrizioni agonistiche greche* (Rome 1953) 105–107. Cf. Gullath, *Geschichte Boiotiens* 199–207.

26. [Plut.] *mor.* 851F.

27. Habicht, *Untersuchungen* 25 n. 25 and 78 n. 15.

28. This will be shown by K. Clinton, who kindly made his manuscript available to me.

Sunium. A decree of the deme of Rhamnus honoring the *strategos* Epichares (published in 1967) indicates that Rhamnus had reverted to Athenian control before the start of the Chremonidean War, although the precise date remains unclear.[29] Sunium, on the other hand, was held by the Macedonians when the war began, and this is why the Ptolemaic general Patroclus could not disembark there, but had to settle for the small island of Gaidaronesi offshore.[30] The island of Salamis, captured by Demetrius in 295, clearly remained occupied by Macedonian forces until 229.[31] Lemnos and Imbros, islands in the northeast Aegean returned to Athens by Antigonus I in 307,[32] were lost again after the battle of Ipsus and must have fallen under the control of Lysimachus when he conquered Macedonia in 288. In any case Seleucus' defeat of Lysimachus in 281 made him ruler of Lemnos, and he returned possession of it to Athens in the next few months, just before his death.[33]

Although relations between Athens and the Aetolian League must have returned to normal as soon as the Athenians rid themselves of Demetrius, scholars have been virtually unanimous in believing that Athens took part in a war against the Aetolians and Antigonus in 280. This war, waged by a coalition of Greek states under the leadership of King Areus of Sparta, is known from a single source, the historian Justinus, writing in the third century A.D. Justinus does not specifically name Athens as a participant; it was a German historian, Karl Julius Beloch, who concluded that Athens had been involved, and almost all later scholars followed his lead. Beloch pointed to an Athenian document from the year of the archon Menecles thought to date from 280 B.C. that contained references to war, and saw it as proof that Athens had taken part. In fact, however, Menecles was archon in 267/6, and the conflict to which the document refers is the Chremonidean

29. *AD* 22 (1967) 38–52 (*SEG* 24.154), with a new fragment, *PAA* (1985) 9–10 and 13–14.

30. H. Lauter, *Marburger Winckelmannsprogramm* (1988) 32–33. The archon of *IG* II².1270 (*ISE* 11) was [Mnesi]demos, 298/7, not [Peithi]demos, 268/7; a similar, unpublished inscription found there contains the full name (*AA* [1995] 810). *IG* II².1281 (*ISE* 19) dates from after 229 (Tracy, *ALC* 52).

31. *ISE* 14, p. 30.

32. Diodorus 20.46.4–5; *IG* II².1492.133; Beloch, *GG* 4.1: 152 with n. 1.

33. Phylarch, *FGrHist* 81 F 29; *IG* II².672 (with *Hesperia* 10 [1941] 338); Habicht, *Gottmenschentum* 89–90; W. Orth, *Königlicher Machtanspruch und städtische Freiheit* (Munich 1977) 36–38.

war.[34] Beloch's theory must be abandoned; apart from the failed attempt to retake Piraeus, Athens was at peace with its neighbors from 287 on.

But the next year, when threatened by a foreign invasion, the Athenians, along with other Greeks, resorted to arms.[35] The fierce swarm of attackers that fell upon Greece in 279 must have reminded them of the Persian attack 200 years earlier. This time the invaders were Celts who overran the Balkan peninsula in several waves. One of these armies, under a leader named Bolgios, besieged and killed Ptolemy Keraunos, who had made himself king of Macedonia after murdering Seleucus I only a year before. Another army of Celts commanded by the leader Brennos invaded and laid waste the neighboring area of Paeonia; it returned again in 279 and pressed farther south. As the Celts ravaged Thessaly without organized resistance from a now leaderless Macedonia, it became clear that Brennos' ultimate aim was to bypass Thermopylae and reach the sacred city of Delphi. Although Phocians had plundered the shrine two generations earlier, it still possessed rich treasures collected over centuries.

To ward off the danger the Greeks assembled an army consisting mainly of the peoples most immediately threatened: Aetolians, Boeotians, and Phocians (in whose territory Delphi lay). They were joined by Locrians, the city of Megara (on the isthmus of Corinth), and Patras, the only participant from the Peloponnese. The Athenians also sent a contingent, and two kings, Antigonus Gonatas and Seleucus' son Antiochus I, each sent 500 mercenaries. The Celts did bypass Thermopylae when the Greeks tried to stop them there and reached Delphi itself, but in heavy fighting they were driven out of the city, suffering enormous losses. As the Greeks forced them to retreat, Bren-

---

34. For a detailed refutation see Habicht, *Untersuchungen* 83–85. Among earlier historians, only B. Niese expressed doubts about Athens' participation in this campaign (which proved unsuccessful); *Geschichte der griechischen und makedonischen Staaten seit der Schlacht bei Chaeronea*, vol. 2 (Gotha 1899) 11. More recently it has been doubted by G. Marasco, *Sparta agli inizi dell'età ellenistica: Il regno di Areo I* (Florence 1980) 66. To my previous discussion of the topic should be added one further consideration: Sparta's decision to go to war against the Aetolians may have been influenced by the loss of an outpost; in 280 the Aetolians forced Heraclea in Trachis, near Thermopylae, to join their League (Pausanias 10.20.9); Heraclea had been founded as a Spartan colony in 426 (Thucydides 3.92–93).

35. The most important study for the following passage is G. Nachtergael, *Les Galates en Grèce et les Sôtéria de Delphes* (Brussels 1977), which deals with the Celtic expansion in the area of the Danube (3–14), the sources relevant to the invasion of Greece (15–125), and the invasion of Macedonia and Greece (126–205).

nos, within sight of his goal, killed himself. Legends sprang up at once about the intervention of the gods and the role played by local heroes in the dramatic rescue of the sacred site. A "festival of deliverance" (Soteria) was created to commemorate the event; the Amphictionic Council took charge of organizing it for the next thirty years. In 246 the Aetolians took over and turned it into an even larger festival celebrated every four years. Greek states from near and far were invited, and several inscriptions recording the acceptances (from the years 278 and 246) have survived.[36] The Athenians played a creditable role in these events but did not have the preeminence ascribed to them by Pausanias, the most detailed and important source. In his *Description of Greece,* he devoted five chapters to an account of the Celtic invasion of 279/8 in book 10 (dedicated to Phocis), and added further material in two other parts of the same work.[37] Pausanias' account and the role played in it by Athens and the Athenians have often been analyzed.[38] It is colored by close imitation of Herodotus (since Pausanias treats the invasions of the Celts and the Persians as more or less equivalent), particularly Herodotus' description of the battles at Cape Artemision and Thermopylae in 480. Pausanias also followed Herodotus in his strongly pro-Athenian standpoint. Thus, for example, Pausanias turned Callippus of Eleusis, leader of the modest Athenian contingent, into the supreme commander of the Greek allied forces, and placed every seaworthy ship in the Athenian fleet at the scene. When the Celts bypassed Thermopylae, he gave the Athenian navy the starring role as rescuers of the infantry troops, just as Herodotus had made the Athenians, along with the gods, the saviors of Greece in the struggle against Xerxes.

Scholars have long recognized that the exaggeration of the Athenian role and the imitation of Herodotus were later additions to Pausanias' original version that can easily be detached from the whole narrative. With these partisan excesses removed, there remains a precise account rich in concrete and often verifiable details, based on the work of an extremely well-informed contemporary. The historian most likely to

36. Nachtergael has collected the inscriptions and provides detailed commentary, ibid., 391–495. D. Knoepfler persuasively argues that the original festival was held every second year; *BCH* 119 (1995) 152–154.

37. Pausanias 10.19.4–23; 1.3.5–4.4; and 7.15.3.

38. See the analysis in Habicht, *Untersuchungen* 87–94, with all the details. Nachtergael and I independently reached the same conclusions on central points.

have produced such a report is Hieronymus of Cardia, the author of a history of the *diadochoi* that followed events down to the death of Pyrrhus in the fall of 272.

The report on which Pausanias is thought to have drawn gave the troop strengths for all participating Greek states in the separate categories of hoplites, light-armed infantry, and cavalry and named all fourteen commanders. The Athenian commander was Callippus, son of Moirocles, and his portrait painted by Olbiades was hung in the Council chamber in his honor. The Athenian forces consisted of 1,000 footsoldiers and 500 cavalrymen. The archons in the year of the invasion and the following year were named Anaxicrates and Democles. The relatives of a particularly brave soldier named Cydias killed in the battle had an epigram inscribed on his shield (which Pausanias cites in full) and presented it as an offering to "Zeus the Deliverer" (Zeus Eleutherios). All these facts have been verified: Callippus was really the son of Moirocles and a member of a prominent Athenian family from Eleusis. An Assembly decree of 246/5 responding to an invitation from the Aetolians to the festival of the Soteria was introduced by none other than Cydias' son Cybernis,[39] and this son of the hero of 279 received honors at that time in Delphi.[40] The decree also confirms that a contingent from Athens took part in the fighting against the Celts, for it mentions that the city sent the cavalry and the corps of elite soldiers known as *epilektoi* (which may well have numbered 1,000, the number given by Pausanias). From another decree passed in 282/1, only three years before the events, we know that the Athenian cavalry was increased from 200 to 300,[41] but it would have been quite feasible to bring it up to a strength of 500, the figure Pausanias mentions, at the time of the Celtic invasion. Cybernis' decree makes no mention of the fleet; its participation was evidently invented by a later writer who wished to create a further parallel with the events of 480.

We see that at most 1,500 Athenians fought with the Greek forces, which must have numbered about 25,000 altogether, commanded by Aetolian rather than Athenian generals. No doubt the Athenians acquitted themselves well, and Cydias particularly distinguished himself; but the brunt of the fighting was borne by the Aetolians and Phocians.

39. *IG* II².680. This family with members named Cydias and Cybernis from the deme of Halimus is well known.

40. *FD* III.2.159.

41. *ISE* 16. See also G. Bugh, *The Horsemen of Athens* (Princeton 1988) 186–188.

Thus while the last-ditch defense of Delphi does not constitute a high point of Athenian history, it was a heroic moment for Greece, remembered as such for centuries not only on the mainland but also in the Greek communities of Asia Minor. The same fierce Celts, who became known there as "Galatians" or Gauls, attacked them only a year later. The Spartans did not participate in the defense of Delphi; Areus, their king, had wanted to drive the Aetolians out of Delphi himself only the previous year.

Their shared victory in an hour of great danger brought the Athenians and the Aetolian League even closer. At this point after a long absence the Athenian delegate resumed his seat at the meetings of the Amphictionic Council, if he had not already done so before. The main Athenian participants in the Soteria at Delphi were the festival guild artists, and it is no accident that in 277 they were granted valuable privileges by the Amphictionic Council, including dispensation from taxes and immunity from arrest throughout Greece.[42]

The Gauls were driven out of Macedonia only two years after the battles at Thermopylae and Delphi, a fact fraught with consequences for Athens. After Ptolemy Keraunos was killed fighting the Gauls, his brother Meleager managed to hold on to the throne for only two months, while Cassander's nephew Antipater reigned for only forty-five days in 279, thereby earning himself the nickname "Etesias," roughly "the Dog-Day King." A Macedonian nobleman, Sosthenes, refusing an offer of the crown, took charge of organizing resistance against the Gauls with some success, but he did not survive long either. By the fall of 278 Macedonia was in a state of anarchy, and it seems highly improbable that the Gauls had left after their first attack in 280. But then Antigonus Gonatas won a celebrated victory against them at Lysimacheia, surprising them with deceptive tactics, the details of which are not known. This momentous victory freed the country from a scourge and finally brought the long-sought crown of Macedonia to Antigonus, who had been for so long the ruler only of scattered outposts, in essence a "king" without a country. The Athenians must have found it a troubling development: Demetrius' son, who had maintained a garrison in Piraeus for the past ten years, had now firmly established himself as monarch of the country from which his father had been driven out eleven years earlier.[43]

42. *IG* II^2.1132.1–39. The Delphic copy is *FD* III.2.68.61–94.
43. Walbank, *Macedonia* 254–258.

Very soon, however, Antigonus found himself challenged for its possession. In the fall of 275 Pyrrhus, once king of Macedonia himself, returned to Epirus from Italy. The next year he attacked Macedonia, won a signal victory against one of Antigonus' armies and his Celtic mercenaries,[44] and occupied large portions of the country. Clearly, his goal was to regain the crown, but he aroused the wrath of the population when he failed to punish his Celtic mercenaries after their plunder of some royal graves in Aegae (Vergina).[45] Then in 272, threatened on another front by a member of the Spartan royal family, Pyrrhus mounted an assault on Sparta. The city emerged victorious after long and heavy fighting, thanks largely to Antigonus' dispatch of support troops from Corinth. Pyrrhus withdrew from Laconia and by late fall 272 reached Argos to confront Antigonus, who had taken up a position with his army nearby. But Pyrrhus was killed in a street fight, and the pressing danger to Antigonus' crown was removed.

During these campaigns the Athenians had participated with other Greek states in the spring of 272 in an embassy to Pyrrhus, which reached him in Megalopolis in Arcadia on his march toward Laconia.[46] No record of their discussions exists, but almost certainly the Athenians wanted to stay in favor with the king, and perhaps tried to enlist his support for an attempt to drive out Antigonus' occupying forces. Pyrrhus' death put an end to such hopes, and as regaining control over Piraeus remained a vital aim of Athenian policy, events began to drift toward war with Antigonus. It would be upon them within only a few years.

2. Life in the City

Once Athens had freed itself from Demetrius' rule in the spring of 287, the city's most urgent problem for the next several years was procuring adequate food supplies. Not only did the Athenians pass decrees awarding honors to foreign grain merchants (as also occurred at other times)[47] and show recognition to their fellow citizens for service in the same cause;[48] they also turned to foreign rulers for aid. The number of

44. Pausanias 1.13.2–3; Plut. *Pyrrhus* 26.10; *AP* 6, no. 130; *Historische griechische Epigramme* (Bonn 1926), no. 94.
45. Walbank, *Macedonia* 259–267; N. G. Hammond, *ABSA* 86 (1991) 79.
46. Justinus 25.4.4.
47. *IG* II².651 and 670; see also G. Marasco, *Athenaeum* 62 (1984) 286–294.
48. *IG* II².698 and 792.

Athenian delegations who visited foreign courts to plead for grain during these years is quite striking, as well as the number of these rulers mentioned or honored as donors.[49]

Presumably this question of survival, the reestablishment of diplomatic relations with various powers, and the reorganization of national defense (for which the city was again itself responsible) absorbed much of Athens' energies and financial resources for a number of years. The Great Panathenaea of 286 had to be canceled, and the festivities did not resume until 282. Another festival created in the year 284/3 clearly belongs in the same context of national liberation. This celebration was the work of the poet Philippides, chosen as director of the dramatic competitions that year. Philippides not only paid all the expenses (usually covered by the public treasury) out of his own pocket but also created an additional competition in honor of Demeter and Kore to commemorate the return of independence.[50] Not long afterward, sometime between 283 and 270, the number of tragedies competing at the Greater Dionysia increased by one; this innovation, unlike Philippides', was intended to be permanent.[51] The citizenry turned its attention to religious and cultural affairs as soon as the most urgent problems of survival were under control. The main festivals of the year 282/1 must have been particularly splendid, for there was not one *agonothetes* that year, but two, both members of distinguished families: Phaedrus of Sphettos, who served at other times as a general and an ambassador (and brother of Callias, who frequently held high office himself); and Glaucon, brother of Chremonides. The decree later honoring Phaedrus bestows high praise on his management of the sacrifices and the competitions.[52] For Glaucon no such decree has been found, at least not in his home city, but he was well known far beyond the borders of Attica as a victor in the four-horse chariot race at the Olympic Games, and as a consul *(proxenos)* of Delphi, Rhodes, and

49. The list includes Ptolemy I (*IG* II².682.28–30), Ptolemy II (*Hesperia Suppl.* 17 [1978] 3, lines 47–55), Lysimachus (*IG* II².657.33–36), Spartocus of Bosporus (*IG* II².653), Audoleon of Paeonia (*IG* II².654), as well as officials of both Ptolemy I (*IG* II².650) and Audoleon (*IG* II².655).

50. *IG* II².657.38–45. Another *agonothetes,* Eurycleides of Cephisia, did the same thing two generations later to celebrate another liberation from Macedonian rule (*IG* II².834.23–24).

51. This new competition is not mentioned in the decree honoring Philippides (*IG* II².657) and is first documented in the decree honoring Callias (*Hesperia Suppl.* 17 [1978] 4, lines 92–94). D. Peppas-Delmousou, *Acts (Praktika) of the 8th International Congress for Greek and Latin Epigraphy* (Athens 1984) 65–67.

52. *IG* II².682.53–56.

Orchomenus in Arcadia; later he was honored by the Hellenes assembled at Plataea, and Ptolemy III erected a statue of him at Olympia.[53]

The decrees passed by the Athenian Assembly in the early third century frequently mention military forces. The new democratic regime of 307 had greatly altered the corps of ephebes, which provided military training for young men, by transforming it from a compulsory into a voluntary organization and reducing the time of service from two years to one. These reforms may have resulted from a basic decision of the state to cut support for the ephebes' equipment and living expenses and to require them to defray these costs themselves, in part if not in full. Scholars now believe that the ephebes entering the corps in the year 306 served under the new regulations, and the rapidly declining numbers of the new cohorts in the following years show that the reform dates from before the turn of the century, that is, from the period of democracy under Demetrius' rule. In the early third century, at some time before the outbreak of the Chremonidean War, the office of the superintendent of the ephebes of his tribe disappears.[54]

The assignment of some *strategoi* to specific areas began in the postclassical era and continued into the early third century. The task of protecting Attica was divided into two commands, one for land defenses based in Eleusis with oversight of the fortresses Panakton and Phyle, and one for the defenses of the coastal area with bases in Sunium and Rhamnus. Perhaps Demochares' recapture of Eleusis between 287 and 270 prompted the innovation.[55] The inscription in honor of Epichares mentioned earlier reveals that the division took place before the Chremonidean War, since he is documented as holding the coastal command in the first year of the war.

Ranking just below the *strategoi* were the twelve taxiarchs, infantry commanders of the twelve tribes. Their counterparts in the cavalry, the phylarchs, took orders not from the infantry generals, the *strategoi*, but from the two hipparchs. Citizens from the ages of eighteen through fifty-nine were expected to bear arms, forty-two year-classes in all

---

53. The documentation is cited by Habicht, *Gottmenschentum* 32 n. 20. Since then the decree of the Hellenes for him has come to light; *BCH* 99 (1975) 51–75.

54. O. Reinmuth, *The Ephebic Inscriptions of the Fourth Century B.C.* (Leiden 1971) 101–102, 115, and 121; P. Gauthier, *Chiron* 15 (1985) 151–161; C. Habicht, *ZPE* 93 (1992) 47–49. The *sophronistai* are documented for 303/2 but have disappeared by 267/6.

55. For Epichares see note 29 above; for the division into two commands see Habicht, *Studien* 43–44. Aphidnon was also part of the coastal command; *Praktika* (1990 [1994]) 21–24, no. 1.

including the ephebes; the number of year-classes called up at a given time depended on the urgency of the threat. As a rule, some tribes' regiments *(taxeis)* would be assigned to secure fortresses, while others were deployed as regular infantry. For a ten-year period from the early third century we have five decrees honoring all the taxiarchs of a given year: one in 281/0, two in 276/5, and one each in 275/4 and 272/1. Two of these decrees were proposed in the Assembly by the same man, Leon, son of Cichesias of Aixone, a member of a prominent Athenian family that played an especially active role in military affairs in the Hellenistic age.[56]

During this period, in 282/1, the strength of the cavalry was increased from 200 to 300 and the election of phylarchs regulated by a new law. The cavalry corps (increased to a strength of 500 on this particular occasion) joined the elite infantry troops in repelling the Celts.[57] Each member of the corps had to provide his own horse, but the state offered loans for the purchase of a horse and paid a part of the maintenance as long as the animal passed the annual inspection. Despite this government assistance, however, only the well-to-do could afford to serve in the cavalry, probably the same elite group that continued to join the corps of ephebes after its reform. Occasionally the members of the cavalry awarded honors to their commanding officers, the hipparchs and phylarchs; this occurred in 281/0, 187/6 (on the motion of another Cichesias from the family in Aixone mentioned above), and again around 160.[58] After Athens regained control of Lemnos through the goodwill of Seleucus, another hipparch was stationed there; one of the first was Comeas, an officer later honored for his service by the entire citizenry.[59]

The evidence indicates that maintaining and improving the city's defenses continued to be a priority. The strongly nationalistic tone of Assembly decrees from this time up to the decree of Chremonides around 268 supports this assumption. After the costly failed attempt to drive out the Macedonian garrison at Munychia in 287, Athenian

---

56. *ISE* 15; *IG* II².685; *Hesperia* 2 (1933) 156, no. 5; *ISE* 18. On the family of Leon and Cichesias see Habicht, *Studien* 194–197. More recent documents are still unpublished.

57. *ISE* 16 documents the increase in cavalry strength. For more on the *epilektoi* see P. Roussel, *RA* 2 (1941) 220–222; L. Tritle, *Ancient History Bulletin* 3 (1989) 54–59. For the Athenian cavalry of this period see esp. J. H. Kroll, *Hesperia* 46 (1977) 83–140; and Bugh, *Horsemen* 184–206.

58. The documentation for the decree of 281/0 is *ISE* 16; for that of 187/6, *AM* 76 (1961) 127, no. 1; and for that of ca. 160, *AD* 18 (1963) 107.

59. *IG* II².672 and (from a second copy) *Hesperia* 10 (1941) 338.

policy still aimed above all else at regaining Piraeus and the fortresses[60] or, to put it another way, at reunifying the city and the harbor.[61] At least four men active in politics in this period received the highest honors the citizenry could award, namely a statue and the right to take meals at public expense. (The latter honor, inherited by the eldest son in the male line, stayed in the family.) Demosthenes received this honor posthumously in 280/79, on a motion introduced by his nephew Demochares, and after Demochares' death, his son Laches proposed him for an award in 271/0. The poet Philippides and Callias of Sphettos received awards during their lifetimes, in the fall of 283 and the winter of 270/69 respectively.[62] Since Demosthenes had been ostracized and then committed suicide with Antipater's hired killers on his heels, the city's decision to rehabilitate and honor him was tantamount to a declaration of war against Macedonia.

In all four decrees the honorees were celebrated as leaders in the struggle for democracy and identified as victims of an oligarchy. After the democratic constitution fell, they were forced into exile and their property confiscated. The motion submitted to the Council (and later approved) even claims that Demochares was the only politician of his generation never to have given his support to an antidemocratic movement. As people saw it then, democracy had been suspended not only between 322 and 318, but also under Demetrius of Phalerum from 317 to 310, and during the second regime of Demetrius, between 294 and 287. Moreover, Philippides accused Stratocles, whose policies had driven him into exile in 304 or 303, of having destroyed democracy.[63] In fact the term "democracy" had become a matter of interpretation, since political leaders claimed they represented democracy even in times when citizenship depended on a new census figure for which many Athenians would no longer qualify. For this reason their opponents, the "genuine" or radical democrats, would occasionally expand their definition of the term to clarify exactly what they understood by it: "democracy that includes all Athenians."[64]

---

60. *IG* II^2.657.35–36, from late summer 283.

61. *ISE* 14.28–30, from the winter of 282/1.

62. [Plut.] *mor.* 850F–851C (Demosthenes; cf. *P.Oxy.* 1800, fr. 3, col. 2.29–39); 851D–F (Demochares); *IG* II^2.657 (Philippides). *Hesperia Suppl.* 17 (1978) (Callias). Cf. also Habicht, *Studien* 124–127; and Gauthier, *Cités* 79–89.

63. Philippides, *PCG* 8.347 F 25.

64. In the decree for Callias, *Hesperia Suppl.* 17 (1978) 4, lines 81–83: "His actions never contravened the laws or the principles of a democracy that includes all citizens." Further examples are in Habicht, *Untersuchungen* 28 n. 48.

It has often been assumed that even the philosopher Epicurus was affected by the dominant nationalist and anti-Macedonian mood of the times, since in a letter of 283/2 he was believed to have expressed a wish for the destruction of "the detested Macedonians." Some scholars find this outspoken statement of a political opinion either offensive or contradictory, for Epicurus' own doctrine taught that the wise man should remain aloof from politics and state affairs. Others argue that the rejection of political activity in principle did not mean total "flight" or "escape" from the world around or a ban on holding opinions.[65] However, a recent revision of the text, which has come down to us in the form of a fragmentary, not easily decipherable papyrus, indicates that the letter contains no such statement and even casts doubt on the identity of the writer.[66]

The scarcity of source material from this era does not allow a clear picture of the Athenian political scene; we do not even know the names of all the leading politicians, much less the kind of men they were. Olympiodorus, the hero of the liberation of 287, clearly played a leading role, as did Demochares after his return from exile. The brothers Phaedrus and Callias of Sphettos were also important figures (whenever the latter was not in the service of the Ptolemies), along with the brothers Chremonides and Glaucon of Aethalidae.[67] Other known political leaders are Callippus of Eleusis and Aristeides of Lamptrai, both of whom served as ambassadors to Orchomenus in Arcadia. Callippus had previously served as commander of the Athenian troops sent to assist in the defense of Delphi, and was one of two Athenian delegates in the council of allies during the Chremonidean War.[68] Others who introduced important bills in the Assembly,[69] represented

---

65. Most recently H. Steckel, "Epikuros," *RE Suppl.* 11 (1968) 591, with further literature.

66. T. Dorandi, *CronErc* 12 (1982) 99 (text) and 112 with n. 94 (commentary).

67. For Glaucon, see note 53 above. For Chremonides, see below. Eteocles, their father, had already been honored by the state with a statue (*IG* II^2.3845).

68. C. Habicht, *Chiron* 6 (1976) 7–10.

69. Euchares of Conthyle, the man entrusted with drawing up the revised law code toward the end of the fourth century (*IG* II^2.487), introduced the motion honoring Callias in 270/69; Epicharmus of Colonae introduced two decrees in 286/5 and 276/5; Eubulus of Melite introduced two further bills in 271/0, and Leon of Aixone has already been mentioned (see note 56 above). Others who introduced motions are revealed as members of the elite, since they belong to families whose members served as *trierarchs* in the later fourth century, including Niceratus of Cephale (Davies, *APF* 14239), Phytius of Thorikos (Davies, *APF* 367, no. 9667), and Agyrrius of Collytus (Davies, *APF* 279, no. 8157).

Athens on missions to royal courts or foreign governments,[70] or held important offices at home such as director of festival competitions,[71] certainly belonged to the political elite of this time.

Better known than the politicians of the time are certain outstanding figures of the intellectual and literary life of Athens, both citizens and foreign residents. A number of them died during this period. Menander perished—while swimming, tradition has it—in 292/1, when Athens was still under Demetrius' rule. Around the time of liberation, in 288/7 or 287/6, came the death of the Peripatetic philosopher Theophrastus, followed ten years later by that of Metrodorus, Epicurus' closest associate. Crantor, a philosopher of the Academy, died in 276/5; Epicurus and probably Straton, head of the *Peripatos,* in 271/0; and finally Polemon, the head of the Academy, in 270/69. Polemon's successor at the Academy, Crates, died during the Chremonidean War, and a year after its end, in 262, the Stoa lost its founder, Zeno.[72]

During that period, and especially in the decade from 270 to 260 (approximately the time of the Chremonidean War), scholars have noted a shift in the practice and teaching of philosophy in all the various schools.[73] While interest in the natural sciences fell sharply, and dialectics almost ceased to be taught, epistemology grew to be regarded as the fundamental problem of philosophy, with skepticism a dominant tendency. Practical ethics continued to be a widely discussed subject pertinent to daily life. The practice of citing the doctrines taught by a founder grew increasingly common, particularly in the school of Epicurus and the Stoa of Zeno. The neglect of speculative thought and empirical research led to a crisis in philosophy, since philosophers had lost the naive faith in constant human progress that had motivated Aristotle in his youth.

During the war literature lost the comic playwright Philemon,[74] and

---

70. Besides Demochares, Phaedrus, Callias, Callippus, Glaucon, and Aristeides, e.g., the *hipparch* Comeas of Lamptrai, ambassador to Seleucus I in 281/0 (see note 59 above).

71. Besides Philippides, Glaucon, Phaedrus, and his son Thymochares, e.g., Thrasycles of Dekeleia (Davies, *APF* 7341), Deinias of Erchia (Davies, *APF* 3163, where the source for the *agonothesia* of 266/5 has been overlooked: *Hesperia* 37 [1968] 284, no. 21), and Theophanes of Euonymon in 270/69 (*IG* II^2.3081–82 and 3851).

72. The only problematic dates are those of the deaths of Crantor and Polemon; see T. Dorandi, *Filodemo, Storia dei filosofi: Platone e l'academia* (Naples 1991) 56–58; for all others see idem, *Ricerche*.

73. This passage is based on P. Steinmetz, *Antike und Abendland* 15 (1969) 122–134.

74. *PCG* 7.222 T 6.

after the war Antigonus put to death the noted local historian Philochorus. How long Timaeus of Tauromenium, the historian who lived in Athens, survived after completing his account of Greek civilization in the western Mediterranean in 265/4, is unknown.[75] In any event, the deaths that occurred during these years left such gaps in the ranks of leading Athenian intellectuals that one may justifiably conclude that Athens' defeat in the war coincided with the end of a cultural era.[76] With Philochorus' death ended not just the writing of local history, but the chronicling of Athenian political history altogether.[77]

3. The Chremonidean War

Four years after the Athenians had attempted to oppose Antigonus of Macedonia by joining forces with his enemy Pyrrhus, they formed a strong new alliance and declared war.[78] Already in ancient times the conflict was known as the Chremonidean War, since the immediate cause of the outbreak of hostilities was a decree from the archonship of Peithidemos (still in existence) declaring an alliance with Sparta, proposed by the Athenian Chremonides of the deme of Aethalidae. Although Antigonus was clearly not the instigator, but the attacked party, it is less clear which of the allies took the initiative. The three strongest powers of the larger alliance were Egypt under Ptolemy II Philadelphus, Sparta under Areus I (who had fought on Antigonus' side against Pyrrhus as recently as 272), and Athens. Chremonides' decree reveals that both Sparta and Athens had formed an alliance with Ptolemy before concluding their own direct pact, a circumstance that

75. For Philochorus and Timaeus see Chapter 4, Section 4.

76. Walbank, *Macedonia* 287.

77. F. Jacoby, *Atthis: The Local Chronicles of Ancient Athens* (Oxford 1949) 108–111. He says, among other things, that "the scholar Philochoros found successors, but the historian did not."

78. A representative view of the subject is H. Heinen's detailed account, *Untersuchungen zur hellenistischen Geschichte des 3. Jahrhunderts v. Chr.* (Wiesbaden 1972) 95–213. Older accounts include Will, *Histoire* 1: 219–233; and Walbank, *Macedonia* 276–289. I concur with these scholars in assuming here that Peithidemos' year as eponymous archon was 268/7 (IG II^2.1534.145 is of no consequence for the chronology, since, as S. Aleshire has demonstrated, this text does not refer to the archon [*The Athenian Asklepieion* (Amsterdam 1989) 293–298], and that King Areus was killed sometime in 265/4. However, T. Dorandi has argued convincingly that the archon Antipatros, during whose term Athens capitulated, served in 263/2 and not in 262/1; *Ricerche* 23–28.

makes Ptolemy a likely actual initiator of the war. At the same time the decree strikingly emphasizes the wishes of Ptolemy's sister and consort, Arsinoë II, to liberate the Greek states from Macedonia. That statement recently acquired more weight when it emerged that Arsinoë died not in 270, as previously assumed, but less than two months before passage of the decree, on 1 or 2 July 268.[79] The tenor of this passage goes well beyond a mere gesture of posthumous respect. Quite likely the king was under her influence almost up to the start of the war.

The royal couple probably viewed the growing strength of Macedonia with concern, especially its intensive efforts under way to enlarge the fleet. Antigonus had strong bases and excellent harbors in Demetrias, Chalcis, Piraeus, and Corinth, and his occupation of Acrocorinth gave him control over the land bridge of the isthmus. Numerous cities on the Peloponnese were ruled with Antigonus' support by tyrants who not only blocked the attempts by Areus of Sparta to expand his territory and influence, but also perpetuated an undemocratic form of government regarded as outdated and hated by the Greeks. Finally Athens strove for twenty years to regain full sovereignty over its territory, not only Piraeus first and foremost, but also several fortresses. With military aid from the two kings the Athenians hoped finally to attain this goal. My earlier assumption that Athens was the driving force toward what was chiefly an "Athenian war" may go too far, but the fact that Sparta had entered into an alliance with Ptolemy before making a pact with Athens does not refute it, because the same holds true for Athens itself.

Thus, although the goals of the allies may have differed on essential points, they could all be achieved only through the weakening of Macedonia; a common enemy brought and kept them together. Possibly Athens' decision to ally itself with Sparta was triggered by Antigonus' siege of Eretria on Euboea.[80] Almost all the Peloponnesian states allied themselves with Athens and Sparta: Elis, the half-dozen cities of the new Achaean League (refounded in 280), the Arcadian cities of Mantinea, Orchomenus, Phigalia, and Caphyae, and several towns in Crete with ties to Sparta. Quite probably Athenian diplomats were active in persuading a number of these cities to join the coalition

79. E. Grzybek, *Du calendrier macédonien au calendrier ptolémaïque* (Basle 1990) 103–112. For Arsinoë's role in the events leading up to the war, see H. Hauben, *Studia Hellenistica* 27 (1983) 114–119.

80. D. Knoepfler, *BCH* 117 (1993) 339–341 and 119 (1995) 141–144.

(as Demosthenes and others had done in 323), and the award of honors by the city of Orchomenus to three influential Athenian politicians during the same period raises this likelihood to a virtual certainty.[81] The three recipients were Glaucon, brother of Chremonides; Aristeides of Lamptrai, known to have served as *strategos* in 290/89; and Callippus of Eleusis, previously commander of the Athenian troops who faced the Celts in 279. Callippus, and probably Glaucon as well, were elected as the two Athenian delegates to the allies' joint council of war when hostilities broke out.

Chremonides' bill,[82] proposing to add an alliance with Sparta to the existing alliance with Ptolemy, was passed by the Assembly in the summer of 268, on the forty-first day of the Attic year (which began in July). The text of the pact is appended to the bill. It states that the aim of the alliance is the general liberation of Greece, to be achieved in a joint campaign with Ptolemy. The opponent is not specifically named, but the treaty does mention past campaigns against the Persians in which Athens and the Peloponnesians had been comrades-in-arms in the cause of Greek freedom. Thus the king of Macedonia is indirectly branded as a new Xerxes.

Hostilities began within the year of Chremonides' bill, as revealed by a decree passed by the Athenian deme of Rhamnus for the general Epichares.[83] The decree adds important contemporary information to the extremely meager accounts of later writers. We learn, for example, that pirates fought on the side of the Macedonian king (something that had occurred in earlier wars). But more important, the decree tells us that Patroclus, one of Ptolemy's generals, landed in Attica with an army and tried to offer the Athenians more effective support than was previously assumed on the basis of the old sources. Almost simultane-

81. *ISE* 53; Habicht, *Chiron* 6 (1976) 7–10.

82. *IG* II^2.686–687; now *StV,* no. 476; Heinen, *Untersuchungen* 117–142.

83. B. C. Petrakos, *AD* 22 (1967) 38–52; emended text in Heinen, *Untersuchungen* 152–154. There is a new fragment in *Praktika* (1985 [1990]) 9 and 13–14. See further D. Knoepfler, *BCH* 117 (1993) 327–341. In the year of the archon Peithidemos, Epichares was *strategos* for the coastal district and defended it and the fortress of Rhamnus during the war (lines 5–7). Stone-shot (for catapults) recently discovered in Rhamnus offers evidence that it was stormed or besieged by the Macedonian army (Petrakos, *Ergon* 39 [1992] 5). The existence of a state of war in the following year 267/6 is documented by *IG* II^2.665.8; see also the decree in *Hesperia* 59 (1990) 545. For Rhamnus in 263/2, the last year of the war, see *IG* II^2.1217, with *Praktika* (1991) 37–39, no. 13.

ously, new archeological evidence on the Koroni Peninsula confirmed this new information.

On the east coast of Attica between Rhamnus and Sunium, American archaeologists came across the remains of a camp that showed signs of hasty construction. It had been built by an army that arrived by water and expected an attack by land, but as the findings showed, it did not stay long. Of the several dozen coins found there, twenty-four, more than three-quarters of the total, dated from the reign of Ptolemy II; the most recent had been minted either in 267/6 or 265/4. All indications suggested that this was the camp erected by Patroclus' troops during the Chremonidean War. The only obstacle to this dating arose from the pottery fragments, which appeared to be about twenty years older. But the other evidence seemed so convincing that scholars reexamined the chronology of Athens' Hellenistic pottery; the result was a general lowering of previously accepted dates.[84] The presence of Ptolemy's troops in Koroni during the war can be considered as certain. Ptolemaic soldiers from this era left traces in other parts of Attica as well, such as Vuliagmeni on the west coast halfway between Piraeus and Sunium, in Rhamnus, and also in Heliupolis, surprisingly close to the city. The alliance with Ptolemy and the presence of royal troops are also reflected in a series of Athenian coins minted during the war that conform to the Ptolemaic standards of weight and correspond to Ptolemaic coin types; they were produced for at least three years.[85]

However, although Ptolemy's army under Patroclus' command had a more active role and came closer to Athens than was previously assumed, it could not save the city. Clearly, Antigonus' forces surrounded Athens right after the outbreak of war. According to Patroclus' own estimate, his troops were too weak to relieve the besieged inhabitants alone; his plan was to have the Spartans attack the enemy

84. E. Vanderpool, J. R. McCredie, and A. Steinberg, *Hesperia* 31 (1962) 26–61 and 33 (1964) 69–75; McCredie, *Hesperia Suppl.* 11 (1966). Several points in their findings have been modified by H. Lauter-Bufe, *Marburger Winckelmannsprogramm* (1988) 67–102. A report on the work leading to a modification in the chronology of Attic pottery of this period is given by S. Rotroff in H. A. Thompson and D. B. Thompson, *Hellenistic Pottery and Terracottas*, ed. S. Rotroff (Princeton 1987) 4–6 and 183–184.

85. McCredie, *Hesperia Suppl.* 11 (1966) 30–32 (Vuliagmeni); E. Varoucha, *AE* 1953–54, part III (1961) 321–349. All the relevant sites are clearly marked on the map in Walbank, *Macedonia* 281. Coins of Ptolemy II have also been found in Rhamnus (*Ergon* 39 [1992] 5). For the Athenian minted 5-obol coins, see Kroll, *Coins* 11.

from the front, approaching on land by way of Eleusis, while his forces attacked from the rear. Athens' fate was sealed when the planned combined operation never took place. Areus of Sparta advanced several times toward Attica, but he was stopped either at the isthmus or before reaching the Thriasian plain. On his last advance in 265/4 a battle took place near Corinth in which the Spartans were defeated by Antigonus and Areus himself was killed.[86]

Athens held out for a long time, with or without further aid from Ptolemy. The Athenians may have won a reprieve because Pyrrhus' son Alexander invaded Macedonia and forced Antigonus to return to defend his own country. This may even have led to a temporary truce. But when Antigonus, having defeated Alexander, resumed the siege, Athens' situation became critical. The king destroyed the shrine of Poseidon Hippios ("Lord of Horses") outside the city walls near the Academy, the headquarters of the Athenian cavalry; small as this force was, it could have inflicted considerable damage on the besiegers.[87] Ultimately the city had to capitulate in 263/2, the year of the archon Antipater. Athens had failed to achieve its goals of liberating Piraeus and the fortresses in Macedonian hands at the beginning of the war; as in 295, a royal garrison returned to the city, and other troops occupied the remaining fortresses such as Rhamnus. Antigonus appointed an Athenian citizen to govern the city, just as Cassander had appointed Demetrius of Phalerum fifty-five years earlier. And he chose none other than the grandson and namesake of the previous regent of 317–307.[88]

Whether military operations at sea, about which virtually nothing is known (apart from the rich documentation of Patroclus' activities in the area of certain islands),[89] had any significant influence on events

86. Heinen, *Untersuchungen* 197–202. The hypothesis of C. B. Welles (*Klio* 52 [1970] 477–490) that the Seleucid king Antiochus I sent Gallic mercenaries as support for Antigonus is derived from an epigram from Maroneia (*ISE* 115). Will (*Histoire* 1: 227) and Walbank (*Macedonia* 280 and 282 n. 1) followed him, wrongly, since it has long been recognized that the epigram mentions not the Spartan king Areus, but the god of war Ares; moreover, the text is considerably later than the Chremonidean War.

87. Pausanias 1.30.4; P. Siewert, in *Arktouros: Hellenic Studies Presented to Bernard M. W. Knox* (Berlin 1979) 280–289.

88. The sources have been assembled with commentary in *StV*, no. 477. Cf. further Habicht, *Studien* 13–20.

89. M. Launey, *REA* 47 (1945) 33–45. In addition to the sources named by Launey we now have the "Epichares" inscription from Rhamnus (above, note 83); the archaeological finds in Koroni, Vuliagmeni, and Heliupolis; and the honors awarded to Patroclus in Samos

and the outcome of the war is not at all clear. In particular, the date of a naval victory by Antigonus against Ptolemy's fleet off the island of Cos either at the end of the Chremonidean War or in the next decade (255) is in doubt.[90]

As long as scholars believed that Athens was under Antigonus' rule at the start of the war, it was justifiable to see the city's entry into a coalition against him as an act of rebellion.[91] But since it has become clear that Athens was independent and self-governing after 287 (though not in control of all parts of Attica), characterization of the Chremonidean War as "the Greek revolt led by Athens and Sparta" seems rash.[92] All the participating Greek states were independent of Macedonia when they entered the conflict. They fought not for their own freedom, but rather for the freedom of other Greeks who indeed were under Macedonian rule. This does not mean the Athenians had no interests of their own to pursue at the same time; they certainly did, but their activity cannot be called a rebellion or a revolt.

Very little documentary evidence from the war years has survived in Athens. A statue of Chremonides must have been erected on the Acropolis either shortly before the war broke out or in its early stage; to place a monument there, an Assembly decree was necessary.[93] Apart from the decree of the deme of Rhamnus for Epichares, two Assembly decrees mention the war. The first, from the fall of 266, honors the ephebes of the previous year and their instructors. It relates that "while the war had the city in its grip" the young men carried out all their assignments, which included guard duty and defending the Museum hill.[94] The second decree dates from the winter of 266/5 and awards

---

(*Chiron* 20 [1990] 67–68, no. 2). The islet Gaidaronisi opposite Cape Sunium was called "Patroclus' Island" after Ptolemy's commander (Pausanias 1.1.1) and undoubtedly served as one of his bases. Similarly, a group of small islands in the Saronic Gulf were called "Pelops' Islands" after another high-ranking officer of Macedonian nationality serving under Ptolemy in this period (Pausanias 2.34.9).

90. See K. Buraselis, *Das hellenistische Makedonien und die Ägäis* (Munich 1982) 146–151, with the voluminous literature. See also G. Reger, *AJAH* 10 (1985 [1993]) 155–171.

91. Ferguson, *HA* 137 and 187.

92. Walbank, *Macedonia* 280. A. Momigliano uses the term *ribellione; Terzo contributo alla Storia degli Studi Classici e del Mondo Antico* (Rome 1966) 31.

93. *ISE* 21.

94. *IG* II^2.665.8–13. The same corps of ephebes and its *kosmetes* Ameinias is honored by the Council in *IG* II^2.3210, if Aleshire's identification of Nicias as the eponymous archon of this year is correct (*Asklepieion* 79).

honors to the metic Strombichus, once an official of Demetrius. A member of the royal garrison in the city at the time of the uprising in the spring of 287, Strombichus had gone over to the Athenian side and taken part in Olympiodorus' storming of the Museum hill. In the Chremonidean War he again fought on the side of the citizens, who in gratitude awarded him Athenian citizenship.[95]

A further surviving decree was passed not by the Athenian Assembly but by the citizen soldiers stationed in Eleusis, showing that an Athenian force was still occupying the fortress in 267/6.[96] It is impossible to say whether direct communication between Eleusis and Athens still existed at that point, or whether the region around the fortress was largely under Macedonian control. Two decrees of the Assembly dating from the first phase of the war reveal only that the times were unusual. The first, from 266/5, mentions the normal annual sacrificial offerings by the eponymous archon for the welfare of the Council and the city, but it contains an unusual addition: sacrifices for the safety of the crops in the rural part of the country were included in the archon's dedications, since the harvest was endangered by the presence of foreign troops on Attic soil that year.[97] The other text, of slightly earlier date, namely March or April 266, honors two religious officials (and was introduced in the Council by the brother of one of them, serving a term as councillor); appended to the usual phrases about offerings to the gods for the Council and the people are the words "and for the friends well disposed toward the people." The expression must refer above all to Athens' allies.[98] A list of officials for 266/5 makes no reference to wartime, but it has not survived in its entirety. The list does reveal that the festival of the Great Panathenaea was celebrated in the summer of 266.[99] And the resolution of a private group devoted to

95. *IG* II[2].666 and 667.

96. *IG* II[2].1272.

97. *IG* II[2].668.8–10. Similarly, one of Epichares' chief tasks as *strategos* in 268/7 was to ensure the safety of the farmers in his command area as they brought in the harvest (lines 10–12 of the above-mentioned inscription). Callias, under similar conditions in 287, was equally concerned to rescue the harvest before the enemy could seize it. Two unpublished decrees from Rhamnus also illustrate the efforts of the generals in charge to secure the harvest, one dating from the war of 307–302, the other from the war between Antigonus Gonatas and his nephew Alexander of Corinth (Chapter 6, Section 2).

98. *IG* II[2].661.17–19. The same formulaic phrase occurs in *IG* II[2].690.1–3 and is dated to approximately the same time by Kirchner ("ca. 262/1").

99. *Hesperia* 37 (1968) 284, no. 21.

the cult of the god Ammon, passed in the first month of the last year of the war, reads as if it were written in the most peaceful of times.[100] Despite this negative evidence the country was at war; the military conflicts of antiquity, however, were usually far removed from the totality of modern warfare.

100. *IG* II^2.1282.

SIX

Renewed Subjugation
(262–229)

1. The Royal Governor

Defeated in the war against Macedonia, Athens lost its independence, falling under the rule of Antigonus Gonatas, son of the King Demetrius who had deposed the regent Demetrius of Phalerum in 307. After Demetrius' defeat at the battle of Ipsus in 301, the Athenians had prevented him from returning; in 295 he had regained control of the city, only to lose it again in the uprising of 287. Naturally, Antigonus, mindful of his father's experience, had an interest in establishing firm and lasting control over Attica. The garrison his father had left behind in Piraeus remained loyal to the son when Demetrius was taken captive by Seleucus, and so the harbor had served as a base for Antigonus' operations without interruption since 285. Some Attic fortresses, such as Eleusis and Rhamnus, and perhaps others, had returned into Athenian hands, and a few remained Athenian up to the end of the war. In 262, however, the king's troops reoccupied them. A force of occupation returned to Athens as well, taking up quarters on the Museum hill overlooking the city. Securing military control over Attica was a relatively simple matter after the victory.[1]

The king also had to acquire political control over both the city and the countryside. He certainly succeeded in this aim, for down to the year 229, more than a generation later, the resolutions of the Athenian Assembly, of the Council, and of nongovernmental organs are full of assurances of loyalty to the king and the royal house of Macedonia.

1. For more on the subject see Habicht, *Studien* 13–20 (the city under the rule of the victors).

Before the start of every Assembly session, the *prytaneis* (the rotating committee in charge of the Council that set the Assembly's agenda) dedicated a sacrifice to the gods, asking for their favor toward the Council, the people, the king, the queen, and their children.[2] Awards of honors to *strategoi* appointed by the king or serving under his command stress their loyalty to the ruling dynasty.[3] From these and other indications it is obvious that the king exercised a decisive influence on Athenian politics.

How he did it, on the other hand, is unclear, documented only by a single—and ambiguous—piece of evidence. It dates from more than a century later and stems from Apollodorus, whose chronicle (now lost) was quoted by Philodemus, a scholar from the time of Cicero and Julius Caesar. The passage cited states unequivocally that the city lost its independence in the year of the archon Antipater, who directly preceded Arrheneides, and that occupying troops took up a position on the Museum hill. Then, according to the excerpt, traditional public offices were abolished, and "everything became subject to the will of one man."[4] Evidence from the following years, however, shows that all major offices did continue to exist; they are referred to as functioning in the Assembly decree honoring the recently deceased philosopher Zeno, which was passed in the middle of the year following the capitulation.[5] For this reason it appears that the correct restoration of the decisive passage has not yet been discovered; it cannot refer to the abolition of public offices, but only to a limitation of the officeholders' powers that in fact made all decisions dependent on the will of a single individual. We should probably understand it to mean that this one man had binding authority and could also veto decisions made by subordinate officials.

This means in effect that the king placed one man in charge of supervising Athenian politics, just as Cassander had earlier installed

---

2. See the numerous documents assembled by S. Dow, *Hesperia Suppl.* 1 (1937) 48–50, with additions by Habicht, *Studien* 148 n. 137. Most of these references were expunged in 200 B.C. (see Chapter 8, Section 1), but many stones were overlooked and spared. For one such inscription, an Assembly resolution from 246/5, see *Hesperia* 52 (1983) 52.19–25.

3. *IG* II².677, 1225, 1299; and *ISE* 25.

4. For Apollodorus' text see *FGrHist* 244 F 44, quoted with commentary in Habicht, *Studien* 15–20. The text, restored with slight modifications by Cirillo and M. Gigante, is also in T. Dorandi, *ZPE* 84 (1990) 130.

5. Diog. Laert. 7.10–12; see also C. Habicht, *Bathron: Festschrift H. Drerup* (Saarbrücken 1988) 173–175.

Demetrius of Phalerum as head of the city's government and King Demetrius had given command of Boeotia to the historian Hieronymus. Apollodorus must have spoken of a royal governor, but in his abridged excerpt Philodemus gave neither his name nor his title. Whoever he was, he remained in office only until the mid-250s, for according to Eusebius' chronicle, in 255 the king "gave the Athenians their freedom."[6] The fact that Antigonus withdrew his troops from the city sometime after the war ended should no doubt be viewed in connection with this event.[7] However, the gift of their "freedom" and removal of the Macedonian garrison from the city did not mean that the Athenians were as independent as they had been before the war, but only that the king's exercise of his power had become less visible. Piraeus and the fortresses of Attica were still occupied by his commanders and soldiers, and this fact was sufficient to ensure that the city could pursue no policies contrary to the king's interests. The Athenians may have regained a certain measure of freedom in their contacts with other foreign powers, something apparently not permitted during the royal governor's rule; in any event there is not the slightest evidence of such contacts during those seven years.

The prevailing opinion among scholars is that the king also appointed the archons during that period,[8] although there is no evidence for this either. Why would he have taken the trouble when the powers of all Athenian officials were already limited by the royal governor? For a long time many scholars were also convinced that during the entire period of Macedonian domination, that is, from 262 to 229, the king played a role in the selection of Athenian generals that greatly limited the influence of the general electorate.[9] This view is based on Adolf Wilhelm's reconstruction of a later resolution by the soldiers at Eleusis awarding honors to the *strategos* Demetrius. This view has since been recognized as incorrect, and abandoned in the most recent studies.[10] More likely the king had a strong influence on the choice of *strategoi*

6. Eusebius, *Chronica,* ed. A. Schöne (Berlin 1866) 2: 120.
7. Pausanias 3.6.6.
8. The literature is cited in Habicht, *Studien* 17 n. 19.
9. Ibid., 47–55.
10. Ibid. and Walbank, *Macedonia* 286–287. The inscription is *IG* II^2.1285; for A. Wilhelm's reading see (1925) 36 in *Akademieschriften* 1: 496.

for Athens only in the years in which the governor ruled under the laws of the military occupation. A single instance is documented.[11]

A report by Hegesander, who wrote about a century after the events under discussion, should probably be interpreted in connection with Apollodorus' reference to the appointment of a royal governor.[12] Hegesander reports that Demetrius of Phalerum, grandson of the regent of the same name appointed by Cassander, lived in a lavish style offensive to many of his fellow Athenians, and was summoned to answer for his conduct before the Areopagus, the council of former archons that functioned as arbiters of moral standards. When he was commander of the cavalry *(hipparch)* and led the cavalry parade during the Panathenaea, for example, he allegedly built a viewing stand for his mistress Aristagora of Corinth so tall that it dwarfed the nearby *hermai* (square pillars capped with busts of the god Hermes), and that for the Eleusinia he had built her a throne next to the temple. He threatened to thrash anyone who tried to stop him. Hegesander says further that the speech Demetrius offered in his own defense before the Areopagus was so outspoken and aggressive that he was let off without censure, so that it was the reputation of several judges that suffered damage. Antigonus Gonatas, supposedly impressed by so much independence and firmness, deemed him just the right man to appoint as *thesmothetes*.

The *thesmothetai* in Athens were the six archons "at large" without the specific responsibilities assigned to the eponym, the *basileus* ("king"), and the *polemarchos* ("warlord"). Like all archons they were chosen by lot, one from each tribe, among a previously selected group. The *thesmothetai* had virtually no power. A royal appointment was a violation of the Athenian constitution, but the king knew that Demetrius possessed certain qualities and clearly chose him for that reason. With this appointment the monarch made known his intention to intervene visibly in the government of the city. In this instance the word *thesmothetes* cannot have its normal meaning, and the event must fall in a period when the king could follow or ignore the constitution as he pleased; it would have to be after the city had capitulated and before its "independence" was restored, that is, immediately after Antigonus' victory. I have therefore suggested that Demetrius was the royal gov-

11. *ISE* 22.
12. In Athenaeus 4.167E–F.

ernor between 262 and 255. Instead of assuming the title of *epistates* ("overseer"), however, which would have emphasized the citizens' subservient status, Demetrius adopted the less offensive name of *thesmothetes,* which recalled its original, all-but-forgotten sense of "giver of ordinances."[13]

Support for this supposition has recently emerged from an unexpected quarter. A large pedestal found in Eleusis and known since the eighteenth century, with its inscription in a good state of preservation, was at one time surmounted by a statue of general Demetrius, son of Phanostratus, of Phalerum.[14] The monument was erected by the citizen soldiers of Eleusis, Panakton, and Phyle and was always thought to honor the regent from the time of Cassander, even though these soldiers represented a military command (inland Attica) not created until after 287. Eight wreaths engraved in the base testify to further honors awarded to this Demetrius: by the Council, the people, the deme of Eleusis, and the cavalry. They reveal that Demetrius served both as hipparch (as the younger Demetrius did, according to Hegesander) and at least three times as *strategos,* and that he won chariot races at the Great Panathenaea (in which connection Hegesander again mentions the younger Demetrius) and at the Hermeia and Delia festivals. Stephen Tracy has recognized these inscriptions as the work of a stone carver active in the period 270–235, and thereby shown that the monument honors the younger Demetrius of Phalerum, grandson of the regent (both of whom had fathers called Phanostratus), the one mentioned by Hegesander and appointed as *thesmothetes* by Antigonus.[15] Further evidence shows that this same Demetrius also served, apparently somewhat later, as a member of the Council and treasurer of the *prytaneis.*[16]

Thus, it appears that two different kings of Macedonia appointed a member of the same Athenian family as regent of the city: first Cassander, son of Antipater, and later Antigonus Gonatas, who appointed the grandson of the elder Demetrius of Phalerum, the man his father, Demetrius Poliorcetes, had ousted in 307 and sent to seek refuge with Ptolemy, the sworn enemy of the Antigonid dynasty.

Some scholars have assumed that the victor imposed further restric-

13. Habicht, *Studien* 17–20.
14. *IG* II^2.2971.
15. S. V. Tracy, *Boiotia antiqua,* vol. 4 (Montreal 1994) 151–161.
16. J. S. Traill, *Hesperia* 47 (1978) 280–282.

tions on the vanquished in the period following the Chremonidean War. However, Ferguson's theory that the institution of *ephebia* was suppressed for a time is obviously incorrect.[17] Just as incorrect was my previous supposition that the office of hoplite general had been abolished at this time and not reinstituted until the liberation of the city in 229, a theory based on the lack of all documentation referring to this office in the relevant period. The dating of the inscription *IG* II^2.1705 was for a time a matter of some controversy, with some scholars favoring 250–240 and others the period immediately following 229. But this inscription, which contains a list of officials, and names Eurycleides of Cephisia as hoplite general, most likely dates from the end of the 240s after all.[18] It is more difficult to determine whether the victorious king revoked the city's right to mint its own coins, as has often been assumed, and how long such a prohibition may have lasted, if it was ever imposed. Athens apparently ceased to mint silver coins for a time after 262, but the reasons for such a hiatus—by no means unique in the history of Attic coinage—are completely unknown. In any event there is no firm evidence to show that Antigonus suppressed the production of coins in Athens for any length of time.[19] The need for money was filled after the Athenian defeat by the king's own silver and bronze coins, many of which were in circulation at the time; 160 of the bronze coins have been found in the Agora alone.[20]

Of all the Athenian politicians who played a role in events before and during the Chremonidean War, only one is mentioned as present in the city after the war's end, Phaedrus of Sphettos, by then an old man who had served as *strategos* under the tyrant Lachares in 296/5. In the 250s, shortly before or after the end of the military occupation of Athens, the citizens awarded him honors for his forty-year career in politics. His son Thymochares also enjoyed the respect of his fellow citizens and served as *agonothetes* ("director of the games") under the archon Eubulus in 256/5, at about the time his father was honored.[21] Phaedrus was

---

17. See Section 2 below.

18. Habicht, *Studien* 44–47; refuted by S. V. Tracy, *Hesperia* 57 (1988) 314–315.

19. Discussion in Habicht, *Studien* 34–42; for views published since see H. Nicolet-Pierre and J. H. Kroll, *American Journal of Numismatics* 2 (1990) 1–35; and Kroll, *Coins* 12–13, 16, 35–36, and 51–52.

20. Kroll, *Coins.*

21. *IG* II^2.682; Gauthier, *Cités* 77 ff. The eponymous archon of one of the first postwar years (*IG* II^2.700) is more likely to have been this Thymochares rather than his cousin of the same name, who was the son of Callias.

certainly no "Macedonian sympathizer," as many scholars have assumed, but rather an Athenian patriot who understood better than many of his compatriots how to get along under every kind of regime; he was furthermore descended from one of the families whose services the city could always use whenever they did not serve a king, as Phaedrus' brother Callias had done for a long period. Another pair of brothers very active in politics, Chremonides and Glaucon, are mentioned after the war ended, but abroad rather than at home. They had managed to escape before the city fell, and reappear a short time later as advisers and "coadjutors" (paredroi) to Ptolemy II. His successor, Ptolemy III, had a statue erected to Glaucon in Olympia in recognition of his achievements.[22] Inspired by Ptolemy II, sometime after the end of the war the "Hellenes" assembled in Plataea, where they had won their great victory over the Persians in 479. There they celebrated Glaucon as a champion of Greek independence and unity, evoking the memory of the Persian wars in the resolution honoring him; just as previously Chremonides' decree had done, they drew an implicit comparison between the Macedonians and the eastern barbarians.[23] Chremonides fought a naval battle for Ptolemy II against the Rhodians near Ephesus, probably in the 250s, in which he was defeated by the Rhodian admiral Agathostratus.[24]

Although the victorious Macedonian king treated the conquered city harshly, at least in the first few years after their defeat, almost as soon as the fighting stopped he offered posthumous honors to a foreigner who had made his home in Athens fifty years earlier. Zeno, founder of the Stoa, a philosopher whose lectures Antigonus had occasionally attended as a young man and whom he had tried to attract to his court, had died a few months after the war ended, in the fall of 262. When this news reached Antigonus, he suggested to Thraso, an Athenian ambassador at court at that time, that Zeno be awarded honors. The resolution Thraso introduced in the Assembly has survived and begins with the following words: "Whereas Zeno, son of Mnaseas, of Citium

22. Teles[2], ed. O. Hense, p. 23; W. Dittenberger and K. Purgold, Die Inschriften von Olympia (Berlin 1896) 296.

23. BCH 99 (1975) 51–75. For some of the copious literature on this subject see R. Etienne, La Béotie antique (Paris 1985) 259–263; Walbank, Macedonia 277; A. Erskine, The Hellenistic Stoa (London 1990) 89–90.

24. Polyaenus 5.18. The Rhodian admiral is further documented in the inscriptions I Lindos 88.1–2 and IG XI.1128.

was active in our city for many years as a teacher of philosophy, and not only showed himself to be a man of excellent qualities in general, but also exhorted the young men who came to him for instruction to virtuous and rational conduct, teaching them the best principles by serving as a model to them in his own life and actions in perfect harmony with his own doctrines, the people have decided to commend Zeno." The philosopher was honored posthumously with a golden crown and a grave in the state cemetery.[25]

2. A Satellite of Macedonia

The four decades from the outbreak of the Chremonidean War to Athens' liberation from foreign rule in 229 are one of the least known periods in the city's history. There are several reasons for this shortage of information, the most important being the loss of all the writings of contemporary historiographers, and then the loss of political freedom itself. The defeat put an end to Athens' independent diplomatic relations with other states, at other times at least partly reflected in surviving decrees of the Assembly. The definitive work on the history of this period, Phylarchus' history, has not survived. Phylarchus, who was either an Athenian or lived in Athens (like Timaeus of Tauromenium), wrote a history of the Greek world in twenty-eight books, taking up where Hieronymus of Cardia had left off. It began with the last campaign of Pyrrhus in 272 and ended with Antigonus Doson's defeat of Cleomenes of Sparta, a leader Phylarchus admired, in 222 and Cleomenes' death in Alexandria shortly thereafter. Phylarchus' history was continued by Polybius, but in contrast to Polybius' work only random scraps (in the form of quotations) have survived. In these surviving fragments the history of Athens, which must have been covered extensively in the original, does not figure at all.[26]

Another reason for the paucity of material for this period is the fact that the city was once again subject to foreign rule. After the great patriotic upsurge that set in with the liberation of 287 and lasted into the years of the Chremonidean war, their defeat must have had a

25. Diog. Laert. 7.10–12; for Thraso and the king, 7.15.

26. For an edition of the fragments with commentary see F. Jacoby, *FGrHist* 81. See further J. Kroymann, "Phylarchos," *RE Suppl.* 8 (1956) 471–489; P. Pédech, *Trois historiens méconnus* (Paris 1989) 391–493. For the general history without specific citations, see Will, *Histoire* 1: 315–354.

paralyzing effect on the Athenians' spirit and morale. It is no accident that the chronicles of local history known as *Atthides* came to an end at this time. The corps of ephebes, which by the end of the Chremonidean War had been for some time an organization of volunteers, attracted only twenty to forty young men per year in the next three decades. This drastic drop in numbers has been viewed, no doubt correctly, as a consequence of political circumstances and Macedonian policy toward the city.[27] Presumably the only young men who still volunteered were those with ambition (and good prospects) to become *strategoi* one day. Political activities were even more seriously restricted, not only in the first years after the war, when every initiative required the approval of Demetrius, the king's governor, highly unpopular with his fellow Athenians. But even after 255, when the city became officially independent again, the king still dictated foreign policy. The Assembly met as regularly as before but had little or no latitude to make political decisions. Its authority was limited to routine administrative matters such as awards and commendations for officials, members of the Council, ephebes and their instructors, priests and priestesses, and religious officials.[28] Decrees honoring figures in political life virtually ceased to exist, except for recognition of a meritorious citizen's entire career, as in the case of Phaedrus of Sphettos in the 250s.[29] Honors were awarded to foreigners when the king gave his approval or even proposed them himself (as in the case of Zeno). The honorees included officers and other high-ranking officials in the king's service,[30] and in one case a general of the Aetolian League named Charixenus, who received an award in connection with the reorganization of the "festival of deliverance" (Soteria) in Delphi, first established by the Amphictionic Council in 278 and which took place annually or biannually to celebrate the defeat of the Celts; in 246 the Aetolian League turned it into a larger, pan-Hellenic festival held every four years.[31]

27. C. Pélékidis compares the numbers of Athenian ephebes with those of Boeotia and observes, "There is no doubt that the political condition of Athens was definitely inferior to that of Boeotia"; *Ephébie* 167. For the numbers of ephebes in the fourth century (roughly 460–500 per year), see L. Gallo, *ASNP* (1980) 403–412.

28. For a detailed discussion of the subject see Habicht, *Studien* 20–26.

29. *IG* II².682. The initiative for the award came from Phaedrus himself (line 94); Gauthier, *Cités* 83–89.

30. *IG* II².477, 677, and 777.

31. *BCH* 51 (1927) 349, no. 2 from the year 246/5, in connection with *IG* II².680. For this contact between Athens and the Aetolian League to occur, Macedonia and Aetolia had to be on good terms. Cf. G. Nachtergael, *Les Galates en Grèce et les Sôtéria de Delphes* (Brussels 1977) 330 n. 131 and 333.

Several Athenians received similar honors from the Aetolian League in Thermus during this period, at least before the outbreak of the "War of Demetrius" between Macedonia and Aetolia in 239. Two brothers from Bate were honored first, and five more citizens in the following year. Since the awards of the first year went to a pair, those of the second year to a group of three Athenians and another group of two, it appears that all the honorees were members of diplomatic or festival delegations. The editor assigned the relevant inscriptions to the years 239/8 and 238/7, but they could be earlier, from the latter half of the preceding decade.[32] Thus despite evidence of contacts with other states during this time, the Athenian state had no foreign policy as such. Few diplomatic or other links existed between Athens and other states, and those that did either served the interests of the king of Macedonia or at the very least did not run counter to them.[33] And if any awards of Athenian citizenship were made to foreigners during this time, they had become extremely rare.[34]

As far as the organization of the government was concerned, the conventional institutions of democracy such as the Assembly, Council, public officials, and courts continued to exist, but with limitations on their powers incompatible with democratic ideology, even after the royal governor was recalled. It now seems certain that the archons of this period were no longer chosen by lot, but either appointed or (more likely) elected, for a striking number of them have names identical with those of socially prominent men and are presumably the same persons; a lottery could not have achieved such a result, even if it had been preceded by some form of preselection.[35] Recently it has become clear that other normal democratic practices were interrupted or suspended in this period as well, such as the traditional method of selecting a secretary for the Council: clearly, the annual rotation of this office

32. G. Klaffenbach, *IG* IX.1^2.25.37–42, 69–72, and 72–75.

33. *Hesperia* 13 (1944) 246, no. 9, on the cult of Aphrodite Stratonikis in Smyrna. Good relations between Macedonia and Seleucus II (246–226) were a prerequisite for passage of this resolution. See also *IG* II^2.769 + 441, a decree concerned with Rhodians; and *IG* II^2.778–779, on contacts with the city of Lamia in Malis and the Boeotian League (P. Gauthier, *Symbola* [1972] 172 and 337–338).

34. M. J. Osborne assigns three decrees granting citizenship to foreigners (D 87–89) to this period; *Naturalization* 1: 185–189. It is now virtually certain that the first of these pertains to the elder Bithys and must therefore date from the 280s (Chapter 5, note 7). The two others (*IG* II^2.707 and 570) may also be from before 262; see A. S. Henry, in *Owls to Athens: Festschrift K. Dover*, ed. E. M. Craik (Oxford 1990) 182–183.

35. This group included Thymochares, Callimedes, Diomedon, Theophemus, Eurycleides, Mneseides, and Lyceas.

among the twelve tribes in their official order was altered or possibly dispensed with altogether.[36]

A more problematic question is whether the financial administration of Athens was placed on a new footing in 262. According to the traditional view, during the periods of the third century when the democratic constitution was in force, a board of two or more officials supervised city finances, whereas under undemocratic regimes or foreign rule—the two usually went together—oversight and control were in the hands of a single commissioner.[37] Several dozen pieces of evidence of one sort or another supported this view, but the recent discovery of an Assembly decree from the archonship of Polyeuctus (246/5, a year of foreign rule) that mentions a board of finances with several members has cast doubt on it.[38] Since then there have been numerous attempts to preserve the old view and explain away that single deviation from the norm; one (rather unlikely) supposition was that of a short-lived change in political climate.[39] Other scholars have argued that there always was a board of several financial commissioners after 287 and that the decrees refer to it in varying ways, either in the plural (addressing the group) or in the singular (addressing one of its members).[40] This is possible, but difficult to reconcile with the evidence, which is consistent with just a single exception. The question must be left unanswered for the present.

Like the corps of ephebes, the cavalry continued to exist after the war, but in reduced numbers.[41] Although its strength had been increased to 300 in 282/1, the official size of the cavalry corps after the war appears to have been only 200. In recent years a unique find has provided strong evidence for this view and provided many other in-

36. M. J. Osborne, *ZPE* 78 (1989) 209–242. New evidence and new research make it likely that some dates will have to be slightly adjusted, bringing Polyeuktos to 247/6, Diomedon to 245/4, etc. See provisionally J. D. Morgan, *AJA* 100 (1996) 395; and D. Knoepfler, *BCH* 119 (1995) 158–159.

37. This view was propounded by Beloch (*GG* 4.2: 57–58) and has since been supported by further new evidence (Habicht, *Untersuchungen* 70–71).

38. *Hesperia* 52 (1983) 48–63.

39. A. S. Henry, *Chiron* 14 (1984) 74–77 and *ZPE* 72 (1988) 129–136; M. J. Osborne, *ZPE* 78 (1989) 212 n. 9 and 239.

40. J. and L. Robert, *Bulletin épigraphique* (1983) 96–97, no. 153; P. J. Rhodes, in *Tria Lustra: Festschrift J. Pinsent,* ed. H. D. Jocelyn (Liverpool 1993) 1–3; J. Tréheux, *Bulletin épigraphique* (1991), no. 236.

41. For more on the subject see K. Braun, *AM* 85 (1970) 129–269; J. H. Kroll, *Hesperia* 46 (1977) 83–140; G. Bugh, *The Horsemen of Athens* (Princeton 1988) 184–191.

sights into the operation of the cavalry at that time. Hundreds of lead tablets, relics of the annual inspection of cavalry horses by the Council, were discovered in wells in the Cerameicus and in the Agora. The state gave every Athenian cavalryman a loan for the purchase of a horse, and an annual sum for its upkeep as long as the citizen remained with this horse in the corps. In annual inspections the value of each horse was determined—its value fell by 100 drachmas a year on average—and the owner received compensation equal to the last appraised sum (not the purchase price) if the horse was lost. The lead tags give the owner's name (occasionally with an addition to distinguish him from other identically named men), a brief description of the horse, and its appraised value in hundreds of drachmas. The (seldom occurring) minimum was 100 drachmas, and the (arbitrarily fixed) maximum was 1,200. The average value, which lay a little below 700, was significantly higher than it had been in the fourth century, precisely because the cavalry had grown smaller and more exclusive. Many corps members must have owned horses with an actual value far in excess of 1,200 drachmas, meaning that in case of loss, they stood to lose a great deal of their own money.

Archeological evidence and study of the names on the tablets indicate that the owners served in the cavalry between 260 and 240, and that the tablets themselves were all thrown into the wells in the cemetery and the Agora sometime between 240 and 220, when they had ceased to be relevant. The cavalrymen acquired new horses relatively often. Many of their names can also be found in the donors' list of 244/3 and undoubtedly refer to the same individuals.[42]

Antigonus came to Athens more frequently after the war and on such visits stayed in Piraeus, at the house of his governor, Hierocles. Many Athenians thronged to pay their respects to the monarch, but Arcesilaus, the head of the Academy at the time, refused to go, no matter how much his friend Hierocles pressed him. He also refused to send a congratulatory message after the king defeated Ptolemy's fleet (in a battle off Cos or Andros). Arcesilaus did once agree to go to Antigonus' Greek court at Demetrias on the Gulf of Volos as an ambassador for Athens, but failed in his mission.[43]

The city's subjugation by the Macedonian king compelled it to fight

---

42. See Habicht, *Studien* 33.
43. Diog. Laert. 4.39.

on his side whenever he went to war. From 251 Antigonus Gonatas was at war with Alexander, son of his stepbrother Craterus. He had made Alexander his governor over Corinth and Euboea (with the important fortress of Chalcis), but Alexander proved disloyal and assumed command in his own name. The nephew's revolt encouraged several cities in the Peloponnese to rebel against their own tyrants, who were either supported by Antigonus or had been appointed by him. The driving force behind this rebellion was Aratus of Sicyon, who had overthrown Nicocles, the tyrant in his own city, and brought Sicyon into the Achaean League as a member. The league had the most to gain from the democratic opposition to Macedonia; thus it is hardly surprising that it formed an alliance with Alexander. On the other side, the king's allies included Athens and those cities on the Peloponnese, such as Argos under its leader Aristomachus, in which tyrants had been able to retain their hold on power. From two Attic inscriptions—*IG* II².1225, a resolution passed by the Athenians living on Salamis awarding honors to the royal *strategos* Heracleitus (an Athenian citizen himself);[44] and *IG* II².774, honoring Aristomachus of Argos—we know that battles were fought. From the second decree we learn that Alexander offered a truce to Aristomachus in exchange for a sum of money; Aristomachus demanded that the conditions of the truce be broadened to include the Athenians; when Alexander agreed but raised the price by fifty talents, Aristomachus paid the entire sum himself, thereby securing peace for both Argos and Athens.[45] A striking aspect of this document is the fact that the king, without whose approval none of this could have been arranged, receives no mention at all. Another relic of this period is an epigram on a young Athenian named Leon, killed in one of the battles over Salamis. The epigram exhorts his contemporaries to show as much valor as this young man, for Leon showed himself worthy of his "ancestors who [once] slew the Persians" at the same site.[46]

An Athenian resolution passed during the war promises the recipient

---

44. Heracleitus is also the subject of the decree *IG* II².677, which contains proofs of his loyalty to the king. Emended text by W. S. Ferguson, *CP* 24 (1929) 13 n. 1; and A. N. Kondoleon, *Akte des 4. Internationalen Kongresses für Griechische und Lateinische Epigraphik, Wien 1962* (1964) 196–197. An unpublished decree from Rhamnus honoring the coastal commander Archandrus will undoubtedly provide new insights regarding this war. Archandrus succeeded in keeping the Rhamnousia free despite attacks by pirates on the surrounding territory (*Ergon* [1993] 7–8).

45. A. Wilhelm (1925) in *Akademieschriften* 1: 475–494.

46. *ISE* 24.

greater honors commensurate with his merits "as soon as there is peace," the peace referred to being the end of this war in the 240s.[47] Hostilities are still reported for 245/4, but peace was achieved soon thereafter. Not long afterward Alexander died, enabling Antigonus to reseize Corinth. He did not hold the city and fortress long, however, for in 243 a bold attack by the Achaeans under Aratus proved successful. The Achaeans pressed their advantage, and Aratus led a further attack on Attica and Salamis in 242, hoping to force Athens to join their league.[48] The Athenians' need to improve their defenses is reflected in an appeal to the citizens from the spring of 243, calling for contributions "to save the city and secure the countryside."[49] The practical goal of the measure was to ensure that the harvest could be gathered in the coming months. An interesting provision sets the minimum allowable donation at 50 drachmas and the maximum at 200. As was customary, the appeal was addressed to resident foreigners as well as citizens, and among the foreigners who responded was Lyco of Alexandria in Troas, the current head of the Aristotelian school, who appears as "Lyco the philosopher" in the list of contributors.[50]

In the winter of 241/0 Antigonus made peace with the Achaeans. After agreeing to the terms, however, in the spring of 240, the Achaeans (who had returned their Athenian prisoners after the offensive of 242 without demanding ransom in hopes of winning Athens over to their side) attacked Piraeus, still occupied by a Macedonian garrison. This was a clear breach of the peace treaty, and although Aratus tried to lay the blame on a subordinate, he and the Achaeans were discredited.[51]

Antigonus Gonatas died in 239 and was succeeded by his son Dem-

---

47. *IG* II^2.845, interpreted and restored by Wilhelm (1936) in *Akademieschriften* 2: 531–542; and by W. K. Pritchett and B. D. Meritt, *The Chronology of Hellenistic Athens* (Cambridge, Mass., 1940) 104–108. S. V. Tracy's identification of the stone cutter reliably places the inscription between ca. 270 and 234, showing that the peace that is expected soon must refer to the end of hostilities with Alexander; *Hesperia* 57 (1988) 320.

48. Plut. *Aratus* 24.3; R. Urban, *Wachstum und Krise des Achäischen Bundes* (Wiesbaden 1979) 51–54.

49. For the Athenian decree see Habicht, *Studien* 26–33; and L. Migeotte, *Les souscriptions publiques dans les cités grecques* (Québec 1992) 28–34. The man in charge of the military treasury at that time was Eurycleides of Cephisia, the later liberator of 229, who served as hoplite *strategos* in the 240s and as eponymous archon in the 230s.

50. He donated 200 drachmas. In the same period Lyco was honored by the Amphictionic League of Delphi; *FD* III.3 167. Lyco is elsewhere mentioned as an adviser to the Athenians who gave them most valuable service (Diog. Laert. 5.66).

51. Plut. *Aratus* 33. 2–4.

etrius II.[52] Soon after ascending the throne the new monarch, allied by his marriage to Princess Phthia of Epirus with that neighboring kingdom, found himself at war against the newly allied Aetolians and Achaeans. This conflict, known as the "War of Demetrius," broke out in 239 or 238, when Lysias was eponymous archon in Athens,[53] and lasted until the king's death some ten years later. Since Athens was inescapably tied to the king's side, Attica once again became the scene of battles, perhaps to an even greater degree than in the preceding war against Alexander of Corinth. Immediate relief on the northern front, however, came when around 236 the king made allies of Boeotia, which had been completely dependent on the Aetolian League since 245, and the city of Opus in Locris. This move transformed Athens' long-hostile neighbor to the north into a friendly power and led King Demetrius to return full control of the military region of Eleusis (with the fortresses of Eleusis, Panakton, and Phyle) to the Athenians.[54]

To the south, the Achaeans forged alliances with the cities that had traditionally allied themselves with Macedonia. Megara, Troizen, and Epidaurus now gave in to Achaean pressure and joined their league. An attack on Argos led by Aratus failed, but the entrance of Megalopolis in Arcadia into the league in 235 made up for this setback. Aratus, whom the league chose as its *strategos* every other year, kept up the pressure on Athens. He led repeated raids into Attic territory, hoping to pressure the Athenians into joining him and to seize Piraeus with their aid. But with royal Macedonian forces on their soil, the Athenians' hands were tied. At the same time the Aetolians were raiding their coasts.[55] In Rhamnus, the fortress on the east coast, the war caused a shortage of animals for sacrifices, interrupting for a time the offerings for "the festival of Nemesis and the king."[56] As Ludwig Deubner recognized, the veneration of the king was "connected with that of the

---

52. Walbank, *Macedonia* 317–336.

53. *IG* II^2.1299.56–57.

54. *IG* II^2.1299. See Habicht, *Studien* 57–59; and Walbank, who agrees, *Macedonia* 326–327.

55. A state of war existed in 238/7 (the year of the archon Aristion) at any rate, according to *SEG* 24.156.3. Further mention of the war is made in the decree passed by the Attic community of Rhamnus honoring the royal officer (and Athenian citizen) Dikaiarch in the year 236/5; *ISE* 25. The ravages inflicted on the coasts of Attica by the Aetolian Bukris are mentioned in the first Athenian decree honoring Eumaridas of Cydonia (Crete) in 229/8; *IG* II^2.844.4–10.

56. *ISE* 25.27–30.

goddess Nemesis."[57] His insight has been confirmed for a somewhat earlier time by a newly discovered decree of the deme of Rhamnus, which orders "sacrifices to be made to the king [Antigonus Gonatas] on the nineteenth of Hecatombaion, at the gymnastic contest of the Great Nemesia."[58] The decree reveals not only the date of the festival but also the important fact that Antigonus was venerated as a god in this Attic community and by the Athenian state during his lifetime.[59]

Two extremely fragmentary texts of this time also mention Athens' involvement in military combat: the first mentions Antigonus, a war, and "the independence of the Hellenes";[60] the second is an Assembly decree honoring foreign soldiers, clearly mercenaries serving side by side with Athenian forces, to defend the city and the fortresses.[61]

The two surviving Athenian decrees honoring *prytaneis* from the reign of Demetrius—in addition to the traditional sacrifices to Apollo Prostaterios ("the Protecting"), Artemis Boulaia ("of the Council"), and other gods—mention offerings to "the saviors," a term otherwise unknown in such texts. It must refer to the ancestors of the present king, Antigonus and Demetrius Poliorcetes, who were venerated as "saviors" in their lifetimes and whose cult was either reactivated at that time or given particular prominence.[62]

In all these years Demetrius himself had to concentrate on operations in northern Greece and had relatively few forces to send to the Peloponnese. This circumstance made Aratus overconfident, and sometime between 235 and 232 his lack of caution led to a severe defeat at the hands of the royal general Bithys near Phylacia (in Arcadia?). Various rumors reported that Aratus had been either taken prisoner or killed. On hearing a false rumor of his death Diogenes, Demetrius' commander in Piraeus, is supposed to have demanded the surrender of Corinth from the Achaeans. Aratus himself happened to

57. L. Deubner, *Attische Feste* (Berlin 1932) 219 n. 3.

58. *Ergon* (1989) 7–8 (= *Praktika* 1989 [1992] 31, no. 15).

59. Cf. Habicht, *Gottmenschentum* 79–81 and 256–257, where I characterize as "doubtful" the widely held opinion that Antigonus prohibited such veneration of his person; this view, however, has recently been restated by P. Green, *Alexander to Actium* (Berkeley 1990) 835 n. 87. The new decree from Rhamnus is unambiguous and more than an offering "in honor . . . of the sovereign" (P. Roussel on the decree for Dikaiarch, *BCH* 54 [1930] 275), namely an offering to Antigonus the god. See C. Habicht, *SCI* 15 (1996) 131–134.

60. *Hesperia* 30 (1961) 214, no. 9.

61. *IG* II².732, from after 299 according to Tracy, *ALC* 259.

62. *Agora* XV.111.4–5 and 115.12. See V. J. Rosivach, *PP* 42 (1987) 270–274.

be in the city when his messengers arrived, however, and they were made to look ridiculous. The same rumor caused great celebration in Athens, angering Aratus so greatly when he learned of it that he undertook yet another offensive against Attica. He advanced as far as the grounds of the Academy, immediately outside the city walls, but was then persuaded to turn back.[63] After one such raid, while "fleeing" across the Thriasian plain in northwestern Attica, Aratus injured his leg and had to be carried on a stretcher.[64] It is quite possible that the Athenians saw these incursions into their territory, which did not pass without damage, less as attempts to liberate them than as hostile acts, and it is significant that Aratus once returned their prisoners without asking for ransom, as a way of lessening their animosity and perhaps winning them over.[65] However, no decisive change in the situation occurred until after Demetrius' death in 229.

3. Official Religion and the Royal House

In the first chapter of his book on Athenian popular religion, titled "Priority of the Divine," Jon Mikalson stated succinctly: "The gods came first." Every political group opened its meetings with religious rituals; meetings of the *ekklesia* began with the purificatory sacrifice of a pig, fumigations, and prayers by the herald.[66] Only then did the members move on to the agenda of the day, and there as well the sacred took priority over the profane. Before the members discussed political or governmental affairs, for example, priests might report on a sacrificial offering they had made on behalf of the community and the omens observed. No fundamental change in this respect occurred during the Hellenistic age; the priority of religious matters remained undisputed. Nor is there any indication that foreign occupation caused the citizens of Athens to alter the practice of their religion, except for the obligation to mention the king and the royal family in all official

63. Plut. *Aratus* 34.1–4. Walbank observes that the "persuasion" may have consisted of a bribe. He also doubts the authenticity of Diogenes' alleged demand and the celebrations in Athens (*Macedonia* 332). The pro-Aratus tendency of Plutarch's account (which is based on Aratus' own memoirs) is evident, yet while it may justify doubts about the interpretation of events, it does not necessarily place the events themselves in doubt.

64. Plut. *Aratus* 33.6.

65. Ibid., 24.4.

66. *Athenian Popular Religion: 405–323 B.C.* (Chapel Hill 1983) 13–17; quotations 13, 15.

prayers, such as those recited at the opening of Assembly sessions. The herald would not address prayers to them as if they were gods, but he would seek the gods' special blessing for them in his prayers as he did for the entire population. An innovation during this period was that a smaller unit, the Attic village or deme, could recognize kings as higher beings and award them divine honors, as is known to have occurred with Antigonus Gonatas and Demetrius II in Rhamnus. One important factor in this case may have been that Rhamnus, unlike almost all other Attic demes, was first and foremost a fortress, occupied in those years by a mixed garrison of Macedonian and Athenian soldiers. An official state cult for Antigonus Gonatas, like the one established in 307 for his grandfather and for his father, has recently become known from the very same inscription, a surprise to many scholars who were convinced that the king was not prepared to accept divine honors.

In all other respects, religion and religious rituals probably continued to be observed in the traditional manner. Indeed, there seem to be a particularly large number of Assembly decrees devoted to religious matters from these years, as if the observance of official piety had increased after the Athenian defeat. This may have been the case, but appearances may also be deceiving, since, in contrast to earlier years, almost no political Assembly decrees have survived. In this section I shall not attempt to sketch the traditional state religion (a topic that should be treated in the context of the history of religion),[67] but instead to present several notable documents from the time, which shed light on particular aspects of the official cult. It should be kept in mind that these aspects were only formal rituals the individual citizen was expected to perform: "The official religion was part of the state and did not affect one's personal beliefs."[68]

Just ten years ago, the site of the sanctuary of Aglauros was discovered on the east slope of the Acropolis. Aglauros was the legendary daughter of Cecrops, first king of Athens, and the consort of Ares, the god of war.[69] Also found at the site it had occupied since ancient times was a completely preserved copy of an Assembly decree from 246/5 honoring her priestess, who had conscientiously performed all the

67. U. von Wilamowitz-Moellendorff, *Der Glaube der Hellenen,* vol. 2 (Berlin 1932) 261–427. M. P. Nilsson, *Geschichte der griechischen Religion*[3] (Munich 1974) 2: 1–309; Deubner, *Attische Feste.*

68. Wilamowitz, *Der Glaube der Hellenen* 2: 271.

69. G. S. Dontas, "The True Aglaurion," *Hesperia* 52 (1983) 48–63.

duties of her office. These included making sacrificial offerings for the health and well-being of the Council and citizens, women and children, King Antigonus, Queen Phila, and their offspring. Timocrite, the priestess, had not been known before this find, but undoubtedly she came from a prominent family, like her recent predecessor Pheidostrate, sister of the famous brothers Chremonides and Glaucon.[70] However, the great surprise of this discovery was that the sanctuary itself, which the Persians had bypassed as they stormed the Acropolis in 480,[71] lay not, as scholars had expected, on the northern slope, but on the even steeper eastern side. The discovery of the sanctuary's site also revealed the exact location of the spot where the ephebes were inducted into the corps and took the ephebic oath to protect their country. Eleven divinities are mentioned in the pledge they swore, with Aglauros, the divinity to whom the site was sacred, coming first, before Hestia, Ares, Athena, Zeus, and other gods. It must have been in the presence of this priestess, Timocrite, that the ephebes of 246/5, the year of the decree, took their oath; many of them are known by name, including Theotimus of Rhamnus, who some thirty years later served several times as coastal *strategos* and is also known from other inscriptions.[72]

Lysistrate, the priestess of Athena Polias ("Guardian of the City") at the time, was from the same social class as Pheidostrate and Timocrite; as daughter of Polyeuctus of Bate and wife of Archestratus of Amphitrope, she was connected with two of the city's first families. The sister of her grandfather Lysistratus had been priestess of the same goddess before her. In another surviving decree Lysistrate was also honored by the Council and the people for conscientious service, and in her case as well the duties of the office included performance of sacrifices to assure the safety and well-being of the country and the royal family.[73]

In the same year in which Timocrite was officiating at the sanctuary of Aglauros, two citizens whose names have been lost served as elected commissioners for the Eleusinian Mysteries. They were responsible for the practical organization of the festival and the procession to Eleusis,

70. *IG* II^2.3548–49.

71. Herodotus 8.53.

72. *IG* II^2.681 (the ephebic inscription); *ISE* 32 and *Praktika* (1979) 24, no. 2 (Theotimus as *strategos*); J. Pouilloux, *La forteresse de Rhamnonte* (Paris 1954) 145, no. 34 (Theotimus as introducer of a motion).

73. *IG* II^2.776. For the older priestess see *IG* II^2.3455.

but not for the actual religious rites. The decree recognizing their service also mentions their sacrificial offerings for the welfare of the Council and citizens, women and children, and members of the royal family.[74] These examples show that the royal family had to be mentioned in every official rite and prayer, but that they had not usurped first place from the Council and citizens.

Two other documents from this period refer to the little-known goddesses Basile and Calliste. The evidence for Basile as a goddess is limited to Athens, where she was known as ruler of the underworld with Hades, a variant of Persephone and a chthonic divinity. Her priestess is mentioned in an Assembly decree from 239/8, based in large measure on her report.[75] Calliste ("Fairest") is usually one of the manifestations of Artemis, but in Athens she had her own separate cult; the officiator was not a priestess, however, but a male priest, as we know from a decree honoring him in 235/4. There was an image of Calliste and her counterpart Ariste ("Best") in a shrine of Artemis outside the city walls near the Academy.[76]

Every year an *agonothetes* was chosen to organize the games and contests at the major festivals, and sometimes even two—one for the dramatic and acting competitions at the Dionysia and another for the Panathenaea. These officials always came from affluent families, for even though the main costs were covered by the state treasury from the end of the fourth century on, the citizens expected directors to add special events, such as an extra competition, to mark a particular occasion, and to pay for them out of their own pockets. Such special touches and embellishments might cost up to several talents.[77] In the 240s Agathaeus of Prospalta was honored for his service as *agonothetes* immediately after the Dionysia in the spring, because he had carried out his duties (including the obligatory offerings for the welfare of the state and monarchy) to the satisfaction of all. Exactly one year later, after serving out his term and presenting a final report in summer, he was honored again, as had been promised to him on the condition of

74. *IG* II².683. For the office of Eleusinian commissioner see K. Clinton, *Hesperia* 49 (1980) 280–282; Rhodes, *Commentary* 636–637; R. Garland, *ABSA* 79 (1984) 116–117.

75. *Hesperia* 7 (1938) 132, no. 25.

76. *IG* II².788 (cf. 789); Pausanias 1.29.2.

77. *IG* II².798.18–19: a cost of several talents; 834.4–5: 7 talents. See *IG* II².657.43–45 for the sponsorship of an additional competition (*epithetos agon*) to celebrate the liberation of 287, and 834.23–24 to celebrate the liberation of 229.

good performance.[78] This same Agathaeus had made a private financial contribution a few years earlier to the *athlothetai,* the group in charge of the gymnastic, artistic, and equestrian competitions at the Great Panathenaea every four years.[79] Presumably his generosity recommended him in the eyes of the citizens for the office of director of the games, to which he was elected shortly thereafter.

The longest surviving document related to an official religious cult dates from 244/3, the year in which the government appealed for donations to help secure the harvest from attack. It is an inventory catalogue 200 lines long (many incompletely preserved) from the shrine of Asclepius, the god of healing, at the foot of the Acropolis.[80] The catalogue is preceded by the Assembly decree ordering an inventory of gift offerings at the shrine and the election of ten men to carry it out in cooperation with the priest at the shrine and several others. Apparently the priest that year deemed it necessary to clean house and organize the operation of his shrine, and persuaded the Council and Assembly to act.[81] The catalogue itself lists all the offertory gifts received in the fifteen or twenty years since a particular priest had been in office. Each annual occupier of the office is listed with the donations received during his term, mostly representations of parts of the human body and coins. Every priest is also identified by his deme, revealing to which of the twelve tribes he belonged. This enabled scholars long ago to determine that the office of priest of Asclepius rotated among the tribes like the office of secretary of the Council. Nothing shows more clearly than this inventory that Asclepius was the subject of a true folk cult with a direct appeal to men and women alike.[82]

4. Hellenistic Athens as Seen by a Contemporary

As good luck would have it, a description of Hellenistic Athens from the third century, about two pages long, has survived. It is found at

78. *IG* II².780; both resolutions are inscribed on a single stone. Cf. M. J. Osborne, *ZPE* 78 (1989) 238. See *IG* II².798 for the *agonothetes* of a slightly earlier year.

79. *IG* II².784; Habicht, *Untersuchungen* 137–141; Osborne, *ZPE* 78 (1989) 212–213.

80. *IG* II².1534B, 1535. A new critical edition with an English translation and groundbreaking commentary is S. Aleshire, *The Athenian Asklepieion* (Amsterdam 1989) 249–336; on 372 is a list of the names of priests from this period. A new fragment of *IG* II².1534 was published by Aleshire and A. P. Matthaiou in S. B. Aleshire, *Asklepios at Athens* (Amsterdam 1991) 5–11; and *Horos,* 8–9 (1990–91) 45–51.

81. Aleshire, *Asklepieion* 301.

82. Ibid., 56.

the beginning of the "City Sketches" by a certain Heracleides (nick-named either "the Cretan" or "the critic")[83] and was written after the founding of the city of Demetrias in 294, for it mentions the city's existence. Despite many scholars' best efforts no more precise date within the century has been established.[84] It has even been impossible to determine whether Athens was independent or under Macedonian control at the time: Heracleides was not interested in the political conditions of the places he described.[85] For him the important aspects of a city were its geographic situation; the quality of its dwellings, public buildings, local products; and the appearance and character of its inhabitants. The work's numerous very personal observations, sometimes in the form of aphorisms or burlesque remarks, make it exceptionally vivid but also raise doubts about the author's objectivity.[86]

At the beginning Heracleides praises the beauty of the route that brings the visitor into the city from the south, since it leads through beautiful planted fields that delight the eye. But he finds the city itself ugly, with irregular streets and not enough water. Most dwellings are so mean that at first glance strangers would find it hard to credit that this is the celebrated "city of the Athenians"—until convinced by the public buildings, one of the most splendid sights on earth: "A theater worthy of notice, large and admirable; a magnificent shrine to Athena, removed from the bustle and worth a visit; the Parthenon, situated above the theater, where it makes a formidable impression on the beholder. The Olympieum, only half finished, but impressive in its layout alone; it would have been a magnificent structure had it ever been completed. And three gymnasia: the Academy, the Lyceum, and the Cynosarges, all surrounded by trees and lawns."

This opening chapter of the surviving text ends with a description of the wealth of the city's cultural offerings: "Many different festivals, temptations and refreshments for the mind from a variety of philoso-phers, many amusements, and constant exhibitions." Thus, with char-acteristic brevity, does the author list what seems to him worth men-

83. The older literature is summarized by F. Pfister, *Die Reisebilder des Herakleides: Einleitung, Text, Übersetzung und Kommentar, SB Wien* 227 (1951). For the author's epithet see 18–19. An interesting characterization of the work is G. Pasquali, *Hermes* 48 (1913) 198–219. See also E. Perrin, *REG* 107 (1994) 192–202.

84. I concur with the great majority of scholars in thinking the most likely date to be around or after the middle of the century. None of the arguments advanced for a more precise date is conclusive.

85. "He includes whatever strikes his fancy"; Pasquali, *Hermes* 48 (1913) 200.

86. "Heracleides' style is rhetorical through and through"; ibid., 213.

tioning. The passage is the sole mention of cultural matters in the entire work, and its uniqueness, rather than its brevity, emphasizes the exceptional character of Athenian cultural activity.

Heracleides notes further that the agricultural products of Attica are outstanding in quality but insufficient in quantity to feed the population. It was common knowledge that Attica depended on grain imports; therefore, he says, although the inhabitants are no strangers to hunger, nevertheless dramatic performances and lectures (or leisuretime activities, *scholai*) help the lower classes to forget it. Artists and the arts enjoy high prestige among Athenians, and audiences in the city are both knowledgeable and demanding. The urban population makes a more favorable impression than the inhabitants of rural Attica; the latter are hardworking but garrulous, suspicious, and inclined to denounce everything foreign. By contrast, the Athenians themselves are described as generous, open, and reliable, except for certain corrupt lawyers who try to exploit rich foreign visitors; when exposed and found guilty by their fellow citizens, however, they face severe punishments. Just as cities in general offer better and more pleasant living conditions than the hinterlands, concludes Heracleides, Athens exceeds all other cities in its attractions—although visitors must be on their guard against the enticements of harlots. Athens is the one city in Greece everyone should see; all visitors are entranced, and those who must depart again are the poorer for it.

Heracleides depicts Athens as a city untouched by war, where one can find the good life. He gives no indication whether it was free then or ruled by the king of Macedonia, and he devotes not one word to the political activities of its citizens. His Athens is a timeless idyll, its perfection disturbed only by the presence of a few rapacious lawyers, whose importance fortunately pales by comparison with the city's abundant charms.

SEVEN

Freedom and Neutrality
(229–200)

1. Precarious Freedom

Demetrius II died in early 229, leaving behind a son named Philip only nine years old. The unstable situation in Macedonia offered Athens another opportunity to regain its independence, and this time the attempt was both successful and, unlike the revolt of 287, accomplished without violence. Diogenes, the royal governor in Attica, probably an Athenian citizen himself, was persuaded to place Piraeus, the island of Salamis, and the fortresses of Munychia and Rhamnus once more under Athenian control and to disband his Macedonian troops. The 150 talents needed to pay the soldiers off were quickly collected.[1] Athenian Assembly decrees show that the independence movement was led by two brothers, Eurycleides and Micion of Cephisia. Eurycleides had already held several high offices, and in the following decades he and his brother dominated Athenian politics. In addition to these two men, the decrees mention the role played by "the people."[2] Both Pausanias and Plutarch agree that the Athenians took the initiative in the effort to regain their freedom, but in their accounts they assign a decisive role to the Achaean statesman Aratus, an old enemy of Athens who had often attacked Attic territory. Recognizing the excellence of his character, the citizens now invited Aratus to intercede on their behalf. Though so ill that he had to be carried on a litter, he allegedly came to Athens and not only persuaded Diogenes to give up his military bases, but also contributed twenty or twenty-five talents to the

---

1. For more on this subject see Habicht, *Studien* 79–93.
2. *IG* II².834.10–14; *BCH* 80 (1956) 57, no. 1; and 102 (1978) 103–108.

soldiers' pay fund. Both Pausanias and Plutarch drew on Aratus' own memoirs for their histories, and it is clear that his role is therefore greatly exaggerated.[3]

Before July 229, when the new Attic year began, the city and rural areas were free for the first time since the end of the Chremonidean War, and the harbor finally free after sixty-six years. The Athenians even began a new tablet for recording the names of eponymous archons, and placed the name of the man who took office in July 230 at the top, to emphasize that a new epoch of freedom had begun.[4] For a long time fragmentary inscriptions were interpreted as showing that the two Boeotian cities of Thebes and Thespiae lent Athens money to help pay off the occupying troops, but a recent study has revealed that the foundation on which this conclusion rests is very weak.[5] Ptolemy III (reigned 246–221), who subsidized Aratus and is believed by some scholars actually to have incited the attacks on Athens, has often been seen as another contributor, but there is no evidence for this view.[6] However, it is certain that appeals were made to citizens and foreigners residing in Attica to contribute to a fund "for freedom" mentioned in several inscriptions. The sum collected may have gone toward paying off the soldiers of the royal garrison. Money donated at the time was also used to strengthen the walls around the city, Piraeus, and the harbor installations.[7] Obviously both officials and ordinary citizens exerted themselves to ensure that their independence would not be threatened again. They had to expect an attack sooner or later, since it was hardly likely that Macedonia would accept the loss of its bases in Attica without a fight.

Aratus now hoped that Athens would finally join the Achaean League voluntarily, after all his attempts to bring this about by force had failed. The city was again free to conduct its own foreign policy, and he may well have expected that his financial assistance would make

3. Plut. *Aratus* 34.5–6; Pausanias 2.18.6.

4. *IG* II².1706, with commentary by S. Dow, *Hesperia* 2 (1933) 430–434. Manifestations of this kind in Greek cities' lists of eponymous officials are relatively common; see Habicht, *Studien* 80 and n. 3.

5. The view taken in older studies (including Dittenberger, Ferguson, Feyel, and Habicht) has been corrected by L. Migeotte, in *Boiotika*, ed. H. Beister and J. Buckler (Munich 1989) 193–201. In addition, D. Knoepfler argues that *IG* II².2405–6, previously seen as belonging in the context of 229, actually belongs to the period around 285; *Chiron* 22 (1992) 475.

6. R. Urban, *Wachstum und Krise des Achäischen Bundes* (Wiesbaden 1979) 52–54.

7. Habicht, *Studien* 81–82.

the citizens more responsive. But the Athenian government resisted, adopting instead a policy of strict neutrality for which the brothers Eurycleides and Micion are thought to have been responsible. Aratus revealed his bitter disappointment in his memoirs, on which the Achaean historian Polybius based the following passage:

> The Athenians under the leadership of Eurycleides and Micion, freed from fear of Macedonia and believing themselves already to be in secure possession of their liberty, took no part in the other Greeks' affairs. Rather they followed the wishes and initiatives of their leaders and curried favor with all kings, but first and foremost with Ptolemy. They voted every sort of decree and proclamation, however humiliating, and damaged their reputation because of their leaders' servility.[8]

Such was the strong language Polybius used to denounce Athenian policy as pacifistic, opportunistic, even craven. Coming from him, the accusation of isolationism and lack of solidarity for Greek concerns can only mean that he expected Athens to participate in *Achaean* affairs, and above all to join the Achaean League. His bitterness derives from the fact that in the 220s, just after Athens' liberation, the League suffered its worst crisis, driven to the brink of destruction and disintegration by Cleomenes of Sparta.[9] This would never have happened if Athens had acceded to Aratus' wishes and become a member. Even worse was Athens' refusal to come to the Achaeans' aid when they asked for help in the fall of 225: although a majority of the citizens leaned toward support, according to Plutarch, Eurycleides and Micion succeeded in maintaining the city's neutrality.[10] The Achaeans had no choice but to seek help from Macedonia against Sparta, even though for the past fifty years opposition to Macedonia, its greatest foe, had been the League's main purpose. In order to stay in power Aratus had to humiliate himself and renounce all his previous political aims. King Antigonus Doson came to his aid and rescued the League by defeating Cleomenes and Sparta at Sellasia in 222, but at a high price: the Achaeans were forced to give back to the king both Corinth and the fortress of Acrocorinth, Aratus' greatest conquests. Nor was that all; for the next twenty-five years the Achaeans had to accept the status of

8. Polybius 5.106.6–8.
9. Urban, *Wachstum und Krise* 117–214.
10. Plut. *Aratus* 41.3.

"allies" of the Antigonid dynasty (in fact a satellite), until they traded one form of dependence for another in 198 and joined a coalition with Rome.

While Aratus' and Polybius' dissatisfaction with Athens' policy after 229 is thus perfectly understandable from the standpoint of Achaean interests, their anger at Athenian overtures to Ptolemy III also stems from another source. During the League's great crisis, Ptolemy not only stopped his subsidies to Aratus but transferred them to Aratus' worst enemy, Cleomenes. Under these circumstances the amicable relations prevailing between Ptolemy and Athens must have indeed embittered the Achaeans. Furthermore, the accusation of servility toward Ptolemy derived from a very specific source of offense—the Athenians' foundation of a cult devoted to the king in 224/3 (see below).

Polybius' criticism may appear justified from the Achaean point of view, but it fails to do justice to the Athenians' situation. The preservation of their newly won freedom—that is, safety from Macedonian attack and the maintenance of their own sovereignty—had to be their chief priority. Entry into the Achaean League would have considerably diminished the latter. Eurycleides and Micion had a difficult course to steer, asking for the support of a stronger power while giving up as little independence as possible. Circumstances dictated as before that this power could only be Egypt.

After gaining its freedom in 229, Athens was again able to conduct its own foreign policy. The citizens resumed their diplomatic activity at once, traces of which have been preserved in the very fragmentary surviving documents. The city strove to create good relations with as many powers as possible while avoiding entanglements and refraining from all actions that might further provoke Macedonia. The "War of Demetrius" had continued after Demetrius' death as a conflict between Macedonia and Aetolia. Profiting from the instability caused in Macedonia by the uncertain succession, the Aetolians took the offensive and in 229 wrested key areas of Thessaly from Macedonian control. But stability soon returned to Macedonia when Antigonus Doson, a nephew of Antigonus Gonatas chosen to serve as tutor to Philip, the young heir to the throne, came to power that same year. Antigonus Doson quickly took control and cemented his authority by marrying Demetrius' widow, Phthia, Philip's stepmother. After defeating the

Dardani in the north, he drove the Aetolians out of Thessaly and in 228 attacked the region of Doris (in central Greece), associated with the Aetolian League.[11] By then he may already have assumed the title of king of Macedonia. The Aetolians had Ptolemy III as their ally, for the Egyptian dynasty had traditionally opposed the Antigonids.[12] It was probably about this time that the Aetolians placed numerous statues of members of the Egyptian royal family in their principal shrine at Thermus, in a new exedra built to house them.[13] Despite this alliance the Aetolians were forced to make peace with Antigonus, who next extended his campaign across the Aegean to Asia Minor, conquering a series of cities near Mylasa in Caria.[14] It quickly became apparent that Athens would need to be on guard against him, and prudence dictated remaining aloof from the Aetolian-Egyptian alliance. Furthermore, the Athenian government seems to have taken its time normalizing relations with the Aetolians, with whom they had been at war until 229, for they waited about fifteen years before resuming their seat (one of two traditionally reserved for the Ionians) in the Amphictionic Council at Delphi, which the Aetolians controlled.[15] Such a policy can only have arisen from a desire to avoid giving offense to Macedonia and its king.

The city also established direct contact with Antigonus, a fact revealed by an Assembly decree from September 226. It awards honors to Prytanis of Carystus, a philosopher of the Aristotelian school whom Antigonus held in high regard and had appointed to draft a new law code for the Arcadian city of Megalopolis. When approached by the Athenians, Prytanis agreed to negotiate with Antigonus on their behalf.[16]

---

11. The fundamental study is J. V. A. Fine, *TAPhA* 63 (1932) 126–155; see also Walbank, *Macedonia* 337–342. For more on the invasion of Doris see the recently published documents from Xanthus in Lycia: J. Bousquet, *REG* 101 (1988) 12–53; dating corrected by F. W. Walbank, *ZPE* 76 (1989) 184–196. See also S. Le Bohec, *Antigone Dôsôn roi de Macédoine* (Nancy 1993) 154–162.

12. *Pap.Haun.* I.6.18; Habicht, *ZPE* 39 (1980) 1–2.

13. *IG* IX I².56 (*ISE* 86); cf. *FD* III.4.233.

14. The inscriptions from Labraunda have provided new information on the subject: J. Crampa, ed., *Labraunda: The Greek Inscriptions,* part 1 (Lund 1969). Cf. Walbank, *Macedonia* 343–345; Le Bohec, *Antigone Dôsôn* 327–361.

15. R. Flacelière, *Les Aitoliens à Delphes* (Paris 1937) 256 n. 1.

16. *ISE* 28, with commentary by Moretti. Le Bohec considers there is no foundation for the hypothesis that the Athenians' decision to send Prytanis on a mission to Antigonus reflects their fear of the king's intentions toward them; *Antigone Dôsôn* 184–189.

Presumably the Athenians sought from the king some indication that he was prepared to accept the status quo. From the wording of the text it is clear that the Athenians regarded Prytanis' mission as one of extreme delicacy; the decree praises the philosopher for accepting the chore without making excuses and without regard to the trouble and dangers it entailed. It also commends him for addressing the king "with frankness." At the same time there is no indication that he achieved any notable results. Antigonus Doson was certainly not inclined to give the Athenians any guarantee of respect for their sovereignty.

It is perhaps no accident that another honorary decree was passed in the same month of September 226 for a high-ranking Ptolemaic official named Castor of Alexandria.[17] Both documents date from the time the Achaeans, following their defeat at Hecatombaeum that summer, began sounding out the possibility of an alliance with the Macedonian king.[18] These contacts must have alarmed Athens, suggesting as they did not only that the two traditionally opposing powers might reach an accord, but also that Macedonia might intervene on the isthmus and in the Peloponnese. Such fears would have been increased by the news, first, that a political faction led by the Theban family of Ascondas and Neon, which sought to come to terms with Macedonia, was gaining the upper hand in Boeotia; and second, that the Boeotian League had renewed its alliance with the Achaeans in 228 or 227. No doubt the danger of Athens' becoming isolated was real. And a political initiative led by Antigonus Doson in 224 did result in the foundation of a new "Hellenic League," modeled on those of 337 and 302, which consisted of the Boeotian and Achaean Leagues, together with Macedonia and its satellites such as Thessaly, Epirus, Acarnania, Phocis, Locris, and Euboea.[19] The confederation was directed primarily against Cleomenes of Sparta, but concern that some or all of its members might one day turn upon Athens was clearly justified. Shortly after this, in 224/3, the Athenians resolved to found a cult honoring Ptolemy III. Clearly, the motives behind this step were political in nature (as had been the case for all earlier cults of Hellenistic rulers).

17. *IG* II².838. Castor's son Philo received honors at Delphi in 188/7 and was made honorary consul (*proxenos*) by the Aetolian League around 175/4 (*Syll.* 585.146; *IG* IX.1².31.141).

18. J. V. A. Fine, *AJPh* 61 (1940) 144.

19. *StV*, no. 507.

2. The 220s

In the same year that Macedonian rule over Athens came to an end, a philosopher named Cleanthes of Assos died at a very advanced age after serving thirty-two years as Zeno's successor at the Stoa; his tenure as head of the school had coincided exactly with the period of foreign domination, for Cleanthes assumed the office of the recently deceased founder the year after Athens capitulated. Antigonus Gonatas had revered Zeno and urged the city to grant him posthumous honors; he also took Zeno's pupil Persaeus into his service for a time. But now, with the deaths of both Antigonus' and Zeno's successors, Demetrius II and Cleanthes, the close ties between Athens and the Antigonid court were broken.

Not surprisingly, the citizens' attitude toward the rulers to whom they had previously paid homage cooled rapidly. Surviving inscriptions show that references to the king of Macedonia and his family were immediately stricken from public prayers, state decrees, and the liturgy of official sacrifices. Royal bronze coins, in common use in Attica for the past thirty years, were restruck with Athenian symbols and continued to circulate as currency of the independent republic.[20] Similarly, the evidence shows that the deme of Rhamnus ceased to include the king in its offerings to the goddess Nemesis.[21] But just as in 301 and 287, the two tribes Antigonis and Demetrias, named after the Antigonid rulers Antigonus I and Demetrius Poliorcetes, kept their names, and with them the cult of their two royal namesakes.

The new political order was reflected in positive evidence as well, such as the highly unusual honorary decrees for the former royal commander Diogenes and the creation of a new religious state cult. Diogenes, whose actions had made liberation possible, was officially titled a "benefactor" (Euergetes) and as such received a special seat at the theater: a costly marble chair inscribed with his name, which passed

20. Previously I argued for 200 as the date when the coins were overstruck. Now J. H. Kroll has made a very strong case for the years immediately following 229 (*Coins* 51–52). In the summer of 228 the royal family is no longer mentioned in the prytanies' sacrifice for the well-being of the state, as performed at the opening of an Assembly, and they are absent from all later documents.

21. *ISE* 29.16–18, an inscription from Rhamnus from 225/4, shows that the king has been eliminated from the cult of Nemesis.

to his eldest male descendant at his death. It is safe to assume that he also received the right to take meals at state expense, another hereditary privilege awarded only to citizens of exceptional merit. A new gymnasium, the "Diogenium," where the young men of the city could exercise, was named after him. More than a century later Diogenes' decisive contribution to Athenian liberty was still commemorated yearly at a festival also named after him, at which the ephebes sacrificed a bull in his honor. The city continued to demonstrate its gratitude long after its benefactor had died.[22]

Just as Philippides had once endowed a new contest honoring Demeter and Kore after the liberation of 287,[23] Eurycleides now created a competition commemorating the recent liberation.[24] In addition, probably quite soon after the events of 229, he introduced a resolution, which the citizens passed, to build a new shrine honoring the personified *demos* and the Charites (Graces), daughters of Zeus.[25] The grounds of this shrine were marked out and enclosed northwest of the Agora, on the north slope of the Agora hill, but apparently the temple was never built. The priesthood of the new cult seems to have been made hereditary in the family of Eurycleides and Micion. About a century later another member of the family named Eurycleides, while serving as mint magistrate in 122/1, commemorated the founding of the cult and his family's association with it by striking coins bearing images of the three Graces.[26] The priest enjoyed the same privilege of *prohedria* (privileged seating) at the theater as Diogenes and his descendants, and a marble seat with the corresponding inscription has been found in the theater of Dionysus.[27] Very soon after the shrine's creation and for a long time to come, statues of men who had distinguished themselves in the city's service were dedicated and placed there, and that the cult was intended as a religious and ideological

22. For details see Habicht, *Studien* 83–84; and Gauthier, *Cités* 64–65. For the Diogeneion see St. G. Miller, "Architecture as Evidence for the Identity of the Early *Polis*," in *Sources for the Ancient Greek City-State*, ed. M. H. Hansen (Copenhagen 1995) 207–209.

23. *IG* II^2.657.43–45.

24. *IG* II^2.834.23–24; the text is almost identical with that of the decree for Philippides.

25. For a detailed discussion of the cult and its significance in the life of the city, with a review of the earlier literature see Habicht, *Studien* 84–96, including a key piece of evidence from Aristotle contributed by H. A. Thompson (see note 29 below).

26. M. Thompson, *The New Style Silver Coinage of Athens* (New York 1961) 604 (where only the chronology is in need of revision).

27. *IG* II^2.5029a and 5047. M. Maass, *Die Prohedrie des Dionysostheaters in Athen* (Munich 1972) 109 and 121.

symbol of the new independent and democratic state was never in doubt.

Representations in personified form of the *demos,* the body of citizens that constituted the state, were not new. In his *Knights* Aristophanes introduced as early as 422 a character named "Demos," and the figure is shown in relief on numerous fourth-century inscriptions.[28] However, the cult and cult image were new, created in commemoration of the liberation of 229. As for the Charites, their identity in Athens has long been disputed, with scholars divided over whether there were only two of them (Auxo and Hegemone), three, or even four (adding Thallo and Karpo). The priest of the new cult attended the ceremonies for the new ephebes every year (as did their commander), and Thallo, Auxo, and Hegemone numbered among the divinities invoked in the ephebic oath. For this reason scholars believed these were the three Charites venerated in Athens at that time. It is known with certainty that an older, modest shrine to the Charites existed earlier at the entrance to the Acropolis, but it was destroyed during the Age of Pericles to make room for the Propylaea. The Charites' association with the corps of ephebes shows that their cult was connected with the welfare of the young; their association with the personified citizenry reflects the belief that citizens' concern for the welfare of young people offered the best guarantee for the well-being of the state. The meaning of the word *Charites,* "thanks," "expressions of gratitude," may also have expressed the founders' intention to display in the new cult their gratitude for their liberation from foreign domination and the help they had received.[29] Sometime later, probably around the middle of the second century B.C., the goddess Roma became associated with the cult, making the priest of the *demos* and the Charites also Roma's priest.[30] This connection confirms the dominant role that political ideology played in it from its beginnings. The later, expanded cult was

---

28. Cf. C. Habicht, *AM* 105 (1990) 259–263. For more on the reliefs see M. Meyer, *Die griechischen Urkundenreliefs* (Berlin 1989).

29. Aristotle, *Nicomachean Ethics* 5.1132b–1133a. M. P. Nilsson sees the cult as having arisen out of a need "to create, as a counterpart to the cult of rulers symbolizing monarchy, a cult clearly symbolic of independence and democracy"; *Geschichte der griechischen Religion*[3], vol. 2 (Munich 1974) 144–145.

30. The oldest documented sacrifices to Roma in Athens do not belong in the year 184 B.C. (as stated earlier in Habicht, *Studien* 91 n. 67), since the archon Pleistaenus mentioned in the inscription *Agora* XV.180.11 did not hold office until midcentury; see Tracy, *ALC* 141–142; for a different opinion, see J. S. Traill, *ZPE* 103 (1994) 109–114.

intended to express the inseparable union of the Athenian citizenry and the Roman republic.

The creation of the cult to the *demos* was followed a few years later by the founding of still another official cult: in 224/3 Ptolemy III Euergetes was added to the Athenian pantheon.[31] A new tribe was created, the thirteenth such division of the citizenry, and named Ptolemais in his honor. Since every tribe sent fifty representatives to the Council, the number of councillors rose accordingly from 600 to 650. To form the new tribe, one deme was taken from each of the twelve old tribes, and a new deme was created for it, named Berenicidae in honor of Queen Berenice.[32] As eponym of a tribe, Ptolemy earned a place on the monument of the founders in the Agora, and his statue was duly added to the others. A festival called the Ptolemaea was created in his honor and a priesthood founded for his cult; Ptolemy's priest also served as priest for Queen Berenice.

The various cult honors correspond down to the minutest details with the honors granted Antigonus I and Demetrius Poliorcetes in 307. A further exact parallel was created in 200 in the cult of King Attalus I of Pergamum. It is not difficult to see that the basic motive in all three cases was the same, namely gratitude for the restoration or preservation of freedom (and democracy) after a period of Macedonian oppression or the threat of one. In 307 the Macedonian ruler was Cassander, in 224/3 the threat came from Antigonus Doson, and in the year 200 from his successor King Philip V. As a result of its isolation in the 220s, Athens sought support and protection from the king of Egypt, as it had so often in the past. The cult to the king was the city's expression of thanks for aid in a moment of peril. As W. S. Ferguson recognized many years ago, Ptolemy was "almost the official protector of the neutrality of Athens."[33]

The Athenians at this time awarded citizenship to a high official of the king named Thraseas, who joined the newly created tribe of Ptolemais as a compliment to the monarch.[34] A document from Arsinoë in

---

31. For detailed documentation and the dating of the cult, which is no longer a matter of controversy, see Habicht, *Studien* 105–112; and idem, *CA* 11 (1992) 68–90.

32. J. Traill, *Hesperia Suppl.* 14 (1975) 33, 61, and plate at 62–63.

33. *Athenian Tribal Cycles in the Hellenistic Age* (Cambridge, Mass., 1932) 143. Alexandrian influence on Athenian pottery of this period is confirmed by S. Rotroff, *Hellenistic Pottery: Athenian and Imported Moldmade Bowls, Agora* XXII (Princeton 1982) 11–13.

34. *IG* II².836, with commentary by A. Wilhelm (1936) in *Akademieschriften* 2: 546–550. Cf. Habicht, *Studien* 115–116.

Cilicia published in 1989 has provided much new insight into Thraseas' identity and background.[35] The family came from Aspendus in Pamphylia, located east of Antalya on the southern coast of present-day Turkey. In 253/2 Thraseas' father, Aetus, served in Ptolemy's empire as eponymous priest of Alexander the Great and the divine royal couple of the *Theoi Adelphoi,* a high office reflecting membership in elite circles of the monarchy. He also served as Ptolemy II's governor of the province of Cilicia in southeastern Asia Minor and founded the city named after Queen Arsinoë. Cilicia was later lost to the Seleucids, but reconquered by Ptolemy III in 246/5. Thraseas followed his father as governor, and the recently published document narrates his activities. He brought about a settlement between the new city of Arsinoë and its neighbor Nagidus, a city founded centuries earlier by Samos that had been forced to cede some of its territory for the founding of Arsinoë. Thraseas' son was the same Ptolemy known from Polybius, other writers, and inscriptions as the man Ptolemy IV appointed governor in Coele Syria and Phoenicia after a brilliant career in the army. After the Egyptian monarch's death, however, Ptolemy entered the service of the Seleucid king Antiochus III and handed over the province to his new master. Other members of the family, including two other sons of Thraseas, are documented as having held high positions under the Ptolemies and the Seleucids.

From this it is clear that Ptolemy had chosen a man in whom he placed great trust to send as envoy to Athens in 224/3. Thraseas returned a second time shortly afterward with gifts from the king.[36] The monarch must have set great store by renewing the ties interrupted in 262. The foundation of a new gymnasium in Athens named the Ptolemaeum, endowed by the king, also served to strengthen these ties. (The name more likely refers to this king than to his third successor, Ptolemy VI Philometor [reigned 181–145].)[37] For their part the Athenians strove to cement and publicize the ties with Egypt by inviting

35. Published by E. Kirsten and I. Opelt, *ZPE* 77 (1989) 55–66; emended text and detailed commentary by C. P. Jones and C. Habicht, *Phoenix* 43 (1989) 317–346; for Thraseas' family see esp. 335–346. Further emendations have been offered by P. Gauthier, *Bulletin épigraphique* (1990) 304.

36. *IG* II².836; see note 34 above.

37. Pausanias 1.17.2. M. Thompson has argued for Ptolemy VI as the gymnasium's patron, *ANS MusN* 11 (1964) 119–129; for his identity as Ptolemy III see Habicht, *Studien* 112–117. See further Miller, "Architecture as Evidence" 202–207; and H. Schaaf, *Untersuchungen zu Gebäudestiftungen in hellenistischer Zeit* (Cologne 1992) 73–83.

other states to participate in the Ptolemaea. A surviving decree honors the city of Ephesus and the diplomats who announced the Ephesians' intention to send a delegation to the games.[38] The city belonged at that time to the Ptolemaic empire. Celebrations of the new festival continued for more than a century, and perhaps up to the end of the monarchy in 30 B.C.[39]

In the spring of 228, a year after the liberation, Athens had its first contact with the rising new power in the Mediterranean, the Roman republic. After acquiring its first two overseas provinces, Sicily and Sardinia, Rome had experienced an upswing in maritime trade, but this commerce was increasingly hindered by Illyrian pirates. When diplomatic embassies to the Illyrian queen Teuta proved fruitless, the two Roman consuls led a campaign against her, known as the First Illyrian War, and in 228 compelled her to sue for peace. Among other things the terms prohibited her from allowing warships to operate south of Lissa (modern Lesh in Albania); this was Rome's first intervention on the Balkan peninsula. L. Postumius Albinus, one of the two consuls, remained behind in Illyria in 228 and sent envoys to explain the reasons for the Roman operations in the Balkans to the assemblies of the Aetolian and Achaean Leagues (who had themselves also fought against the Illyrians). Soon thereafter the Senate sent envoys on the same mission to Corinth (a member of the Achaean League) and Athens.[40] Scholars are divided on whether these embassies were merely acts of diplomatic courtesy or possessed greater political significance.[41] It is undeniable, however, that both Aetolia and the Achaeans were at war with Macedonia at the time, and that Athens had just freed itself from Macedonian rule. Under these circumstances the failure of both Postumius and the Senate to send messengers or envoys to the royal court at Pella can hardly be an accident. To assume that Rome was seeking to isolate Macedonia would be going too far, but it seems

38. *ISE* 30, from the years 224–222.

39. Habicht, *CA* 11 (1992) 83–85.

40. Polybius 2.12.4–8.

41. The view that the missions had little or no political significance is argued by M. Holleaux, *Rome, la Grèce et les monarchies hellénistiques au III*^{e} *siècle av. J.-C.* (Paris 1921) 113–119; and Walbank, *Commentary* 1: 165–167. W. V. Harris takes the opposite view in *War and Imperialism in Republican Rome, 327–70 B.C.* (Oxford 1979) 137–138: "The target of this policy, it must have been clear, was Macedon." According to a late source (Zonaras 8.19.7), the Roman emissaries were awarded citizenship and allowed access to the Eleusinian Mysteries.

certain that the Senate wished to gain among Macedonia's enemies approval of the new conditions prevailing in Illyria, to which Macedonia could hardly remain indifferent.

Athens had a further connection with the events taking place in Illyria. After the Illyrian campaign the Senate approved an alliance with several cities there, including the island city of Pharos. The treachery of Prince Demetrius of Pharos led to an attack by the Roman army in 219, the Second Illyrian War, during which heavy damage was inflicted upon the city. Nonetheless Rome repeated its offer of an alliance with the city. Following the war Pharos sent embassies to its mother city, Paros, and to Paros' mother city, Athens, with appeals for "renewal" of the relationship and help in rebuilding.[42] The text of the inscription is incomplete, and so it remains uncertain how the Athenian government responded to the request. The nature of the relationship indicates that Pharos expected a positive answer, and the very fact that Athens is mentioned in a text chiseled in stone and intended for public display suggests they received one.

3. Athens as a Neutral Power

When in the fall of 225 the Athenian government rejected the Achaeans' plea for help in beating back the attack of Cleomenes of Sparta (a refusal that still rankled with Polybius several generations later), their desperation drove them into the arms of the king of Macedonia, whom they had previously regarded as an enemy. In response to the isolation that threatened it in consequence, Athens sought and found a strong ally in Ptolemy of Egypt. Relying on this source of support, the city continued on the course of political neutrality that its leaders had set in 229.

Such a policy could be successful only if the city was in a position to defend itself in case of necessity, now that it lacked a strong Macedonian garrison to guarantee its safety. Accordingly, the Athenians embarked on a program to strengthen the walls of the city, Piraeus, and the harbors. Further measures aimed at maintaining and improving the

---

42. The fundamental interpretation of the inscription found in Pharos was offered by L. Robert, *Hellenica* 11–12 (1960) 505–541; the role of Athens is mentioned on 515 and 524–525. Robert's conjecture that the events date from 219 has been confirmed by P. S. Derow, *ZPE* 88 (1991) 261–270. Derow cites the passage of the Pharos decree relevant to Athens on 262 (lines 10–16), with notes on 263.

country's fortress defenses. Recent discoveries of documents at Rhamnus in eastern Attica, honoring the coastal generals and their subordinates, indicate that a great deal of activity occurred there over a period of thirty years.[43] Rhamnus is unlikely to have been an exception; the greater frequency of finds there than at Eleusis, Sunium, and other fortresses may simply be accidental. It appears that a decision was made not to repair the Long Walls connecting the city and the harbor, for according to Polybius they were half in ruins by the end of the century. Apparently those in command had become convinced that each could be more effectively defended separately, and that keeping the link between them open under wartime conditions was no longer a high priority or perhaps even possible. Conceivably financial constraints played a role in this strategy, which to a certain degree abandoned the idea of city and harbor as a unit. Certainly it seems revealing that, from the end of the century on, Assembly decrees refer to the *astu* ("town") and Piraeus as the "two cities" of the Athenians. The same sober appraisal of the realities and financial possibilities probably ruled out all thought of building up the navy.[44]

Whereas after the liberation of 287 it was possible for Athenian leaders to hope that a clever policy of alliances would allow the city to go on playing an independent role on the larger political stage, Eurycleides and Micion were convinced that they could best maintain Athens' independence by avoiding all international entanglements. Alcibiades, Leosthenes, and Chremonides had been bolder, had aimed higher and risked more, but in the end they had all failed to achieve their ambitious aims and brought disaster on the city. There is no good reason to condemn as unheroic or misguided the policy of the brothers from Cephisia, which avoided such great risks.

During the last three decades of the third century, three major wars, each lasting several years, took place on Greek soil: the war of Cleomenes of Sparta (228–222) against first the Achaean League and, after

43. See the yearly reports by B. C. Petrakos in *Ergon* and *Praktika*, most recently *Praktika* (1990 [1994]) 21–24, nos. 1–2; and *Ergon* (1993) 8.

44. For details see Habicht, *Studien* 128. The reference to the walls "half in ruins" is Livy's citation of Polybius (Livy 31.26.8). On the other hand Livy gives the impression that the walls connecting the city and harbor were either still or once again intact (or at least worth a visit) when Aemilius Paullus visited Athens in 168 (45.27.11). The first documented reference to the two cities (πόλεις) occurs in 204/3 (*Hesperia* 45 [1976] 298, lines 16–17), with frequent references thereafter; see P. Gauthier, *REG* 95 (1982) 275–290; and *Agora* Inv. I 7581.8–11.

224, its allies (Macedonia and the Hellenic League); next the Social War (220–217), in which the coalition that had defeated Cleomenes, now under the leadership of King Philip of Macedonia, took the field against the Aetolian League; and finally, the First Macedonian War (212–205), between the same coalition on the one side and the Aetolian League and Rome on the other. Athens was the only major power on the mainland to avoid being drawn into these conflicts. Its leaders managed "to keep the city in peace while the rest of Greece was racked by devastating wars."[45] The peace agreement at Naupactus in 217 that ended the War of the Allies was the last peace treaty concluded on Greek soil without the participation of Rome.

The War of Cleomenes took place entirely on the Peloponnese.[46] In order to obtain assistance from Antigonus, the Achaean League had been forced to cede to him the fortress of Acrocorinth. During the fighting Antigonus captured the Arcadian city of Orchomenus from the enemy but, instead of returning it to the Achaeans, kept it for himself. The war ended with the victory of the king and his allies over Cleomenes and the Spartans at Sellasia in 222. Cleomenes fled to Egypt, and Sparta joined the Hellenic League. With these events the Macedonian monarchy again achieved a dominant position in Greece. The news of Antigonus' sudden death at a relatively early age shortly after his defeat of Cleomenes must have been received with relief in Athens. His successor, seventeen-year-old Philip V, was not seen as posing much of a threat for the immediate future.

Within less than a year, however, a new war broke out, sparked by the antagonism between the Aetolian and Achaean Leagues.[47] After a coup Sparta switched sides and joined the Aetolians, while Philip and his Hellenic League remained allies of the Achaeans. The battles of this war, waged with unexpected energy by the young king, took place at widely scattered sites with different outcomes, giving the advantage first to one side and then to the other. In the north and northwest, the regions affected were Epirus, Acarnania, Aetolia, Thessaly, and the area of Pieria in Macedonia; after the Aetolians plundered the undefended shrine of Dion at the foot of Mt. Olympus in an offensive in 219, Philip took revenge the following year by committing similar excesses at the

45. Beloch, *GG* 4.1: 641.
46. For more on this war see Walbank, *Macedonia* 337–364.
47. More on this "Social War" can be found in F. W. Walbank, *Philip V of Macedon* (Cambridge 1940) 24–67.

Aetolians' shrine of Thermus. The main fighting on the Peloponnese occurred in Elis, Laconia, and Arcadia.

Though not directly involved in the war, Athens was once seriously threatened after a crisis in Philip's camp.[48] Before his death Antigonus had created a council of seasoned leaders to assist his young successor. During the war a profound conflict arose between the king and several of these influential advisers, led by a Macedonian named Apelles, in which Aratus appears to have sided with Philip. It ended with Apelles' execution and the deaths of others who had opposed the monarch or merely fallen out of favor (218). One of them, a man named Megaleas who headed the royal chancellery, escaped and asked for asylum in Athens, but his request was denied "by the generals." He then turned to Thebes, where, faced with extradition, he committed suicide.[49]

Athens had a long and honorable tradition of granting asylum to petitioners seeking protection. The city's refusal in this instance must have been based on instructions given by the Assembly to the *strategos* in charge. Since Megaleas had come to Attica from Corinth, the general of the region of Eleusis would have been responsible, and in 218/7 this was Theophrastus.[50] Like the request for asylum from Harpalus, Alexander's treasurer,[51] a century before, Megaleas' petition placed the Athenians in a predicament: if they granted it, they would face open conflict with Philip, perhaps even war; but if they denied it they would commit an act contrary to principles on which earlier generations had prided themselves. In the end they decided on a course more politic than honorable. When Polybius reproached the Athenian politicians of this era for currying favor with *all* kings, he must have had this incident in mind as well as the kings at the Egyptian court.[52]

Athens was also in direct contact with the warring powers during these years. The Athenian Demaenetus of Athmonon went on a mission to Philip and the Aetolian League in 220/19, the first year of the war; then, after serving as *strategos* in the military command of Eleusis in 219/8, he appears to have visited both several times as an envoy in 218/7, to ensure "that the people [of Athens] will continue to enjoy

48. For details on what follows see R. M. Errington, *Historia* 16 (1967) 19–36.
49. Polybius 5.27.1–2.
50. For Theophrastus the general see *ISE* 31, a decree awarding him honors. His immediate predecessor was Demaenetus of Athmonon (*IG* II².1304.13).
51. See Chapter 1, Section 4.
52. Polybius 5.106.7.

the friendship of both in peace, and not be drawn into the fighting on either side."[53] The chief aim of his mission was thus to make clear to the adversaries Athens' intention to remain neutral and the reasons behind it. It is possible that Demaenetus also attempted to mediate, since all the noncombatants had an interest in seeing the war come to an end.

A peace agreement was reached at Naupactus in Aetolia in September 217. By then all the participants were weary of the war, and the news Philip had received about events in Italy allegedly provided additional motivation to bring hostilities to an end: the news that Hannibal had defeated the Romans near the lake of Trasimene. The Romans' presence in Illyria gave Philip cause for considerable concern; their campaign there in 229 had been only a brief episode, but since the Second Illyrian War in 219 they had established strong ties to the region.[54] Although they did not establish a base, they did make pacts with several cities and tribes, and thus had a handy pretext for further military intervention if they chose. This "Roman protectorate" in Illyria served as a kind of bridgehead to the Balkan peninsula at Macedonia's back, similar to the bridgehead of Saguntum on the border of Carthaginian territory in Spain (until Hannibal captured it in 219). Ending Roman influence in Illyria was an essential and legitimate goal of Macedonian policy.

The war against Hannibal seemed to offer an opportunity, and Philip took the initiative, sending an Athenian in his service, Xenophanes, to make first contact with Hannibal. In 215, only a few months after the Roman defeat at Cannae, Philip and Hannibal reached an agreement, the text of which has been preserved in Polybius' history.[55] The only provision of interest in the present context is its guarantee that Philip would have control of the Roman sphere of influence in Illyria, should the alliance be victorious.[56] However, no combined operations of the allies ever took place either there or in Italy. Philip was left to try to conquer Illyria on his own. His attempts to do so were tantamount to

---

53. *IG* II^2.1304, with comments by Habicht, *Studien* 132–135.

54. E. Badian, *PBSR* 20 (1952) 72–93; E. S. Gruen, *The Hellenistic World and the Coming of Rome*, 2 vols. (Berkeley 1984) 359–368; R. M. Errington, *CAH* 8^2 (1989) 85–106.

55. Polybius 7.9.1–7; *StV,* no. 528.

56. Polybius 7.9.13: "that the Romans shall not be rulers over Corcyra, Apollonia, Epidamnus, nor over Pharos, Dimale, the Parthini or Atintania." Philip was thus given a free hand in these areas.

an attack on Rome, which responded by forming an alliance with the Aetolians in 212.[57] Philip had considerable success in his Illyrian campaign; he conquered Lissa and subdued the tribes of the Atintans, Ardiaeans, and the Parthinians.[58]

The conflict spread when Attalus I of Pergamum, Elis, Messene, and Sparta joined the coalition against Philip in 211/0. Battles took place almost everywhere on the Balkan peninsula. Athens could no longer remain a passive onlooker when the Roman proconsul Sulpicius Galba conquered the island of Aegina opposite Athens in the Saronic Gulf, plundered it, and then handed it over to the Aetolians, as provided by the treaty between Aetolia and Rome. The Aetolians proceeded to sell the island to Attalus. In June 209 Athens joined with other neutral powers to try to put an end to the fighting. Envoys from Ptolemy IV Philopator (reigned 221–204) from Rhodes, Athens, and Chios assembled at the headquarters of Philip and the Aetolians on the Malian Gulf to negotiate a peace among the combatants. It was a concerted attempt, coordinated mainly by Egypt, to mediate a political settlement in which both the Romans and Attalus would agree to leave Greece. A further aim was certainly the wish to reestablish normal conditions for trading, which had suffered from the ongoing hostilities. The mediators obtained a thirty-day cease-fire, along with an agreement to continue negotiations at the assembly of the Achaeans in Aegeum. However, these talks proved fruitless.[59]

Over the next two years Ptolemy and Rhodes continued to press for peace; Byzantium, Chios, and Mytilene are mentioned as playing a role in the efforts of 207. The Athenians receive no mention in these years and were presumably no longer involved. In any event it is clear that Egypt had a strong interest in seeing the war brought to an end. In the final third of the century (until 204) Egyptian policy was determined by Sosibius of Alexandria, who as eponymous priest of Alexander and the deified Ptolemies in 235/4 held an office reserved for the king's most important councillors. It is probably largely as a result of Sosibius' influence that Athens participated in the mediation effort of 209, and there are other signs that he strove to maintain ties with the city: in all likelihood he is the Sosibius celebrated in a poem by Callimachus, who

57. All the evidence, including the fragment of the treaty itself, published in 1954, is in *StV*, no. 536, with detailed commentary by H. H. Schmitt.

58. Walbank, *Philip V* 80; Hammond, *Macedonia* 391–399.

59. Livy 27.30.3–6 and 10–15; see Habicht, *Studien* 135–137.

won victories at the pan-Hellenic Isthmian and Nemean Games at the Great Panathenaea and the Ptolemaea in Alexandria, no doubt in the horse or chariot races.[60] Not long afterward Polycrates of Argos, who had been taken into Ptolemy's service about 220 and rose to chancellor of the Ptolemaic empire, won a victory at the Panathenaea, where members of the Egyptian royal family were also victors.[61]

As long as Eurycleides and Micion ruled Athens, they endeavored to maintain or create friendly relations with all other states. By 229 relations must have become normalized with the Aetolian League, against whom the Athenians had previously fought on the side of Macedonia; numerous awards to Athenian citizens were granted in the 220s by the city of Delphi, associated with the League.[62] However, corresponding honors from the Aetolian League in Thermus did not occur until after the peace of 217. Relations were clearly formal and correct, but not close. Athens could not have held its seat in the Amphictionic Council during the period of Macedonian domination, and it is highly significant that it did not resume its place in 229. The Aetolians, who controlled a majority in the Council after their territorial expansion during the third century, faced hostility on this account, and in the war of 220 one of the declared goals of the Hellenic League was to end this dominance and restore traditional representation on the Council.[63] To achieve their aim would have been possible only if the opponents of Aetolia had succeeded in liberating the regions that had once had independent seats in the Council but lost them through annexation by Aetolia. They failed in this aim, and the question of representation on the Council played no role in the peace of 217. Immediately thereafter Athens again began sending a delegate chosen in an annual election. As long as the Aetolian hegemony was under such forceful attack, the Athenians did not want to commit themselves

---

60. For more on Sosibius see E. Olshausen, *Prosopographie der hellenistischen Königsgesandten*, vol. 1 (Löwen 1974) 43–45; and W. Huss, *Untersuchungen zur Außenpolitik Ptolemaios' IV.* (Munich 1976) 242–251. For the poem by Callimachus: fr. 384 Pfeiffer. Doubts have occasionally been raised about whether the victor is identical with the king's minister, e.g., by Pfeiffer, *Callimachus,* vol. 2 (Oxford 1953) xl–xli. However, the identification has been generally accepted since Beloch. The man celebrated by Callimachus must have been both of high rank and very wealthy, and thus could hardly be anyone other than the famed courtier.

61. *IG* II^2.2313.62; 2315.48–51; cf. *Hesperia* 60 (1991) 230.

62. *FD* III.2.78, 79, and 158 (229–227 B.C.), 74, 76, 82, and 166.

63. Polybius 4.25.8; A. Giovannini, *Ancient Macedonia,* vol. 1 (Thessaloniki 1970) 148.

to a position or to compromise themselves in the eyes of the king of Macedonia, who was leading the Hellenic League in trying to put an end to that hegemony.

In Boeotia, several Athenians were honored by the Boeotian League with the award of *proxenia* during the 220s,[64] and others after the peace of 217.[65] The Athenian guild of craftsmen for Dionysus voted in 215 to take part in the festival of the Muses in Thespiae, which the city and Boeotian League had revived.[66] The war had interrupted many religious festivals that were resumed or celebrated in an altered form after the peace of Naupactus. The Acarnanian League took over responsibility for the festival of Apollo at Actium from the city of Anactorium, because the city could no longer finance it after the war.[67] Polybius writes of the Achaeans: "They revived the traditional sacrifices and festivals and other religious customs in their various cities, which had almost fallen into oblivion in most places because of the incessant series of wars."[68] In the federal capital of Megalopolis celebration of the Lycaean festival was resumed, and a fragmentary decree of the Athenian Assembly records the city's acceptance of an invitation to participate.[69]

Eurycleides was still alive in 211 but almost certainly dead by 201.[70] It is impossible to determine whether he participated in the peace initiative of 209. Toward the end of his career he was honored by an Assembly decree still partially preserved, which summed up a lifetime of public service. The surviving fragment reflects very clearly that he played a leading role in the political life of the city. In addition to service in a variety of offices, the decree mentions sizable contributions from his personal fortune for the city's welfare, the decisive role he played in its liberation, his rebuilding of defenses in the fortresses and harbor, his initiatives in restoring agriculture to areas devastated by war, his construction of sacred and secular buildings, and finally his success as a statesman in winning over other Greek cities and monarchs as allies.[71]

64. *IG* VII.246.302 and 308.

65. Copious documentation is in Habicht, *Studien* 132 n. 64.

66. *IG* VII.1735 as reconstructed by M. Feyel, *Contribution à l'épigraphie béotienne* (Le Puy 1942) 88–117, esp. 94–96. See also J. and L. Robert, *Bulletin épigraphique* (1942) 69.

67. *IG* IX^2.583, with commentary by C. Habicht, *Hermes* 85 (1957) 85–122.

68. Polybius 5.106.2–3.

69. *IG* II^2.993; S. Dow, *HSCP* 48 (1937) 120–126.

70. Habicht, *Studien* 121.

71. For a more detailed analysis of the inscription see Habicht, *Studien* 118–127, with the substitution of "kings" for "allies." For the date of Eurycleides' term as hoplite *strategos,*

After 229 Athens must have maintained regular diplomatic relations with a number of foreign states, but only slight traces of these exchanges have survived. The existing evidence does at least show that ties existed with regions far beyond the Greek mainland and included both islands (such as Crete)[72] and Asia Minor, where there is documented contact with Ephesus and Miletus in Ionia,[73] and Antioch and Magnesia-on-the-Maeander in Caria.[74] The resumption of contacts between Athens and the Seleucid court in Antioch in northern Syria after a long hiatus is documented before the end of the third century.[75]

As far as life in Athens itself during this period is concerned, only a single decree in honor of ephebes was known up to 1937. This and the fact that the ephebes in the year of the decree must have been few in number were seen as evidence of Athens' poverty at the time.[76] Since then ten ephebic decrees from the period have come to light, not counting those estimated to date from "around 200"; but the number of ephebes—between 20 and 55 per year-class—remains low.[77] It seems that the numbers did not rise again until an upswing in economic activity occurred in the second century.

---

see Chapter 6, note 18. For the family see *Studien* 179–182, where certain details require amplification and correction.

72. *IG* II^2.844 and P. Brulé, *La piraterie crétoise hellénistique* (Paris 1978) 17–24.

73. *ISE* 30 (Ephesus); *Milet* I.2, no. 12, an Athenian award of honors for the Milesian statesman Lichas from shortly before 200. As the epigram added to the monument shows, Lichas was a leading politician and general of his city.

74. *Hesperia* 47 (1978) 49–57 and M. J. Osborne, *ZPE* 38 (1980) 99–101 (Antioch). I *Magnesia* 37 is an Athenian decree for Magnesia.

75. C. Habicht, *Chiron* 19 (1989) 9–14.

76. S. Dow, *HSCP* 48 (1937) 109.

77. A list is in S. V. Tracy, *Hesperia Suppl.* 19 (1982) 158–169; further *Hesperia* 30 (1961) 218, no. 14.

EIGHT

Alliance with Rome
(200–167)

1. Against Philip

The policy of neutrality pursued for a generation by the brothers Eurycleides and Micion of Cephisia (named by Polybius as its originators) was based on the assumption that external events would not draw Athens into conflicts beyond the borders of Attica.[1] The strategy functioned well as long as the different powers on the Balkan peninsula were left more or less to their own devices, but continuing it became impossible in the altered political circumstances of the late third century. After its defeat at Cannae in 216, Rome viewed as a provocation Hannibal's alliance with Philip the following year and determined on a policy of intervention in Greece, with, as a first step, the formation of its own alliance with the Aetolians. In 212 Attalus I of Pergamum joined Rome and Aetolia against Philip, in a conflict that became known as the First Macedonian War. Attalus' initiative was soon rewarded with the acquisition of the island of Aegina, on Athens' doorstep.

During this period the groundwork was laid for Roman domination of Greece. The powers named above played the main roles. Although the importance of individual events may be disputed, it cannot be denied that Rome's decision in 229 to use force to stop the Illyrians' piracy (to which their queen Teuta was turning a blind eye) set in motion a long chain of events that in the course of two generations

---

1. For the general history of this period see Will, *Histoire* 2: 101–301; E. S. Gruen, *The Hellenistic World and the Coming of Rome*, 2 vols. (Berkeley 1984) 359 ff.; Hammond, *Macedonia* 441–557; J.-L. Ferrary, *Philhellénisme et impérialisme* (Rome 1988) 45–218; R. M. Errington, *CAH* 8[2] (1989) 244–289; and P. S. Derow, ibid., 290–323.

made Rome ruler of the Balkan peninsula. Polybius, a contemporary observer of much of the period, recognized and articulated this fact accurately.[2] It is arguable, to be sure, whether the events of that first year aroused great fear or much unease in Greece or Macedonia. But even if the initial appearance of Roman armies in Illyria passed without undue alarm, their return in 219 caused serious concern to Macedonia and its young king Philip. Demetrius of Pharos may have influenced the king's decision; after Demetrius betrayed his pact with the Romans, they drove him out in 219, and he found asylum at the court in Pella, where he may have persuaded Philip to seek an alliance with Hannibal. A provision of the pact of 215 between Rome and Macedonia awarded the Roman-controlled regions of Illyria to Macedonia in the event of a victory.[3]

Athens avoided being drawn into the First Macedonian War, although it participated with other powers in efforts to make peace. After the Aetolians concluded a separate peace with Philip, the general peace treaty between Rome and Macedonia was signed in Phoenice in Epirus in 206.[4] A list of the allies on both sides was appended to the document, six powers on the side of Philip (namely Prusias I of Bithynia and the members of the Hellenic League of 224), and seven on the side of Rome. With two exceptions, all had been combatants, and it was therefore necessary to include them in the peace treaty. The two exceptions were both on the Roman side, namely Ilium at the top of the list and Athens at the bottom. Although some scholars disagree, it has been clear for a long time that both are later (that is, Roman) additions to Polybius' original account. The mention of Ilium is an obvious interpolation designed to make the site connected with Rome's legendary origins (Troy/Ilium) appear an early protectorate of the republic, while the mention of Athens is intended to justify in retrospect Rome's aggression against Macedonia in 200, by presenting it as intervention on behalf of an ally protected under the peace agreement of 206. The forgery was probably perpetrated in the first century B.C. by the annalist Valerius Antias, who is known to have interpolated one clearly inaccurate statement into the work of Polybius, namely the claim that in 196, after the Roman victory over Philip, Athens was rewarded with the

2. Polybius 2.12.7.
3. Polybius 7.9.13; text of the pact with commentary in *StV*, no. 528.
4. Livy 29.12.11–16.

islands of Lemnos, Imbros, Delos, and Skyros. With these embellishments he apparently wanted to present Rome's declaration of war against Philip merely as the fulfillment of a six-year-old treaty obligation after Philip attacked Athens, and to show that Rome offered compensation to the victims of Macedonian aggression afterward.[5] In fact, however, Rome had no ties of any sort with Ilium or Athens in 206 and 200.

Nevertheless, the appearance of Rome and Pergamum as new powers on the scene in Greece was only one reason why Athens was no longer able to maintain its policy of neutrality; a further factor was an acute crisis in the Ptolemaic monarchy, its traditional protector. Ptolemy IV Philopator died in 204, leaving a six-year-old heir, his son Ptolemy V Epiphanes. A series of rapidly succeeding regents governed in his stead: first Agathocles of Samos, followed by Tlepolemus of Lycia and Aristomenes of Acarnania. Power struggles created a situation akin to civil war in Alexandria, and the obvious weakness of the dynasty virtually invited exploitation by rivals. An earlier attempt by Antiochus III to seize territory had failed with his defeat at the battle of Raphia in 217, but now he succeeded in taking southern Syria and Palestine (202–200), and in 201 Philip wrested Samos from Egypt.

At the same time Athens faced acute danger of attack from Macedonia after many years of peace. The city appealed to the friendly regime in Egypt, but circumstances did not permit it to send effective help. Athens was forced to turn to the powers that had opposed Philip in the recent war: Attalus, Rome, and Rhodes, which had just recently become an enemy of Macedonia. In 200 the citizens of Athens declared war on Philip.[6] At this point Rhodes and Attalus were already at war against Philip, and Roman emissaries in Athens let it be known that Rome would shortly enter the conflict on the side of the allies.

Polybius, who condemns so harshly the Athenian policy of neutrality

---

5. A more detailed discussion is in Habicht, *Studien* 138–142. For publications since then see J. W. Rich, *Proceedings of the Cambridge Philological Society* 210 (1984) 150 with nn. 209–210; and Ferrary, *Philhellénisme* 25 n. 81. E. S. Gruen makes an ingenious attempt to prove that the naming of Ilium is authentic—he makes no mention of Athens—in *Studies in Greek Culture and Roman Policy* (New York 1990) 27–33 and 150. But his equating of Ilium and Pergamum is incorrect and would mean that Attalus had permitted a city belonging to his empire to be mentioned separately, something incompatible with the character of monarchical rule. For the peace of 196 see Valerius Antias in Livy 33.30.11 and Holleaux, *Etudes* 5: 104–120.

6. Habicht, *Studien* 142–158.

in the preceding decades, is equally harsh regarding the circumstances in which the city abandoned it. While offering pointed criticism of Philip's aggression in this period, he nonetheless asserts that the Athenians became involved in the war against him for an unworthy cause.[7] The background was the following: During celebration of the Eleusinian Mysteries in September 201 two young men from Acarnania inadvertently took part in ceremonies reserved for initiates. Even though the offense was unintentional, it constituted sacrilege in the eyes of the Athenians, who executed the two perpetrators. The step was not only extreme overreaction but also politically rash, for the Acarnanians had been loyal allies of Macedonia for the previous twenty years. They complained bitterly to Philip and received his permission to retaliate. An Acarnanian force augmented by Macedonian soldiers raided the coast of Attica, inflicting severe damage and carrying off rich booty. At the same time the Macedonian royal navy seized four Athenian warships.[8] Obviously, Philip was seeking a confrontation with Athens.

The Athenian Assembly responded in the spring of 200 with a declaration of war and simultaneously abolished the two "Macedonian" tribes created more than a century before, Antigonis and Demetrias. In addition they voted to destroy all monuments to Philip and his ancestors in Athens, to expunge references to members of the royal families in public decrees, and to anathematize and ban all Macedonians—henceforth no Macedonian would be permitted to set foot on Attic soil.[9] Numerous surviving inscriptions from which the names of Macedonian kings, their relatives, or the tribes of Antigonis and Demetrias have been obliterated still bear witness to the implementation of this decree. A gilded equestrian statue of Demetrius Poliorcetes was also taken down at that time and destroyed.[10]

When war was declared, it happened that Attalus and emissaries from Rhodes and Rome were in the city. Attalus and the Rhodians had come to persuade Athens to join them in the war they were waging against

7. In Livy 31.14.6.

8. Polybius 26.16.9; Livy 31.15.5.

9. Livy 31.44.2–9 and 41.23.1. The priesthoods of the two tribes' heroes, Antigonus and Demetrius—Livy's *sacerdotes* (31.44.4)—disappeared along with the tribes themselves.

10. The evidence was collected by S. Dow in *Hesperia Suppl.* 1 (1937) 48–50, to which many more recent discoveries have been added: Habicht, *Studien* 148 n. 137. For the statue of Demetrius see *Hesperia* 42 (1973) 165–168 and plate 36; cf. *SEG* 32.151.

Philip, while the Roman envoys had business with Attalus. Because the king was unwilling to address the Assembly himself, a statement was read aloud in which he called upon the Athenians to join the war, warning them that otherwise they would not share in the fruits of victory. The citizens were particularly well disposed toward the Rhodians, who made a similar appeal, because they had recaptured the four Athenian ships seized by Philip and returned them.[11] In honor of the Pergamene monarch the Assembly voted to create a new tribe to be named Attalis, to which each of the old tribes would contribute one deme. With this the number of tribes, which had just dropped from thirteen to eleven, rose again to twelve. The cult of the tribe's hero Attalus replaced that of the Macedonian tribes' heroes; the cult of Ptolemy III continued in existence. The new cult resembled the latter down to matters of detail: just as in 224/3 a new deme named "Berenicidae" in honor of the Egyptian queen had been added to the new tribe, a deme named "Apollonieis" after Apollonis, queen of Pergamum, was created in 200 and incorporated in the new tribe of Attalis.[12]

Immediately after the declaration of war the citizens sent a delegation led by Cephisodorus of Xypete to Rome. The existence of this delegation inspired the hypothesis by Roman annalists (which can be encountered in Livy) that an appeal by Athens for help *(preces Atheniensium)* led Rome to enter the war against Philip.[13] However, in fact Rome had reasons of its own; the Senate had determined upon war (and made that known to Attalus in Athens) even before the Athenian envoys arrived.[14] The end of the war against Hannibal allowed Rome to resume a conflict only temporarily interrupted by the peace of Phoenice. Deserted by its Aetolian allies, Rome had been forced to make major concessions in the treaty, such as ceding to Philip the Illyrian region of Atintania. The Romans saw this not as compromise,

11. Polybius 16.26; Livy 31.15.

12. Polybius 16.25.8–9; Livy 31.15.6; J. S. Traill, *Hesperia Suppl.* 14 (1975) 30–31. For *IG* II^2.2362 see idem, *Demos and Trittys* (Toronto 1986) 52–76; and R. S. Stroud, *JHS* 109 (1989) 253. The priesthood of Attalus is documented for the first time in the early second century (*Agora* XV.259.86) but was not created then, as H. Mattingly erroneously states, *Historia* 20 (1971) 28.

13. Livy 31.1.9 and 45.22.6. Despite earlier doubts about the accuracy of Pausanias' account (1.36.5–6), the historical authenticity of the delegation was confirmed by the decree awarding honors to Cephisodorus, *ISE* 33, published in 1936.

14. Polybius 16.25.4 and 26.6; Livy 31.15.4. For more detailed discussions see Habicht, *Studien* 150–158; Rich, *Proceedings of the Cambridge Philological Society* 210 (1984) 150–151.

but as humiliation.[15] It was the old score still to be settled with Philip that led them to declare war, not an appeal from the Athenians, to whom Rome had no obligations at all. Nevertheless, once the Romans had decided on war, they cited Philip's actions against Athens as one reason for it,[16] and it was Roman troops advancing after landing in Epirus in the late summer of 200 that rescued Athens from grave danger.

For Athens, although it had declared war on Philip, was incapable of waging one. It was not even able to defend its own hinterland effectively. The king did not conduct the campaign personally, for he was besieging Abydos on the Hellespont at the time. The Macedonian attack on Athens was led by Philip's generals Nicanor (who advanced as far as the Academy, directly outside the gates of the city, and met with the Roman envoys near Athens) and Philocles; the latter had been provided with a rather modest force of 2,000 footsoldiers and 200 cavalry.[17] It was clearly not these troops, but another Macedonian army from the fortress of Corinth that invaded Attica by way of Megara. In addition naval squadrons stationed in Chalcis on Euboea threatened Athenian shipping routes and the Attic coasts.[18] The reports convey the impression that in this phase of the war Athenian forces were virtually nowhere in evidence on land or sea, and limited their activities to defending the city, harbor, and some few selected strategic points.[19] The sources mention that Attalus and the Rhodians did too little during these critical months, and nothing indicates that they sent troops to help.[20] In Eleusis religious rituals were canceled several years in a row "as a result of circumstances," as a later decree honoring the hierophant Aristocles phrased it, perhaps referring to the years of this war.[21]

Effective help came from the Romans. On landing at Apollonia in

15. For Atintania see Livy 29.12.13. The peace is called "a humiliating reverse" for Rome by Rich, *Proceedings* 151.

16. Polybius 16.34.5.

17. Polybius 16.27.1–3; Livy 31.16.2.

18. Livy 31.22.6.

19. For Eleusis see Livy 31.25.2; for Piraeus, 31.26.7. For the city, harbor, and fortresses generally, see *IG* II^2.886.10–12, honoring a Pergamene who interrupted his studies of philosophy to help defend Athens.

20. Polybius 16.28.1 ff.; Livy 31.15.8 ff.; *IG* II^2.894.3–4 seems to suggest that Attalus provided support in the form of money and grain.

21. Clinton, *Officials* 24, no. 11.17–18.

Epirus Consul Sulpicius Galba found Athenian envoys who described the city's precarious situation. He at once dispatched twenty warships and 1,000 soldiers to positions in Piraeus. They stabilized the situation immediately, and the attacks from both Corinth and Chalcis ceased. The Roman fleet was soon joined by three Rhodian and three Athenian warships.[22] After receiving some information from exiles, the Roman commander was emboldened to use this force for a surprise night raid on the strong Macedonian fortress at Chalcis. The allies burned down royal storehouses and arsenals, freed prisoners from the dungeon, and destroyed statues of the king. However, their small numbers made any thought of holding Chalcis impossible, and the attackers retreated to Piraeus.[23]

The bold venture placed Athens at risk again, for Philip decided to retaliate. He hurried to Chalcis from Demetrias in the Gulf of Pagasae and prepared to launch an assault. The Athenians, warned just in time of the impending attack and assisted by a corps of mercenaries and a detachment from Attalus, prevented Philip from entering the city through the double gateway. The next day Pergamene reinforcements arrived from Aegina, and Roman reinforcements from Piraeus. Philip had to abandon his hopes of a surprise attack, and he also failed in a follow-up raid on the fortress of Eleusis, where the garrison proved alert and prepared; the king took his troops on to the Peloponnese.[24]

During Philip's absence his *strategos* Philocles led another assault on Attica from Euboea with a force of 2,000 men. He, too, failed to take Eleusis by storm and met up with Philip's army on its return from Achaea. Philip again tried to take Eleusis but was repulsed by reinforcements brought from Piraeus by Roman ships. When his next plan, a simultaneous two-pronged attack on Athens and Piraeus led by himself and Philocles, proved no more successful, the sources report that the king and his general resorted to the time-honored strategy of ravaging the undefended countryside, particularly the rural shrines and temples.[25]

---

22. Livy 31.14.3 and 22.5–8. Possibly the presence of some warships from Byzantium, whose commanders were honored by the Athenians around this time, belongs in this context; see *IG* II².884 (*Syll.* 580). Ships from Byzantium had taken part in the battle of Chios against Philip the previous year (Polybius 16.2.10).

23. Livy 31.23.

24. Livy 31.24.1–25.2.

25. Livy 31.26.1–13; H. A. Thompson, *Hesperia* 50 (1981) 352–354.

These events ended the first year of the war, and also the phase in which Athens suffered directly; later battles affected the city only marginally. Still, it remained encircled by enemies for some time: Euboea and Corinth continued to house strong Macedonian garrisons, and the Boeotians remained allied with Philip. Clearly, the Athenians had to give first priority to defending the city and harbor, and then to protecting the rural areas and crops. Thus it is understandable that little or nothing is heard of Athenian participation in the ensuing war outside Attica, either on land or on sea. Beyond protecting its own territory Athens could offer no military support to the allies' cause, although the city did undertake some diplomatic initiatives. Wherever they could, Athenian politicians sought to persuade neutral states to enter the war on the side of the Romans and to convince Philip's allies to drop out. In March 199 the assembly of the Aetolian League in Naupactus heard first the envoys of Macedonia, and then the Athenians; at their own request the Romans spoke last. The Romans gave precedence to the Athenian representatives because they had so recently endured the king's attacks and could testify to the outrages he had committed at sacred sites.[26] For the moment the Aetolians were unwilling to commit themselves, but they made preparations enabling them to join the fighting at any time it might appear opportune.

We do not know who led the Athenian delegation; if Polybius gave any names, Livy did not repeat them. The same holds true for the next major diplomatic intervention of the Roman allies at the assembly of the Achaean League, which was on Philip's side. At the meeting in September 198 in Sicyon Philip's representative Cleomedon spoke, urging the Achaeans not to desert Macedonia or at the very least not to change sides in the conflict. The opposing side was represented by L. Calpurnius for Rome and by envoys from Attalus, Rhodes, and Athens. The entire first day of the three-day convocation was devoted to addresses by the foreign ambassadors. Calpurnius spoke first, followed by Attalus' emissaries, the Rhodians, then Cleomedon for Philip, and finally the Athenians, whose position was designed to neutralize any effect Cleomedon's speech might have on the Achaean delegates.[27] The Athenians' address had in fact the greatest vehemence, since of all the participants they had suffered the most at Philip's hands. The

---

26. Livy 32.29.1–32.5; the Athenians' speech is reported in chap. 30.
27. Livy 32.29.12: "ut refellerent Macedonum dicta."

outcome was a split decision by a deeply divided Achaean League to repudiate its old ally Macedonia and to join the war on the Roman side.[28]

With the addition of the Achaeans to the coalition against Philip, Athens' importance must have diminished considerably. As time passed and the memories of Philip's ravages in Attica faded, the Athenians' suffering was less likely to stir up strong emotions, and in military terms the Achaeans were far stronger; Athenian troops had not distinguished themselves anywhere since the end of Macedonian rule in the city in 229. Now the decision of the Achaean League to join the allies relegated the Athenians to an altogether insignificant supporting role.

This is probably why the Athenians are not mentioned in any of the diplomatic activities that followed, neither in the peace negotiations held at Nicaea on the Malian Gulf in November 198,[29] nor at the assembly of the Boeotians in Thebes early in 197.[30] In both cases mention of the Achaeans replaces the Athenians in the sources, a clear sign that Achaean strength had pushed the Athenians into the background. While it is highly likely that the latter were represented at both Nicaea and Thebes, the weight of their opinion and their military contingent were too insignificant for historians to take separate note of them.

Nonetheless, while the growth of the coalition through the entry of the Achaeans and later the Boeotians (both previously allied with Philip) may have reduced Athens' role, the city's name and reputation must have contributed to the prestige and attraction of the allies' cause. Their contribution to the allied fleet remained relatively modest apart from their provision of a well-fortified and centrally located harbor at Piraeus. The Roman and other allied forces stationed there—reinforced by numerous light Illyrian warships as the fighting continued[31]—managed to pin down Macedonian troops in Corinth and the cities of Euboea, preventing Philip from deploying them elsewhere.

---

28. Livy 32.19–23; cf. Pausanias 7.8.1–2 and Appian *Maced.* 7.

29. Polybius 18.1–12; Livy 32.32.9–37.5; Holleaux, *Etudes* 5: 29–79. The Athenians' presence at these negotiations is generally assumed, particularly as afterward the Athenian Cephisodorus traveled with delegates of the other allies to Rome, where the negotiations were continued before the Senate (Polybius 18.10.11; Pausanias 1.36.6; *ISE* 33.22–23). See, e.g., F. W. Walbank, *Philip V of Macedon* (Cambridge 1940) 159 n. 6. Only A. Aymard tends to assume that the Athenians were not present; *Les premiers rapports de Rome et de la confédération achaïenne (198–189 av. J.-C.)* (Bordeaux 1938) 115 n. 5.

30. Livy 33.1–2.

31. Livy 31.45.10 and 32.21.27.

The war, waged with caution by the first two Roman commanders, entered a new phase with the arrival of the young consul Titus Flamininus in May 198. With a combination of energy and luck Flamininus maneuvered Philip out of his firm position on the Aous River in Epirus. A year later the Roman consul won a decisive victory at Cynoscephalae in Thessaly, which brought peace. Large parts of Greece were declared free and independent of Macedonia, including Corinth, Phocis, Locris, the island of Euboea, and Thessaly with its territories Achaea Phthiotis, Magnesia, and Perrhaebia. A new Thessalian Confederacy was created, for which Flamininus himself drew up the constitution, based on the predominance of the wealthy.[32]

During the war Athens was visited by all four successive admirals of the Roman fleet,[33] and at least three times by King Attalus: in the spring of 199, in September of the same year (when he was initiated into the Mysteries at Eleusis), and in the late fall of 198.[34] Years before he had warned the citizens that they would come away empty-handed at the end of the war if they took no part in it. The Athenians had joined his cause, but failed to receive the anticipated benefit all the same. During the truce of the winter of 198/7 their statesman Cephisodorus had returned to Rome, this time with other allied delegates to present Athens' claims before the Senate. It is possible that either on this occasion or after the war Athens demanded the return of the islands of Lemnos, Imbros, and Skyros, which had traditionally been Athenian before they were lost to Macedonia. Many scholars have interpreted Polybius' statement regarding the Athenians' request in 167/6 that the Senate award them Delos and Lemnos in this way: "As far as Delos and Lemnos are concerned, there is no objection to their wish, since they have already laid claim to these islands before."[35] However, it is possible that Polybius merely meant to say that the Athenians claimed old rights of possession to these islands (a reading that seems to fit the context better).[36]

Whether or not Athens presented claims in the peace negotiations of 196, the city won no additional territory. Attalus, who could have

32. Livy 34.51.4–6; *Syll.* 674 b 50–53 and 63–64; H. Kramolisch, *Die Strategen des Thessalischen Bundes vom Jahr 196 v. Chr. bis zum Ausgang der römischen Republik* (Bonn 1978) 22–23.
33. Livy 31.14.3; 21.5; 45.1; 32.16.5; and frequently elsewhere.
34. Livy 31.45.1 and 47.1–2; 32.23.13.
35. Polybius 30.20.3. The passage is understood in this sense by Holleaux, *Etudes* 5: 108 n. 1, and others.
36. F. W. Walbank clearly read the text thus; *Commentary* 3: 443.

served as their advocate, had died about the time of the battle of Cynoscephalae. Athens thus emerged from the war without significant losses, but also without gains. Significantly for the future, the city had also bound itself closely to Rome, though without concluding an official alliance.

2. Against Antiochus

Although Athens had played no part in the Roman Senate's decision to settle its score with Philip of Macedonia after the end of the war against Hannibal, the city derived a certain benefit from it. Athens was already at war with Philip itself, and Roman soldiers provided greater protection than the insufficient Athenian forces could muster. Yet if the Athenians were counting on the Romans to make a swift and permanent withdrawal from Greece after winning the First Macedonian War, they were quite mistaken. First of all, Roman troops remained in the country for several years, as new political structures were established in the areas wrested from Macedonian control: Flamininus took several years to carry out this task with the assistance of a commission appointed for the purpose (consisting of ten members of the Senate). Secondly, after the victory Flamininus immediately became embroiled in a fierce and rapidly escalating conflict with the Aetolians. In 192 this would lead to a major war between the formerly allied powers when the Aetolians declared that the Romans had merely replaced the Macedonians as foreign tyrants in Greece and called on the Seleucid king Antiochus III ("the Great") to liberate them. In consequence the Roman armies, which had finally returned to Italy in 194, promptly reappeared in 192 to prevent this from happening.

The conflict with Aetolia had arisen not only from personal animosities between the autocratic Roman general and the intransigent Aetolians, but also from serious political differences.[37] The Aetolians made extensive demands for territory at the end of the war, which Flamininus opposed, supported by the other Greek allies. The Aetolians' goal was to destroy Philip completely and to take possession of most of his territory, which they claimed on the basis of the treaty signed with Rome in 212. This granted them sole rights to the entire territory that might be won, while the Romans would receive all portable goods and chattels. Flamininus refused categorically to recognize the pact as valid,

---

37. D. Musti, *ANRW* I.2 (1972) 1146–49; Ferrary, *Philhellénisme* 69–72.

since the Aetolians had violated its terms by concluding a separate peace with Philip in 206. An open rift resulted, and from that time on the Aetolians never tired of denouncing the Romans as the new oppressors of Greece.

Athens played a very small role in these developments, which pointed toward renewed war. It is noteworthy that the victors considered it unnecessary to offer Athens any reward under the terms of the peace. Indeed, the Athenians failed to receive even the island of Lemnos seized from Philip, to which they had an excellent claim; the Senate declared it independent instead.[38] Attica had suffered considerable damage at the start of the war, and Athens had provided crucial support to the allies, at the very least, by placing its indispensable harbor at their disposal. But it appears the victors saw this debt as canceled out by the role their troops had played in defending the city. The Athenians were probably disappointed by their failure to gain anything under the peace settlement, yet although the sources are full of Aetolian complaints and resentment, significantly they do not mention any Athenian discontent: conditions had changed so materially that the city had ceased to merit the chroniclers' attention except when it participated in some political process involving the major powers. Frequently Athens came to play the role of mediator, particularly between the Romans and various vanquished Greek opponents. After the war against Philip, Athens and the Achaeans mediated between Rome and the Boeotians; after the war against the Aetolians, Athens and Rhodes mediated between Rome and the Aetolian League; and after the war against Antiochus, Athens joined Rhodes and other powers in mediating between Miletus and Magnesia-on-the-Maeander.

In Boeotia Philip's defeat created an explosive situation. Although the Boeotians, led by the Theban commander Brachylles, had fought on the Macedonian side, Flamininus had allowed them to return home without hindrance. There they made no secret of their continuing partisanship for Philip. In the fall of 197 they elected Brachylles, whose family had maintained close ties with the Macedonian royal family for the previous thirty years,[39] to the chief office of the Boeotian League and filled other high posts with more friends of Macedonia. The leaders

38. Polybius 18.44.4 (Livy 33.30.3) and 18.48.2 (Livy 33.35.3).
39. See the articles on Brachylles, Neon, and Askondas in *RE Suppl.* 1 (1903), with the sources. In addition surviving inscriptions refer both to Brachylles (*ZPE* 17 [1975] 1 ff.) and his father, Neon (*SEG* 11.414.30 and *IG* VII.3091). Brachylles' son Neon carried on the traditional alliances of the family.

of the anti-Macedonian, pro-Roman faction in Boeotia thereupon formed a plan to murder Brachylles. When they approached Flamininus he refused to have anything to do with the plot directly, but he told them he would place no obstacles in their path. In fact he went so far as to recommend the Aetolian *strategos* Alexamenus to them as a man who could take charge of the matter. Alexamenus lived up to expectations, and his hired assassins killed Brachylles early in 196. In his reworking of Polybius Livy suppressed the role of Flamininus, as it shows him in a very unfavorable light: Flamininus and Brachylles had met face to face less than a year before, when Brachylles had accompanied Philip to negotiations with the Roman commander.

The outraged Boeotians retaliated by murdering Roman soldiers, allegedly no fewer than 500, and dumping their bodies in Lake Copaïs. When they refused to comply with Roman demands to hand over the ringleaders and pay 500 talents in reparation, Flamininus led his army into Boeotia and at the same time sent envoys to Athens and Achaea to persuade them that his cause was just. The ravages he inflicted on their territory compelled the Boeotians to sue for peace, but now Flamininus refused to admit their ambassadors. At this juncture Achaean and Athenian negotiators intervened and mediated a settlement. Livy, who on this point follows Polybius, explicitly gives the Achaeans the greater credit, reporting that they carried more weight with the Romans than did the Athenians, and that it was through Achaean efforts that Flamininus finally consented to receive the Boeotian envoys.[40] While Polybius may have exaggerated his compatriots' role, the report appears credible, for it corresponds to the known political realities. The most notable aspect of the two states' mediation efforts is that they occurred in response to messages from Flamininus and perhaps at his invitation.

In the conflict between Flamininus and the Aetolians the Athenians acted as strong advocates for the Romans, as became clear at a conference organized by Flamininus in Corinth in the spring of 195. Before delegates from Achaea, Thessaly, Macedonia, Pergamum, and Rhodes, and in the presence of Flamininus himself, the Athenian representative praised Roman engagement in Greece in such strong terms that it provoked a heated reply from the Aetolian delegate Alexander. The

---

40. Livy 33.29.11–12 and, most recently, D. Knoepfler, *Festschrift S. Lauffer* (Rome 1986) 599–600.

Aetolian leader pointed out that the Romans were occupying Demetrias, Chalcis, and Acrocorinth, the very fortresses long occupied by
Macedonia and referred to by Philip himself as "the three shackles of
Greece"; the Romans remained there for the identical purpose of
controlling the country. Alexander bitterly reproached the Athenians,
once leaders in the struggle for Greek independence, who had now
sunk to the role of Roman toadies, willing to champion the cause of a
foreign ruler.[41] This remark in turn provoked protests from the other
Greeks.[42]

At this time the Athenians maintained friendly relations with Antiochus, although increasingly they came to regard him as a potential ally
of the Aetolians in a war against Rome, and were on better terms with
the kings of Egypt and Pergamum.[43] And although Athens' official
policy was to prevent further war in Greece as far as possible, the city
left no doubt that should armed conflict break out, it would fight on
the side of Rome. When in 192 the Senate sent to Greece four high-
ranking members—three of whom had already been consul—to combat the Aetolians' saber-rattling and Antiochus' propaganda, they first
visited Athens, accompanied by Flamininus. They contented themselves with sending written dispatches to the Achaean League, on
whose loyalty they believed they could count. One may see in this a
sign that the emissaries were aware that official Athenian policy by no
means enjoyed the full support of the citizens, as succeeding events
would very soon show. Flamininus asked for Athenian backing in his
request to address the Aetolian assembly; the Athenians appeared
suited for this particularly sensitive task "because of their state's distinguished reputation and their traditional friendship with the Aetolians."[44] The Athenians spoke after the representative of Antiochus
and recommended moderation, but they had great difficulty persuading the assembly to admit Flamininus at all and hear him out, succeeding only with the help of several Aetolian elder statesmen. In the end
the assembly ignored Flamininus' warnings and invited Antiochus to
come and liberate Greece: They would let Antiochus determine the
outcome of the strife with Rome.[45]

41. Livy 34.22.7–23.11.
42. Livy 34.24.1–5.
43. C. Habicht, *Chiron* 19 (1989) 10–14.
44. Livy 35.23.5 and 31.3; quotation from 32.7.
45. Livy 35.32.8–33.11.

The Roman emissaries met with better success in Thessaly, Magnesia, and Chalcis in Euboea. In the last-named city the pro-Aetolian politician Euthymidas was exiled and forced to seek refuge in Athens. As his attempt, undertaken jointly with the Aetolians, to bring down the pro-Roman government in Chalcis and to go back there almost succeeded, Flamininus and King Eumenes thought it advisable to strengthen Chalcis' defenses with 500 Pergamene soldiers. Eumenes himself made a trip to Athens to see how matters stood.[46]

The war itself began when Antiochus landed in Greece in October 192; in Athens his supporters became so vocal, according to Livy (whose report is based on Polybius), that it approached sedition. The existing authorities prevailed only when the government called in Flamininus, who brought 500 Achaeans with him "to protect Piraeus." Leon of Aixone, one of the most respected politicians in the city, succeeded in having his rival and supporter of the king, a man named Apollodorus, sentenced, and Apollodorus went into exile. (Unfortunately, this name is so common that it is impossible to determine his identification with any one bearer.)[47]

The consul of the year 191 responsible for conducting the war in Greece was Acilius Glabrio; to serve under him as military tribune the Roman people had elected Marcus Porcius Cato, who himself had served as consul in 195. As soon as the Roman army landed in Epirus, Glabrio sent Cato on a political mission to their Greek allies. After visiting several cities in Achaea, he proceeded to Athens where, in early 191, he addressed the Assembly in Latin; his speech was translated for the delegates by an interpreter.[48] The occasion for the appeal was probably Roman doubts about Athens' reliability as an ally, but after the defeat of Apollodorus and his supporters the mood in the city was firmly pro-Roman.

Events in Greece took a decisive turn in the spring of 191, when the

46. Livy 35.37.4–39.2. An inscription from the Aetolian shrine of Thermos shows that Euthymidas had become the Aetolians' *proxenos* (consul) by 208/7; *IG* IX.1^2.31.67. The assumption that at that time Eumenes received the same honors in Athens that his father received in 200 is incorrect (B. Virgilio, *Studi ellenistici* 5 [Pisa 1993] 52), for evidence would surely have survived if a new phyle had ever been created in his honor and named after him. No thirteenth phyle was created until Hadrian was so honored.

47. Livy 35.50.4. For Leon and his family see Habicht, *Studien* 194–197, and further below; the publication of new inscriptions will produce further documentation for members of this influential family.

48. Plut. *Cato maior* 12.4–5; A. E. Astin, *Cato the Censor* (Oxford 1978) 56–57.

consul (whom Cato had rejoined) defeated the combined armies of Antiochus and the Aetolians at Thermopylae. Glabrio thus forced Antiochus to leave Greece, and the Aetolians were on the defensive in their own territory. The war against them dragged on for some time, but the brothers Publius and Lucius Scipio ended the war against Antiochus with their victory at Magnesia at Sipylum (in Asia Minor) early in 189.

Just as in the previous war against Philip, Athenian military participation in the war against Antiochus and the Aetolians was on a very modest scale; once again their main contribution was to make the harbor of Piraeus available to their allies. Four successive Roman admirals used it as a base of operations from 191 to 188, supported by contingents from Rhodes and Pergamum. Athenian warships are known to have taken part in Aemilius Regillus' operations in 190.[49] Nonetheless, there is no indication that Athens inflicted serious damage on the enemy or suffered any itself. At the same time nothing suggests that the Romans expected more from their Athenian allies.

Matters stood differently in the Aetolian campaign, where Athens played a central role. It was Athenian politicians who, over and over again, negotiated for peace on behalf of the hard-pressed Aetolians. Polybius and Livy (who follows Polybius closely here) report these diplomatic efforts in some detail, finally crowned with success after a year and a half, although the mood in the Roman Senate remained hostile.[50] In the spring of 190 Glabrio had laid siege to the Aetolian city of Amphissa, and just as the Scipios (Lucius as consul of 190 and Publius Scipio Africanus as his legate) arrived to relieve him, a delegation arrived from Athens, headed by Echedemus of Cydathenaion, the city's leading statesman after Leon.[51] The Aetolians wished to make peace, as did the Scipios, who wanted to be free to move against Antiochus. However, they were bound by strict instructions from the Senate. Echedemus traveled three times between Amphissa and the Aetolian authorities in Hypata without reaching an agreement. Finally

49. Livy 27.14.1–2. These Athenian ships are also mentioned as participants in the naval war of 190 in the Delian decree *IG* XI.751, for which F. Durrbach has provided a commentary, *Choix d'inscriptions de Délos* (Paris 1921), no. 67.

50. Polybius 21.4–5; 25; 29–31. The corresponding passages in Livy are 37.6–7; 38.3; and 38.9–10. For the chronology see Holleaux, *Etudes* 5: 249–294.

51. For Echedemus see Habicht, *Studien* 189–193, and a new inscription revealing his role in the reorganization of the Amphictionic Council in Delphi, *Hesperia* 56 (1987) 65 (see note 57 below); and further P. A. Pantos, *Hesperia* 58 (1989) 277–288.

he urged the Aetolians to ask for a six-month truce, and this was granted.

When the Romans defeated Antiochus the next year, the Aetolians lost all hope of receiving further help from their ally and asked the republics of Rhodes and Athens to negotiate a peace for them in Rome. Both cities agreed, but before sending their representatives to Rome they sent them to confer with Fulvius Nobilior, the new Roman consul; he was carrying on the war against the Aetolians in Epirus, where he had laid siege to the city of Ambracia, once the residence of King Pyrrhus. In the summer of 189 the mediators negotiated a temporary peace settlement, soon ratified by the Aetolian assembly. To persuade the Senate to ratify it, the Athenians and Rhodians accompanied the Aetolian negotiators to Rome. Having received new information from Philip, the Senate was again extremely annoyed with the Aetolians' behavior, and ratification of the peace treaty appeared to be in serious jeopardy. In this situation it was the Athenian Leon, the same man who had prevented Athens from turning against Rome in the fall of 192, whose speech (paraphrased by Polybius) so impressed the senators that they approved the treaty in the form agreed upon by the consul.[52] The Aetolians' bestowal of the title *proxenos* on the Athenian citizen Lysicles in 189/8 probably belongs in the context of the city's effort to help the Aetolians end the fighting.[53]

The Roman peace treaties with the Aetolians and King Antiochus in 189 and 188 brought the Athenians no territorial gains. However, the city did profit within Greece by acquiring greater influence and prestige in Delphi. The loss of the war to Rome ended the Aetolians' century-old control of the shrine, and also their dominant position in the Amphictionic Council, in which they once had controlled fifteen of the twenty-four votes. The Romans effected the reforms previously announced by the Hellenic League as one goal of its war against Aetolia in 220, which it had been unable to achieve in the Social War. Now reorganization of the Council and a new distribution of votes had become imperative. The representatives of Athens, the Boeotians, and the Cephallenians had not attended the meeting of 193/2, clearly because they wished to avoid giving offense to the Romans, then close

52. Polybius 21.31.5–16; Livy 38.10.4–6.
53. *IG* IX.1^2.1, no. 4b.

to war with Aetolia.[54] The Thessalians had also been absent, either for the same reason or because the Aetolians had not allowed them to return.[55] The first surviving list of delegates attending the Council dates only from 178;[56] nonetheless, several surviving inscriptions show with sufficient clarity what had happened in the meantime.[57] Apparently the city of Delphi hoped to acquire sole control of the shrine, the Pythian Games, and the festival of the Soteria, and to prevent the return of an international oversight committee, for immediately after the Aetolians' withdrawal Consul Glabrio wrote to the city, assuring them he would use all his influence to preserve the city's and the temple's old rights. As potential opponents to such a plan he mentioned the Thessalians "and others."[58] This reference to foreign states reveals that he had a supranational organization in mind, namely the Amphictionic Council, in which the Thessalians had traditionally played a decisive role.

The fears expressed were not without foundation. On the basis of an inscription from Delphi of 184/3 it has long been known that the Thessalians were in fact instrumental in the reorganization of the Amphictionic Council after the Aetolian War. An inscription discovered more recently in Athens, from 185/4, reveals that Athens played an equally prominent role in collaboration with the Thessalian Confederacy. It emerges that both powers, represented by Nicostratus of Larissa (known to be a member of the Thessalian aristocracy) and the three leading Athenian politicians, Echedemus (who had mediated between the Scipios and the Aetolians), Menedemus, and Alexion, succeeded in pushing through their plan for the Council, finally approved by the Senate in Rome. The new composition and organization of the Council were the work of these two powers and entailed a rejection of Delphi's own wishes. The only sugar-coating to this bitter pill was the assurance that the city's two representatives would in future be listed at the top of the roster of delegates.[59] These events marked the beginning of a

54. R. Flacelière, *HSCP Suppl.* 1 (1940) 479.

55. Daux, *Delphes* 261 n. 1. The Thessalians owed their liberation from Macedonian control and their new constitution to Flamininus. Their ties and loyalty to him would not have recommended them to the Aetolians.

56. *Syll.* 636, where only the representative of the Dorians from the Peloponnese is missing.

57. C. Habicht, *Hesperia* 56 (1987) 59–71.

58. R. K. Sherk, *Roman Documents from the Greek East* (Baltimore 1969) 224.

59. *Syll.* 613 A, a decree of the Amphictiony honoring Nicostratus of Larissa; the base of a statue erected to him at the time is *BCH* 73 (1949) 274 §25. For more on Nicostratus as

process in which Athens' ties to the Delphic shrine grew stronger and stronger, also increasing the city's international prestige.

Although it is clear that ties were created between Athens and Rome by their common opposition first to Philip, and later to Antiochus, it has remained unclear whether their common interests and military alliance ever resulted in a formal treaty *(foedus)*. The only mention of such a treaty is in Tacitus, who did not write until some three centuries later. In his account of Prince Germanicus' visit to Athens in 18 A.D. (100 years before his own time), Tacitus reports that out of respect for the alliance existing between the two states, Germanicus entered the city accompanied by only one lictor.[60] Few scholars argue outright against the existence of such a treaty, but those who think it probable disagree about when it was concluded. Several historians assume it came about during the Second Macedonian War (200–196) or soon thereafter.[61] Others argue that Athens was too weak at the time for Rome to have granted it a *foedus*.[62] Still others believe a pact was concluded either before 167[63] or after 146.[64]

It is certain that no treaty obligations existed in 200, when Cephisodorus asked the Romans to intervene against Philip V. And when an Athenian faction publicly supported Antiochus in 192, Livy does not mention this as constituting a violation of existing treaty agreements.[65] A reference to Athens as a "friendly and allied" state in a Senate decree from the late second century is not sufficient proof that a formal treaty existed above and beyond the informal ad hoc alliance.[66] Some time ago Sterling Dow pointed out one significant indicator: from the early

one of the most powerful men in Thessaly, see *ISE* 102, col. 2.15, with commentary by C. Habicht, *Chiron* 13 (1983) 24, no. 6. For the Athenian decree, see idem, *Hesperia* 56 (1987) 59–71; and J. Bousquet, *Etudes sur les comptes de Delphes* (Paris 1988) 79. For Menedemus, who presented the Athenian point of view to the Senate, see Habicht, *Hesperia* 56 (1987) 63; and for Alexion, Habicht, *Studien* 185–188.

60. Tacitus *Ann.* 2.53.3.

61. H. Horn, *Foederati* (Diss. Frankfurt 1930) 65–67; Accame, *Dominio* 101; G. De Sanctis, *Storia dei Romani* IV.3 (Florence 1964) 80 n. 6a.

62. A. Heuss, *Die völkerrechtlichen Grundlagen der römischen Außenpolitik in republikanischer Zeit* (Leipzig 1933) 32–34; Gruen, *Hellenistic World* 24.

63. R. Bernhardt, *Imperium und Eleutheria* (Diss. Hamburg 1971) 86.

64. E. Täubler, *Imperium Romanum* (Leipzig 1913) 228.

65. Gruen, *Hellenistic World* 24.

66. Sherk, *Roman Documents*, no. 15.8–9 and 55–56, from 112 B.C. This is normal diplomatic language in correspondence with friendly powers, even those with which no formal treaty has been signed.

second century on, prayers accompanying sacrifices for the welfare of the state included the phrase "and for that of our allies." Dow dated the first occurrence of this addition to the period just after 200.[67] Since then a greatly increased volume of more precisely dated material allows us to identify it as the time between the summer of 191 and the end of 188, that is, during the war against Antiochus.[68] For the next twenty years the reference to allies' welfare is never lacking, as far as present evidence shows. Dow is most likely correct when he concludes there are good reasons to assume that Athens was a formal treaty partner of Rome.[69] It was thus during the years the city was at war with Antiochus and the Aetolians that Athens, under the leadership of men such as Leon, Echedemus, Alexion, and Menedemus, concluded an official pact with Rome.

It appears that the city's ties to Rome, which rapidly grew stronger after they were first established in 200, were also commemorated in its bronze coinage. At least Kroll believes that the type of helmet Athena is depicted as wearing on these coins represents a borrowing from the Roman *denarius*. *Denarii* were minted from 212 or 211 on, and were probably brought to Attica by Roman troops. Kroll sees the borrowing as a compliment to Rome as the new protector of Athenian independence, and assigns the corresponding series to the years 196–190.[70]

3. Against Perseus

The peace agreement of 196 that followed Philip's defeat at Cynoscephalae marked the end of Macedonia as a constant potential threat to Athens' political independence. The monarchy continued in existence, but after the loss of the fortresses Demetrias, Chalcis, and Corinth and dissipation of its influence on various Greek tribes such as the Thessalians, it ceased to be a menace to the Greek states. In the two remaining decades of his life, King Philip devoted his energies to consolidating and strengthening the truncated realm that he still ruled. However, Polybius, the historian of this era, interpreted the king's

---

67. Dow, *Hesperia Suppl.* 1 (1937) 9.

68. The last inscription without the addition dates from the summer of 191 (*Agora* XV.187.43); the first surviving inscription with the added phrase is from the end of 188 (*Agora* XV.174.11).

69. Dow, *Hesperia Suppl.* 1 (1937) 9.

70. Kroll, *Coins* 51; the coins are illustrated on 63, nos. 78–80.

every action as showing his determination to resume the conflict with Rome someday and believed that by the time of Philip's death in 179 he had passed on this resolve to Perseus, his son and heir. And indeed open conflict did again break out with Rome in 171, in the Third Macedonian War. It ended in 168 with a Roman victory at Pydna, after which Perseus was imprisoned in Italy and the monarchy abolished, thus bringing to an end the kingdom of Philip II and Alexander the Great.

Polybius' claim that Philip and Perseus wanted this war and maneuvered to bring it about is unsupported by any other evidence. Philip scrupulously observed the conditions of the peace treaty, fulfilling even some arbitrary demands of the Senate that must have offended him. And for his part Perseus did everything in his power to avoid renewed conflict with Rome. In this effort he went to the limits of what could have been expected of him, and perhaps even beyond. The war was forced upon him, provoked no doubt by a faction in Rome whose breaches of faith disturbed even some senators.[71]

Athens, which had sought Roman protection from attack by Macedonia a generation earlier and continued a firm alliance with Rome ever since, had no choice but to declare itself on the Roman side after the outbreak of hostilities. Now tied to Rome by a formal treaty as well, the city did so unconditionally and without hesitation, offering its entire army and navy to Roman commanders in the first year of the war. The offer was refused, although the Romans did demand huge amounts of grain to feed their soldiers. Attica's poor soil made the Athenians themselves dependent on imported grain for their own citizens and even for some of their own farmers, but they nonetheless managed to supply the required amounts and declared their willingness to supply other goods if needed.[72] If they had an idea that cooperation was the right course, they were proved correct, for those Greek states that complied with Roman wishes in a hesitant or halfhearted manner were severely punished after the war. The Senate was pleased with Athens' readiness to do its bidding, as became apparent even before

71. The major recent studies of this period are Will, *Histoire* 2: 255–285; Hammond, *Macedonia* 488–569; and P. S. Derow, *CAH* 8[2] (1989) 290–323. Cf. A. Giovannini, *AJAH* 9 (1984 [1988]) 33–42. For criticism of the perfidious methods employed by Roman negotiators see Livy 42.47.1–9 and J. Briscoe, *JRS* 54 (1964) 66–77. For the "Roman Manifesto" summarizing Roman accusations against Perseus (*Syll.* 643), see J. Bousquet, *BCH* 105 (1981) 407–416.

72. Livy 43.6.2–3. The demand was for 100,000 Roman *modii*, equaling almost 900,000 liters or approximately 28,000 bushels; cf. R. P. Duncan-Jones, *ZPE* 21 (1976) 51–52.

the end of the war: when many Greek delegations traveled to Rome in 170, the Athenian emissaries were admitted and allowed to address the Senate first, always a sign of particular favor. The rewards later granted to Athens by the Senate reflected the same favored status.

The war dragged on for several years without any significant advantage to either side. The Roman commanders of the army and navy, a consul and praetor respectively for a one-year period, inflicted as much damage on their Greek friends and allies through plundering, extortion, and raids as did the enemy in the field; the Senate was forced to intervene, responding to the massive and well-founded complaints by tightening discipline among the troops and by trying to prevent the outrage from spreading to the general population. The Greeks were instructed henceforth to comply with such demands only when expressly authorized by the Senate. There is no indication that Athenian forces participated in the fighting. The outcome was decided on 22 June 168, when Consul Lucius Aemilius Paullus defeated King Perseus overwhelmingly at Pydna, near Olympus. Not long afterward Perseus was taken prisoner by the Romans on the island of Samothrace. An inscription found in the Athenian Agora reveals that at least one Athenian citizen, Calliphanes of Phyle, took part in the battle on the side of the victors, namely the Romans and the Pergamene princes Attalus and Athenaeus. He arrived in the city with the news of this victory shortly before the end of the Athenian year, and the *strategoi* immediately had the Council call a special session of the Assembly. It took place on the last day of the year, and the messenger was awarded honors.[73]

Only a few months later, in the early fall of 168, Aemilius Paullus came to Athens himself. Accompanied by his son (the younger Scipio) and one of the Pergamene princes, he was on a tour of Greece to visit the principal sights of the country. His travels took him from Macedonia via Thessaly to Delphi, Lebadea in Boeotia, Chalcis, Aulis, Oropus, and Athens. The consul offered a sacrifice to Athena on the Acropolis and probably visited the other sights recommended by Livy: "the harbors, the walls connecting Piraeus and the city, the ship-houses, and images of the gods and men created in all different materials by masters of all kinds."[74] He is also said to have asked the citizens to grant him a wish and lend him their most respected philosopher to tutor his

73. *ISE* 35.
74. Livy 45.27.11–28.1; Polybius 30.10.3–6; Plut. *Aemilius* 28.1–2. For the Long Walls see Chapter 7, Section 3.

children, as well as a painter to commemorate his victory at the triumphal procession in Rome. The Athenians thereupon chose Metrodorus, a master in the fields of both scholarship and art, and Paullus found both requests well fulfilled. The consul may also have taken a statue of Athena, which he placed in a temple of Fortuna.[75] From Athens he traveled on to Olympia by way of Corinth, Sicyon, Argos, and Epidaurus.

After the war it immediately became clear that Athens would continue to enjoy the favor of the Senate; the favorable treatment accorded the city stood in sharp contrast to the punishments meted out to Rome's three oldest and most important allies, the king of Pergamum, the republic of Rhodes, and the Achaean League.[76] Rome suspected or accused all three of having shown insufficient zeal or loyalty toward the Roman cause during the war; Eumenes II of Pergamum was charged with secretly maintaining contact with Perseus. The king wanted to defend himself in person, but when he landed in Italy the Romans brusquely asked him to leave at once, and the Senate even proclaimed the independence of Galatia, a part of Eumenes' realm. The Rhodians lost the Romans' goodwill because, on Consul Marcius Philippus' encouragement, they had dared to speak of a negotiated peace in 169 and offered to serve as mediators. Certain factions in the Senate even wanted to declare war on them, but in the end peace prevailed. The Rhodians lost the regions of Caria and Lycia, given to them after the war against Antiochus, but which were now declared independent. They also lost the lucrative tariffs associated with the island of Delos when its status was changed (as will be discussed below). The Romans could hardly reproach the Achaeans with any serious offenses; their worst crime was to have tolerated (like most Greek states) a political faction that favored Perseus or at least wished to see Macedonia preserved as an independent state. Even so, 1,500 Achaeans named by the pro-Roman politician Callicrates were seized without trial and held in Italy for fifteen years; during this time the Senate repeatedly refused to grant the captives individual trials or to allow the Achaean League to investigate their cases. One of the internees was Polybius, a man about thirty years old in 170 who had served as hipparch of the League and whose father was a prominent opponent of Callicrates, the strongly pro-independence politician Lycortas. Befriended by Scipio

---

75. Pliny *Nat. hist.* 35.135 and 34.54.
76. For more on what follows, see the general histories listed in note 71 above.

Aemilianus, son of the victor at the battle of Pydna, Polybius' involuntary sojourn enabled him to study Rome and the Romans at first hand for fifteen years.

After the war states both large and small from all parts of the Greek world sent envoys to Rome to present their congratulations to the Senate and either remind it of their loyal support or dispel any lingering doubts about their zeal; Athenian diplomats numbered among them. Part of their mission, though not their principal aim, was to intercede on behalf of the citizens of Haliartus in Boeotia. In 171 the praetor Gaius Lucretius had stormed the city and taken it after fierce fighting; the entire population was killed except for 2,500 armed men who retreated into the fortress. When they capitulated the next day, they were sold into slavery.[77] The Athenian attempt to "rescue" them was linked with a request that those whose freedom was bought be allowed to refound their city. When the Senate refused, the Athenians acted on their previous instructions and requested the territory of Haliartus for themselves instead, along with the islands of Delos and Lemnos. The Senate granted this second petition.

In his commentary on these events Polybius remarks that the Athenians deserved no reproach for seeking Delos and Lemnos, for both islands had been under Athenian rule before, or at least claimed by them. However, they did merit censure for robbing the citizens of Haliartus of all hope for the future, rather than pleading as energetically as possible for the rebuilding of one of the oldest cities in Boeotia. Here they had shown themselves unworthy of their own great past. Polybius goes on to say that their acquisition of Haliartus earned Athens more ill will than benefit, and the return of the two islands to Athenian rule was accompanied by a host of difficulties as well. However, it is not at all certain that his criticism is justified.[78] Haliartus became an Athenian enclave within Boeotian territory.[79]

77. Livy 42.63.11.

78. Polybius 30.20.1–8, with Walbank, *Commentary* 3: 443–444; Strabo 10.5.4, p. 486. P. Roussel, *Délos, colonie athénienne* (Paris 1916; enl. ed. 1987) 2 n. 2, expresses doubt about whether Polybius' reproach was justified. Athenian sovereignty over the region of Haliartus is confirmed by three border stones and an honorary decree for the Athenian governor in Haliartus (*ABSA* 28 [1926–27] 137–138, nos. 10–11; *Chiron* 22 [1992] 481; *IG* VII.2850; better text in P. Roesch, *Etudes béotiennes* [Paris 1982] 168–171, from the year 122/1). The area was still Athenian during the Augustan era (Strabo 9.2.30, p. 411). The Athenians may have asked for Lemnos as early as 196.

79. J.-M. Bertrand, *Sociétés urbaines, sociétés rurales dans l'Asie Mineure et la Syrie hellénistiques et romaines,* ed. E. Frézouls (Strasbourg 1987) 100.

Seleucus I had given Lemnos back to the Athenians after his victory over Lysimachus in 281. At some later time the island passed under Macedonian control. Several decrees and a dedication of the Athenian community in Hephaestia have survived from the second half of the third century,[80] but these inscriptions do not reveal who the island's rulers were at that time, any more than Livy's report, which says only that the Roman commander Publius Sulpicius and Attalus I put in at Lemnos in 208, during the First Macedonian War.[81] A letter from Philip V to the Athenians in Hephaestia, in which he announces his intention to undergo initiation into the mysteries of the Cabiri on the island, also contains no information on Lemnos' political status.[82]

Imbros and Skyros in the northern Aegean were probably given back to Athens at the same time.[83] It is not easy to see why Delos lost the independence it had enjoyed for almost 150 years; perhaps it occurred because a Macedonian admiral had used the island as his base of operations during the war. The Senate linked its award of Delos to Athens with the condition that it must be a free harbor; that is, no import or export tariff, which usually amounted to two percent of goods' worth, could be imposed. This provision may have been pushed through by Italian traders. As a result a large proportion of the Mediterranean trade, particularly between Italy and Syria and Palestine, began to pass through Delos instead of Rhodes; the Rhodians' income from tariffs fell at once by 85 percent, from one million to 150,000 drachmas per year.[84]

In the thirty-two years after King Philip first posed an acute threat to Athenian safety in 200, the city participated in three major wars, always on the side of Rome. It emerged from these conflicts without any glory, but essentially unscathed, and the third war brought it considerable profit. No large-scale military efforts had been required of the Athenians after their successful defense against the attacks of 200. Small squadrons of the fleet participated occasionally in naval battles, and

80. *ASAA,* n.s. 3–4 (1941–1943) 79 ff., nos. 3–5 and 9.

81. Livy 28.5.1.

82. S. Accame, *RFIC* 69 (1941) 179–193; P. M. Fraser and A. H. McDonald, *JRS* 42 (1952) 81–83; Walbank, *Commentary* 2: 611; R. K. Sherk, *ZPE* 84 (1990) 270–272.

83. B. Niese, *Geschichte der griechischen und makedonischen Staaten seit der Schlacht bei Chaeronea,* vol. 3 (Gotha 1903) 189 n. 6; Holleaux, *Etudes* 5: 107–108.

84. Polybius 30.31.12 with Walbank, *Commentary* 3: 459–460; D. van Berchem, *MH* 48 (1991) 129–145; Will, *Histoire* 2: 300–301.

possibly a detachment of Athenian soldiers saw action at the battle of Pydna, unless Calliphanes fought as a lone volunteer. No significant destruction of Attic territory took place after 200, and it does not appear that the population suffered much loss of life during these wars.

At the end of this period the Athenian state found itself in a far stronger position than at the beginning. The danger that had threatened from Macedonia for almost two centuries had now vanished, for the Romans had taken King Perseus and 250 Macedonian nobles captive and interned them in Italy; the monarchy was replaced by four independent republics. And although Athens lagged far behind the Achaean League and Rhodes (not to mention the king of Pergamum) in influence and military power in the first quarter of the second century, it emerged with gains from the Third Macedonian War, which it owed less to its own newly acquired strength than to the penalties imposed on the other powers by the Roman Senate. In contrast to its rivals, Athens continued to enjoy the Senate's favor, which even increased over time. The city owed to this body the great territorial gains of 167: Delos, Lemnos, Imbros, and Skyros (all of which had been under Athenian sovereignty for some considerable time in the past) and the region of Haliartus.

It is clear that after 168 Rome exercised decisive power in Greece, even though it had not yet annexed any Greek territory nor established a permanent garrison on Greek soil. Although in the following years the course of events was not always dictated by the Romans' will, nothing of consequence could occur that ran counter to their wishes. The Greeks had watched in horror as the Roman armies took their departure. Before embarking for Italy on the Adriatic coast, the commanders Aemilius Paullus and Anicius Gallus carried out their instructions from the Senate and passed formal judgment on the Molossi, a tribal group in Epirus that had fought on the Macedonian side. After promising mercy, they demanded that the population surrender all its money and valuables. Thereafter all the houses in seventy villages were plundered and destroyed in a single day, and 150,000 people were herded together and sold into slavery for the benefit of the Roman soldiers.[85]

---

85. Polybius 30.15; Livy 45.34.1–6; Walbank, *Commentary* 3: 438–439.

NINE

Times of Peace
(before and after 167)

1. Contacts with Kings

The Roman treaty with Philip V in 196 ushered in a century of peace for Athens. The city was hardly touched by Rome's wars with Antiochus and Perseus and did not become involved in armed conflict again until 88, when it joined King Mithridates of Pontus in his war against the Romans. With the coming of peace lively diplomatic relations with other states were resumed, in strong contrast to the isolationist policy pursued by the brothers Eurycleides and Micion in the closing years of the third century. In addition general prosperity increased, greatly stimulated by Athens' acquisition of Delos and Lemnos.

During the third century Athens had maintained its closest relations with the dynasty of the Ptolemies; Egypt protected the city from the rival Antigonid dynasty of Macedonia more than once in this period, with varying success.[1] Faced with the difficult situation of the year 200, the Athenians turned as usual to the court at Alexandria, sending Cephisodorus with a plea for help, but Egypt was too preoccupied with its own problems; it was involved in a major war with Antiochus III, which ended with Egypt losing Palestine and southern Syria. The king of Egypt, Ptolemy V Epiphanes, was only a child at the time, and a series of regents, acting as his tutors and running the affairs of state, were never able to maintain their hold on power for any length of time. For these reasons Egypt was in no position to provide Athens with any effective assistance, and other powers stepped in to fill the gap. Attalus of Pergamum and the Rhodians were of some help, but the most

---

1. Athenian relations with the Ptolemaic empire are discussed in detail in C. Habicht, *CA* 11 (1992) 68–90; for the early second century see esp. 75–86.

important support in this predicament came from Rome, with whom the Athenians soon developed close ties. Relations with Egypt did not suffer, however. Three decrees honoring high officials in the service of Ptolemy V have survived from the decade 190–180.[2] They reveal that contacts between the two powers were frequent and that large numbers of Athenians traveled to Egypt, chiefly to buy grain and to trade other goods. Two other Athenian decrees show that lively contacts were also maintained with Cyprus, then governed by a Ptolemaic official.[3]

It is practically certain that Athens sent a delegation to Alexandria for the festival commemorating Ptolemy I every four years, and that the Egyptian court was regularly represented at major Athenian festivals such as the Great Panathenaea and the Eleusinian Mysteries; delegates probably attended the Athenian Ptolemaea in honor of Ptolemy III as well. The kings of Egypt were also honorary citizens of Athens and members of the tribe of Ptolemais. It is known that on one occasion in 169—a date not especially favorable to diplomatic activity, since the sixth Syrian War between Ptolemy VI and Antiochus IV was raging—three Athenian delegations were in Egypt at the same time; we know that one of them dealt with the Panathenaea and one with the Mysteries.[4] However, nothing illuminates the intensity and cordiality of relations between the two powers as clearly as the number of Panathenaean victories won by members of the Egyptian royal family and high officials of the crown between 182 and 158; they included King Ptolemy V, his son and successor Ptolemy VI (once as prince and twice as king), his consort Cleopatra II, Polycrates (a minister whose sister Polycratea was the mother of King Perseus of Macedonia), his wife Zeuxo of Cyrene, their three daughters, and Eirene and Agathoclea, who as priestesses of the dynastic cult belonged to the ruling elite.[5] And this surviving evidence certainly gives us only a partial view of the complete picture.

Contrary to a theory advanced by Ferguson and adopted by other scholars, no break in diplomatic relations occurred between Athens and the court of the Ptolemies in the fifty years following the death of Ptolemy VI in 145, nor was there any cooling of their cordial entente.[6]

2. *IG* II^2.891, 893a, 897, and perhaps also 888; Habicht, ibid., 77.
3. *IG* II^2.908 and 909. Details on their content and dating are in Habicht, ibid., 80–81.
4. Polybius 28.19.4.
5. Habicht, *CA* 11 (1992) 78–79.
6. For more details see ibid., 83–85. Since then a new inscription concerning the celebration of the Ptolemaea in Athens in 117/6 has come to light; *Ergon* (1991) 5.

About the middle of the second century the Ptolemies began to dismantle their bases in the Aegean and ceased to be in a position to offer Athens much protection. However, by that time Rome had long since assumed the role of the city's main protector.

During the third century Athens had only sporadic contact with the court of the Seleucids. Closer relations were hindered not only by geographic circumstances but also by the fact that the Seleucid and Ptolemaic dynasties engaged in constant disputes over rival claims to southern Syria. If the Athenians had attempted to establish firmer ties to the court at Antioch, they would have run the risk of alienating their Egyptian protector. At the end of the third century Antiochus III, having returned from his "Anabasis" in the east, tried to gain the goodwill of the various Greek states, including Athens.[7] Scholars disagree as to whether the aegis of gilded bronze with the head of the Medusa dedicated to Athena on the Acropolis came from him or his son Antiochus IV.[8] Most likely the offerings registered at an Athenian shrine in 181/0 from a Queen Laodice were the gifts of his consort.[9] An Athenian decree from 184/3 shows further that in the years before the war against Antiochus broke out in 192, Athenian envoys and festival delegations traveled with some regularity to the royal court at Antioch on the Orontes.[10] Thus diplomatic relations with Antioch did exist, at the very least, and they were cordial, though perhaps no more than routine. When hostilities broke out, some citizens in Athens would have preferred to support Antiochus rather than be drawn into the war on the opposite side by the Romans.

When the war ended, and Seleucus IV succeeded his father Antiochus III on the throne soon afterward, it did not take long for good relations between the two powers to be restored. This happened at the latest in the spring of 186, when an emissary from the king was honored in Athens.[11] A decree from the clans of the Kerykes and Eumolpids from about the same time documents the existence of diplomatic contacts between Athens and the king's court.[12]

7. For more on what follows see C. Habicht, *Chiron* 19 (1989) 7–26; for Antiochus III and his sons Seleucus IV and Antiochus IV, 10–21.

8. Ibid., 11–12.

9. *Hesperia Suppl.* 4 (1940) 145, lines 8–9.

10. *IG* II^2.785.10–13.

11. W. K. Pritchett and B. D. Meritt, *The Chronology of Hellenistic Athens* (Cambridge, Mass., 1940) 117–118.

12. *IG* II^2.1236; Habicht, *Chiron* 19 (1989) 18. For the date see Tracy, *ALC* 95.

But cordial relations reached their peak when Seleucus' younger brother succeeded him as Antiochus IV Epiphanes at the end of 175, for this king became a great benefactor of Athens and the city's declared favorite. Personal contacts undoubtedly played a role in the friendship. When Antiochus III reached a peace settlement with the Romans in 188, he was forced to send his son Antiochus to Rome as a hostage. After some time the king's grandson, Seleucus' son Demetrius, was sent to take the prince's place. It was thought that this exchange occurred in 175, shortly before Seleucus' death (or murder), but a recently published decree in honor of young Prince Antiochus reveals that he must have been released earlier, for he is described as residing in Athens in the autumn of 178.[13] He thus spent several years in Athens as a young man instead of returning to Antioch, where his brother now occupied the throne. After his brother's death in 175 regents claimed the throne in the name of Seleucus' younger son, still a child, but Antiochus set out for home determined to seize it for himself. He had the full support of Eumenes II of Pergamum and his brothers, former enemies of the Seleucid dynasty, and with their aid soon achieved his aim. The citizens in Athens were so delighted by Antiochus' success that they thanked the Pergamene ruler and his brothers with an effusive decree, unearthed in Pergamum.[14] As the text reveals, statues of the new king already stood in Athens, probably erected during his stay there, demonstrating the citizens' affection for the prince.

Once crowned king, Antiochus rewarded the Athenians royally for their kindness toward him. He sponsored resumption of construction on the huge temple of Olympian Zeus, begun in the sixth century but never completed. The king made magnificent plans and chose—rather surprisingly—a Roman master builder by the name of Cossutius to carry them out. Although the project was not finished in Antiochus' own lifetime, the scale of the plans immediately earned it a place among the most famous temples in the Greek world.[15] At about this time, presumably in 173/2, the Athenians also awarded honors to Arridaeus, commander of Antiochus' royal guard.[16] Athenian envoys again met

13. *Hesperia* 51 (1982) 60, no. 3.
14. *OGI* 248, interpreted by Holleaux, *Etudes* 2: 127–147; Appian *Syr.* 233–234.
15. Sources are listed in Habicht, *Chiron* 19 (1989) 19 n. 63; they include *AP* 9, nos. 701 and 702.
16. *ISE* 34.

the king face to face in Egypt in 169. They had been sent to the court of the Ptolemies, who were at war with Antiochus and had requested emissaries from several Greek states, including Athens, to visit Antiochus' camp and negotiate a peace settlement. According to the story, however, Antiochus made such a strong case that his hearers became persuaded of the justice of his cause.[17] The news of his death in 164 must have affected the Athenians deeply, for the king's benevolence toward them was known far and wide. Even the Jews who rebelled against him in distant Palestine were impressed by his kindness toward Athens, a fact reflected in the second book of Maccabees.[18]

As far as is known, the first contacts between the Attalids and Athens took the form of gifts to the Academy and the Peripatetic School (or their heads).[19] Under Attalus I (reigned 241–197), who took the title of king after victories over the Galatians in Asia Minor, official contacts began and soon took on a political character. This was inevitable after the First Macedonian War, when Attalus acquired control of the island of Aegina in the Saronic Gulf, for in a manner of speaking it made him a neighbor. He was also the prime mover behind the Athenians' decision to enter the war against Philip V in 200, during which he supplied them with soldiers, money, and grain. Attalus seems to have concerned himself further with Athenian prisoners of war, meaning in all probability that he supplied funds for their ransom.[20] A considerable number of scholars assume that it was Attalus I who sent the Athenians the sculpture of the "small Attalid dedication group" sometime around 200, in order to remind them of his early victories over the Galatians and to present himself as a champion of Greek civilization. However, many other scholars believe the group to have been a gift of his son Attalus II, who, before ascending the throne, not only took part in the campaign against the Galatians led by the Roman consul Manlius Vulso in 189 but also, with his brother King Eumenes, had to weather the great Galatian uprising of 166, which plunged the dynasty into a severe crisis.

Whatever the correct answer to this question,[21] it is certain that from

---

17. Polybius 28.19–20.

18. 2 Maccabees 9.15. See also C. Habicht, *HSCP* 80 (1976) 3.

19. For more on the subject see C. Habicht, *Hesperia* 59 (1990) 561–577. For more on Attalus I and his time, cf. H.-J. Schalles, *Untersuchungen zur Kulturpolitik der pergamenischen Herrscher im dritten Jahrhundert vor Christus* (Tübingen 1985).

20. *IG* II².886.17.

21. For a recent summary of this controversy see F. Queyrel, *RA* (1989) 278–296. B. Andreae argues for the later dating in *Studi ellenistici*, ed. B. Virgilio, vol. 4 (Pisa 1994)

the year 200 on no other royal house, not even the Ptolemies, maintained closer and more cordial relations with Athens. Upon the outbreak of the Second Macedonian War, Attalus was in a position to remind the city of the favors it had received from him, and as the Athenians were abolishing the cult of the Antigonids, they replaced it with one for Attalus, modeled directly on the Antigonid cult and that of Ptolemy III.

As allies of Rome and Athens, both Attalus I and later his son Eumenes (reigned 197–158) visited the city (or Piraeus) more than once during the wars against Philip V, Antiochus III, and Perseus. And during the war against Antiochus at least three men in Eumenes' service were honored in separate Athenian decrees: Menandros, the king's personal physician; Theophilus of Pergamum; and Pausimachus.[22] Similarly, Athenian emissaries visited the Pergamene court soon after Antiochus' defeat. Like the male members of the Ptolemaic dynasty, Eumenes and his brothers were honorary citizens of Athens, registered as members of the tribe named after their father. All four are thus identified in the list of victors at the Great Panathenaea of 178.[23] That same year the Seleucid prince Antiochus, sojourning in Athens, was awarded honors by the city—the prince whom Eumenes and his brothers later installed on the throne that by rights should have gone to his nephew Demetrius, still a prisoner in Rome. The Athenians took the Pergamene act of assistance to Antiochus IV in 175 as an occasion to award new honors to the members of that dynasty. They added an individual decree for the third brother, Philetaerus, in 174, and a statue in Olympia as one of their benefactors.[24]

Not long afterward, perhaps during the war against Perseus, the Athenians passed honorary decrees for Hicesius of Ephesus, the royal governor in Aegina, and for Philtes of Cyzicus, another of the king's

131–133. According to Andreae (133) the group ("really one of the greatest monuments of all time," p. 133) was worked on by, among others, the "Pergamene court artist" Phyromachus of Athens, who had previously set his stamp on the style of the Great Altar of Pergamum; the monument was dedicated to Athens sometime between 166 and 150. Cf. R. R. R. Smith's review of Andreae's thematically related book *Laokoon und die Gründung Roms* (Mainz 1988) in *Gnomon* 63 (1991) 351–358.

22. *IG* II².946 and 947.9–21; Osborne, *Naturalization* 1: D 100. Habicht, *Hesperia* 59 (1990) 564–567.

23. *IG* II².2314.84–91; for the dating see S. V. Tracy, *Hesperia* 60 (1991) 217–221; for preservation of the tribe of Attalis, ibid. 189, col. 1.38 and 48.

24. *IG* II².905; W. Dittenberger and K. Purgold, *Die Inschriften von Olympia* (Berlin 1896) 312.

officials. In the summer of 167, in a special session of the Assembly called on the last day of the year, they honored a certain Diodorus described as "a friend" of the king and his brothers.[25]

The monuments erected in Athens by the Attalids were virtually the equals of the temple of Olympian Zeus, which their friend Antiochus IV had brought closer to completion. These were the stoa of Eumenes on the southern slope of the Acropolis, a full 163 meters long, which sheltered audiences at the theater of Dionysus in case of bad weather; and the two-story stoa to the east of the Agora (116 meters long), which Attalus built after succeeding his brother as king in 158.[26]

The Athenians honored Eumenes II and Attalus II with colossal statues on the Acropolis above the theater; the name of the Roman triumvir Marcus Antonius was later substituted for the names of the kings on the inscribed bases.[27]

Athens also maintained friendly relations with a neighboring monarch and rival of the Pergamene dynasty, King Pharnaces of Pontus. Although his expressive face is familiar from the portrait on his silver coins, he remains otherwise a shadowy figure, and we know very little more about him today than what Eduard Meyer wrote in 1879 in his history of the kingdom of Pontus. The dates of Pharnaces' reign have still not been determined, although it seems likely that he died during the year 171/0; Polybius devotes a passage to him under that year's heading that must almost certainly be understood as an obituary.[28] Pharnaces makes a sudden appearance in history with his conquest of Sinope on the Black Sea in 183, an independent city that the Rhodians had protected from earlier attacks by his father. Pharnaces' act of aggression led to a war of several years' duration against Eumenes of Pergamum and various other allies. A peace treaty concluded in 179 forced Pharnaces to relinquish most of his conquered territories— above all in Galatia, it is thought—but he managed to hold onto Sinope, which he then made the capital of his realm.[29]

In the year of the archon Tychandrus the Athenian Assembly drew

25. Osborne, *Naturalization* 1: D 106; *IG* II^2.955 as restored by Habicht, *Hesperia* 59 (1990) 576–577; *IG* II^2.945, where the name of the sponsor can be completed as Aris[tion], following *Agora* XV.212.110.

26. H. Schaaf, *Untersuchungen zu Gebäudestiftungen in hellenistischer Zeit* (Cologne 1992) 84–111.

27. Plut. *Antonius* 60.6; cf. Cassius Dio 50.15.3.

28. Polybius 27.17. For the portrait of Pharnaces: R. Smith, *Hellenistic Royal Portraits* (Oxford 1988) 113 and plate 77.10.

29. C. Habicht, *CAH* 8^2 (1989) 328–330.

up a rather long decree in honor of Pharnaces and his new queen, a member of the Seleucid royal family named Nysa; an inscription on a stone tablet was set up in Delos and excavated there.[30] Until recently scholars agreed that Tychandrus' term of office was 160/59, which prevented reading Polybius' text on Pharnaces for 171/0 as an obituary. Now, however, Stephen Tracy has demonstrated that Tychandrus served in 196/5, and that the Athenian decree for Pharnaces dates from April or May 195.[31] The surviving opening fragment states that the king's ancestors were already friends of the city and that Pharnaces made certain promises to the Athenians, but had to ask the city's emissaries for a postponement in fulfilling them because he had not yet established his rule firmly enough. The king and queen are praised for their benevolence, and the intention to erect statues to both in Delos is announced. A citizen is named and charged with personally delivering a copy of the decree to the king; he should make use of the opportunity, it states further, to remind the king tactfully of his promise to send a gift of money, if at all possible; the yearly installment would be most welcome. This is the only firm evidence of diplomatic relations between the city and the monarch; many other documents must have been lost. There is no proof at this time of Athenian contact with the kings of Bithynia in northwestern Asia Minor, Prusias I (reigned until 183) and his son and successor, Prusias II (reigned 183–149).

The preceding survey of Athens' diplomatic relations during the second century has shown that a great deal of construction on a large scale was undertaken but no longer financed by the city itself, as it had been in the time of Lycurgus. Instead, the sponsors were the kings in Pergamum and Syria, prompted to display their wealth and power in Athens because of the city's great prestige.

2. Contacts with Independent States

Once the difficult years of the Second Macedonian War and the wars against Antiochus and the Aetolians were over, a new spirit of confidence arose among the citizens of Athens. Together with the

---

30. *IG* XI.4.1056 (I *Délos* 1497 *bis*).

31. S. V. Tracy, *AM* 107 (1992) 307–314, where he also cites the epigraphic evidence for Pharnaces' reign from Odessus, Amaseia, and Chersonesus. Virginia Grace proposed Pharnaces as the donor of the "Middle Stoa" in the Athenian Agora; *Hesperia* 54 (1985) 1–54. She demonstrated that its construction began around 183 B.C., that is, during his reign, but the link with the king of Pontus remains unproved.

Thessalian Confederacy, now independent of Macedonia, the Athenians brought about a redistribution of seats in the Amphictionic Council at Delphi, made necessary by the disappearance of Aetolia as its major force. The two powers were astute enough to gain the Roman Senate's approval for their plan to reorganize administration of both the shrine and the Pythian Games.[32] Although these steps frustrated the hopes Delphi itself seems to have entertained for a larger role, no lasting friction between that city and Athens resulted. Some time around 180/79 Delphi asked Athens to provide a mediator for its quarrel with a neighboring community over territory and certain holy places. The Athenian Apollodorus resolved the matter, and Delphi awarded him honors for his services. The other party in the dispute is not named, but probably it was the Locrian city of Amphissa, known to have been involved in a similar quarrel at the same time. The parties to that controversy requested mediators from Rhodes, and the Rhodians sent them a panel of nine of their citizens.

Two documents describe the disputes in virtually identical language,[33] so that it seems reasonable to suppose they refer to the same events. If this is the case, then the question naturally arises how both groups could have mediated the same dispute and, if so, what their different duties might have been. Various explanations are possible, such as a division of responsibility in which the Rhodians worked out the general framework of a settlement while Apollodorus, the Athenian, took charge of its implementation and any specific problems arising in that connection.

Another fragmentary decree found in the Agora in Athens relates to religious matters in a city in Boeotia, Attica's neighbor to the north; in all likelihood it concerns Athenian participation in the festival of the Muses in Thespiae.[34] As might be expected, the city and the Aetolian League were on good terms during the 180s, after the Athenians supported them in their efforts to obtain peace from Rome; cordial relations are reflected in a surviving document from about 182.[35] In

32. A. Giovannini, *Ancient Macedonia,* vol. 1 (Thessaloniki 1970) 147–154; Habicht, *Hesperia* 56 (1987) 59–71.

33. *FD* III.2.89 (the decree for Apollodorus) and III.3.383 (the decree for the Rhodians). Cf. Daux, *Delphes* 277–280; and G. Daverio Rocchi, *Frontiera e confini nella Grecia antica* (Rome 1988) 132–142. The dating follows from *Syll.* 585.216–224.

34. G. Lalonde, *Hesperia* 46 (1977) 268–276, dating from the period 210–170; Tracy, *ALC* 75. For the reorganization of this festival at the end of the third century, see M. Feyel, *Contribution à l'épigraphie béotienne* (Le Puy 1942) 88–132.

35. *IG* II^2.4931.

the early second century, some time between 198 and 168, the city also concluded a mutual legal assistance pact with the Achaean League, over which differences arose later between the two states.[36]

It appears that during the second century other states increasingly turned to Athens and Athenian citizens for help in mediating conflicts. An important document from Miletus deals with the peace made following a war between Miletus and Magnesia-on-the-Maeander in which both sides had suffered heavy losses.[37] Thirteen other states, primarily from the Aegean and Asia Minor, participated in the peace negotiations under the leadership of Rhodes. Besides the Athenian delegation, five Achaean envoys came from the mainland—one representing the League, one each representing Megalopolis and Antigonea (Mantinea), and two from Patras. For a long time after the peace treaty was discovered on the eve of the First World War, it was assigned to the year 197. Not long ago, however, Malcolm Errington proved convincingly that the treaty must have been concluded between 185 and 182, after the troops of Philip V and Antiochus III had departed from Asia Minor, and the peace of 188 had given the Rhodians control of Caria south of the Maeander (where Magnesia was situated).[38] The only participating states from the continent, Athens and the Achaeans, were at that time Rome's most influential friends in Greece; Athens was particularly involved as the "mother city" of the Ionian communities. The Athenian delegation consisted of three men from prominent families, and its leader, Alexion, had participated in the reorganization of the Delphic Amphictiony a few years earlier. He was thus an experienced diplomat, and participated in yet another diplomatic mission only a short time later.[39]

At about the same time as this peace treaty (perhaps a few years before or afterward) three Milesians, all from influential families in their home city, visited Athens as festival delegates, possibly for the Panathenaea, and received honors there. It is easy to see why these particular men were chosen for the trip, as the father of Euandridas, their leader, was the descendant of an Olympic victor named Antenor, who had received honors in Athens in 306. Euandridas' fellow delegate

36. Polybius 32.7.3; P. Gauthier, *Symbola* (Nancy 1972) 173; W. Ziegler, *Symbolai und Asylia* (Diss. Bonn 1975) 63. See Chapter 10, Section 1.

37. I *Milet* 148 (*Syll.* 588).

38. R. M. Errington, *Chiron* 19 (1989) 279–288.

39. For Alexion's family see Habicht, *Studien* 185–188, and the new document concerning his role in Delphi after the war against Antiochus, *Hesperia* 56 (1987) 65, line 15.

Hermophantus was the son of Lichas, a leading statesman of Miletus in the late third century who was awarded crowns in many cities, including Athens.[40]

Other Athenian decrees show the city in contact with Crete and with Ceos in the Cyclades.[41] Athenian relations with Crete in the early second century are reflected in a fragmentary inscription containing the decree of a city in the western part of the island. It prohibits its citizens from seizing booty on Athenian territory and establishes penalties for infractions; the Athenian representatives present in Crete in this connection, Lysicles and Thrasippus, two brothers from a well-known family of Gargettus, are also made *proxenoi* of the Cretan city.[42] Their mission was related to the growing problem of Cretan piracy, from which various Greek cities were seeking relief by obtaining guarantees from Cretan communities; a number of such official promises have been preserved.[43]

Athenian cooperation with the Thessalian Confederacy in 186–184 for the purpose of reorganizing the Amphictionic Council has already been mentioned. Slightly earlier, in the first few years after the refounding of the Confederacy, a Thessalian named Alexander was awarded honors. I have proposed the year 194/3 for the Athenian archon Dionysius, in whose term the award was made, but there is one difficulty in this connection: Nicias, the sponsor of the motion, was then a member of the Council but is also known to have belonged to the Council in 193/2. Although it was possible to serve twice in the Council, successive terms were not permitted.[44]

On the Peloponnese, after Sparta and Messene joined the Achaean League conflict smoldered for years between League officials and various political factions in the two cities. In Sparta there was tension between supporters of Nabis, the tyrant murdered by the Aetolians in

40. *IG* II^2.992; Habicht, *Chiron* 21 (1991) 325–329.

41. *IG* II^2.844.49–70 and 978.

42. M. Guarducci, *Inscriptiones Creticae*, 4 vols. (Rome 1935–1950) 2: 313, no. 3.1–12, found in Athens and also printed as *IG* II^2.1130. For the family of the two brothers see C. Habicht, *Hesperia* 60 (1991) 227.

43. P. Brulé, *La piraterie crétoise hellénistique* (Paris 1978) 23–24 and 75.

44. *IG* II^2.850, which certainly dates from the 190s. The sponsor Nicias, son of Polyxenos, appears in line 3 and in *IG* II^2.844.50 from 193/2. The permissibility of serving two terms in the Council is documented by *Ath. Pol.* 62.3, but as departing members had to submit an account of their activities, an interval must have been required by law (G. Busolt, *Griechische Staatskunde*^{3}, ed. H. Swoboda, vol. 2 [Munich 1926] 1022; cf. P. J. Rhodes, *The Athenian Boule* [Oxford 1972] 14–16).

192, and the opponents he had exiled; factions for and against the union with the Achaeans opposed each other in both cities.[45] The protracted disputes, in which the Roman Senate had to intervene repeatedly, were finally settled as a result of the Achaean mission to Rome led by Callicrates in 180. At that time the Senate directed the Achaeans to readmit the Spartans and Messenians still living in exile, and sent copies of the order to Aetolia, Epirus, Athens, Boeotia, and Acarnania (presumably all places currently harboring such exiles) with instructions to cooperate.[46] Callicrates had persuaded the senators that the interests of Rome and its allies among the Greeks would suffer if they did not intervene; clear directives from Rome would be necessary to end the constant strife. The senators' reaction showed they had adopted his viewpoint (which Polybius condemned as unpatriotic). Their instructions also reflect the expectation that independent Greek states such as Athens would carry out Rome's wishes without protest. The presence of emissaries from the Achaean League in Athens in 178/7 may have been connected with this matter. The envoys apparently negotiated with a three-member Athenian commission, headed by the same Alexion of Azenia who had played a leading role in the reorganization of the Amphictiony in 186/5 and led the Athenian delegation involved in making peace between Miletus and Magnesia sometime around 184.[47]

Very soon after the war against Perseus ended, Athens was approached by the old royal city of Ambracia in Epirus and the Acarnanian League, its neighbor to the south, for a panel of judges to settle ongoing disputes between the two states (or some of their citizens). Ambracia had been the scene of long and fierce fighting in the Roman-Aetolian war and had suffered terribly; in the end, in 189, the city surrendered to the Roman consul Marcus Fulvius Nobilior in obedience to the orders of Aetolian officials, who could not obtain a peace agreement on any other terms. Fulvius' train included the Roman poet Ennius, who composed a piece, now lost, on the siege of Ambracia. The consul plundered the art collection in the royal palace, assembled

45. Livy 35.37.1. The report that copies of the treaty that made Sparta a member of the League in 192 were displayed on the Capitol in Rome, in Olympia, and on the Acropolis in Athens (Livy 38.33.9) may be nothing more than a decorative invention of a Roman annalist.

46. Polybius 24.10.6. For more on these events see R. M. Errington, *Philopoemen* (Oxford 1969) 200–205.

47. *Hesperia* 26 (1957) 210, no. 58.

largely by King Pyrrhus, taking a record number of works back to Italy with him. Shortly thereafter, in 187, the Senate declared Ambracia a free city. During the war against Perseus the Romans had stationed a large garrison of troops there,[48] straining its resources so severely that near the end of the war (or immediately thereafter) the city was forced to appeal to friendly states for financial assistance. Substantial portions of a decree passed by the Thessalian Confederacy have survived in which they agree to provide the requested relief.[49] Once the war ended, Ambracia tried to place relations with surrounding states on a new footing, as is revealed by a recently published document regarding Charadrus, its neighbor to the west.[50] Two other documents concerning Athamania to the northeast may date from this period (the chronology is a matter of controversy),[51] but a fragmentary Athenian decree from 167/6 definitely belongs in this context.[52] It shows that Athens had received requests for judges from Ambracia and the Acarnanians, and the *ekklesia* agreed to send them. Five citizens were chosen and sworn in; the decree lists them by name, and among them was a member of the famous family of sculptors to which Praxiteles and Cephisodotus belonged.[53] This appeal from states in the northwest demonstrates that Athens continued to enjoy great prestige, and that Athenian citizens appeared specially qualified as judges and mediators in international disputes, even to ethnically different groups in distant regions.

At about the same time Athens became involved in settling a dispute between two states on the Peloponnese. The cities of Troizen and

48. Livy 38.44.4–6 (the Senate decree); 43.17.10 and 44.1.4 (on the garrisons).

49. C. Habicht, in *Demetrias,* ed. V. Milojcić and D. Theocharis, vol. 1 (Bonn 1976) 175–180.

50. P. Cabanes and J. Andréou, *BCH* 109 (1985) 499–544 and 753–757; C. Habicht, *ZPE* 62 (1986) 190–192; J. Tréheux and P. Charneux, *BCH* 112 (1988) 359–373; P. Gauthier, *Bulletin épigraphique* (1989) 265.

51. *ISE* 91, a letter from the Roman praetor P. Cornelius Blasio to Corcyra and the (unpublished) decision of the Corcyrans on the back of the same stone about redrawing the border between Ambracia and Athamania; Holleaux, *Études* 5: 433–448.

52. *IG* II^2.951, interpreted by A. Wilhelm (1916) 23–30 in *Akademieschriften* 1: 447–454. According to the new inscription from note 50 above, line 3 should be completed as γραμ[ματίστα]. For the dating of the archon Nikosthenes, see Habicht, *ZPE* 62 (1986) 190–192. The federal *strategos* of the Acarnanians at that time was Chremas, the notorious head of the local faction controlled by Rome; Walbank, *Commentary* 3: 332, 435, and 522.

53. Davies, *APF* 286–290.

Arsinoë (formerly Methana) were at loggerheads over the rights to two pieces of land, one a mountainous area that served both communities as pasture, and the other a strip of coast used by tuna fishermen. As the conflict escalated, Troizen resorted to reprisals, seizing goods and taking three citizens of Arsinoë hostage. Mediators appointed by Ptolemy (who maintained a military base in Arsinoë at the time) obtained an agreement from both parties to share the disputed territory in the future; the terms of the settlement also provided compensation for private parties, including those whose personal or property rights had been infringed. Finally, the parties agreed to request a delegation of three judges from Athens to oversee the implementation of the treaty; after adjudicating specific cases, such as the amount of compensation owed, they were to place their decisions on public display in the shrine of Poseidon in Calauria, the temple of Asclepius in Epidaurus, and the Acropolis in Athens.[54]

3. Conditions at Home

Among the features that continued to play a role in the city's life during the first half of the second century were the small *ephebia* (understood as an elite school for future leaders) and the major state festivals. In contrast, a new phenomenon of the period was the annual minting of a new type of coins known as "New Style silver."

The institution of *ephebia,* well known from the Aristotelian *Athenaion Politeia,* had been greatly altered by a reform in the closing years of the fourth century.[55] The participation of all healthy young men ceased to be compulsory, and the period of service was reduced from two years to one. In addition ephebes were now required to provide their own arms. In the wake of these reforms, the year-classes dropped abruptly to one-tenth or even one-twentieth of their former size, from approximately 500 to somewhere between 20 and 50 mem-

54. Copies of the decree of Troizen containing the background of the dispute and the agreement (*IG* IV.1^2.77) were found in Epidaurus and Troizen. The essential commentary was provided by A. Nikitsky, *Hermes* 38 (1903) 406–413. The text was correctly explained as a decree from Troizen by B. Bravo, *ANSP* (1980) 745, 805–806, 865, and 868. For a long time the identity of the other city involved in the dispute was in doubt. That it was Arsinoe was recognized by L. Robert (*Bulletin épigraphique* [1961] 318; cf. *OMS* 3.1465), who realized that *IG* IV.1^2.76 is part of the same decree (76.32–38 = 77.1–7).

55. See Chapter 5, Section 2.

bers. They remained at this modest level for the next 135 years, until the end of the war against Perseus.[56] Whereas formerly there might have been a total of 1,000 ephebes serving in the two year-classes, in this period there were sometimes only 20, just 2 per tribe on average. This greatly reduced corps continued to be trained in various forms of athletics and the use of weapons, and to patrol rural Attica under the command of the hoplite general, but it no longer represented a significant military force.

Since after the reform the state ceased to provide each ephebe with a set of hoplite arms, the only enlistees necessarily came from families that could afford to buy the equipment and to dispense with the young man's labor or earning power for a year. The corps of ephebes thus became a sort of club for the sons of the upper class. It appears that many of the young men who joined had ambitions of rising to high rank in the army, either in the hoplite regiments or in the elite cavalry corps with its few hundred members.

Thirteen more or less complete extant decrees concerning the corps of ephebes are known from the first thirty years of the second century.[57] They provide information first of all on the leaders of the corps. The commander of the corps, the *kosmetes,* had to be at least forty years old and was elected annually by the citizens. No case is known of a *kosmetes* who served more than one term. By contrast, the instructors for physical fitness (the *paidotribes*) and the weapons experts (for fencing, spear-throwing, archery, and the catapult) generally served for ten to twenty years. From 267 to 176 the post of gymnastics instructor was held by members of a single family from Acharnae; after this period a different *paidotribes* appears every year, an indication that the post had become an annual office like that of *kosmetes.* All the instructors in this era were still Athenian citizens, with the exception of the archery teachers, some of whom were from Crete. (Throughout antiquity Cretans were considered outstanding archers.)

Several well-preserved decrees from this period, much more detailed

56. The numbers fluctuated between 18 and 47 in the third century (Pélékidis, *Éphébie* 165–172), and between 35 and 50 from 200 to 172. In 177/6 there were 48 ephebes enrolled, and in 172/1 there were 50. The numbers rose after the war against Perseus, soon passing 100 but never reaching 200 members.

57. A list is in Tracy, *Hesperia Suppl.* 19 (1982) 158–159; also *Hesperia* 51 (1982) 58, no. 2, and two as yet unpublished documents from 197/6 and 177/6. What follows concerning the activities of the ephebes is taken from these decrees.

than earlier ones, offer a vivid picture of the variety of activities in which the ephebes engaged during their year in the corps. Besides physical training and instruction in the use of weapons, the young men were expected to continue their education in the "sciences" *(mathemata)*, including some lectures at the schools of the philosophers. Great importance was attached to ephebes' participation in the religious life of the community and to the inculcation of patriotism; to strengthen the latter, the corps was frequently required to take part in ceremonies honoring the heroic tradition of their ancestors at the time of the Persian wars. At the end of each year the Assembly passed a decree listing the activities of the departing year-class and summing up its performance. The departing ephebes were granted crowns and other honors, and finally their instructors were honored as a group, receiving crowns as well. In a second decree honoring the *kosmetes*, the same activities were described from his perspective, so that the two decrees complement each other.

The year began with sacrifices in the Prytaneum, where the eternal flame burned. The ceremony was attended by the *kosmetes*, the fathers of the new ephebes, and the fifty members of one tribe currently serving as *prytaneis* (the executive committee) in the Council. Next the names of the ephebes were entered in the official list for the year, and the young men swore the oath of service. Throughout the year religious ceremonies formed an important part of their activities, above all sacrifices to the gods and the benefactors of the state. As is known from other sources, the latter included Diogenes, the former military commander of the Macedonian forces in Attica, who had played a central role in the liberation of 229; the Romans were also treated collectively as "benefactors." The ephebes took part as a distinct group in many, perhaps even all, state festivals; at some, such as the Theseia (after 165), they held tournaments. At the Great Mysteries of Eleusis they had the task of lifting the sacrificial bull onto the altar, and they performed the same duty at the Proerosia, another festival in Eleusis.[58] At the Dionysia and the other festivals of Dionysus (the Lenaea, the Peiraea), the ephebes escorted the sacred image of the god into the theater.[59]

Other rites were performed in commemoration of heroes and heroic

58. L. Ziehen, *Hermes* 66 (1931) 227–234; S. Dow and R. F. Healey, *Harvard Theological Studies* 21 (1965) 14–17; J. D. Mikalson, *The Sacred and Civil Calendar of the Athenian Year* (Princeton 1975) 67–69.

59. Pélékidis, *Ephébie* 239–247.

ancestors on pilgrimages to various sites in rural Attica. For one such event the ephebes went to the shrine of Amphiaraus near Oropus, where they performed a sacrifice to the healer. Other places had associations with Athens' heroic past, such as Marathon, site of the great battle of 490, which the ephebes visited every year to lay a wreath on the common grave of the fallen[60] and to hold games in their honor, "for they considered showing proper respect to those who had given their all for freedom a noble part of their duties." On another occasion they would board a ship (for they were also supposed to gain experience at sea) and row to the *tropaion* of Themistocles on the hill of Cynosura, where they offered a sacrifice to "Zeus the Averter," who had forced the Persians to turn and flee at the battle of Salamis in 480; the monument to Themistocles preserved the memory of this great event for centuries afterward.[61] On the festival of Ajax Telamonius they sailed to Salamis and marched in a procession with their arms to make a sacrifice to Ajax, Asclepius, and Hermes.[62] During the year, on repeated excursions to the countryside, they performed these rituals at all the fortresses and chief holy places.

To keep physically fit, the ephebes ran footraces in the *gymnasion;* to gain experience with their weapons and get to know the entire country and its borders, they went on marches commanded by the corps leader, the hoplite general, and the master at arms. The ephebes, led by the *kosmetes* and in full military uniform, attended meetings of the Assembly in both the city and Piraeus,[63] not as participants—they acquired the vote only after completing their year in the corps—but as observers (similar to the sons of Roman senators in the *curia*), to learn how political decisions were made. Finally, at the end of the year, they passed in review before the Council in the Panathenaean stadium of Lycurgus during the festival of Epitaphia and performed drills to demonstrate the skills they had learned.

As the surviving decrees indicate, the ephebes were expected to display unconditional obedience and to endure the rigors of their

---

60. Pausanias 1.32.4; W. K. Pritchett, *The Greek State at War,* vol. 4 (Berkeley 1985) 126–129.

61. E. Kirsten, Τρόπαιον, *RE* (1939) 673, no. 2; W. C. West III, *CP* 64 (1969) 15–17; P. W. Wallace, *AJA* 73 (1969) 299–302; G. R. Culley, *Hesperia* 46 (1977) 291–298.

62. Pélékidis, *Ephébie* 247–249. Cf. P. Von der Mühll, *Ausgewählte kleine Schriften* (Basle 1976) 454–455 and 466–467.

63. Pélékidis, *Ephébie* 273–274.

service without complaint. In the final honorary decree, the name of each ephebe, the names of his father and deme, and all the instructors were engraved in stone along with the text of the decree, and set in a public place where it could be seen by all. Many features of this Hellenistic *ephebia* recall the cadet corps of the modern era, and all the evidence indicates that the institution served the state's goal of training a small elite of young citizens as future leaders in the army and navy, politics, and public administration and inculcating in them both democratic values and a sense of patriotism.

The Athenians celebrated numerous festivals honoring their gods and heroes;[64] particularly informative sources survive for two of these: the Great Panathenaea, the main festival of the city's patron goddess Athena; and the Theseia, held in honor of Theseus, the mythical king venerated as the founder of the Attic state. The surviving documents shed little or no light on the religious aspects of the festivals (for which one must consult sources from earlier and later eras), but they do impart a great deal of information about the gymnastic and equestrian games, in which athletes, riders, and chariots participated. Since both festivals were specifically Athenian rather than pan-Hellenic (such as the Olympic, Pythian, Isthmian and Nemean Games), most of the events were open only to Athenian citizens; some few, however, were open to outsiders. The Panathenaea and, to a lesser extent, the Theseia thus occupy a middle position between the exclusively national and the great international festivals; like the games in Olympia and Delphi they were celebrated at four-year intervals rather than every year.

Since ancient times the Athenians had held an annual festival in honor of Athena, patroness of the city. Beginning in the era of the tyrant Pisistratus in the sixth century, they celebrated it in a particularly splendid manner every fourth year, whence it came to be called the "Great Panathenaea."[65] The colonies, including the cities of Ionia, that regarded Athens as their mother city participated by sending festival delegations and gifts. In the fifth century, at the time of the Athenian

---

64. The subject is treated in detail by A. Mommsen in *Feste der Stadt Athen im Altertum* (Leipzig 1898); see also L. Deubner, *Attische Feste* (Berlin 1932); and E. Simon, *Festivals of Attica* (Madison 1983).

65. Besides the works cited in the previous note, see G. R. Edwards, *Hesperia* 26 (1957) 320–349. For the history of the festival in the second century, the lists of victors are particularly valuable: *IG* II^2.2313–17 and three new lists published with commentary by Tracy and Habicht, *Hesperia* 60 (1991) 187–236.

empire, every member of the Naval Confederacy was required to send Athens a bull and a complete set of arms to mark the occasion. The athletic and dramatic competitions attracted participants from near and far; as prizes the victors received a varying number of amphorae filled with oil. Pictorial depictions of the games appear on many pieces of black-figured pottery from the sixth and early fifth centuries. In the Age of Pericles, the festival procession was carved on the frieze of the Parthenon by Athens' best artists.

When the Athenian empire collapsed in 404, most foreign states probably ceased to participate. But after some time had elapsed the colonies, at least, resumed the practice of sending delegations to the Great Panathenaea. Alexander the Great and several of his successors also sent gifts on the occasion of the Panathenaea, even though no ties of this sort bound them to the city.[66] Soon kings, queens, and princes entered the contests themselves, as they did at other Greek games. They did not appear in person but sent their horses, jockeys, and charioteers to compete in their names. We do not know when this custom first began, as no documents listing the Panathenaean victors have survived from before the end of the third century. At another festival, the Lycaea, celebrated by the Arcadian Confederacy, a son of Ptolemy, then satrap of Egypt and later king, won a contest in 315.[67] A whole series of Athenian lists of victors in the athletic and equestrian events at the Panathenaea, more or less complete, from 202 to 146 have been known for some time, and recently similar lists for the years 170, 166, and 162 have been added to it. Among the victors are members of the Ptolemaic, Seleucid, and Attalid royal families, as well as the Numidian prince Mastanabal and high dignitaries from the same courts. In 178 four members of the Pergamene royal family won four different chariot races, namely Eumenes II and his three brothers Attalus, Philetaerus, and Athenaeus; in 162 the victors included Ptolemy VI Philometor and his sister-consort Cleopatra II.[68] In 169, during the Third Macedonian War and Sixth Syrian War between Antiochus IV and Ptolemy VI, an Athenian delegation visited Alexan-

66. For Alexander see Chapter 1, note 23; Ptolemy, Chapter 5, note 49; Lysimachus, *IG* II^2.657.14–15.

67. *Syll.* 314 B 8–9 as dated by L. Moretti, *Olympionikai, i vincitori negli antichi agoni olimpici* (Rome 1957) 131.

68. For the Attalids: *IG* II^2.2314.83–90. Ptolemy VI and Cleopatra II: *Hesperia* 60 (1991) 188–189, col. 3.31–33 and 21–22. Mastanabal: *IG* II^2.2316.42–45.

dria in connection with the Panathenaic festival.[69] The Macedonian dynasty of the Antigonids is a striking exception to the rule: its members had been placed under a solemn ban in 200 that obviously remained in effect until the collapse of the monarchy and were prohibited from setting foot on Attic soil. Rather than participating himself, Ariarathes V of Cappadocia offered his respects to the city and its goddess by serving as *agonothetes* around the middle of the second century. This fact no doubt means that he contributed a large sum toward the cost of the festival and was rewarded with the honorary title of head of the games, while an Athenian citizen carried out the practical duties of the office.[70]

Like the four pan-Hellenic festivals, the Panathenaic competitions attracted entrants from throughout the Mediterranean world and beyond: from Italy and the Ligurian coast in the west; from Asia Minor, Syria, and Mesopotamia in the east; from Egypt, Cyrenaica, and Numidia in the south; and from Epirus and Corfu in the north. The athletic events were open to foreigners and took place in the stadium of Lycurgus in different classes according to age.[71] The three usual categories in Greek games were boys, youth (*ageneioi*, literally "those without beards"), and men. The boys' events consisted of footraces over three different distances, wrestling, boxing, and "all-in" or "freestyle" wrestling *(pankration)*, a combination of wrestling and boxing. In the youth class there was only one footrace, over a distance of one *stadion* (about 200 yards); the other events included the same three wrestling and boxing competitions as in the boys' division, plus the pentathlon, consisting of running, broad jump, disc and spear throwing, and wrestling. The men's class included all six events of the boys' class plus the pentathlon, a four-*stadion* footrace, and a footrace in full hoplite armor. It is assumed that these games took two days, one for the boys' and youth competitions and one for the men's events.

The horse and chariot races, possibly also dressage competitions, took place at two different sites. The events carried out in the Agora were of a quasi-military character, and participation was limited to Athenian citizens. One set of events was open only to members of the cavalry, and another only to the commanders of the twelve cavalry

69. Polybius 28.19.4.
70. J. and L. Robert, *Bulletin épigraphique* (1951) 79.
71. For the roster of events see Tracy, *Hesperia* 60 (1991) 196–201.

units. In these disciplines the owners rode or drove their own cavalry horses. About fifteen further events were carried out at the hippodrome, or racetrack, some of them open only to foreigners. There were horse and chariot races in various classes, for colts and adult horses and for two- and four-horse chariots. These events were highly professional in character, and professional jockeys, racehorses, and race drivers competed. Persons of royal blood sent entries exclusively to these horse and chariot races at the hippodrome.

At the Great Panathenaea and the other (annual) festivals, the names of foreigners who had acted as benefactors of the city and been awarded honors by the people were solemnly announced by heralds. Such proclamations acquired a particular resonance through the presence of so many delegations from foreign states, Athenian colonies, and the cities of Ionia.[72]

Beginning in the early fifth century the Athenians celebrated an annual festival in honor of Theseus. At that time Cimon, son of the victor of Marathon, Miltiades, discovered a grave on the island of Skyros, where Theseus was believed to have died. Declaring the remains to be those of the king, he moved them to Athens in 476/5, where they were ceremonially reinterred in a new shrine. A festival called the Theseia was created and observed every fall thereafter in commemoration.[73] Little is known about it in the classical period, but several surviving inscriptions from the second century shed considerable light on how it was celebrated in the Hellenistic age. The inscriptions are decrees honoring the organizers of the Theseian Games for a given year, followed by a list of the events and the winners in each.[74] The sources reveal that by then few if any traces remained of the original celebration beyond its name; it had become a quadrennial event and, like other such festivals, was observed with particular pomp and splendor. It opened with competitions for trumpeters and heralds,

---

72. There is documentation for the participation of the Ionian cities of Priene, Colophon, and Miletus in the Hellenistic age: F. Hiller von Gaertringen, *Die Inschriften von Priene* (Berlin 1906) 45; A. Wilhelm, *Anatolian Studies Buckler* (Manchester 1939) 349; Habicht, *Chiron* 21 (1991) 329. *IG* II².886 probably documents the participation of an Ionian city in the realm of Attalus I before 200. For Athens as the "mother city" of the Ionians: Gaertringen, *Inschriften von Priene* 109.47–49. Cf. W. Günther, *Epigraphica Anatolica* 19 (1992) 135–143.

73. Mommsen, *Feste* 278–307; and G. R. Bugh, *ZPE* 83 (1990) 20–37. The description in the text follows Bugh in the main points.

74. *IG* II².956–965 from 161/0 through 109/8.

followed by games similar to those of the Great Panathenaea: athletic, equestrian, and chariot events, many of them in different classes for boys, young men, ephebes, and members of the cavalry. The extant inscriptions all stem from the shrine of Theseus, whose precise location has not been found; it is known to have stood near the later Roman agora. Those from the years 161, 157, and 153 are the best preserved; the earliest of them thus dates from the era in which Athens regained possession of the island of Skyros in 167. Scholars believe, almost certainly correctly, that the return of Skyros offered the Athenians an opportunity to reorganize the Theseia on a grander scale and that they probably first celebrated them in the new manner in 165. If that is the case, the inscriptions documenting the first celebration have not survived.[75]

Entrants in the various events were almost exclusively Athenians, a natural circumstance in games honoring the nation's founder. However, from the beginning, two competitions were open to foreigners, provided they were mercenaries in Athenian service; those were group rather than individual events, the first a test of general physical fitness and the second a contest for the best maintenance of weapons and equipment. Prizes were awarded in three categories: the elite soldiers, the cavalry, and the foreign mercenary units. Only later do the names of individual foreigners crop up in the athletic events, almost certainly mercenaries in the Athenian military forces.

The official organizers of the festival came without exception from the most prominent families in the city. In the decrees in their honor the people praise them for arranging the procession and the sacrifice to Theseus in the appropriate traditional manner; for making sure that the torch race and athletic events were carried out safely, so that no one suffered injury; and finally for overseeing the prizes and the stone tablet commemorating the victors. To attract the 600 councillors to the festival, the sponsors offered them two drachmas each for expenses. While the basic cost of the festival was covered by the state treasury, all the extra expenses such as the remuneration for the city councillors came from the sponsors' own pockets. The inscriptions note that one such *agonothetes* donated more than 3,390 dramas, and a second more than 2,690.[76]

---

75. Pélékidis, *Ephébie* 229–230 and 295–300; Bugh, *ZPE* 83 (1990) 25.
76. *IG* II[2].958.15–16 and 956.18–19.

The information that councillors' presence was desired at the Theseia may at first appear to be at variance with Aristotle's statement that the Council met daily except on those days for which there was a specific "dispensation." Aristotle does not identify these days, but a survey of all documented Council sessions shows that the free days coincided with the celebration of annual—and of course the even more important quadrennial—festivals, while on the lesser, monthly holidays the Council met as usual.[77] The Assembly sessions were less frequent, being called neither during the great annual and quadrennial festivals nor on the lesser holidays each month.[78] The state calendar was thus arranged so that all citizens were free to take part in the major festivals, and only members of the Council were prevented from attending the minor ones. Not a single session of either the Council or the Assembly is documented for the dates of the Great Panathenaea, between the twenty-third and thirtieth Hecatombaion, and the same holds for dates when the Theseia might have fallen. The main festival is known to have been held on the eighth Pyanopsion, and no doubt the celebration as renewed after 167 lasted more than one day. Other possible dates are then limited to the seventh, ninth, and tenth of that month, for two Council sessions are documented for the sixth and two Assembly sessions for the eleventh Pyanopsion.[79]

The Athenian state appears not to have minted any coins for about twenty years, from approximately 183 to 164. Then, presumably in 164/3 or shortly before, the Athenians began producing new kinds of one-drachma and four-drachma pieces, which were soon circulating far beyond the borders of Attica. From then on a new set of coins was struck annually under the supervision of two magistrates who served one-year terms. While the obverse of these "New Style" silver coins all bore a head of Athena in a helmet, the images on the reverse contained some constant features but also others that changed from year to year or even month to month. The unvarying elements consisted of an amphora surmounted by an owl, the symbol of both the goddess and the city, together with the abbreviated *ethnikon* AΘE, "from the Athenians." The new and variable elements identified the two magistrates in charge of the mint, at first by monograms and later by full or

77. *Ath. Pol.* 43.3; Mikalson, *Calendar* 193–197.

78. Mikalson, ibid., 182–193.

79. Ibid., 67 and 72, and for the 11th Pyanopsion a second, as yet unpublished text from 176/5.

abbreviated forms of their names. For approximately fifty years, from 136/5 to 88/7, the name of a third citizen, the so-called third magistrate, appeared as well. The reverse of the coins is further marked by a letter from *alpha* to *nu*, standing for the numbers 1 to 13 and indicating the month of the year in which the coin was struck. With the aid of these dates it can be seen that as a rule the third magistrate changed every month. In addition, each year had its own symbol, which the magistrate named first was responsible for selecting. All the elements on the reverse were surrounded by an olive wreath.[80]

Today 111 annual monetary emissions are known from an estimated total of 120. Thus only a few years of the series are missing, probably from the beginning or end of the period, when production was lower. Observation of reverse dies common to more than one issue made it possible to establish the relative order of the extant coins, and today there is general agreement that the years 145–77 are represented without a break. The key to absolute dating is the coin from the seventy-eighth year in the series, which names King Mithridates and Aristion as masters of the mint and contains the Pontic symbol of a star between two crescents; without doubt this coin dates from 87/6. Working backward from there, and assuming that coins from every year have survived, we can calculate that the minting began in 164/3, or slightly earlier if it is assumed that one or two years are missing. The series ended with the 111th emission, perhaps in 54/3, or more likely in the 40s, as toward the end of the period one or more years may be missing or coins were no longer struck every year.[81]

The weight and quality of the metal in New Style coins show that the state had no lack of fine silver, but the source of that silver is another question. Presumably the mines at Laurium could no longer supply the need. However, since the minting of the series began shortly after the collapse of Macedonia and after Athenian acquisition of Delos, it is possible that royal Macedonian coins were collected, melted down, and restruck, along with some of the silver brought to Delos by interna-

---

80. The fundamental modern study of the subject is M. Thompson, *The New Style Silver Coinage of Athens,* 2 vols. (New York 1961). For the preceding interruption of production at the Athenian mint, see Kroll, *Coins* 50.

81. Decisive work on the absolute chronology of New Style silver was done by D. M. Lewis, *NC* (1962) 275–300. See also O. Mørkholm, *ANSMusN* 29 (1984) 29–42; M. Price, *Essays Kraay-Mørkholm* (Louvain-la-Neuve 1989) 223–243; H. Mattingly, *NC* (1990) 67–78.

tional trade.[82] The profit from Delos and the success of the new currency probably contributed to the rising prosperity observable for this era. Furthermore, these coins provide direct information about historical persons and social history. The names of several hundred Athenian citizens appear on them, with precise dates. Nearly all of these men, including the "third magistrates," are known from other inscriptions from Attica, Athenian Delos, or from other sources, or can at least be assigned to known families.[83] We may therefore conclude that the remaining, otherwise unidentified officials probably came also from wealthy or affluent families and were otherwise active in politics, and that only men of this type were considered for magistracies at the mint. It is thus not without significance that among the mint magistrates in this period we find sculptors and poets. Frequently two relatives served together as first and second magistrates of a given year, such as the cousins Polycles and Timarchides of Thoricus, both members of a noted family of sculptors, in 149/8; and Timostrates and Poses, brothers from Phalerum, in 102/1. Poses was a comic poet, as his father and grandfather had been before him, and as his son would be after him.[84]

In a number of cases the name of a mint magistrate explains the choice of a particular symbol for the coins of his year. Eurycleides, for example, who was mint magistrate in 112/1, chose a depiction of the three Graces to recall his famous ancestors Eurycleides and Micion, the liberators of 229 and founders of the cult of the Charites. Another Micion, mint magistrate in 137/6, recalled the victory of a member of his family in a chariot race at the Great Panathenaea by depicting a figure of Nike and a chariot. An earlier Micion is in fact documented as having won such an event.[85] The trophy in Salamis chosen by Themistocles, the magistrate of 117/6, was a reminder of the great naval victory won by his famous namesake; while a certain Apellicon,

---

82. A. Giovannini, *Rome et la circulation monétaire en Grèce au IIe siècle avant Jésus-Christ* (Basle 1978) 62; M. Price, *The Coinage of the Roman World in the Late Republic*, ed. A. M. Burnett and M. H. Crawford (Oxford 1987) 95–96; S. Lauffer, *Die Bergwerkssklaven von Laureion*[2] (Wiesbaden 1979) 165–166 and 284–285; Lauffer cites Seltman's observation that the volume of Athenian coin production at this time was greater than that of Pergamum, Rhodes, or Syracuse.

83. Habicht, *Chiron* 21 (1991) 1–23.

84. M. Thompson, *New Style Silver Coinage* 600–607. The dates have been altered to match Lewis' chonology.

85. *IG* II[2].2314.76.

an immigrant from Teos in Ionia, chose the image of a griffin for his coins in 88/7 as a symbol of his home city.

The use of symbols to express a political orientation is relatively rare in New Style silver coins, but in one instance hardly any other interpretation is possible: in 134/3 the use of an anchor, a symbol of the Seleucid kings, appears to be an act of homage to Antiochus VII Sidetes, who had just sent a particularly trusted emissary to Athens on a diplomatic mission.[86] The clearest use of political symbols in New Style coins, however, occurs around the time of the First Mithridatic War. In 90/89 the goddess Roma was chosen as emblem, a clear proclamation of where Athenian loyalties lay; the next year Roma appeared with the goddess of victory, presumably a reference to Roman military successes in the Social (or Marsic) War of 90–88. This was the year preceding the one in which Medeius, the archon supported by the Romans, lost political control of Athens. A year later, with Apellicon's election as mint magistrate, the office was filled by a supporter of the king of Pontus; the year after that the king himself was named master of the mint, together with his Athenian vassal Aristion, and the emblem chosen was Pontic. The depiction of the tyrant-slayers in 84/3 announced the success of the countercoup in which the "tyrants" Athenion and Aristion were overthrown and Athens was brought back into the Roman fold by Sulla.

New Style Athenian silver was a spectacular success throughout mainland Greece and beyond. Before long even the Amphictionic Council of Delphi, which claimed to speak for all Greeks, gave it a uniquely favored status.[87]

86. The symbol was related to Antiochus IV Epiphanes by M. Thompson (*New Style Silver Coinage* 606) in a chronology now recognized as mistaken. For Antiochus VII and Athens see Chapter 12, Section 1.

87. See Chapter 12, Section 2.

TEN

Athenian Delos

1. The Cleruchy

After Antigonus the One-Eyed drove the Athenians out of Delos in 314, he declared the island's independence. In fact, however, Delos became the cultural center of Antigonus' new confederacy of island communities, the League of the Islanders or Nesiote League, which he and his son Demetrius dominated for almost thirty years. Then the Egyptian kings Ptolemy I and II replaced them as Delos' protectors and overlords, until their naval supremacy was destroyed in battles against the fleets of Macedonia and Rhodes. But regardless of who controlled the island, it remained sacred to Apollo and was kept accessible to pilgrims from all parts of Greece, its temples gradually filling with offerings and gifts from royalty and private citizens, city-states and confederacies, and later Roman generals and dignitaries. Every year Delian officials took inventory of all the offerings, descriptions of which might then be copied again and again in the annual catalogues of temple treasures. These inventories, continued by the Athenians after they reacquired possession of the island in 167, offer perhaps the most vivid and concrete picture of Delos and its international character in that period. In addition the Ptolemaic, Macedonian, and Pergamene kings endowed festivals that were named after themselves and celebrated annually.[1]

At the end of the Third Macedonian War, Delos again lost its independence. The Roman Senate awarded the island to Athens and

---

1. The fundamental study of the island for this period is C. Vial, *Délos indépendante* (Paris 1984). See further M.-F. Baslez and C. Vial, *BCH* 111 (1987) 281–312; G. Reger, *Regionalism and Change in the Economy of Independent Delos* (Berkeley 1994).

ordered its inhabitants to leave Delos, allowing them to take their personal property. An inscription (known for some time but never published) apparently mentions military operations of some kind in conjunction with the transfer of power.[2] The population of the island emigrated to Achaea, where the Delians were permitted to become citizens of the cities in the Achaean League.[3] The Athenians sent out a group of citizens as colonists, or "cleruchs," to resettle Delos and take over its administration. Their government was led by a governor *(epimeletes)* elected by the people annually from the group of former archons who made up the Areopagus. A second term in office was unusual but is documented twice in the decade after 130. In the eighty-year period between Athenian resettlement and the outbreak of the First Mithridatic War, two-thirds of these commissars are known by name, primarily from Delian inscriptions. Almost all came from known families and served in other offices and positions of honor in both Delos and Athens.[4] In one house on Delos destroyed in 69 B.C. excavators found a private archive containing thousands of impressions of seals, including seventeen inscribed with the title "the *epimeletes* in Delos."[5]

The island's independence came to an end in late 167 or early 166.[6] After a long scholarly controversy it has now been established that the first gymnasiarch on Delos held office in 167/6 (not 166/5): Pausanias of Melite, the tenth Athenian occupant of this office, served as gymnasiarch in the year of the archon Pyrrhus, 158/7, according to an unpublished decree of the Athenian Assembly; counting back, we find that Aristomenes of Acharnae, the first gymnasiarch, held this post in 167/6. Although he certainly did not serve out a full year's term in Delos, he must have taken office sometime before the summer of 166.[7]

At about the same time an Athenian decree introduced by

---

2. J.-M. Bertrand, *Sociétés urbaines, sociétés rurales dans l'Asie Mineure et la Syrie hellénistiques et romaines,* ed. E. Frézouls (Strasbourg 1987) 100 n. 53.

3. The classic work on Athenian Delos is P. Roussel, *Délos, colonie athénienne* (Paris 1916; enl. ed. 1987). Most of our knowledge about the island in this period is derived from several thousand inscriptions found there; P. Bruneau, *Recherches sur les cultes de Délos à l'époque hellénistique et à l'époque impériale* (Paris 1970); P. Bruneau and J. Ducat, *Guide de Délos*[3] (Paris 1983). The results of the French excavations are published in *EAD.*

4. For more on the *epimeletai* see Roussel, *Délos* 97–125; and C. Habicht, *Hermes* 119 (1991) 194–216.

5. M.-F. Boussac, *Les sceaux de Délos,* vol. 1 (Athens 1992).

6. Vial, *Délos indépendante* 3.

7. The list of gymnasiarchs is I *Délos* 2589. P. Roussel argued that the list began in 167/6, while A. Plassart proposed 166/5 (see the commentary on I *Délos* 2589). The Athenian

Theainetus of Aigilia named a commission of Areopagites, with Micion at its head, and instructed them to go and negotiate with the outgoing Delian officials about transferring oversight of the shrines and their treasure. The leader of this delegation must certainly have been a member of the famous family of Eurycleides and Micion of Cephisia, who brought about the liberation of Athens in 229. The activities of this commission are also mentioned in an inventory list dating from the early years of Athenian rule, which reveals that the commission made various changes in the disposition of offerings.[8] After Athens took possession of the island, Athenian officials took over the task of inventorying the shrines' offerings. The oldest evidence of their work, dating from about 166 and found not on Delos but in the Athenian Agora, consists of four fragments listing mostly vases in the shrine of Apollo, presumably the only such catalogue inscribed and exhibited in Athens as well as in Delos.[9]

In 170 or 169, during the Third Macedonian War, the Delians had awarded crowns to the Roman people and the Senate as an expression of their solidarity; coming so soon afterward, the Senate's decision to evict them from their island must have provoked considerable bitterness.[10] Nonetheless, not many years later the Delians, now citizens of Achaea, were addressing an appeal to the Senate to settle a controversy. According to Polybius, emissaries from Athens appeared in Rome during 159/8—their names, missing from his text, were probably dropped by the Byzantine abridger of his history—at the same time as an Achaean delegation led by Thearidas (Polybius' older brother) and Stephanus. The parties requested a decision from the Senate in a dispute between them bearing directly on the former inhabitants of Delos. When the Romans (and Athenians) had evicted them from the

---

decree honoring Pausanias (*RA* [1948] I 263–264) mentioned by J. Delorme decides the controversy in Roussel's favor.

8. I *Délos* 1403Bb.I.23–29 with commentary by F. Durrbach and P. Roussel (13).

9. *Hesperia* 3 (1934) 51, no. 39 (three fragments), interpreted by P. Roussel, *BCH* 58 (1934) 96–100. The fourth fragment appears with the other three in *Hesperia* 13 (1944) 254–257 with Meritt's commentary.

10. I *Délos* 465.c.20 and J. Tréheux, *BCH* 109 (1985) 489–490. Inscriptions from Delos reveal that some Delians remained on the island during the first few years after the Athenians had taken it over, and that toward the end of the century others had returned (M.-T. Couilloud, "Les monuments funéraires de Rhenée," *EAD* 30 [1974] 66–67 and 128, no. 182). They cannot have been numerous at any time, however.

island, they had promised the Delians that they would be allowed to take all their possessions with them, but some of them had nonetheless lost considerable amounts of property. Once they had become Achaean citizens, the former Delians claimed recompensation, citing a pact concluded between Athens and Achaea at the beginning of the second century establishing mutual recognition of legal claims. The Athenians refused to pay, saying the agreement applied only to those who had been Achaean citizens at the time of its signing. The former Delians then urged the Achaeans to impose sanctions on the Athenians, the usual escalation in such disputes. The Achaeans must have complied, for it is hard to see how the matter could have gone all the way to the Senate in Rome otherwise. When Polybius remarks, in his discussion of the Romans' award of Delos to Athens, that the Athenians had much bad luck in their clash with the island's inhabitants, he probably had this controversy in mind, for, as was only fair, the Senate ruled in favor of the Delians.[11]

The new settlers of the island, who called themselves "the community of Athenians residing in Delos," represented a cross-section of Athenian society. In the administration of their own internal affairs they were as independent as the 139 demes of Attica.[12] They differed from the demes in having their own legislative bodies, Council and Assembly, while the demes had only one legislative assembly, known as the *agora*. The Athenians on Delos elected at least some of their secular and religious officials. They were permitted to award their own honors to such officeholders and to foreign citizens, but if they wished to award honors to higher officials chosen in Athens, their decree had to be ratified by the Assembly at home.

In addition to the *epimeletes,* this group of consisted of the head of the public bank, two overseers of the island temples and sacred treasure (who replaced the officials known as *hieropoioi* in independent Delos),[13] three overseers of the markets, an administrator of the exchange, also responsible for weights and measures, and finally a gymnasiarch. The last was responsible for the gymnasium, the competitions held there,

---

11. Polybius 32.7.1–5 with P. Gauthier, *Symbola* (Nancy 1970) 173, 200, and 204; Walbank, *Commentary* 3: 525–526. The earlier passage is Polybius 30.20.9.

12. For more on the subject see Roussel, *Délos* 33–96. For the limitations placed on local autonomy by the Athenian state, see C. Habicht, *Gnomon* 31 (1959) 706–707.

13. For these offices see Roussel, *Délos* 126–144; for the public bank and its heads see also R. Bogaert, *Banque et banquiers dans les cités grecques* (Leiden 1968) 187–192.

and the Delian ephebes; in this respect he was the Delian counterpart of the Athenian *kosmetes*.[14]

The oldest surviving decree of the cleruchs dates from 165/4; as in all such decrees the year is identified by the name of the eponymous archon in Athens. The last extant decree passed by the Athenian cleruchs independently is from 145/4. A decree known to date from between 145/4 and 126/5 was passed not by the cleruchs alone, but by them and "the Romans present in Delos."[15] In a decree from 126/5 these two groups are joined by "the merchants, shipowners, and foreigners present" on the island.[16] Several decrees of 124/3 were passed by "the Athenian cleruchs, the Romans on Delos, and the merchants and shipowners,"[17] followed the next year, 123/2, by a decree in the name of "the Athenians, Romans, and other foreigners present or resident in Delos,"[18] and finally by a decree in the name of all these last groups plus the merchants and shipowners, who are again given separate mention.[19]

Clearly, around 130 the cleruchs ceased to manage local affairs exclusively; other groups had won the right to share in the government of the island: members of other nations, such as the Romans; of new occupational groups, the shipowners and merchants; and finally, individuals who did not reside in Delos but were merely there for some period. Within a few decades the island community had grown noticeably more international and more mercantile. Obviously the establishment in 167 of a free harbor (where no customs duties or tariffs were charged) played a central role in this development; other important factors were the rerouting of some Aegean trade after the Romans destroyed Corinth in 146[20] and the founding of the Roman province of Asia in 129.[21] There may be some connection between these events and the fact that soon after 130 two *epimeletai* served a second year in office. While the foreign population on the island consisted chiefly of Romans and Italians, there were growing Near Eastern contingents,

14. Roussel, *Délos* 179–198. I *Délos* 2589 contains a complete list of the Delian gymnasiarchs from 167/6 to 112/1, although not all the names are complete.

15. I *Délos* 1643; cf. I *Délos* 1644 and 1703 from the same year.

16. I *Délos* 1645.

17. I *Délos* 1647, 1648, 1649.

18. I *Délos* 1650.

19. I *Délos* 1652.

20. Strabo 10.5.4 (p. 486); Roussel, *Délos* 55.

21. R. Etienne, *Tēnos*, vol. 2 (Paris 1990) 129–130.

immigrants from the cities of Syria and Phoenicia, most of whom merchants and traders.[22]

It is difficult to estimate how many of the Athenian citizens present on the island at any one time were actually long-term residents, and how many were there only on business or to serve a term of office. It is likely that most of the officials elected in Athens and dispatched from there remained only as long as their duties required, returning to their careers and homes on the mainland as soon as they could. A very large number of the citizens then active in politics are documented as having held office both in Athens and on Delos.

Administration of the cults indigenous to Delos passed to the Athenians when the Delians left. The new officials maintained the same cults, for the Athenians continued to show respect to the Delian gods.[23] Nevertheless, they introduced certain innovations, such as the cult of Pythian Apollo, celebration of the festival of the Theseia (similar to the one held in Athens), and a local festival known as the Delia. During the period of independence the Delians had accepted a number of Egyptian divinities, including Isis, Sarapis, and Anubis. The immigration of foreigners on a large scale during Athenian rule gradually led to further enlargement of the pantheon as Syrians, Phoenicians, Jews, Arabs, and Italians brought their religions to Delos. Their gods and rites remained private, however, and no state cults for them were established.

As a site sacred to Apollo and home to many other gods, the island under Athenian rule continued to receive attention from many Hellenistic monarchs. Besides being the site of important shrines, Delos was also a popular place for the display of wealth and honors, with many monuments erected by and for royalty, high-ranking dignitaries, and meritorious individuals. One such monarch was Ptolemy VI, who kept his throne in 168, after a Roman fiat ended the war against Antiochus IV, and reigned until 145, when he was killed in battle in Syria. After a successful campaign in Cyprus in 154 his Cretan soldiers passed a resolution honoring him and erected his bronze statue in Delos. On the same occasion they voted honors for their commander, Aglaus, a man from a prominent family of Cos; two statues of him were to be erected, one in Cos and one in Delos. The resolution called for an

22. Roussel, *Délos* 84–96 and *BCH* 55 (1931) 447–448.
23. For more on this subject see Bruneau, *Recherches* 659–662.

ambassador to visit both Athens and Cos to request a site for the monument.[24] A man named Chrysermus, another official of Ptolemy VI and head of the Museum at Alexandria, was honored by a private citizen of Athens, who had his statue erected on Delos.[25] Many other inscriptions document the continuing interest of the Egyptian royal family in Delos during the last third of the second century, even after the dominance of the Athenian cleruchy had ended.[26] At the same time they reveal that relations between the court and Athens remained unclouded during this whole period, without the fifty-year span of cool, hostile, or even severed relations often assumed to have existed.[27]

The Ptolemies were not alone in their wish to be recognized on Athenian Delos. Antiochus IV Epiphanes, the preeminent benefactor of Athens in this period, was honored in Delos with a statue by a grateful Athenian citizen.[28] The obvious question of whether Delos itself also profited from the king's generosity is answered in the affirmative by the ancient authors. Polybius says of the king that "he outshone all earlier monarchs in the magnificence of the offerings he made in different cities and the reverence he showed to the gods. This can be observed at the Olympieum in Athens and in the statues surrounding the altar at Delos." Antiochus must have donated a group of costly statues to embellish the altar to Apollo,[29] perhaps in the early years of the Athenian cleruchy (167–164), or possibly earlier, in the period 175–167. Shortly before the middle of the century a private association active on Delos put up a statue to Menochares, a minister of Demetrius I of Syria (reigned 162–150) and the second most powerful man in the Seleucid empire.[30] The royal governor for the province of Seleucis, either under this king or under his son Demetrius II, was an Athenian citizen who dedicated two or three statues on the island.[31]

---

24. I *Délos* 1518 and 1517. Aglaus was also honored by a larger-than-life statue on Paros; *AD* 20 (1965) 119–133. For the background of these honors see Walbank, *Commentary* 3: 553–554.

25. I *Délos* 1525, which also documents the family of Chrysermus as having been in the service of the dynasty for generations.

26. I *Délos* 1526–35.

27. See Chapter 9, note 6.

28. I *Délos* 1540. There is a similar dedication, probably for the same king, in I *Délos* 1541.

29. Polybius 26.1.11 and, following him, Livy 41.20.8–9. Excavations have uncovered no trace of these statues; Bruneau, *Recherches* 27.

30. I *Délos* 1543. For Menochares see C. Habicht, *ZPE* 74 (1988) 214.

31. I *Délos* 1544 and 1545, possibly 1546 as well. I *Délos* 1547–53 are later documents concerning Seleucid kings and dignitaries.

The Attalid rulers of Pergamum are documented often in independent Delos, but very rarely during the time of the Athenian cleruchy, which coincides rather exactly with the final three decades of the dynasty. Attalus II (reigned 158–138) placed a statue of one of his most trusted retainers in Delos: Apollonides, a native Pergamene who had been raised with the king but was later also granted Athenian citizenship.[32] The people of Athens also erected a statue to Attalus' queen, Stratonice. The daughter of Ariarathes IV of Cappadocia, she married first Eumenes II of Pergamum, thus uniting the two royal houses, and then his brother Attalus II.[33] The fact that the inscription on the base of the statue refers to her as queen points to a time after her marriage, and the Athenian origin makes a year after 167 most likely. On the other hand, the lack of any reference to a royal husband suggests that she was either still unmarried or already widowed. Various dates have been proposed, ranging from before 189 to the period 138–134.[34]

The royal house of Cappadocia is not represented in surviving inscriptions from Delos until after the end of the cleruchy, the earliest dating from the last third of the second century. However, older inscriptions exist for the monarchy of Pontus. The oldest, from the period of Delian independence, is an Athenian decree of 195 awarding honors to King Pharnaces and his consort Nysa. The Delian statue of Pharnaces' sister Laodice originates from before 171/0 and thus also predates Athenian rule.[35] The two pedestals for statues of Mithridates V Euergetes fall in the period of the cleruchy (one datable precisely to the year 129/8),[36] and most probably the statue of his Athenian courtier Boethus as well.[37] This king, who made donations to the temple and had the palaestra on the lake rebuilt in a new form, was a particular benefactor of the island.[38] Mithridates VI Eupator, his successor and the dynasty's most important monarch, maintained extremely close contacts with Delos. Seventeen extant Delian inscriptions, all from the

32. I *Délos* 1554. For Apollonides and his family see C. Habicht, *Hesperia* 59 (1990) 565–567.

33. I *Délos* 1575.

34. Details are in H. Müller, *Chiron* 21 (1991) 393–424, where Müller himself favors a date between 159 and 156.

35. I *Délos* 1555.

36. I *Délos* 1557 and 1558.

37. I *Délos* 1559.

38. L. Robert, *JS* (1978) 151–163 (= *OMS* 7.283–295); cf. Bruneau and Ducat, *Guide de Délos* 195–197.

period after the cleruchy, commemorate him in one form or another. It was Mithridates VI who began the war against Rome that brought ruin upon Delos and put an end to its flourishing culture in 88.

The Delian evidence related to the kingdom of Bithynia in northwest Asia Minor is somewhat older. Prusias II (reigned 183–149) maintained contacts with Delos in the period of its independence.[39] His son Nicomedes II, who rebelled and deposed him in 149, clearly had the support of old King Masinissa of Numidia (previously an ally of the Romans in their war against Hannibal), for Nicomedes erected statues in Delos to Masinissa and one of his sons; the inscription suggests they were placed there soon after Masinissa's death in 148.[40] Nicomedes himself was honored in 139/8 as a benefactor of the Delian ephebes, who put up a statue to him; while his son and successor, Nicomedes III, received the same honor on the occasion of his succession in 127/6 from the Delian gymnasiarch Dioscurides of Rhamnus.[41]

All these inscriptions reveal that under Athenian sovereignty Delos remained a popular site for displaying tributes awarded to public figures. The international character of the island guaranteed the honorees a maximum of publicity.

2. The Limits of Athenian Sovereignty

Contemporary observers—Romans, Athenians, and other Greeks—were all well aware that Athens had not won Delos back through its own efforts, but had been awarded the island by the Roman Senate. About a decade later, when the Athenian Phocion of Melite made a list of the names of his predecessors as gymnasiarchs on Delos, he noted that it began with "the year in which the people regained the island thanks to the Romans."[42] The Athenians possessed Delos as a gift from Rome, just as the Rhodians had possessed Lycia and Caria south of the Maeander after 188, only to see these territories taken from them by the Senate and declared independent after the war against Perseus. This occurred at the same time Delos was "given" to Athens. These events made it clear that the status and duration of such possessions in the last

39. I *Délos* 455A.41; 1408A.I.27; 1427.4; 1428.II.8; 1430f.5; 1450A.112.
40. I *Délos* 1577 and 1577 *bis*. For Nicomedes' rebellion see C. Habicht, "Prusias," *RE* (1957) 1120–24. Another of Masinissa's sons, Golossa, was honored with a statue in Delos by a different donor; I *Délos* 1578.
41. I *Délos* 1580 (G. Daux, *Hesperia* 16 [1947] 55–57) and 1579.
42. I *Délos* 2589.

analysis depended on Rome's will. Even after "sovereignty" was transferred to Athens, the last word over its fate and future would come
from the Senate.

We have already seen that the Senate did not hesitate to intervene in
Delian affairs and instruct the Athenians on how to manage them. Even
before the Roman mediation in 159/8 in the case of the evicted
Delians who had become Achaean citizens, in one of the first years of
Athenian rule, the Senate passed a decree (surviving in a Greek translation) overruling an Athenian resolution concerning a private cult of
the Egyptian god Sarapis on Delos. The story is an interesting one,
with a background requiring some explanation.

In the early third century an Egyptian priest from Memphis named
Apollonius came to Delos, bringing a statue of Sarapis with him. He
placed it in his rented lodgings and made it the center of a private cult
in which he served as priest. When Apollonius died at the age of nearly
a hundred, his son Demetrius took his father's place as the god's
hereditary priest and was succeeded, after his own death at sixty-one,
by his son Apollonius II. One night this priest, the original priest's
grandson, had a dream in which Sarapis appeared to him and demanded a permanent shrine in place of the rented lodgings; the god
even named the spot where he wanted it built. Apollonius bought the
land and began construction, but as he had apparently neglected to
obtain the necessary building permit, he was soon faced with a lawsuit.
Once again Sarapis came to him in a dream and prophesied that all
would end well. Indeed, the verdict handed down before an expectant
crowd was in Apollonius' favor, and with the aid of many donations
the shrine was completed within six months. Believing that he had won
the case through the god's intervention, the priest expressed his gratitude by putting up a large column inscribed with an account (paraphrased here) of how the cult had come to Delos, followed by a hymn
to Sarapis composed by a certain Maiistas. The column, erected near
the temple of Apollonius sometime around 215, has survived almost
completely intact.[43]

Surviving dedications reveal that the cult experienced a considerable

---

43. *IG* XI.1299; a new edition with commentary by H. Engelmann, *The Delian Aretalogy
of Sarapis* (Leiden 1975). The basic study of Egyptian cults on Delos is P. Roussel, *Les cultes
égyptiens à Délos du IIIe au Ier siècle av. J.-C.* (Nancy 1916); for the private cult mentioned in
the text see 71–98 and 239–262. A summary including more recent findings is in Bruneau,
Recherches 457–466 and *Etudes déliennes* (Paris 1973) 130–136. The temple of Apollonius is
"Sarapieion A" in Bruneau and Ducat, *Guide de Délos* 219–221.

increase in numbers at the new shrine, but soon after the Athenian takeover it was threatened by a new crisis. We learn of it from a second inscription, placed in the same spot in 165 or 164, which has also survived in its entirety. It contains two documents, namely a decree of the Roman Senate in Greek translation and a letter from the government in Athens to the *epimeletes*. From these it emerges that Demetrius, the priest of this private cult and without doubt a descendant of its founder Apollonius, developed a grievance after "the Delians" and the Athenians on Delos began interfering with his cult of Sarapis and the *epimeletes* closed his shrine. Traveling to Rome to protest, he gained the ear of the Senate, which decreed that he ought to be allowed to practice the cult as in all previous years. The Senate informed the Athenian government accordingly, and the matter came before the Council for discussion. The result was the letter from the *strategoi* at home to the *epimeletes,* instructing him to respect the Senate decree and to allow Demetrius to continue the cult undisturbed.[44]

What prompted the Athenians to interfere with Demetrius' practice of his cult is not known, but it was not a refusal to recognize Sarapis' divinity or right to be worshipped, for a public cult had existed on Delos for some time, as had a large state temple devoted to the god (known in modern times as the "Sarapieion C"). His cult flourished both in the independent community and later during the cleruchy. In the context of a history of Hellenistic Athens, the most interesting aspect of the dispute is its revelation that Athenians could act as they saw fit on Delos only so long as they did not incur the disapproval of the Senate. If they did, then the Athenian government, to save face, could bring up the Senate's instructions for discussion in the Council, but in fact it had no other choice but to comply.

Rome's dominance was rarely so obvious as it was in this case, but it is reflected in certain phrases used in decrees of the cleruchs, in which they stress their loyalty not only to the Athenian state, of which they

44. I *Délos* 1510; a more recent edition is R. K. Sherk, *Roman Documents from the Greek East* (Baltimore 1969) 337–339, no. 5; cf. Roussel, *Les cultes égyptiens* 261–262. If the praetor P. Cornelius Blasio belongs not to 165 but to a later year (see Chapter 9, note 51), then the earliest possible date for the Senate decree is not 164 but 165. According to the text of the Senate decree the Athenians were not alone in attempting to prevent practice of the cult; "the Delians" had treated Demetrius in the same manner. Scholars generally agree with Roussel (*Les cultes égyptiens* 94 n. 2) that this term does not refer to the inhabitants driven out in 167/6, but to the new cleruchs on the island. Doubts remain, however, because to assume that the Senate really meant "Athenians" when it said "Delians" is problematic.

are citizens, but also to Rome. Thus in 159/8 public sacrifices "for [the well-being of] Athenians and Romans" are mentioned, and in 153/2 there were "traditional"—meaning regular—sacrifices on behalf of "the Council and the people, the children and women of Athens, the Roman people, and the Athenian cleruchs in Delos."[45] These sacrifices express the cleruchs' sense of direct attachment to the larger Athenian state, but also to Rome as the supreme power.

These loyalties found another expression in the development of the traditional cult of Hestia, which acquired two new "divinities," symbolic representations of the people of Athens and the people of Rome, and thereby a political dimension. The priest of the new trinity appears in a catalogue of Delian priesthoods in 158/7, ranking second in the religious hierarchy of the island after the priest of Apollo. There can be no doubt that the expanded cult was already created in 167/6, especially as a celebration of the Romaea, the new festival in honor of the goddess Roma, is documented as early as 166.[46]

Although the above-mentioned sacrifices were conducted in the name of the Athenian community on Delos, and although the triple cult was created in the name of the Athenian state, most of the numerous dedications found on the island came from individual inhabitants. Many of them express the sense of double loyalty already observed in more official statements, but with a striking time lag. Numerous dedications beginning in 119/8 or shortly before[47] contain the phrase "for the people of Athens and the people of Rome." There are forty-five such cases up to the year 89, and thirty-nine of them contain a reference to the exact year. The great majority of these inscriptions stem from priests of the various cults, and in only two are the Romans mentioned first.[48] No such case occurs after 89.

The question naturally arises why the Romans began to be included in dedications only in 120, and not in 166. There exist a number of dedications offered solely on behalf of "the people of Athens," but they too begin only at that late date: of the thirteen surviving examples of this kind of dedication, none dates from before 115/4.[49] Ten date from the years between 115/4 and 110/9, two most probably from the early

45. I *Délos* 1498.20–21 and 1499.2–8.
46. I *Délos* 2605 and 1950; Roussel, *Délos* 222–223; and Bruneau, *Recherches* 443–446.
47. I *Délos* 2247 is apparently somewhat earlier.
48. I *Délos* 1709 from 99/8 and 1889, of unknown date.
49. I *Délos* 1810–13, 1839, 2038, 2221–22, 2229, 2256, 2607–08, 2614.

years of the first century, and one cannot be assigned a precise date. They reveal that neither phrase was in common use before about 120, when both began to appear almost simultaneously, with the version including the Romans far more popular than the version that mentions only the Athenians.[50] This development undoubtedly reflects the fact that by 120 Romans (and Italians) constituted a significant proportion of the island population.

3. Center of Trade

The destruction of Corinth by the Romans caused Delos, already famed, to grow still further, for the merchants began to shift their wares there, attracted by the tax-exempt status of the shrine and the favorable site of the harbor. The latter is situated conveniently for sailors on their way to Asia from Italy and Greece. The festival is a commercial event, and the Romans, more than others, were regular customers there even while Corinth was still standing. And when the Athenians took over the island, they paid equal attention to the cults and the merchants.[51]

This is how Strabo, a Greek from Asia Minor writing in the Age of Augustus, described Delos at the time of Athenian rule, before events in the war between the Romans and Mithridates VI of Pontus brought the catastrophes of 88 and 69 upon the island. He attributes Delos' great prosperity to the duty-free harbor created in 167;[52] its convenient location as a stopover for ships on their way between Italy, Greece, and Asia; and finally to the destruction of Corinth, its commercial rival, in 146. Recent research has recognized another factor in the creation of Asia as a Roman province in 129, which led, among other things, to a considerable increase in trade and flow of capital between Italy and western Asia Minor.

In another passage Strabo makes it clear that the slave trade, which also passed through Delos, was a particularly profitable enterprise. He describes how the Seleucid empire, consisting in 140 of little more than

---

50. Of the 13 inscriptions in this form, 7 date from 110/9; of these, 6 are dedications by the current *epimeletes*, Dionysius of Pallene.

51. Strabo 10.5.4 (p. 486).

52. It is virtually certain, however, that the Athenians charged visiting ships other fees, such as a toll for using the harbor, in place of the usual customs duty amounting to 2 percent of the value of goods on board.

Cilicia, northern Syria, and Palestine, exhausted itself in internecine struggles for the throne. The breakdown of royal authority was accompanied by a rise in piracy, especially in Cilicia, and all the warring factions, both the rival claimants to the throne and the pirates, sold into slavery many of the prisoners they took in order to raise money. "It was easy to capture slaves, and a great mercantile center was not far away, the island of Delos, which could handle ten thousand slaves a day, taking them in and shipping them out so quickly that it gave rise to a saying: 'Merchant, you need only dock there and unload your cargo; by the time you finish it will already be sold.' The reason was that after the destruction of Carthage and Corinth, rich Romans needed many slaves."[53]

Delos reached its peak of prosperity in the last third of the second century. The surviving inscriptions are most numerous for the period 120–89, and the wealth of dated dedications greater than ever. The Athenian *epimeletai* are known practically without any gaps for this period. Delos brought prosperity to Athens as well, where the minting of New Style silver coins increased considerably beginning in the 140s. Besides Athens, only the Thessalian Confederacy was then minting silver in any notable quantities in Greece.[54]

By that time the Athenian citizens on Delos no longer exercised sole authority; Romans and other foreigners from all regions, most of them merchants, participated in policymaking, regardless of whether they resided on the island or had been there only a short time. Archaeological findings and plentiful inscriptions[55] flesh out Strabo's brief sketch with a wealth of colorful details, conveying the impression of a bustling multi-ethnic society in which many languages were spoken and many different religions practiced, largely united in the pursuit of its mercantile goals.

Two rather long and well-preserved decrees from the middle of the second century provide detailed information on two guilds founded by entrepreneurs from Phoenicia for both religious and commercial purposes. The first is a decree of the Heracleists of Tyre from 153/2,[56]

---

53. Strabo 14.5.2 (p. 668).

54. For the *epimeletai* see Habicht, *Hermes* 119 (1991) 198–200; for the extent of silver minting see Kroll, *Coins* 14.

55. There are about 2,000 from the period of Athenian rule alone.

56. I *Délos* 1519; F. Durrbach, *Choix d'inscriptions de Délos* (Paris 1921) 140–144; Bruneau, *Recherches* 622.

while the second, passed by the Poseidoniasts of Berytus, stems from the same time (the month of Elaphebolion in the spring of 152). The groups that passed the decrees called themselves the "Guild of Merchants and Shipowners of Tyre for the worship of Hercules [Melqart]" and the "Guild of Merchants, Shipowners, and Shipping Agents of Berytus for the worship of Poseidon." A member of the Heracleists named Patron, then serving as priest to the guild, had noted that Hercules (also worshiped as Melqart) was the founder of Tyre and a great benefactor of mankind; he proposed sending an envoy to ask the Council and Assembly in Athens to set aside a piece of land for a shrine to him. The guild passed the resolution and elected the priest himself as emissary. He left on the voyage, assuming all or part of the cost himself, and achieved his aim. The grant of a plot of land by the Athenian Assembly was tantamount to official recognition of the cult. Patron was honored with crowns by both his own association and the people of Athens; the decree was inscribed on a tablet and erected at the new shrine. The location of the shrine has not been determined. One passage of the text refers to the association's members as "the seafaring merchants and shipowners"; another mentions that the association was flourishing at the time, thanks to the favor of the gods. Without doubt this is a reference to commercial success enjoyed by its members in the course of their activities on Delos, which now permitted them to express their gratitude to their patron divinity through establishment of the shrine.

The association of Berytians passed a long and detailed decree of almost a hundred lines honoring a benefactor, the Roman banker Marcus Minatius.[57] Whereas the Tyreans at that point had just been granted a site in Delos on which to construct their precinct for Hercules/Melqart, the Berytians were already adorning the precinct of their god with various structures. Minatius had given them a loan for this purpose, waived the not inconsiderable interest charges, and, to ensure that construction proceed without delay, donated 7,000 drachmas himself. Last but not least, he had invited the association to a sacrifice followed by a banquet.[58] The group thanked him with a variety of honors, some in the form of ceremonies to be repeated monthly or

57. *JHS* 54 (1934) 140–159; I *Délos* 1520. On the dating see L. Robert, *BCH Suppl.* 1 (1973) 486–489; cf. further Bruneau, *Recherches* 622–630.
58. Lines 9–16.

annually; they also granted Minatius the right to a statue and to a painted portrait at the shrine together with the honorary citations to accompany them in the decree. To guarantee that the ceremonies in his honor continued to be performed, the association established penalties for noncompliance; line 65 mentions a fine of 6,000 "New Style" drachmas for violators.

The building complex of Poseidon erected by this group has been identified and excavated.[59] Although it is not known when construction was completed, work was well under way in 153/2, when Minatius was honored. Among the buildings was a chapel with an altar to the goddess Roma.[60]

The two documents convey a vivid impression of one aspect of merchant life in Athenian Delos: the formation of associations or guilds by groups of merchants from the same region, in which they practiced the cult of a god, either the divinity under whose protection they had placed themselves, or the chief god of their home city. Sooner or later these associations expressed their loyalty not only to Athens, on whose goodwill and toleration the practice of their business and cult depended, but also to Rome. The Poseidoniasts of Berytus performed this gesture with their altar to Roma, which serves as yet another indicator of Rome's position as the power above Athens.

The wealth of inscriptions allows us occasionally to follow the history of one family on the island through several generations, at least in broad outline. Such is the case for the family of a man named Dioscurides from the Attic deme of Myrrhinutte, which emigrated to Delos in 167/6 and left behind evidence of their lives in a fortunate combination of archaeological and epigraphic findings.[61] The modest house in the theater quarter where they first lived has been identified, and its ground plan is known. Growing prosperity allowed them to purchase the lot next door and build a large addition that offered greater conveniences and comfort. The members of the family served in local offices, including some, such as gymnasiarch, that required considerable private expenditure; the women served as priestesses. Dioscurides himself was honored in a surviving decree of the Athenian Assembly,

---

59. *EAD* 6 (1921) = C. Picard, *L'établissement des Poseidoniastes de Bérytos*, Bruneau and Ducat, *Guide de Délos* 174–179, no. 57 with plate 46; H. Meyer, *AM* 103 (1988) 203–220.
60. I *Délos* 1779. Cf. 1778 and 1782.
61. M. Kreeb, *Horos* 3 (1985) 41–61.

and in 138/7 he and his wife Cleopatra placed marble statues of themselves in a niche in their house.[62]

At the beginning of the Athenian cleruchy, the *ephebia* on Delos was presumably open only to the sons of Athenian citizens, but it and the gymnasium soon took on a cosmopolitan character. In 144/3 the list of ephebes contains several foreigners, including one Roman; and whereas the six ephebes in a list (or the start of a list) of 133/2 are without exception Athenians, the list of 119/8 contains only six sons of citizens and thirty-four foreigners out of a total of forty. (It may well be that by that time citizens preferred to do their service at home.)[63] The reason for an irregularity that occurred in 141/0 is unknown; in that year the gymnasiarch responsible for the ephebes on Delos was chosen not by the Assembly in Athens, but by the *epimeletes* on the island and by the men who frequented the gymnasium.[64]

The great slave revolt that began in the mid-130s in Sicily spread to Attica and Delos, apparently in 134, but was quickly and decisively suppressed in both places, on Delos by the *epimeletes*.[65] The rebels in Attica were slaves working in the mines, whereas in Delos they were most likely slaves waiting to be sold.

The Hellenistic monarchs remained interested in Delos in the last third of the second century. There are five inscriptions related to the Seleucid dynasty, for statues of Antiochus VIII Grypus, Antiochus IX Kyzikenos, and their ministers.[66] The court of the Ptolemies is represented with four pedestals from 127–116, honoring courtiers of Ptolemy VIII Euergetes II and with five more for his successor, Ptolemy IX Soter II, and several of his high officials, including an Athenian named Stolos, from the years 116–107.[67] The king himself

---

62. I *Délos* 1987. The Athenian decree for Dioscurides is I *Délos* 1508.

63. I *Délos* 2593 from 144/3, 2594 from 133/2, and 2598 from 119/8, with commentary by P. Roussel, *BCH* 55 (1931) 438–449.

64. I *Délos* 2589.31–32.

65. Diodorus 34.2.19; he mentions the *epimeletes*, by whom he must mean the Delian official, particularly since according to Orosius (the only source for the events besides Diodorus) the revolt in Attica was put down by the *strategos* Heracleitus (Orosius 5.9.5); S. Lauffer, *Die Bergwerkssklaven von Laureion*[2] (Wiesbaden 1979) 232–233.

66. I *Délos* 1547–51. A later addition to this group is I *Délos* 1553, an inscription for Seleucus III from around 96–94, dedicated by an Athenian citizen.

67. I *Délos* 1526–29 and 1531–35 (Stolos: 1533–34). One dedication for the health of his king stems from a Roman who took Athenian citizenship; I *Délos* 2037. For Stolos, see *Prosopographia Ptolemaica* 14693.

made a donation to the gymnasium in 111/0, as an offering "to Apollo, the people of Athens, and the young."[68]

At the very end of the century, in 102/1, the donations and dedications from an Athenian named Helianax, priest of the cult of the Cabiri, the "great gods" of Samothrace, document a close relationship with the royal house of Pontus. Sixteen surviving inscriptions relate to his activities.[69] He built a temple known as the Cabirium or Samothraceum for the gods of his cult, and also a small "monument of Mithridates" adorned with thirteen sculpted busts. Helianax dedicated the Ionian Epistyle "to the gods whose priest he is, and to King Mithridates Eupator Dionysus for the people of Athens and the people of Rome."[70] In another inscription Helianax praises the enduring favor shown to the people of Athens by the king of Pontus.[71] In addition to Mithridates VI and several of his courtiers and officers, the busts include members of other dynasties: the Seleucid monarch Antiochus VIII Grypus; the Cappadocian Ariarathes VII, long a protégé of Mithridates; and two courtiers of the Parthian king Mithridates II.[72] These medallion busts were later intentionally damaged, undoubtedly in connection with the events of 88.[73]

A few years later, in 95/4 or 94/3 , the Athenian priest of Sarapis on the island made a dedication "for the welfare of the people of Athens, the people of Rome, and King Mithridates Eupator Dionysus."[74] However, the time was not far off when the inhabitants of the island and the citizens of Athens would have to decide between the king and Rome. They made different choices—the island for Rome, Athens for the king—with ruinous consequences for both.

68. I *Délos* 1531; J. Audiat, *EAD* 28 (1970) 32, with a reproduction of the inscription in plate 6.

69. I *Délos* 1552, 1563–74, 1576, and 1581–82.

70. I *Délos* 1562 with the new fragment *ABSA* 85 (1990) 327–332, which had been carried off to Melos and was discovered there. The Cabirium and monument to Mithridates have been described in some detail by F. Chapouthier, *EAD* 16 (1935) (the monument on 13–42), and more briefly in Bruneau and Ducat, *Guide de Délos* 221–223, nos. 93–94; W. H. Gross, *Antike und Abendland* 4 (1954) 105–117.

71. I *Délos* 1563.

72. I *Délos* 1552, 1576, and 1581–82.

73. Bruneau, *Recherches* 576–577.

74. I *Délos* 2039.

Roman Hegemony

1. Athens and Oropus

After Athens had regained Delos in 167, its expulsion of the islands' inhabitants led to tensions with the Achaean League, which had taken in the exiled Delians and backed them in their claims against Athens. Both sides appealed to the Roman Senate for a judgment, and the senators handed down a decision in favor of the Delians in 159/8. New and far more serious tensions between the two powers soon arose, leading them to the brink of war near the end of the 150s. Apparently the problems stemmed from Athens' aggressive policy toward the city of Oropus on the border between Attica and Boeotia. Throughout its history, control of the city, founded by the Ionian community of Eretria on Euboea, had swung several times between Athens and Boeotia, with rare intervals of independence. The shrine of the healer hero Amphiaraus, a revered site much visited by the sick, lay in its territory.

Oropus had been part of the Athenian state several times during the fourth and early third centuries, from 377 to 366, from 338 (or 335) to 322 thanks to Philip II, and from 304 to about 287 thanks to King Demetrius. Thereafter Oropus belonged to the Boeotian League until the latter's dissolution during the war against Perseus in 171.[1] Since then Oropus had been independent but under threat from its larger neighbors Attica, Thebes, and Eretria. Athens could claim earlier rights of possession, as it had in the cases of Delos, Lemnos, Imbros, and Skyros, all of which it had recovered after the war against Perseus. It was almost inevitable that the Athenians should next cast an eye on

1. L. Robert, *Hellenica* 11–12 (1960) 200–204. See also Chapter 1, note 7.

Oropus. They stood high in Roman favor and were ready to put it to the test to see if they could reannex Oropus and its surrounding territory.

Little is known about what happened next. Polybius dealt with the events at some length in book 32 of his contemporary history, but only a portion of the introduction to that story survives. In that passage Polybius explains why he has summarized events that took place over several years under the heading of 158/7, saying he feared taxing his readers' patience if he spent more time on relatively minor matters.[2] All the same he attached to them a certain importance, less for their own sake than because they represented the first stage of a development that would lead to war between the Achaean League and Rome.

Two other sources supplement Polybius' meager surviving account; one is the much later account by Pausanias in the seventh book (on Achaea) of his *Description of Greece,* from the second half of the second century A.D. Pausanias' version is based on Polybius but contains some errors and misunderstandings. The second source, a decree from Oropus dating from 150 B.C., awarded honors to Hieron, an Achaean who had intervened in the conflict between the two cities on the side of the Oropians.[3]

This much can be ascertained about the course of events: the Athenians raided Oropian territory and plundered it. The cause is not known; there may have been some legal claim behind their action. They probably hoped to intimidate the Oropians into giving up their independence and joining Athens, but instead the Oropians filed a complaint in Rome. The Senate, as it often did in such cases, handed over responsibility for investigating and settling the matter to a Greek community, in this instance the town of Sicyon, a member of the Achaean League. As the Athenians failed to appear on the day appointed for the proceedings, they were ordered to pay a fine of 500 talents, an extraordinarily large sum.[4] Now it was the Athenians' turn to appeal to the Senate to have the fine cancelled or at the very least reduced. They sent

---

2. Polybius 32.11.5–7 with Walbank, *Commentary* 3: 531–533.

3. Pausanias 7.11.4–8; in the following chapters he describes the resulting intrigues and schemes of Achaean politicians, which finally led to the League's confrontation with Rome. The Oropian decree is *Syll.* 675. There is a good discussion in G. A. Lehmann, *Untersuchungen zur historischen Glaubwürdigkeit des Polybios* (Münster 1967) 314–321. See also D. Knoepfler, *MH* 48 (1991) 274–276; Y. Lafond, *JS* (1991) 31–33.

4. It exceeded 460 talents, the first annual contribution Athens demanded from all the members of the Naval Confederacy, based on the assessment of Aristeides.

a delegation to Rome to plead their case, selecting, instead of the usual group of citizens, the heads of three of the main philosophical schools—all of them foreigners, as it happened, although they had lived in Athens for many years. The choice was unusual but not without precedent. The "philosophers' embassy," as it has come to be known, consisted of Carneades of Cyrene from the Academy, Critolaus of Phaselis in Lycia from the Aristotelian school, and the Stoic Diogenes from Seleuceia on the Tigris. Their presence aroused enormous interest in Rome and can be said to have ushered in a new epoch in the intellectual life of the city, for during their stay the three Greeks gave extremely popular public demonstrations of their skills in rhetoric, logic, and debate. The Romans were fascinated, so much so that the elderly censor Cato denounced the presentations as dangerous to youth.[5] He was appalled when Carneades spoke on justice as a principle of international politics on one day, but argued—just as convincingly and with apparently equal sincerity—for the opposing view on the next. Polybius agreed with Cato, and must have had these demonstrations in mind when he referred disparagingly to the academicians' debates as so much smoke and mirrors.[6] But the philosophers not only impressed most of the Roman public; they carried out their mission successfully: after their address to the Senate, for which a senator acted as interpreter, the members voted to reduce the sum to be paid to Oropus to 100 talents.

However, this verdict did not put an end to the matter. The Athenians stalled for time, made no payment to the Oropians, and allegedly—it is difficult to imagine how—persuaded them to accept an Athenian garrison in their territory. When these soldiers began raiding and looting the vicinity, the Athenians refused to accept responsibility, although they declared themselves willing to try the offenders in court. At this point the Oropians, feeling perhaps that they had exhausted all possible means of reaching an agreement, called on the Achaeans for aid. The Achaean League met in Corinth, but the members showed no inclination to pick a quarrel with Athens on the Oropians' account.

5. The numerous documents related to the embassy were collected by G. Garbarino, *Roma e la filosofia Greca dalle origini alla fine del II secolo a.C.*, vol. 1 (Turin 1973) 80–86. Polybius also mentioned this delegation and may himself have heard the philosophers' public lectures in Rome (33.2). For more on their effect on the Roman public, see A. E. Astin, *Cato the Censor* (Oxford 1978) 174–178.

6. Polybius 12.26.c1–4.

Things must have reached this stage when the Athenians, regarding the Oropians' appeal to a third power as a provocation, marched in and occupied the entire territory, driving out the inhabitants who offered resistance. This fact, unmentioned in Pausanias, is documented in the Oropians' decree for Hieron; the events must have taken place in 151/0.

The expelled Oropians now tried bribery. They promised Menalcidas, a Spartan serving as general of the Achaean League, ten talents if he could persuade the Achaeans to intervene. He believed he could achieve this only by gaining the support of Callicrates, whose close ties to the Roman Senate made him then widely considered as the most powerful man in Greece. Thereupon Menalcidas approached Callicrates and promised him half of the proposed sum if he would help. Callicrates agreed, and at a second conference of the League in Argos, Menalcidas pushed through a decree, over objections from Athens and its friends, ordering Achaean forces to evict the Athenians from Oropus.[7] In the event, the threat proved enough, for when the Achaean army set out, they learned the Athenians had already withdrawn, undoubtedly in part out of fear of offending Callicrates.[8] The Oropians returned to their territory at once and paid Menalcides the sum agreed upon, but the general reneged on his bargain with Callicrates, a move that had unexpectedly far-reaching consequences in the Achaean-Roman war of 146, which ended with the utter defeat of the Achaeans and the razing of Corinth.

On their return the Oropians thanked the Achaean statesman Hieron of Aegeira for his help. Hieron came from a family prominent in Achaean politics; his father had been to Rome several times as an envoy, once in 159/8 as one of the two leaders of the Achaean delegation that debated the Athenians before the Senate. The Oropian decree expresses special gratitude to Hieron for attending the Achaean assembly sessions in Corinth and Argos and presenting their case. It was largely as a result of his efforts that the Oropians had regained their homeland.

---

7. If Walbank's summary of the lively discussion on the nature and jurisdiction of Achaean deliberative bodies is correct (*Commentary* 3: 406–414), the regular meeting of the League Assembly at Corinth had no authority to order a military intervention; that was the province of the extraordinary session held at Argos, which had no other agenda. The wording of the Oropian decree for Hieron (*Syll.* 675) is consonant with this interpretation.

8. Pausanias observes that Callicrates made enemies of the Athenians without deriving any advantage from it, since Menalcidas failed to keep his promise (7.12.2).

The Athenians' brief occupation of Oropian territory is documented by two rather large monuments to an Athenian general, one in Delphi and one in Oropus.[9] They list honors awarded to him by the Amphictionic Council in Delphi, various cities and confederations in Greece and Asia Minor, and a number of Athenian groups, including military units in Attica and the cleruchs on Salamis and Imbros. The monument in Delphi notes further honors from the Achaean League and three of its member cities; the monument in Oropus mentions honors from Corinth. Since Corinth was destroyed in 146, the awards must date from before that year. The city of Knossos appears on the monument from Oropus as leader of the Cretan League, a position it could not have achieved before 155/4;[10] and the mention of a unified Epirote League could not have occurred before 156.[11] Both monuments must have been erected between 154 and 146, but honors to an Athenian general could have been awarded in Oropus only at a time when Athens was occupying the territory. The years after 151 must be eliminated, since the Achaean League and its member cities were involved in the "Oropian dispute" on the anti-Athenian side (and then would scarcely have awarded honors to an Athenian general). The awards must therefore date from between 154, when the philosophers' embassy returned from Rome, and 152, when the Athenians retreated from Oropus.

The Oropian dispute had a brief revival in Roman letters. More than a century later Cicero, who had made a thorough study of Hellenistic philosophy, was aware that the philosophers' embassy to Rome had taken place, but knew very little about it. He had learned the date of this event from the *Annals* of his friend Atticus, published two years earlier; in search of more details he wrote to Atticus on 19 March 45 with several questions:[12] What had caused the philosophers to undertake such a mission? (He believed it had to do with Oropus but was not certain.) What was the subject of the dispute? Who was head of the Epicurean school at that date (although, as it happened, that school was not represented on the mission)? And who were the leading Athe-

---

9. *FD* III.2.35; *AE* (1925–26) 11–16, no. 129. L. Robert realized that the two decrees honor the same Athenian general; *Collection Froehner* (Paris 1936) 31 n. 6.

10. H. van Effenterre, *La Crète et le monde grec de Platon à Polybe* (Paris 1948) 268–271.

11. P. R. Franke, *Die antiken Münzen von Epirus,* vol. 1 (Wiesbaden 1961) 218.

12. Cicero *Ad Atticum* 12.23.2. The questions are surely connected with what Cicero then reported in *Acad.* 2.137. At the beginning of his political career, in the year 73, Cicero participated in a Senate debate on the shrine of Amphiaraus near Oropus and belonged to an advisory committee of the consuls consulted before the vote of the Senate (*Syll.* 747.11–12). About 30 years later he made use of what he learned in his work *De natura deorum* (3.49).

nian politicians of the era? Cicero suggested that Atticus could probably find the answers in the *Chronicle* of Apollodorus. Atticus' reply has not survived. While today we are able to name several Athenian political leaders of these years, we do not know who headed the Epicurean school—it may still have been Thespis, or he may already have been succeeded by Apollodorus, nicknamed "the tyrant of the garden."[13]

2. Rome Acquires a Foothold on the Balkan Peninsula

After 229 Roman armies and navies carried out several operations on the Balkan peninsula and in the Aegean, Illyria, Macedonia, and Greece. Each time, after completing their mission, they returned home, leaving behind neither occupying forces nor political administrators. For eighty years Rome had shown no interest in annexing territory or establishing a permanent presence in that part of the world. This policy came to an end soon after the middle of the second century. In 148, after suppressing the revolt of Andriscus, Rome reorganized the territory of Macedonia (which it had divided in 167 into four independent republics) into a Roman province and sent out a governor every year. Then in 146, following the defeat of the Achaean League, the Romans extended the authority of the Macedonian governor to cover those parts of Greece that fought against them; this included Thebes, Chalcis, eastern Locris, Phocis, and the Megarid, in addition to the territory of the Achaean League.[14] The city of Corinth, where hostile crowds had mobbed Roman envoys before the war, was destroyed by consul

13. Dorandi, *Ricerche* 51, who also mentions further literature. Epicurus' school was popularly referred to as "the garden," where the lectures took place.

14. Accame, *Dominio* 1–15; D. W. Baronowski, *Klio* 70 (1988) 448–460; J.-L. Ferrary, *Philhellénisme et impérialisme* (Rome 1988) 186–209; A. Giovannini, *AJAH* 9 (1984 [1988]) 42 n. 1. All these authors have rejected E. Gruen's hypothesis, formulated in opposition to Accame, that regular governors were not appointed for Macedonia until considerably later, and that the Greek states that opposed Rome in 146 remained independent *de jure* after the war (*The Hellenistic World and the Coming of Rome*, 2 vols. [Berkeley 1984] 481–528). As Pausanias reports (7.16.9–10), the Senate commission formed to assist consul Mummius introduced new constitutions based on a census in the defeated states and established the amount of tribute they owed. Pausanias errs in only one respect, when he claims that Rome also sent a governor to these areas annually; this did not in fact occur until Augustus created the province of Achaea in 27 B.C. Whether meanwhile these areas were treated as an "appendage" to Macedonia (as Accame and Baronowski argue) or whether the proconsul of Macedonia was entrusted with their supervision only as an additional and separate task *(provincia)*, as Ferrary believes, is of no significance for the history of Athens.

Lucius Mummius on orders from the Senate; its greatest art treasures were shipped to Rome, and the lesser spoils passed on to Attalus II of Pergamum and other Roman allies.

During these stormy times Athens' role was generally limited to that of passive observer, although the city demonstrated its loyalty to Rome by sending five triremes as naval support during the Third Punic War (149–146).[15] The Athenians cannot have been tempted for a moment to join the Achaeans and their allies against Rome, particularly since their own relations with the Achaean League had been strained for some time.

The surviving documentation for the Achaean war of 146 is very sparse, and Athens is directly mentioned only once, in connection with a visit to the city that spring by emissaries of Metellus, the Roman governor in Macedonia.[16] Yet despite the lack of evidence it is clear that the outcome of the war had a lasting effect on Athens. The Romans established a presence in Macedonia with authority over large areas of Greece, including Attica's immediate neighbors Megara, Thebes, and Chalcis. Even if this control became apparent only through occasional and limited interventions by the proconsul in Macedonia, it was a basic political fact of life that must have inevitably affected the thinking of all mainland Greeks. Contemporaries saw it as a watershed: the Macedonians made 148/7 the start of a new era, and calculated dates starting from this year on thousands on inscriptions over the next several centuries.[17] At least ten cities on the Peloponnese—of non-Achaean nationality but members of the Achaean League until the defeat—began their own new era in 145/4, which continued in use for over a century until replaced by the Actian era of Augustus.[18] And even Athens, which appeared only indirectly affected, made a similar gesture: although it did not introduce a new system of reckoning dates, the city leaders began a new table of eponymous archons in 146/5, just as they had in the year of liberation 230/29, and as they would again after their liberation from the "tyrant" Aristion in 87/6. In Athens as

15. Pausanias 1.29.14.

16. Polybius 38.13.9.

17. M. N. Tod, *ASBA* 23 (1918–19) 206–217 and 24 (1919–1921) 54–67; *Studies Presented to D. M. Robinson*, vol. 2 (St. Louis 1953) 382–397.

18. For more on the "Achaean era," as it is known, see W. B. Dinsmoor, *The Archons of Athens in the Hellenistic Age* (Cambridge, Mass., 1931) 236–237. For the communities involved (in Arcadia, Laconia, Messenia and Argolid), however, that date is more likely to have been regarded as marking their "liberation" from membership in the Achaean League.

elsewhere, the use of a new tablet was always a sign that the opening year was considered a significant transition or the start of a new era.[19] In 146/5 this must have meant that the Athenians welcomed the new order, or, at the very least, that the city leaders wanted to go on record with an official gesture of welcome. In this context it should be recalled that Delos, an Athenian possession, benefited from the destruction of Corinth, and indirectly so did the Athenians themselves.

In one sense Athens had not been entirely a bystander in the Roman-Achaean conflict, since the Athenian raids on Oropus did set in motion the chain of events leading to war. The Oropians, as mentioned, had sought help in 151/0 from Menalcidas, the Spartan commander of the Achaean League's army, and had secured his cooperation with the promise of a large sum of money. But other Achaean politicians became involved in these machinations, and the original bargain—first between Menalcidas and Callicrates, then between the general and his successor in office, Diaeus of Megalopolis—went sour, leading to angry recriminations and finally a full-fledged conflict between Sparta and officials of the Achaean League. Menalcidas and Diaeus appeared as representatives of the feuding parties before the Roman Senate in 149/8, but before the Romans could carry out their much-delayed plan to mediate a settlement, hostilities broke out. Diaeus played a leading role in the conflict after being re-elected Achaean general for 148/7, while Menalcidas was forced to commit suicide. Having finally lost patience with the Achaeans' intransigence, the Senate in the summer of 147 ordered the withdrawal of Sparta, Corinth, and Argos from the League. The embittered Achaeans responded by declaring war on Sparta the following spring, provoking the Roman intervention that ended the League's existence and brought destruction on Corinth.[20]

In recent years some have claimed that at the end of the war Athens reacquired control over Oropus for another sixty years,[21] clearly basing such an assumption on a visit to the shrine of Amphiaraus by Athenian ephebes documented for 123/2. However, the text of the inscription in fact suggests the exact opposite with regard to the sovereignty of the region, for it states that the visiting ephebes returned "to their own

19. *IG* II^2.1713, with Kirchner's commentary. For similar pronouncements cf. C. Habicht, *Demetrias*, ed. V. Milojčić and D. Theocharis, vol. 1 (Bonn 1976) 185–188.

20. J. Deininger, "Diaios," *RE Suppl.* 11 (1968) 521–526.

21. P. Roesch, *Etudes béotiennes* (Paris 1982) 49.

country" on the same day, implying that they had been on foreign soil in Oropus.[22] There is another documented visit of Athenian ephebes to the same shrine from an unpublished decree of 177/6, when Oropus was independent and a member of the Boeotian League. In both cases permission to visit the site must have been sought and granted. By 123/2 the Boeotian League no longer existed, and whether Oropus was still autonomous is doubtful. This is usually assumed, although Denis Knoepfler has recently suggested that it may have been awarded in 146 to Eretria, a city that fought on the Roman side against its neighbor and rival Chalcis in the preceding war.[23] This suggestion is based on the further assumption that Oropus, by seeking help from the Achaean League years earlier, had compromised itself vis-à-vis the Romans and therefore been punished with the loss of its independence.

Whatever the status of Oropus at the time, it was not placed under Athenian sovereignty after the Roman-Achaean war. Nonetheless Athenians welcomed the new order at least to the extent of marking its inception with a new table of archons. It is further possible that in one form or another the city was rewarded for its support of Rome by a Senate decree passed under the chairmanship of Gaius Laelius. The existence of this Roman decree is known only indirectly, from another decree passed by Athenian settlers in Myrina on Lemnos. The rather complex circumstances require some explanation.

The settlers' decree[24] was inscribed by an Athenian mason known to have been active between 169 and 134.[25] Thus the only possible candidate for chairman of the Senate in this matter is Gaius Laelius (called Sapiens, "the Wise"), a close friend of the young Scipio Africanus. He was consul in 140, had been praetor five years earlier, and could have presided over the Senate either as consul or, in the absence of both consuls, as praetor. All other indications point to 145, the year of his praetorship, for the decree mentions a happy event and good news, and further a military alliance against an opponent described as a lawbreaker (whose name is no longer legible). The people of Athens were involved in these events in some way, and the Romans are called

22. *IG* II^2.1006.27–28 and 70–71.
23. D. Knoepfler, *MH* 48 (1991) 279.
24. *IG* II^2.1224, interpreted by A. Kirchhoff, *Hermes* 1 (1866) 217–228. Since then several more fragments have come to light, including the one that names C. Laelius.
25. Tracy, *ALC* 155.

"the common benefactors," a phrase that can only mean they had recently acted as benefactors of Athens. The Senate decree referred to in the text is obviously the cause of the rejoicing, and it must have either awarded or confirmed possession of certain disputed islands to Athens.

These signs suggest that Rome had recently waged a successful war with Athenian support, and the Senate decree most likely has a close connection with the end of this war and the subsequent reordering of political affairs. It came as welcome news to the Athenians because it guaranteed them possession of the islands in question. Taken in conjunction with the two possible dates at which Gaius Laelius could have presided over the Senate—in 145 as praetor, or in 140 as consul—this evidence points to the Achaean war fought in 146 and to 145 as the year of the Roman decree. This date fits well with two names mentioned in the settlers' decree: Heracleitus as Athenian hoplite general and Philarchides as Athenian *strategos* for Lemnos. The disputed islands may have been Skiathos, Peparethos, and Ikos.

Athens' relationship with Rome remained unclouded after the Achaean war. The clearest possible proof for public display of loyalty to Rome is the continuation of official sacrifices to the personified Roman *demos,* the Roman people. Such a sacrifice is mentioned in an Assembly decree from the archonship of Pleistaenus: the *prytaneis* are recorded as having offered a sacrifice for the welfare of Athens not only to all the gods traditionally receiving such gifts but also "to the *demos* of the Romans." As was recently shown, the year in which Pleistaenus was archon should be assigned not to the early second century B.C. but rather to the period immediately following the philosophers' embassy of 155.[26] The sacrifice in question was probably performed for a specific occasion, as this is the only instance in which the Roman people are named along with the traditional gods; there is no parallel mention of the Roman *demos* in fifteen similar decrees from 178 through 154, nor in later texts.[27] The Athenians had been familiar with personification of themselves as a people since the fifth century, and in 229 a state cult of the *demos* and the Charites was created. Showing a foreign *demos* the same reverence was a different matter, however. The first Greek states to pay this kind of homage to the personified *populus Romanus* in-

26. *Agora* XV.180.7–12; for the dating see S. V. Tracy, *Horos* 7 (1989–1991) 41–43.
27. *Agora* XV.194–229 for the texts through 155/4.

cluded the islands of Samos (in 188 or after 168) and Rhodes (in 163) and the city of Laodicea on the Lycus in Asia Minor (at about the same time as Rhodes). Athens was not far behind, although it may have performed the one sacrifice and left it at that, without erecting a permanent special monument as the above-mentioned states did.[28]

There is also only one mention in this period of the Romaea, a festival honoring the goddess Roma and a further sign of Athens' continuing attachment to Rome. It was celebrated in the year of the archon Lysiades, who held office in or around 149/8.[29]

What had appeared for the first time eighty years before as a nebulous possibility, as "the cloud from the West," and then as more and more a probability, finally became a reality in 146: the Romans came to the Greek mainland to stay. Although no one could predict that they would remain rulers for centuries, contemporaries fully recognized that they were experiencing the beginning of a new era. The Romans' barbaric annihilation of an old and famous city could only compare with Alexander the Great's destruction of Thebes in 335; both events mark the start of onerous domination by a foreign power. The horror experienced by the Greeks at the obliteration of Corinth was heightened by the destruction of Carthage that same year at the end of a war that Rome had needlessly provoked. There can be no doubt that Greeks took note of this event, for it became the subject of an essay written in Athens at that time. Hasdrubal, a Carthaginian, had entered the Academy as a pupil of Carneades in 159/8 and taken the Greek name Cleitomachus. He remained in Athens and later succeeded his teacher as head of Plato's school. He responded to the news of the tragedy at home by composing a consolatory epistle to the Romans' Carthaginian captives, which Cicero read a century later.[30]

Rome's allies in the Greek world must have felt a chill as they observed the fate of Corinth and Carthage. Athens had emerged from events intact, but the Athenian state now had noticeably less political latitude.

---

28. For the documents named and other relevant evidence see Habicht, *AM* 104 (1990) 259–268, where, however, an important piece was overlooked: the cult statue of the Roman *demos* with a height of 30 ells that stood in the temple of Athena on Rhodes (Polybius 31.4.4).

29. *IG* II^2.1938.

30. Cicero *Tusc. disp.* 3.54. For Cleitomachus see H. von Arnim, "Kleitomachus," *RE* (1921) 656–659; Dorandi, *Ricerche* 11–16.

3. Athens and Delphi

Relations between Athens and Delphi grew intensively in the second half of the second century. As part of this development, new inscriptions, large and small, filled more and more of the remaining spaces on the walls of the Athenian treasury inside the sanctuary.[31] About 140 Athenian judges mediated a dispute over Delphi's border with Ambryssus and Phlygonion,[32] and two Athenians from extremely prominent and related families received honors in Delphi: Micion of Cephisia, from the family of the liberators of 229, in his capacity as festival delegate to the Soteria;[33] and Leon, son of Cichesias of Aixone.[34] Around 145 a delegation from Delphi came to Athens with a request for judges in a dispute, the subject of which is no longer legible because of damage to the inscription.[35] A group of four inscriptions found in Delphi further reveals that during the second half of the second century Athens was given the task of settling a long-standing quarrel. In this case it is known that the feuding parties were the east Locrian towns of Scarpheia and Thronion, and the dispute was over who should represent eastern Locris in the Amphictiony. Scarpheia, which must have had a decisive voice in the east Locrian confederacy, demanded the seat at Delphi, but Thronion claimed the right to choose the delegate every third year, since it paid a third of the costs of membership in the Council. An Athenian court with several hundred members had earlier decided in favor of Scarpheia, but this time the sixty-one Athenian judges voted fifty-nine to two for Thronion. Although the texts of these inscriptions are not preserved in entirety, their general drift is clear; only the year of the Athenian judgment is a matter of debate among scholars, with Klaffenbach arguing for a date before 146, and the majority favoring a year around 100.[36]

These documents reveal that cordial relations prevailed between Athens and Delphi at this time, that Delphi gave honors to respected

---

31. They have been published by G. Colin in *FD* III.2.
32. *FD* III.2.142; cf. 136.
33. *FD* III.2.140 and 141. For the family see Habicht, *Studien* 179–182.
34. *FD* III.2.93. For the family see Habicht, *Studien* 194–197. A Cichesias was married to Habryllis, daughter of a man named Micion (unpublished inscription).
35. *FD* III.2.243.
36. *FD* III.4.38–41; G. Klaffenbach, *Klio* 20 (1926) 68–88; Daux, *Delphes* 335–341; Klaffenbach, *Gnomon* 13 (1938) 17–19.

Athenian citizens and several times entrusted disputes to Athenian judges. Connections became even closer after 138, when Athens reintroduced a custom that had died out in the fourth century, a festival procession called the *Pythais*, followed by musical and dramatic performances in honor of Apollo. Such processions took place in 138, 128, 106, and 98, and all are documented by numerous inscriptions, chiseled by Athenian stonemasons on the walls of the Athenian treasury in Delphi and containing, among other things, the names of all participants.[37] In the first procession there were 14 festival delegates, 57 ephebes, 39 members of the boys' chorus, with 2 leaders and 11 *canephoroi* (basket-carrying maidens). In 128 the archons also participated, in addition to 60 knights and 59 festival artists, whose numbers grew to approximately 100 by 106/5. More than 500 Athenians in all took part in the *Pythais* that year.[38]

One of the most striking features of the reports on these processions after 128 is the role of the festival artists, who put on their performances to honor Apollo at the site of his oracle. They were actors, musicians, singers, poets, and dancers, organized in guilds dating back to the early third century. The oldest such group was the Athenian guild of the *technitai,* whose membership was limited to Athenian citizens; the Isthmians were next in importance on the Greek mainland. The troupes traveled from place to place to appear at the various festivals. Since their performances were deemed part of religious observance, they were regarded as priests and early on granted special privileges. The Athenian *technitai* were granted personal immunity and dispensation from taxes by the Amphictionic Council in 277, shortly after the Celtic attack on Delphi had been repulsed. The guild of Isthmus possessed similar privileges, reconfirmed by the Roman consul Lucius Mummius in 146 after the destruction of Corinth.[39]

Originally the Soteria at Delphi was celebrated annually (or biannually) under the sponsorship of the Amphictionic Council, with the Athenian guild responsible for organizing the artistic competitions. Eventually the Isthmian guild took over this function. In the late

---

37. *FD* III.2.2–54 and a new fragment, *Etudes delphiques* (1977) 139–157. See A. Boëthius, *Die Pythais* (Uppsala 1918); Daux, *Delphes* 521–583; S. V. Tracy, *BCH* 99 (1975) 185–218 and *Hesperia Suppl.* 15 (1975).

38. Tables are in Tracy, *BCH* 99 (1975) 215–218.

39. *IG* VII.2413–14. Important new insights are to be expected from as yet unpublished inscriptions from Argos, *Deltion* 28 (1973 [1977]) B 126; *SEG* 31.307.

second century, however, the resumption of the Athenian procession gave the city's artists and performers an opportunity to return to Delphi. Although the *technitai* are not mentioned in connection with the *Pythais* of 138, they participated in large numbers in the celebration of 128. It is certainly no coincidence that only six years previously the Amphictiony had renewed the guild's privileges of 277.[40] The mass participation of performers so soon afterward was certainly above all an expression of gratitude. The Council's decree had one significant disclaimer: the privileges were valid "if the Romans have no objections." Clearly, the councillors wished to avoid giving the impression of interfering in areas the Romans might consider their right to regulate; after all, Lucius Mummius had intervened directly in the case of the festival guild of the Isthmus.

A high point of the celebration of 128 was the performance of a new hymn to Apollo, composed by an Athenian named Limenius. His text, inscribed with the notes above it, was placed on the south wall of the Athenian treasury, along with a second similar hymn.[41] Its performance in 128 was carried out by instrumental soloists (including the composer Limenius as one of the zither players), a chorus of fifty-one boys, and the thirty-nine-member chorus of adult *technitai*.[42] Musicologists have sufficiently reconstructed the incomplete text and music to allow a performance with modern reproductions of the original instruments and trained singers.[43]

The hymn itself, a relatively short piece, takes about ten minutes to perform. Brief verses recount the story of Apollo's birth on Delos and his journey to Athens, his arrival in Delphi, his struggle with the Python, the terrible dragon, and the assistance the god gave in driving back the marauding Gauls in 279. The final ode is an appeal to Apollo, Artemis, and Leto to protect Athens, Delphi, the *technitai*, and Rome,

40. *FD* III.2.68. Copies were displayed in Athens by the *technitai* themselves (*IG* II^2.1132.52–94) and by the state (*Hesperia* 39 [1970] 309–310).

41. *FD* III.2.138. There is a new edition in A. Bélis, "Les Hymnes à Apollon," in *Corpus des inscriptions de Delphes,* vol. 3 (Paris 1992). *FD* III.2.137 is a similar hymn, either by Athenaeus or an unknown Athenian, also performed on the occasion of a *Pythais* in 138 or 128.

42. *FD* III.2.47, where the composer is named together with a relative, probably his brother, in lines 21–22. The relative, Thoinus, is almost certainly the man who served as magistrate of the Athenian mint in 114/3 and 113/2 (C. Habicht, *Chiron* 21 [1991] 21–22).

43. Limenius' hymn was first performed in modern times in the ancient theater of Delphi on 19 September 1992 by a French ensemble under the direction of Annie Bélis.

whose empire the gods should cause to grow. It expresses the accord prevailing between Delphi, the Amphictiony, Athens, and its artists' guilds, in which Rome was included.

In repeated interventions by the Senate in a protracted conflict between the rival guilds of Athens and the Isthmus, it emerged very quickly that Athens and its *technitai* were held in high regard by Rome. The various stages of the dispute cannot be clearly reconstructed on all points;[44] evidently, the Senate's first decree attempting to establish cooperation between the two groups failed to achieve the desired effect. Further disputes were heard in 119/8 or 118/7 by Cornelius Sisenna, the Roman proconsul in Macedonia, resulting in a division of the Isthmian guild. A second, equally ineffective Senate decree was finally followed in June 112 by a Senate hearing in which the two parties presented their cases. The Senate finally decided in favor of the Athenians, a verdict that led to the decline and disintegration of the Isthmian guild.[45]

The fact that Rome had any say at all in such a matter, an internal Greek dispute, is explained by two circumstances. First, with its victory in the Achaean war Rome had acquired sovereignty over the parts of Greece in which the Isthmian festival guild had its seat and area of operations; and second, it was the Roman consul Mummius who had confirmed the guild's privileges. Another point (significant within Athenian history) is that the Athenian festival artists had the full and energetic backing of the state, so that, for example, the advocates who pleaded their cause before the Senate were not emissaries of the guild itself but ambassadors of the Athenian state. The Amphictionic Council of Delphi had sided long before with the Athenians and their artists, and in 117, in the midst of the dispute, it passed a decree that read almost like an anthem, "a veritable panegyric to Athens."[46] Borrowing phrases from as far back as Isocrates' panegyric of 380, the author

44. A detailed discussion is in Daux, *Delphes* 356–372. See further F. Poland, "Technitai," *RE* V A.2 (1934) cols. 2504–07.

45. The various stages of the dispute are recapitulated in the Senate decree of 112, *FD* III.2.70; R. K. Sherk, *Roman Documents from the Greek East* (Baltimore 1969) no. 15.

46. *FD* III.2.69 (*IG* II^2.1134.1–63). The quotation is from G. Klaffenbach, *Gnomon* 14 (1938) 20. The traditional assignment of the decree to the year 117 is preferable to Daux's (tentative) proposal of 125 and is rendered all but certain by the more recent fragment in *Hesperia* 45 (1976) 287, no. 3. See Tracy, *ALC* 190–191. In this case the resolution of the "scandal of 125" (Daux, *Delphes* 372–386) also belongs in 117, for both it and the decree are dated in the year of the archon Eucleidas in Delphi.

praises Athens as virtually the origin of all good things on earth. Athens, so runs the text, has tamed the animal nature of man and thereby made communal life possible; the city received the gift of agriculture from Demeter and shared it with the other Greeks; law and morality have their fount in Athens just as do the Mysteries, tragedy, and comedy. Athens attributed these titles of honor to itself, and they have continued to shine across the centuries, creating the lasting legend surrounding the city.[47]

In the documents discussed above dating from between 117 and 112, the Romans figure as "the common benefactors," a term already used several times to describe them in other parts of the Greek world. They are referred to thus by the Athenian state, the Amphictionic Council, and the festival artists, who sacrificed to them regularly along with Dionysus and the other gods.[48] By all indications, these years represent the peak of cordial relations between Athens and Rome. Athens' relations with Delphi are characterized by the same cordiality during the forty-year period in which the resumption of the Pythian processions are documented, from 138 to 98; of these celebrations, the *Pythais* of 106/5 marked a peak in numbers of Athenian participants, and no doubt in expense as well.

47. See E. Buchner, *Der Panegyrikos des Isokrates* (Wiesbaden 1965) 45–64. See further A. Wilhelm (1947) 49–53 in *Akademieschriften* 3: 297–301. Later sources include Cicero *Pro Flacco* 62; Plut. *mor.* 345F from *De gloria Atheniensium;* Pliny *Ep.* 8.24.2; Augustine *De civitate dei* 18.9.

48. *IG* II^2.1134.69 and 103; *FD* III.2.70.45–46. See Ferrary, *Philhellénisme et impérial-isme* 124–132; A. Erskine, *Historia* 43 (1994) 70–87.

The Close of
the Second Century

1. Foreign Relations

Notwithstanding claims that the good relations prevailing between Athens and the court of the Ptolemies in Alexandria suffered a long interruption in the second half of the second century, there are in fact no signs that this was the case. Athenians continued to celebrate the Ptolemaea regularly during the long reign of Ptolemy VIII Euergetes II (145–116), and cordial relations under his son and successor, Ptolemy IX Soter II (116–107 and 88–80), are documented. The latter donated a large sum for the gymnasium in Delos in 111/0,[1] and a few years later the poet Antisthenes of Paphos praised the friendship between Athens, Egypt, and Rome in an epigram.[2] According to Pausanias the Athenians received many favors from this king.[3] As long as the dynasty lasted, from its founder, Ptolemy I, to its last ruler, Cleopatra, Athens could depend on the goodwill of Egyptian monarchs.

Our knowledge of Athens' relations with the Seleucids in this period is sparse, largely because, here as elsewhere, such a small proportion of the ancient evidence has survived.[4] Nonetheless, what we have is informative. One Athenian decree from the second half of the second century honors a courtier of King Demetrius who had provided assistance to Athenian diplomats in Antioch. The king was probably Demetrius II, who occupied the throne from 150 to 140 and again from

1. I *Délos* 1531; J. Audiat, *EAD* 28 (1970) 32. Cf. I *Délos* 1532 and 2037.
2. I *Délos* 1533; H. Hauben, *ZPE* 25 (1977) 225.
3. Pausanias 1.9.3.
4. For more on this subject see C. Habicht, *Chiron* 17 (1987) 7–26, esp. 18–26.

129 to 125; it was during his reign, in June 142, that the Jews led by Simon (father of John Hyrcanus; see below) declared their independence.[5] In 140/39 Demetrius was captured by the Parthians; while a prisoner he married a daughter of the Parthian king, although he was already married to Cleopatra. Cleopatra thereupon married his brother Antiochus, who took over the realm as Antiochus VII in 139/8. The queen had a son by Demetrius, Prince Antiochus, born in 141; she sent him to be brought up in Athens, a sign that the city still enjoyed a reputation as the most suitable place to acquire a higher education.[6]

Antiochus VII Sidetes also strove to remain on good terms with Athens. During his ten-year reign (139–129) a high-ranking emissary of his, named either [Me]nodorus or [Ze]nodorus, was honored in Athens in a long decree containing some interesting details. The king had good reasons for choosing this man to go on a mission to the city, for Menodorus' father, Eumenes, had lived in Athens for a time and had been awarded Athenian citizenship for his assistance to Athenian diplomats in Antioch. While on his mission Menodorus was invited to address the Assembly. In his speech he recalled the gifts Seleucid rulers had sent to the city and the ways in which the ancestors of the present king had acted as benefactors, assuring the citizens that King Antiochus was of the same mind. It thus appears that Antiochus VII himself had not yet had an opportunity to show his favor to Athens; the emphasis is placed on the acts of his forebears, probably first and foremost Antiochus IV Epiphanes. Menodorus' mission may have been to announce the accession of a new king and to assure the Athenians that the new monarch would continue the favorable policies of the past. He received the same high honors that John Hyrcanus would receive somewhat later, namely a golden crown and a bronze statue erected in the Agora next to the statue of the king.[7]

At about the same time or slightly earlier, the Athenians awarded citizenship to Menestheus, son of Apollonius, another man in the service of the Seleucid king. He came from a distinguished family of

5. A. Wilhelm (1915) 21–23 in *Akademieschriften* 1: 195–197; C. Habicht, *CAH* 8[2] (1989) 367–368.

6. Appian *Syr.* 361. The prince himself acceded to the throne in 125.

7. S. V. Tracy recognized that the king who sent Menodorus was himself not Antiochus IV, as had previously been assumed, but rather Antiochus VII Sidetes, and that Antiochus IV belongs in the group of predecessors praised as great benefactors; *GRBS* 29 (1988) 383–388. The mason who carved this decree is documented as active from about 135 to 122.

Miletus that produced many courtiers and officials of the dynasty. His father had served under Seleucus IV and Antiochus IV in the 170s as governor of Coele Syria, while Menestheus and two brothers, Meleager and Apollonius, had accompanied Prince Demetrius to Rome and, in 162, helped him escape to Syria to claim the throne. Whichever king sent Menestheus to Athens, he clearly chose a man of high standing who enjoyed his confidence.[8]

Several precise sources shed light on Athens' relations with Ariarathes V of Cappadocia, who reigned from 163 until 130, when he was killed in the war against Aristonicus. He is documented as *agonothetes* for the Great Panathenaea in an unknown year,[9] a title he received in all probability in return for a large donation, while an Athenian citizen performed the actual duties but without dipping into his own pocketbook. Ariarathes and his consort Nysa were also benefactors of the Athenian festival guild, and he guaranteed them personal immunity and safe conduct within his realm. These facts can be determined from a lengthy decree passed in the king and queen's honor by the festival artists,[10] with which they expressed their thanks. They also created monthly and annual festival days in Ariarathes' honor, and associated him with Dionysus by hanging his portrait next to an image of the god. The decree reveals further that both the *technitai* and the Athenian state sent envoys to the kingdom of Cappadocia. The festival artists chose three of their members to present the decree to the king, and it is clear that the guild had professional interests in Cappadocia and enjoyed royal protection. An Athenian athlete who won more than thirty competitions in Greece, as we learn from the pedestal of his statue in Delos, also received a victor's crown from Ariarathes after winning a contest sponsored by the monarch in Cappadocia.[11]

Athens' greatly intensified contacts with cities in Phoenicia and Syria as a result of its acquisition of Delos have already been mentioned, but the connections extended even further. By chance a unique document

8. *IG* II².982 (Osborne, *Naturalization* 1: D 113); P. Herrmann, *Chiron* 17 (1987) 171–192, esp. 175–179. The Athenian decree, thought by A. Wilhelm to date from about 150, is assigned by Tracy to around 130 (*ALC* 241).

9. *AE* (1948–49) 5–9; see further J. and L. Robert, *Bulletin épigraphique* (1951) 79.

10. *IG* II².1330; see further L. Robert, *Etudes épigraphiques et philologiques* (Paris 1938) 39–40 and *Noms indigènes de l'Asie Mineure gréco-romaine* (Paris 1963) 495–496.

11. I *Délos* 1957. The Athenians awarded citizenship around the middle of the second century to a resident of the city of Ariarathea, founded by this king's predecessor, King Ariarathes IV (Osborne, *Naturalization* 1: D 112).

has been preserved that merits a closer look. It is found in Josephus' *Jewish Antiquities,* a history from the late first century A.D. containing many old documents intended to demonstrate the degree of respect Jews enjoyed in many kingdoms and cities after the revolt of the Maccabees revived the Jewish state in the second century B.C. Among the documents reflecting privileges granted by kings to Jewish subjects or communities within their realms, or by Romans within their empire, is an Athenian decree from the spring of 105 honoring John Hyrcanus, high priest and leader of the Jewish people. The decree expresses the appreciation of the Athenian people for the kindness and helpfulness he had always shown to the people as a whole and to individuals, both diplomats and private citizens, providing a friendly reception and escorts to ensure a safe journey home. Their reports had informed the citizens of his benevolence, the decree states, and his unfailing goodwill toward the city, and for this reason he is awarded a golden crown and a bronze statue in the shrine of the *demos* and the Charites, with further honors being considered for a later date. Finally, the decree mentions the selection of envoys from the citizenry to present the honors to Hyrcanus and request his continuing goodwill for the future.[12]

This decree clearly demonstrates that Athens maintained official diplomatic contacts with the Jewish ruler and that Athenian citizens visited his country, most of them presumably pursuing commercial interests as traders and merchants. Clearly, Hyrcanus took a lively interest in these contacts with Athens and Athenian citizens, not a surprising development in view of the growing secularization and Hellenization of the Hasmonaean dynasty.

A very fragmentary decree found on Delos has a bearing on the creation of the Roman province of Asia and reordering of political structures after the Roman defeat of Aristonicus, the rebel who claimed the throne of Pergamum as King Eumenes III (131–129).[13] For a long time it was not clear whether this decree belonged to the period of Delian independence before 167 or to the era of Athenian rule; its mention of the dispatch of a Roman army to Asia could have referred to either the war against Antiochus or the war against Aristonicus. Nor was it apparent who had passed the decree, which might have stemmed

12. Josephus *Antiq.* 14.149–155. Three of the Athenians named in the text are known from other sources (assuming that slight deviations in spelling are the result of transcription errors); A. Wilhelm, *Philologus* 60 (1901) 487 and *JOEAI* 8 (1905) 238.
13. *IG* XI.713.

from the free community of Delos, from Athens, or even a third state.[14] Ultimately the identification of the letter cutter as a mason active in Athens between 134/3 and 117/6 has revealed that it was passed by the Athenian Assembly and is connected with the war against Aristonicus.[15] The man to whom it awards honors may have been *epimeletes* of Delos during the war.

At the very end of the century Athenian warships provided support for the Romans in a campaign led by proconsul Marcus Antonius against pirates on the southern coasts of Asia Minor (102–100). It was the first serious attempt by Rome to put an end to this plague. The decline of Rhodes's naval power and the progressive weakening of the Seleucid empire, to which Cilicia nominally belonged, and whose irregular coast offered ideal hiding places for pirates, had resulted in an upsurge of piracy. A Latin epigram found in Corinth reports that Antonius' fleet was towed across the Isthmus to the Saronic Gulf and then detained in Athens by bad weather; Antonius left it there under the command of the legate (Lucilius) Hirrus and sailed on himself to Side in Pamphylia.[16] Cicero confirms that the expedition was held up in Athens by rough seas.[17] Tacitus reports further that Byzantium supported Antonius' campaign, and an inscription from Rhodes reveals that Rhodian ships and the Roman quaestor Aulus Gabinius also took part.[18] Athens' involvement is documented by the remains of a large monument erected in honor of an Athenian *nauarch* (admiral) and found in Piraeus; its inscription has been related to this campaign.[19] The name of the naval officer so honored is not preserved, but he belonged to the distinguished clan of the Kerykes and had previously served as its archon. For his service as commander of the Athenian navy he was awarded crowns by the Athenian crews, the Lycian League, and

14. F. Durrbach and A. Jardé, *BCH* 28 (1904) 278–280, no. 5; P. Roussel on *IG* XI.713; M.-F. Baslez and C. Vial, *BCH* 111 (1987) 294 and n. 68.

15. S. V. Tracy, *AM* 107 (1992) 303–306.

16. A. Degrassi, *Inscriptiones Latinae Liberae Rei Publicae*[2] (Florence 1957) 342 (= *Corinth* VIII.2, no. 1), with T. R. S. Broughton, *TAPhA* 77 (1946) 35–40, and esp. J.-L. Ferrary, *MEFRA* 89 (1977) 639–643.

17. Cicero *De or.* 1.82.

18. Tacitus *Ann.* 12.62; *Inscriptiones Graecae ad Res Romanas Pertinentes* (Paris 1906–1917) 4.1116.

19. *IG* II[2].3218. The most important commentaries are L. Robert, *Rph* 70 (1944) 11–17 (= *OMS* 3.1377–83) and *RN* (1977) 24–25 (= *OMS* 6.186–187). See also H. Troxell, *The Coinage of the Lycian League* (New York 1982) 94–95; J. Nollé, *Side im Altertum,* vol. 1 (Cologne 1993) 69–71 and, with a copy of the text, 231–232, TEp 30.

the Lycian cities of Phaselis and Myra, as well as by Side in Pamphylia and Celenderis in Cilicia. The inhabitants of the island of Cythnos honored him for "liberating" them (clearly from the pirates). The decisive clue for dating the monument is the fact that the cities of Side and Phaselis were then still allied with Rome and not in the hands of pirates, as was the case after the First Mithridatic War.[20] This excludes the possibility that the text on the Athenian monument refers to the operations of either Publius Servilius Vatia (78–74) or Marcus Antonius Creticus (74–71) against the pirates, and in fact the latter expedition never even reached the eastern Aegean.

The *nauarch* whom the monument honored must have served in 103/2 or the following year in order to have taken part in the older Antonius' campaign. As it happens, the large inscription listing the donations and contributions to the *Pythais* procession to Delphi in 98/7 names all the Athenian *nauarchs* for the years from 103/2 through 97/6. The admiral we are looking for must have been a member of the Kerykes clan, and in 103/2 the name of the *nauarch* (only partially preserved) was "Cephis[. . .]."[21] He is probably our honoree, since one of the most distinguished families of the clan at that time included a man named Cephisodorus, who served as priest of the altar at Eleusis. Cephisodorus' father, Philistides, and his brother Philoxenides served successively as *daduchos,* one of the two high priests in Eleusis (the other was the *hierophantes*). While the *hierophantes* always came from the clan of the Eumolpidae, the *daduchoi* and the altar priest were provided by the Kerykes.[22] Cephisodorus, the known clan member from Eleusis, was a generation older than the *nauarch* (whose name can now be completed as Cephis[odorus]), but this poses no difficulty if we assume that the *nauarch* was either his son or the son of the priest's brother Philoxenides. And whether or not the *nauarch* has been identified correctly, it is known with certainty that an Athenian flotilla took part in the older Antonius' expedition against the pirates.

In addition to relations with Delphi, there can be no doubt that Athens maintained active contacts with numerous other mainland

20. For Side see Strabo 14.3.2 (p. 664 C); for Phaselis see Cicero *In Verrem* 4.21 and Strabo 14.5.7 (p. 671 C); W. Ruge, "Phaselis," *RE* (1938) 1879.

21. Tracy, *Contributors* 37, line 19.

22. Clinton, *Officials* 51, nos. 9 and 11, and 82, no. 11. The text naming the two brothers in their sacred offices is on 51, lines 42–44 (= *SEG* 30.93).

Greek states on political, economic, legal, cultural, and religious matters. However, the scarcity of documents allows us only a fleeting glimpse of these activities, for reports of such exchanges would first have had to be inscribed in some permanent form, and then have survived the centuries. Not very long ago, on a stone used in building the monastery of Saint Luke in Phocis, was discovered an Athenian Assembly decree from the end of the century. The decree honors at least three citizens of the city of Stiris, but the greatest interest of the find was its surprising mention of an elective official in Athens "for receiving friends and allies." One of his duties was to invite official guests to state banquets at the hearth of the state in the Prytaneion.[23]

One such delegation in 109/8 consisted of several citizens from Larissa in Thessaly. In spite of Athens' close ties to Rome after the Achaean war, many matters involving foreign relations could of course be settled without consulting the Romans. In this instance a dispute had arisen between Athens and the city of Sicyon on the Peloponnese (or between individual citizens of the two cities), which they had agreed to submit for mediation by judges from Larissa. After visiting both cities, a five-member panel persuaded the parties to resolve some of their differences and handed down a decision in the remaining cases. The Athenian decree thanking the city and the judges was found in Larissa.[24] The judges were also invited to the customary state banquet before returning home. That Athens had maintained diplomatic contacts with Larissa, the capital of the Thessalian Confederacy, earlier in the second century is known from two documents: a decree of the city concerning an embassy from Athens from the 180s, and the honors awarded a Larissan politician from a prominent family by the Council and Assembly of Athens in the second half of the century.[25] At about this time, 140, a citizen of Narthacion in Malis, a member city of the Thessalian Confederacy, is documented as *proxenos* of the Athenians.[26]

Two inscriptions carved on one stele that stood on the Acropolis provide information on Athens' relations at the close of the century

23. *AAA* 4 (1971) 439–443 (E. Vanderpool).

24. *BCH* 59 (1935) 66–67. P. Gauthier is preparing an improved edition with commentary.

25. *IG* IX.2.506 from Larissa and the two fragments *IG* II^2.933 and *Hesperia* 29 (1960) 76, no. 154, which have been combined into one decree; C. Habicht, *ZPE* 20 (1976) 193–199.

26. *IG* IX.2.90.13. On the dating see F. Stählin, "Narthakion," *RE* (1935) 1762–63.

with Elis, the town that presided over the Olympic Games.[27] A reflection of Athens' continued high international standing in this period exists further in the text of a pact between the two Cretan towns of Lyttus and Olus from 111/0, which stated that a copy had to be displayed in a neutral city and that they had chosen the Athenian Acropolis as the site.[28] A decree honoring a citizen of the Cretan town of Aptera was found in the Agora.[29]

Toward the end of the century envoys from the Boeotian town of Thespiae were honored in Athens, apparently in connection with the celebration of the Thespian festival of the Erotidia; several Athenian festival delegates are mentioned by name.[30] There is also a connection with Boeotia in the decree passed in 122/1 by a private association in the region of Haliartus. This city was destroyed in 172 and its territory awarded to Athens by the Roman Senate in 167. Since it still belonged to Athens in the 120s, the decree is dated according to the archon of Athens and names an Athenian governor for the area.[31]

2. Conditions at Home

Many signs indicate that the sixty-five years from the end of the war against Perseus to the end of the second century were a time of increasing prosperity for Athens, peaking after 130, when both Athens and Delos had become important stopping-off places on the route between Italy and the new Roman province of Asia. Scholars agree that this was the case, and that the principal reason for Athens' growing affluence was its possession of Delos.[32] Around the middle of the century political leadership was still concentrated in the hands of prosperous, land-owning families such as those of Eurycleides and Micion of Cephisia, Echedemus and Mnesitheus of Cydathenaion, Leon and Cichesias of Aixone, Habron and Ophelas of Bate, Miltiades of Mara-

27. *IG* II^2.1137.
28. *IG* II^2.1135 = M. Guarducci, *Inscriptiones Creticae*, 4 vols. (Rome 1935–1950) 1: 187, no. 9.
29. *Hesperia* 29 (1960) 20, no. 26, with the name corrected by J. and L. Robert, *Bulletin épigraphique* (1961) 156, no. 264.
30. *IG* II^2.1054.
31. *IG* VII.2850. New edition with commentary by P. Roesch, *Études béotiennes* (Paris 1982) 168–171.
32. J. Day, *An Economic History of Athens under Roman Domination* (New York 1942) 50–119; N. K. Rauh, *The Sacred Bonds of Commerce* (Amsterdam 1993).

thon, Nicogenes and Nicon of Philaidai, and their relative by marriage Adeimantus of Icaria.[33] If, a hundred years later, Atticus answered Cicero's questions about who the leading Athenian politicians were in 155, at the time of the dispute over Oropus and the philosophers' embassy, then he certainly mentioned some of the above names.[34] Toward the end of the century, however, if these families had not been entirely pushed aside, they were nonetheless eclipsed by new ones, such as those of Sarapion of Melite, Medeius of Piraeus, Pyrrhus and Byttakus of Lamptrai, and others identified and analyzed by scholars in recent years.[35] These families all had large commercial interests in Delos, through which they had rapidly risen to wealth and influence.[36] While older families continued to be represented in the priesthood and some other offices, by the end of the century the most important political posts, such as hoplite general, were occupied by the newly rich class. After 128 the second most important position in the political hierarchy was herald of the Areopagus, followed by the two chief magistrates of Delos, the *epimeletes* of the island itself and the *epimeletes* of the exchange.[37]

The ever-closer ties between Athens and Delos in this period created a form of economic symbiosis, reflected in the growing number of Italian families with members both in Athens and in Delos, and in general by the rising number of resident foreigners in Athens, particularly from regions that tended to be strongly represented on Delos. They brought more foreign gods and foreign religious cults with them than ever before, and it has been correctly observed that the cosmopolitanism prevailing on Delos influenced Athens in this period, although this is not to say that the Athenians had been closed-minded toward foreigners in the past.[38] The trend is noticeable in the ephebic

33. For the first three families see Habicht, *Studien* 179–182 and 189–197; for the family of Habron: Davies, *APF* 7856; for Miltiades: T. L. Shear Jr., *Hesperia* 40 (1971) 257–258; for Nicogenes: C. Habicht, *Hesperia* 60 (1991) 209; for Adeimantus: Habicht, *Chiron* 21 (1991) 7.

34. Cicero *Ad Atticum* 12.23.2.

35. Tracy, *Contributors* 159–168; D. J. Geagan, *Phoenix* 46 (1992) 29–44.

36. Day, *Economic History* 100; E. Candiloro, *Studi classici e orientali* 14 (1965) 143.

37. The ranking of offices in order of importance and the increasing numbers of high positions filled by citizens with mercantile interests are demonstrated with particular clarity by the large inscription *IG* II^2.2336 for the years 103–96, as studied by Tracy, *Contributors* 86–89 and 172.

38. Day, *Economic History* 76–82.

corps in both places, somewhat earlier for Delos than for Athens. From midcentury on the number of ephebes in the city rose considerably. Whereas up to the end of the war against Perseus year-classes had never been larger than 50, by the 120s the number of Athenian ephebes had passed 100; in 117/6 there were 179, and in the last decade of the second century the number hovered around 140.[39]

These numbers indicate clearly that the general prosperity was spreading to a larger proportion of the population than before. The ephebic corps, always dedicated to the physical training and higher education of young male citizens, was now also open to the sons of well-to-do foreigners. This shift occurred earlier in Delos than in Athens. A surviving list of Delian ephebes contains eighteen names, with citizenship noted in seventeen cases. The list includes five Romans, four Athenian citizens, and six young men from the cities of the eastern Mediterranean, including Alexandria, Antioch, Laodicea in Syria, Sidon and Aradus.[40] Other inscriptions mention ephebes from Tyre, Damascus, and Marathus.

The first foreign ephebes in the capital appear in 119/8; there are 17 of them in a year-class with 124 members; surviving lists from 128/7 and 123/2, with a combined total of almost 200 names, do not contain a single foreigner.[41] For 15 of the 17 foreign ephebes of 119/8 the name of their home city has been preserved; 7 came from Antioch, Beirut, and Laodicea, and 1 from Soloi (whether the city on Cyprus or the one in Cilicia is not known).[42] In contrast to Delos, however, where most of the foreign ephebes must have come from the trading families of the island, many of the foreigners in Athens had undoubtedly been attracted by the city's continuing reputation as a center of higher learning. Cleitomachus of the Academy, the Epicurean Philonides from Laodicea in Syria, and the Stoic Panaetius of Rhodes are only three of the most famous teachers of the era. An inscription from the Ionian city of Colophon mentions a distinguished citizen named Menippus who as a young man about the middle of the century had accompanied a festival delegation to Athens. The inscription states that

39. The year-class for 128/7 numbered 107 (*Hesperia* 24 [1955] 229, line 89); for 117/6 see *IG* II[2].1009 (and *Hesperia* 15 [1946] 213); for the last decade of the second century see *IG* II[2].1011 and *Hesperia Suppl.* 15 (1975) 32–48.

40. I *Délos* 1923.

41. Pélékidis, *Éphébie* 183–196.

42. *IG* II[2].1008, col. IV.111–127.

"he remained there and studied with the best teachers. He gave the first demonstration of the manners and learning he had acquired there to his adopted city, which rewarded him with the rights of citizenship and a crown."[43]

In the decrees honoring the graduating year-classes, a clause appears for the first time in 123/2 praising them for regular attendance at the lectures of Zenodotus in the Ptolemeum and Lyceum and those of other philosophers during their year of training.[44] A few years later each year-class was required to donate 100 books to the library.[45] The ephebes had always participated actively and visibly in the religious life of the community;[46] at this time they acquired an additional function with a political tenor, namely appearing at ceremonial welcomes for high-ranking Romans visiting the city in either an official or a private capacity. This task is first documented for 123/2.[47]

An eloquent example of the success that could be achieved by the mercantile families of Delos is provided by Dies of Tyre. Two of his sons, Heliodorus and Dies, were members of the Delian corps of ephebes in 105/4, at the ages of nineteen and eighteen respectively, and are later documented as citizens of Athens. By the time he reached his mid-thirties Dies, the younger of the two, was 'one of the richest men in Athens and owner of a palatial house that he sometimes lent to prominent visitors, such as Athenion on his return from the court of Mithridates in 88.[48]

There was traffic in the other direction, too, of course; sometimes Italian merchants on Delos attracted Athenian citizens to the island for stays of varying length by offering them work. The marble statue of C. Ofellius Ferus (placed in the agora of the Italians in recognition of his efforts to have the market constructed) is known to be the work of two Athenian sculptors, the cousins Dionysius and Timarchides of

43. L. and J. Robert, *Claros*, vol. I: *Décrets hellénistiques*, fasc. 1 (Paris 1906) 63, col. I.1–10.

44. *IG* II^2.1006.19–20 and 62–65; Pélékidis, *Ephébie* 261–267.

45. *IG* II^2.1009.7–8 (the year-class of 117/6) and 1030.36; *Hesperia* 16 (1947) 171, no. 167.32. The library was probably the one in the gymnasion of Ptolemy (Pélékidis, *Ephébie* 264 n. 1).

46. Pélékidis, *Ephébie* 211–256.

47. *IG* II^2.1006.21: "At all times they met and welcomed visiting Romans, our friends and benefactors." A similar statement appears at line 75.

48. S. Dow, *CP* 37 (1942) 311–314; Posidonius, *FGrHist* 87 F 36 (Athenaeus 5.212D); see further Chapter 13, Section 1. Osborne, *Naturalization* 3–4: 106–107, T 121–122.

Thoricus, members of a family of artists who also worked for Roman dignitaries in Rome.[49] Works by thirteen Athenian sculptors from nine different families are documented on Delos in the second half of the second century.[50]

A long but incompletely preserved Athenian decree from the last quarter of the century contains detailed regulations concerning weights and measures to be used in commerce. The decree establishes norms, some of them new, and procedures for supervision by officials, as well as fines and penalties for infractions. Although it has been suggested that this was nothing more than a local ordinance, most scholars believe the decree was of far-ranging significance, and intended primarily to create clear and easily convertible relationships between Attic and Roman units of both weight and measure. Calculations were simplified; henceforth one Attic mina corresponded to two Roman pounds (totaling 655 grams); and the *choinix,* a unit of dry measure, was also increased to correspond to two Roman *sextarii.* Scholars have further deduced that one of the intentions of the legislation was to regulate foreign trade, and particularly to make trade with Rome easier. While the initiative for the new law may have come from Rome, it need not be the case.[51]

This Athenian decree has been interpreted in connection with a decree passed by the Amphictionic Council in Delphi at approximately the same time. The Amphictionic decree required member states to accept Athenian silver tetradrachs at an exchange rate of one to four drachmas, and at the same time prohibited charging the usual fee for currency exchange. Violators were to be fined, and officials who per-

---

49. F. Queyrel, *BCH* 115 (1991) 389–446; on 461–462 he has taken over the chronology and *stemma* from C. Habicht, *AM* 97 (1982) 178–180.

50. J. Marcadé, *Recueil des signatures de sculpteurs grecs,* vol. 2 (Paris 1957), mostly dedicated to Delos.

51. *IG* II^2.1013, found on the Acropolis; a German translation with commentary was published by O. Viedebantt, *Hermes* 51 (1916) 120–144. English translation in M. M. Austin, *The Hellenistic World from Alexander to the Roman Conquest* (Cambridge 1981) 191–193. A fragment of a second copy, displayed in the Tholos in the Agora, was published in *Hesperia* 7 (1938) 127, no. 27. In addition to two officials in charge of supervising weights and measures, the *metronomi,* Diodorus of Halai was given special oversight responsibilities; as he was supervisor of the harbor in 112/1, this allows the decree to be dated. The minimal interpretation—"It is not obvious that anything more was involved than a simple market-policing operation"—was advanced by Austin 193 n. 2. Relevance for international trade is assumed by Viedebantt 141–144 and by L. Doria, *MEFRA, Antiquité* 97 (1985) 411–430. Both consider it possible or likely that the initiative came from Rome.

mitted violations within their domain were liable to trial before the Amphictionic court.[52] This move created a privileged position for Athenian silver coins vis-à-vis competing currencies. Unfortunately the date of this important decree is quite uncertain. It was traditionally assigned to the close of the second century, but A. Giovannini pointed out that such a regulation made sense only for the period in which the "New Style" drachma was in fact new, and perhaps viewed suspiciously in many quarters, that is, around and soon after 164. Otto Mørkholm then observed further that within the possible range from 168 to 100 the years around 140 were also good candidates, as the outcome of the Achaean war would have considerably reduced the volume of silver coins being minted by the Greek confederations.[53] He agrees with Giovannini that the Amphictionic Council's initiative is unthinkable without at least the tacit consent of Rome. This point and the obvious partisanship of the Council for Athenian interests may make the most likely date sometime after 140 or 130, possibly the same period as the Athenian decree on weights and measures.

Late in the second century there were two revolts by slaves working in the mines of Attica. The first, presumed to have been sparked by the great slave uprising in Sicily in 134, was suppressed in 133; it has already been mentioned in connection with Delos. We know of it only from a brief note in Orosius, who drew on a portion of Livy's history now lost. Heracleitus, the commander who put down the revolt, must almost certainly have been the son of Poseidippus of Icaria; he is known from other sources to have been not only one of the leading figures in Athenian public life in the 140s, but also hoplite general (for the second time) in or shortly after 145.[54] A second insurrection some thirty years later clearly posed a more serious threat to the country. Once again it was the slaves at Laurium, the mining region of eastern Attica, who

---

52. *FD* III.2.139 (*Syll.* 729).

53. Daux, *Delphes* 202; *Chronologie delphique* L 92 (from one of the priesthoods X–XII[1], that is, between 124 and 100); A. Giovannini, *Rome et la circulation monétaire en Grèce au IIe siècle avant Jésus-Christ* (Basle 1978) 64–72; O. Mørkholm, *Quaderni ticinesi* 9 (1980) 148–149.

54. Orosius 5.9.5. The most important documents concerning Heracleitus are in Tracy, *ALC* 155. Tracy recognized that he is the hoplite general referred to in *IG* II[2].1224b.9–10; this inscription is dated through the mention of C. Laelius as praetor in line 13. Heracleitus is also named at about this time in a list of donors, in second place, after Nicogenes of Philaidai, then one of the leading men of Athens (*IG* II[2].2334.6). See also S. Lauffer, *Die Bergwerkssklaven von Laureion*[2] (Wiesbaden 1979) 232–233.

rebelled. They disarmed their guards and seized the acropolis of Sunium, one of the Attic fortresses; they held it for some time, using it as a base from which to ravage the surrounding countryside.[55] Traditionally this second slave revolt was assigned to the period 104–100, as it was thought to be connected with an "oligarchic revolution" presumed to have occurred in 103. This revolution has long been exposed as a myth, however, prompting suggestions that the slave uprising should be dated closer to 100. It is known that only five Attic knights took part in the *Pythais* to Delphi in 98/7 (whereas in 106/5 there had been 125); and an unsettled situation, with troops needed to protect eastern Attica from marauding slaves, would help account for this low number.[56] In any event, two long decrees from the late summer of 101 honoring the ephebes of 102/1 and their *kosmetes* convey the impression of complete tranquillity in Attica. The decrees recount the ephebes' performance of their routine duties, including making sacrifices to their Roman "benefactors," but make no mention of the special military assignments usual in times of crisis.[57] Of course such a period of quiet could have occurred either before or after a slave revolt.

During this general period an increasing number of Romans visited Athens as official guests of the state, most of them no doubt en route to or from the province of Asia. As a young man Quintus Caecilius Metellus (later to become famous for his command in the war against Jugurtha and his resistance to an illegal clause in Saturninus' grain law of 100) attended lectures at the Academy "for many days." Carneades, head of the school at that time, was already an old man, and this visit must have taken place not long before his death in 129.[58] Another visit by a high-ranking Roman was accompanied by an odd scene preserved in a satire by the contemporary poet Lucilius.[59] The praetor Quintus Mucius Scaevola, the Roman governor of Asia (who achieved fame for his expertise in civil law), stopped off in Athens on his way home and

---

55. Posidonius, *FGrHist* 87 F 35.
56. S. V. Tracy, *HSCP* 83 (1979) 232–235.
57. S. V. Tracy, *Hesperia Suppl.* 15 (1975) 32–48.
58. Cicero *De or.* 3.68; L. W. Daly, *AJPh* 71 (1950) 42.
59. Lucilius 2.88–94 (87–95 Krenkel) with commentary by F. Marx, *C. Lucilii Carminum Reliquiae,* vol. 2 (Leipzig 1905) 41–44; W. Krenkel, *Lucilius' Satiren,* vol. 1 (Leiden 1970) 64 and 138–139; and C. Cichorius, *Untersuchungen zu Lucilius* (Leipzig 1908) 237–251. Cicero, who knew the satire, mentions the episode in several places and refers approvingly to Scaevola's ironic dismissal of exaggerated enthusiasm for the Greek way of life.

received the now customary ceremonial welcome from the corps of ephebes. Among the crowd who had joined the ephebes was Titus Albucius, a young Roman from a prominent family who had become in Athens an ardent follower of Epicurus' teachings. His enthusiasm for everything Greek, particularly the language, was legendary, and Scaevola decided to make fun of him not only by greeting him in Greek but also by ordering his entire retinue to repeat the greeting in chorus. The next year, back in Rome, Albucius accused Scaevola of corruption during his term of office in Asia. Lucilius' satire describes the ensuing trial and ascribes to Albucius personal motives of revenge for bringing charges against the former governor. Scaevola was found not guilty. A generation later the young Roman knight Titus Pomponius, known as "Atticus," also found himself drawn to Athens and the philosophy of Epicurus, but in contrast to Albucius he never went to the extreme of wishing to deny his Roman origins.

The frequent presence of Roman dignitaries in the city may have prompted the Athenians to build a special podium for them in the Agora, in front of the stoa of Attalus. This speaking platform is mentioned in 88.[60] Some of the visitors failed to behave with the tact befitting guests in an independent country; occasionally they behaved more as conquerors. Thus the young quaestor Lucius Licinius Crassus (later to become a celebrated orator) showed a flagrant lack of tact when he stopped in Athens on the way home from a year in office abroad. Finding out that he had missed the Eleusinian Mysteries by two days, he demanded that they be repeated for his benefit. Two hundred years earlier King Demetrius had demanded a special initiation and had his request fulfilled by Stratocles' manipulation of the calendar, over the objections of Pythodorus, the priest responsible for the cult. Young Crassus was neither a reigning monarch nor the city's overlord, however, and Athenian officials responded with a curt refusal. Crassus departed in a huff,[61] no doubt having given great offense to many residents of the city.

---

60. Posidonius, *FGrHist* 87 F 36 (Athenaeus 5.212F). The text says it was erected for the Roman *strategoi*, which technically means *praetores* but in nontechnical language simply military commanders. In fact it was probably intended for all official visitors from Rome, including diplomats, who presumably had the right to address the people. See H. A. Thompson and R. E. Wycherley, *The Agora of Athens, Agora* XIV (Princeton 1972) 51, on the location of this podium.

61. Cicero *De or.* 3.75; cf. also 1.45. During his stay Crassus is supposed to have attended lectures by the *summi homines* and *doctissimi viri*.

Although they did not come as conquerors, the Romans had attained a dominant position by the time statues of Romans were first erected by the city authorities on the Acropolis. One of the first such monuments honored Sextus Pompeius, the proconsul of Macedonia killed in battle against the Scordisci, a Thracian tribe, in 120/19 (or perhaps 119/8). A quarter of a century later his son Gnaeus Pompeius received the same tribute, probably after himself serving as proconsul of Macedonia.[62]

The year 124/3 is marked by an oddity in Athenian political life, namely the unique instance of two eponymous archons. Nicias is listed as sole archon at the (undetermined) time a decree for the *prytaneis* was passed,[63] while Isigenes' name is given in the honors awarded to a priest on Delos.[64] Three subsequent dated inscriptions from Delos all bear the notation "in the year of the archon [*sic*] Nicias and Isigenes,"[65] revealing that Isigenes followed Nicias in office within the same year, almost certainly because of the former's death. The peculiar combination of singular and plural in the Delian decree was undoubtedly intentional, as each year could have only *one* eponymous archon: formally and legally, the two men constituted a single official. The only comparable case known to me is the replacement of a secretary of the Council in 175/4, when Leucius of Perithoidai appears in this office in the first prytany, but is replaced in the tenth prytany by Pausanias of Perithoidai. Both were sons of Bioteles and therefore brothers. The implication is that some tribes possessed few men qualified to fill the important post of Council secretary, and that for this reason it was sometimes passed on within a single family; this conjecture receives some support from the fact that still another member of the same family, Bioteles, son of Leucius of Perithoidai, had previously occupied the office in 187/6.[66]

A similar case involving a pair of officials is documented for 110/09, when the magistrates at the mint were replaced. The two officials at the start of the year, Eubulides and Agathocles, were supplanted by

62. *IG* II^2.4100 and 4101.

63. *Agora* XV.251.

64. I *Délos* 2075.

65. I *Délos* 1647–49. The catalogue of archons *IG* II^2.1713 contains the entry "Nicias and Isigenes" in col. I.6–7 for the year 124/3.

66. Leucius: *Agora Inv.* I.7529.65 (unpublished inscription). Pausanias: *IG* II^2.905.2; *Agora* XV.200.2. Bioteles: W. K. Pritchett and B. D. Meritt, *The Chronology of Hellenistic Athens* (Cambridge, Mass., 1940) 117.

Zoilus and Euandrus during the third month. This change of personnel has been interpreted as a sign of political crisis.[67] While such an explanation is certainly possible in this striking case, other causes are conceivable; why Cleomenes replaced Alcidamus as master of the mint early in 113/2 is equally unclear.

The reason for an extreme anomaly found in another set of decrees seems more easily determined. An inscription from 107/6 contains two decrees for ephebes, one dating from the eleventh day of the month Gamelion in the seventh prytany, and one from the sixteenth of Thargelion in the eleventh prytany. Supposedly both sessions of the Assembly in which they were passed were chaired by the same man, one Stratophon, son of Stratocles of Sunium.[68] Were this the case, it would represent a clear and unheard-of violation of the constitution, which allowed a given citizen to hold this office only once in his life, for a single day. In this instance all the evidence suggests an error on the part of either the recording secretary or the stonemason.

---

67. M. K. Kambanis, *BCH* 56 (1932) 37–42.
68. *IG* II^2.1011.63–65 and 73–74.

THIRTEEN

Athens and Mithridates

1. The Break with Rome

In 89 B.C. war broke out in Asia Minor between Rome and King Mithridates VI, and in May or June of the following year Athens decided to end its alliance with Rome and enter the war on the side of the king. With this step the Athenians, for the first time, turned against the nation that had answered their call for help more than a century before, when they were threatened by Philip of Macedonia. In the intervening years they had been a staunch ally of Rome in both war and peace, and had been richly rewarded for their loyalty in 167. The circumstances surrounding this abrupt shift of policy are reported in a lively and detailed account by the contemporary historian Posidonius, but the reasons that prompted it remain unclear. The question remains: What did the citizens of Athens find so attractive about Mithridates, or, to put it another way, what did they find so repellent about Rome? In attempting to answer this question, let us first take a closer look at Mithridates and his kingdom of Pontus.[1]

The region of Pontus, lying on both banks of the River Halys in northern Asia Minor, became an independent kingdom in the first few decades following the death of Alexander the Great, under a ruling family of Iranian origin. Over the years they annexed the Greek colonies along the Black Sea, creating a realm with a Hellenized coast and

---

1. The basic study remains T. Reinach, *Mithradates Eupator, König von Pontos,* German edition by A. Goetz (Leipzig 1895). See further M. Rostovtzeff and H. A. Ormerod, *CAH* 9 (1932) 211–260; and B. C. McGing, *The Foreign Policy of Mithridates VI Eupator, King of Pontus* (Leiden 1986); J. G. F. Hind, "Mithridates," *CAH* 9^2 (1994) 129–165.

an oriental hinterland.[2] The royal house traced its descent from the Iranian prince Mithridates I Ktistes ("the Founder"), who assumed the title of king at the beginning of the third century. Ruling from his inland capital of Amaseia, he gained access to the Black Sea when he annexed the Greek city of Amastris. His grandson Mithridates II created ties to the Seleucid dynasty by marrying his daughter to Antiochus III. The second Mithridates was an admirer of Greek culture and numbered among the monarchs who sent generous help to Rhodes after a devastating earthquake in 227. All the same, the Rhodians prevented him from taking the city of Sinope a few years later. This important center on the Black Sea remained independent of Pontus until Mithridates' grandson Pharnaces I conquered it in 183. His annexation of Sinope led to a four-year war against Eumenes of Pergamum; when it ended Pharnaces was forced to yield almost all the territory he had seized, but he held onto Sinope and made it his new capital.[3] After his death he was succeeded first by his brother, who ruled for about twenty years as Mithridates IV, and then by his son Mithridates V Euergetes. The latter was also a friend of Greek culture and lived on good terms with the Romans and his neighbors in Pergamum. Mithridates V supported the Romans in their last war against Carthage and their campaign against Aristonicus, which resulted in the creation of the province of Asia. In return for his loyalty he was rewarded at the war's end with the region of Greater Phrygia, given to him by the Roman commander Aquillius. A palace intrigue cost Mithridates V his life in 120.

His young son acceded to the throne in the same year, taking the title Mithridates VI Eupator. A capable, ambitious, and ruthless monarch, he increased the territory of the small realm he had inherited to several times its original size. In the early years of his reign he ridded himself first of his mother, who had been acting as his regent, and then of his brother, with whom he shared rule for a time. Mithridates VI suffered a severe blow when the Senate forced him to surrender Phrygia, declaring that Aquillius had exceeded his authority in awarding it to his father, Mithridates V. Powerless to resist, Mithridates VI had to accept the humiliation. Soon afterward, however, he directed his expansionist aspirations at a target outside the Roman sphere of influence:

2. Rostovtzeff and Ormerod, *CAH* 9 (1932) 211.
3. Chapter 9, Section 1.

the Crimea and the Bosporan kingdom across the Black Sea from Pontus. In the Crimea, as elsewhere around the Black Sea, the dominant influence was Greek; the cities on its shores had been founded as colonies of the Ionian city of Miletus. They all possessed fertile territories, which they were defending against Scythian and Sarmatian tribes. When these cities called on Mithridates VI for help, he began the campaigns as their patron and defender but ended by annexing the territories himself, sending one of his sons to rule as vice-king from a new royal seat at Kerch.[4] By leading the struggle of the Greek communities against the barbarians, Mithridates won great prestige throughout the Greek world. He next pushed eastward from Pontus and seized Trebizond, the place where Xenophon's army of 10,000 had reached the sea and safety on their dangerous and exhausting *anabasis* from Mesopotamia. In the Caucasus Mithridates annexed the region of Colchis, and he extended his influence westward along the Black Sea and as far north as Olbia. As conquest followed conquest his power and prestige rose immensely.

However, when he turned his expansionist drive westward and southward, Mithridates began to collide with Roman interests.[5] He was not seeking a confrontation, for he had his eye on the smaller states of Paphlagonia, Cappadocia, and Galatia, outside the boundaries of the Roman empire. Between 101 and 97 he conquered large portions of these regions, in campaigns in which King Nicomedes of Bithynia was first an ally and later an opponent. In 97 the Senate again compelled him to relinquish territory, demanding his withdrawal from all the newly conquered areas, in order to restore the *status quo ante*. A few years later this sequence occurred for a third time: after Mithridates and his son-in-law Tigranes of Armenia seized Cappadocia, the Romans insisted on its surrender. The war was brought on not by Mithridates' ambition but by irresponsible and arrogant Roman officials in Asia Minor. Because Mithridates refused to pay the bribes they demanded, they incited King Nicomedes to invade Pontus. Ignoring Mithridates' just complaints, they even forbade him to defend himself, announcing that they would regard any use of force against Nicomedes as a violation of Roman sovereignty. Mithridates had no alternative;

---

4. Reinach, *Mithradates* 48–72. An important original source is a decree of the city of Chersonesus in honor of the king's commander Diophantus, *Syll.* 709, for which see L. Boffo, *Athenaeum* 67 (1989) 211–259 and 369–405.

5. Reinach, *Mithradates* 72–99.

knowing it would mean war with Rome, he drove the invader out of Pontus and then out of Bithynia, where the first encounter with Roman troops occurred.[6] During the winter of 89/8 his army pushed into Phrygia, which had been part of the Roman province of Asia, and soon Mithridates again controlled large parts of Asia Minor. Some areas remained loyal to Rome and had to be taken by force, but most cities welcomed the Pontic forces as liberators. In many places the population rejoiced to see the Romans defeated after four decades of colonial rule; they celebrated the defeat of their hated oppressor as if it were their own triumph, just as the Greek cities of Asia Minor had once rejoiced over the defeat of the barbarians by Alexander the Great. Oracles prophesied the impending fall of Rome.

The news traveled to the Greek mainland and Athens in the spring of 88, and the same heady, jubilant atmosphere pervaded the city.[7] At the beginning of the year the Assembly had decided to send a delegation to the king headed by Athenion, a philosopher from the school of Aristotle. Athenion's written reports on events in Asia Minor and on pledges made by Mithridates created among the citizens a mood favorable to the king. The letters held out promises that the king would help put an end to "anarchy" and civil strife in Athens; he would restore harmony and a democratic constitution and find a solution to the pressing debt problem (whereby Athenion seems to mean debts owed by private citizens, perhaps to Roman creditors). Athenion's return in the late spring resembled a triumphal procession, which Posidonius describes in a highly rhetorical and satirical passage. Although it contains many precise details, the intended effect is not a sober assessment of historical reality, but rather a depiction of Athenion as a pompous fool and the Athenians as naive and blinded by their illusions.

On his return Athenion delivered an address praising Mithridates' successes and resources and describing the Romans' situation as des-

6. Ibid., 100–205; McGing, *Foreign Policy* 89–131. Inscriptions recently discovered in Aphrodisias in Phrygia have provided new information on events in Asia Minor during this period; see J. Reynolds, *Aphrodisias and Rome* (London 1982).

7. The main source is Posidonius, *FGrHist* 87 F 36 with Jacoby's commentary. See further E. Candiloro, *Studi classici e orientali* 14 (1965) 145–157; and I. G. Kidd, *Posidonius II: The Commentary,* II (Cambridge 1988) 863–887. Further important studies are J. Deininger, *Der politische Widerstand gegen Rom in Griechenland 217–86 v. Chr.* (Berlin 1971) 245–261; E. Badian, *AJAH* 1 (1976) 105–128; Tracy, *Contributors* 164–182; J. Malitz, *Die Historien des Poseidonios* (Munich 1983) 340–357; R. Bernhardt, *Polis und römische Herrschaft in der späten Republik* (Berlin 1985) 39–49; G. R. Bugh, *Phoenix* 46 (1992) 108–123.

perate. Deeply impressed by his speech, the citizens elected him hoplite general and empowered him to nominate all the other officials, who were then elected by acclamation. Posidonius makes it clear that at this point the die was cast, and the transfer of Athenian loyalty from Rome to Pontus a foregone conclusion; his account also suggests the source of Mithridates' appeal: the king appears as an advocate and defender of Greek culture against Rome, a power that had not only humiliated him and violated his rights, but had also kept Athens in thrall, just as the kings of Macedonia had done in bygone centuries.

Nevertheless the Athenians' break with Rome is not easy to understand, given that shortly before, the relationship between the two states had appeared sincerely cordial. The scarcity and brevity of contemporary sources do not permit a truly satisfactory explanation. Some clear indications of a crisis in Athens during the late 90s suggest possible motives for the considerable Athenian animosity toward Rome reported by Posidonius. However, as several inscriptions indicate, circumstances were still quite normal in 98/7.[8] And in 95/4 (or as late as 94/3) the Athenian priest of Sarapis in Delos proclaimed his loyalty to Athens, Rome, and Mithridates; such a public statement must have conformed to the prevailing sentiment among the citizens. In 96/5 and 94/3(?) official documents still referred to the Romans as "benefactors of the people."[9] But when open conflict broke out between Rome and Mithridates, public opinion shifted somewhat in Mithridates' favor as news of the way the Romans had treated him reached Athens. Just as there had been a movement in favor of Antiochus (and against Rome) in 192, so now many citizens must have sided with the Pontic king. The continued depiction of the symbolic figure Roma on Athenian silver coins in 90/89 and 89/8 reflects the official stance of loyalty toward Rome, but under this placid surface a crisis was brewing. One sign is the cancellation of the *Pythais,* due to be celebrated in 90/89. And the year before, 91/0, Medeius of Piraeus had served an

8. After looking at events in the years 103/2–98/7, Tracy concludes that "the government was working as well as it ever had" (*Contributors* 171). In addition the 90s represent a peak of Athenian coin production. In 99/8, for example, the year Demetrius and Agathippus were mint magistrates, no fewer than 47 different obverse stamps were used. In the same year the silver content began to drop sharply, leading to speculation that silver no longer came from the domestic mines of Laurium (perhaps as a consequence of the latest slave revolt) and instead had to be imported. The size of that year's issue was very large, however (Kroll, *Coins* 4 and 14).

9. *IG* II^2.1029.10 and 1030.12. For the priest of Sarapis see Chapter 10, note 74.

unconstitutional second term as eponymous archon (having previously served in 101/0). Evidence of the extent of the growing crisis is even clearer, since he remained in this office for unprecedented third and fourth terms in 90/89 and 89/8.[10]

Clearly, during these years the constitution was suspended, and Athenion's address was an appeal to the citizens to tolerate a state of "anarchy" no longer while waiting for the Senate to intervene. Medeius must have requested this intervention to resolve the existing problems, but in the years 90–88 the Senate was fully occupied with the Italic (or Social) War. Medeius will have lost control of the government in the second half of 89/8, opening the way for Athenion's embassy to Mithridates. No details of how this happened or what became of Medeius are known.[11] Athenion pointed out Rome's difficult position in Italy when he assured the people that the Italians were also allied with Mithridates. Many Athenians doubtless believed at the time that the Romans were losing their power in east and west simultaneously, and that the end of the empire was approaching. They were well aware of the loathing with which Roman tax officials and moneylenders were regarded both in Asia and in the parts of Greece they controlled. When Mithridates ordered the population to rise up and kill all the Romans in Asia Minor on a preappointed day, giving the people an opportunity to vent their hatred, the bloodbath must have awakened a sense of pan-Hellenic solidarity, among other feelings. Reinach saw the king as a "leader in the struggle and the reestablisher of Hellenic freedom at both ends of the archipelago."[12]

The majority of citizens followed Athenion's call to solidarity with Mithridates, but there were many whose convictions and interests led them to remain loyal to Rome. Many residents are said to have left Athens while it was still possible (before Athenion had the gates shut), including the head of the Academy at the time, Philon of Larissa, who arrived in Rome sometime during 88. In this group's opinion Athenion was nothing but a tyrant. It had been thought that his supporters were

10. The supposed successive terms of Argeius (98/7 and 97/6) have long been exposed as a myth, although it is occasionally still referred to, e.g., G. W. Bowersock, *Augustus and the Greek World* (Oxford 1965) 101 n. 4; and D. J. Geagan, *ANRW* II 7.1 (1979) 374. Argeius served as eponymous archon only once, in 98/7.

11. At the beginning of March 86 a member of Sulla's staff was called Medeius, undoubtedly either the former archon or his son of the same name (see note 24 below).

12. Reinach, *Mithradates* 122.

recruited from the poor and underprivileged classes, but newer research has shown this to be wrong; a number of his adherents were
respected citizens from well-known families,[13] as is demonstrated by a
tablet listing the archons of 88/7 (all of whom had been nominated
by Athenion). Interestingly, this list contains no eponymous archon.[14]
His name was never inscribed; the outcome of the war rendered him a
nonperson, whose memory was to be consigned to oblivion. A later
list of archons contains no name for the year 88/7; in its place is written
the word "anarchy," or "no archon."[15] Some years ago I attempted to
show that the eponymous archon of this year was in fact none other
than Mithridates. There are many documented cases of kings as eponymous officials of Greek cities, including in Miletus Mithridates himself.
The king is further documented as one of the two Athenian magistrates
of the mint in 87/6, together with Aristion, who succeeded Athenion
as ruler of the city.[16]

Among those who immediately fell in behind Athenion were the
Athenian festival artists.[17] This is notable because their guild had long
enjoyed active support from Rome in its disputes with rival groups.[18]
Perhaps the celebrations of the king of Pontus in Asia Minor as "a new
Dionysus" led the Athenian *technitai* to regard him in fact as an
incarnation of the god whom they served with their art.

As long as Mithridates was viewed as a firm friend of the Roman
people—that is, at least until the mid-90s—his popularity was as great
on Delos as it was in Athens itself. But when the city shifted its
allegiance, the island population, with its large contingents of Romans
and Italians, refused to follow. Delos remained loyal to Rome. It would
be interesting to know whether the different course of events in the
two places was also influenced by Mithridates' orders for a massacre. It
could be that his orders had not yet been issued or carried out by the
time Athenion left Asia Minor to return to Athens, but that the Delians

13. P. Desideri, *Athenaeum* 51 (1973) 253; Badian, *AJAH* 1 (1976) 112.

14. *IG* II².1714.

15. *IG* II².1713.

16. C. Habicht, *Chiron* 6 (1976) 127–135. Among those who agreed with my conclusions were Kidd (*Posidonius II, The Commentary*, II 878–879) and McGing (*Foreign Policy*
119). Doubts or disagreement were expressed by R. Bernhardt (*Polis und römische Herrschaft*
49) and J.-L. Ferrary (*Philhellénisme et impérialisme* 473–474).

17. Posidonius, *FGrHist* 87 F 36.49.

18. See Chapter 11, Section 3.

had heard about the bloodbath when they refused to transfer their allegiance.

2. War and Its Consequences

With Athenion's election as hoplite general in the spring of 88 the citizens of Athens cast their lot with Mithridates against Rome. There were then no Pontic troops in Greece, and only a very small Roman force, so for the time being the outbreak of hostilities was delayed. However, the defection of Delos required a response. Athenion, who had assumed leadership of the government simultaneously with his election as general, sent a force to Delos under the command of Apellicon of Teos, an Ionian Greek who had become an Athenian citizen. Like Athenion himself, Apellicon was an intellectual and member of Aristotle's Peripatetic school. He was also a wealthy bibliophile who had bought Aristotle's library, and in 88/7 he was serving as one of the two magistrates in charge of the mint. Most likely he owed this office to Athenion, since the citizens had allowed the latter to make all the nominations for that year. The expedition against Delos was a complete fiasco. After Apellicon's forces had reached the island, a Roman squadron led by an officer named Orbius landed at night and killed most of the Athenians in their sleep. Apellicon himself managed to escape. Orbius erected a monument on the beach, and a commemorative altar with an inscription identifying the Athenians as allies of a foreign king and accusing them of planning to plunder the sacred island.[19]

Apellicon's failure must have weakened Athenion's position. However, Athenion's fall was brought about not by opponents or rivals within the city, but by the arrival in Greece of a strong Pontic army commanded by Mithridates' general Archelaus, whom the king had sent to take possession of the Aegean islands and the mainland in his name. Archelaus occupied Delos and killed all the Romans and Italians he could lay hands on, allegedly 20,000 in all. Seizing the treasure of

---

19. The inscription in fact refers to the king of Cappadocia and not to the king of Pontus. The main source for Apellicon's expedition against Delos is Posidonius, *FGrHist* 87 F 36 (Athenaeus 5.214D–215B). For the further course of the war as it involved Athens, the chief sources are Plut. *Sulla* 12–14 and Appian *Mithridateios* 108–159. Cf. also Reinach, *Mithradates* 127–169; McGing, *Foreign Policy* 118–126; and, for Orbius, F. Durrbach, *Choix d'inscriptions de Délos* (Paris 1921) 235–236.

the temple of Apollo, which Apellicon had been instructed to confis-
cate, Archelaus sent it back to Athens with an Athenian citizen in his
entourage named Aristion and 2,000 soldiers. With their help Aristion
made himself "tyrant" of Athens upon his arrival, and thereafter the
historical sources are mute on the further fate of Athenion.[20] Aristion
is also described as a philosopher, but in contrast to Athenion he was
a follower of the teachings of Epicurus. As soon as he had taken power,
he is supposed to have executed some of the Roman sympathizers
among the citizens and handed others over to Mithridates.[21] In 87/6
Aristion shared the office of master of the mint with the king, and their
two names appear on a large number of coins produced at the time.
Meanwhile he and Archelaus brought the greater part of Greece under
their control, turning these areas into official allies of Mithridates.
Archelaus then set up a permanent headquarters in Piraeus.

For this reason, Attica became the main theater of the war for an
entire year. The Roman general Cornelius Sulla, who had served as
consul in 88, was placed in charge of the war against Mithridates the
following year. Arriving in Greece with five legions, Sulla pinned Aristion down in Athens and Archelaus in Piraeus in the summer of 87.
The Long Walls, which had connected the two in earlier times, had
been allowed to fall into ruins, so the Greeks could not mount a
combined defense. But because Sulla had no fleet, Archelaus could
come and go by sea and keep in contact with the outer world.

There was particularly heavy fighting in Piraeus, where the two sides
battled each other with great daring and ingenuity.[22] Sulla procured the
wood needed for his fieldworks and siege fortifications by chopping
down the trees in the groves of the Academy and the Lyceum, the sites
where Plato and Aristotle had taught. The defenders set many of his
siege machines on fire, however, and Sulla finally had to abandon his

20. A majority of scholars agree that Athenion and Aristion were different persons who
ruled Athens in succession; see most recently Bugh, *Phoenix* 46 (1992) 108–123. Others,
however, consider them to have been a single individual; cited by Bugh on 111 n. 8.

21. Plutarch reports that a large number of Athenians who left Athens when Aristion came
to power settled in Amisus, a city on the southern coast of the Black Sea originally settled by
Athenian emigrants (*Lucullus* 19.7). Since Amisus was part of Mithridates' realm at that time,
these citizens may have been the ones Aristion handed over to him.

22. The main source for the fighting around Piraeus and Athens in this period is Appian
Mithridateios 116–157. Archelaus gave one of his soldiers, a Syrian named Apollonius, an
inscribed silver bracelet as a reward for bravery; the words "in Piraeus" show it to stem from
the period of these battles; *BCH* 105 (1981) 566, no. 7, with an illustration.

attempt to storm the harbor fortress. His hopes of starving them out were frustrated by his lack of a fleet; he could not prevent them from provisioning themselves by ship.

In the winter of 87/6 Sulla set up headquarters in Eleusis, while carrying on with the sieges of both city and harbor. At Eleusis, a shrine to the goddesses Demeter and Kore containing an altar dedicated by the Athenian festival artists was destroyed;[23] the Romans may well have perpetrated this act of vandalism, particularly as the guild of the *technitai* had been among the earliest and most vocal supporters of Athenion's rebellion. Meanwhile the population trapped in the city was running short of food, for traitors had informed Sulla several times when Archelaus had planned deliveries of grain, enabling the Romans to intercept them. Despite all the hardships Aristion fought vigorously. He rejected the efforts of a delegation of members of the Council and the priests of the city to persuade him to seek negotiations. (Later, when he did send a group to parley, Sulla brusquely dismissed them.) Finally, during the night of 1 March 86, the Romans breached the western city wall between the Piraeus Gate and the Sacred Gate (very close to the Dipylon) and entered the city. A terrible bloodbath ensued, sparing neither women nor children, which Sulla halted only after Athenian refugees and Roman senators on his staff pleaded with him to end the slaughter.[24] Praising the Athenians of earlier times, he said he was sparing a few (living) for the sake of the many (dead).[25] Aristion set the Odeum at the foot of the Acropolis on fire, to prevent the Romans from using its rafters for their siege machinery, and retreated to the top of the Acropolis. There he held out against Sulla's lieutenant Scribonius Curio for a considerable time, but a lack of drinking water finally forced him to capitulate. The Romans executed him, his bodyguard, and the city officials of that year[26] but spared the officials of the preceding year. With their capture of the Acropolis they acquired an enormous treasury of gold and silver.

The bravery of the starving defenders during the storming of the city

---

23. *IG* II^2.1338.11–12 and 27.

24. Plut. *Sulla* 14.9; the two Athenians named are Meidias and Calliphon. The spelling of the first name suggests that is probably Medeius, either the four-time archon or his son of the same name, who later had a successful career in Athens; Ferguson, *HA* 451.

25. Plut. *Sulla* 14.9.

26. According to Plutarch, Aristion was not killed until after the preliminary peace negotiations between Sulla and Archelaus at the end of 86, when Archelaus demanded his elimination and he was poisoned. Plutarch reports further that Aristion's descendants were proscribed in Athens like the families of the sixth-century tyrants and Lachares (*mor.* 558C).

was praised some three centuries later in an epigram by Asinius Quadratus, who reports that not one of them died from a wound in the back. Whether or not this statement stems from a reliable tradition or is merely a cliché, it is remarkable that its author is a high-ranking imperial official of the Severan age.[27] A much older epigram, probably from the middle of the first century A.D., on the grave monument of an Athenian woman taken captive as a young girl during the storming of Athens, recounts that she was later taken to Rome, where she was freed and obtained citizenship, and died in Cyzicus on the Sea of Marmara.[28]

After taking Athens, Sulla renewed his siege of Piraeus and, little by little, pushed Archelaus back. Mithridates had dispatched a large Pontic army to Greece by the land route, and as soon as it came near, Archelaus abandoned Piraeus by ship to join the advancing troops. Sulla thereupon moved into Piraeus and burned down a number of public buildings, including the docks and the famous arsenal designed by Philon in the era of Alexander the Great. Soon afterward two great battles on Boeotian territory, near Chaeronea[29] and Orchomenus, both of which Sulla won, decided the fate of Greece. The war then shifted to Asia Minor, and ended in the summer of 85 without again touching Athens directly.

The city had paid dearly enough for its alliance with Mithridates in any case, with great loss of life in Delos (both from Apellicon's expedition and from Archelaus' later conquest of the island) as well as in Athens and Piraeus; in addition many works of art were lost either through destruction or seizure as booty by Sulla and the Romans. The victors seized large amounts of gold and silver treasure, and severely damaged buildings in the city and the harbor area. Signs of this destruction are still visible in some places, and archaeologists have discovered other traces. In the Agora the damage was concentrated on the western and southern sides, where shattered sculptures were found along with damage to buildings and to the wall surrounding the

27. *AP* 7, no. 312. For more on the author cf. *FGrHist* 97 and *Prosopographia Imperii Romani*[2], ed. E. Groag and A. Stein (Berlin 1933) A 1244–46.

28. *AP* 7, no. 368 with commentary by C. Cichorius, *Römische Studien* (Leipzig 1922) 304–306.

29. Both Plutarch (in *Sulla* 19.9–10) and Pausanias (9.40.7) mention two Roman victory monuments erected at the site. Plutarch reports that one bore the name of two of his fellow citizens of Chaeronea who enabled the Romans to circumvent a commanding enemy position on a height. This monument was recently discovered on the site; J. Camp et al., *AJA* 96 (1992) 443–455.

monument to the tribal heroes.[30] Pausanias reports that Roman soldiers destroyed the shields that hung in the stoa of Zeus Eleutherios to honor past heroes of the struggles for Athenian independence.[31] Archaeologists ascribe to this defeat further signs of destruction to the shrine of Asclepius at the foot of the Acropolis and to the Erechtheum on the Acropolis itself.[32] But the clearest traces were discovered around the gates near which the Romans penetrated the city walls. Directly south of the Dipylon the Pompeion, a sizable edifice built around 400 B.C., suffered such severe damage that it had to be abandoned. This building was used among other things by the ephebes during their training, as is reflected in a dedication to Hermes, Hercules, and Apollo placed there in 97/6, not long before its destruction.[33] Much evidence of heavy fighting was found in the damaged layer of the Pompeion, including two iron helmets and many large catapult stones. The stones apparently missed their targets, the city gates, and landed in the building next door.[34]

Two sunken ships have been connected with this catastrophe in Athens, one of which went down in the Aegean and one off the coast of North Africa. The first ship sank near Anticythera, between the island of Cythera, south of the Peloponnese, and Crete. It was carrying bronze and marble statues, a number of ceramic pieces such as amphorae, and glass of particularly high quality. While it used to be assumed that some or all of this cargo had been taken from Athens as war booty, this conclusion is greatly in doubt today, since the ship is unlikely to have begun its voyage from Attica or any port on the Greek mainland, the goods are not of Attic origin, and at least a few pieces may date from after 86.[35] The second wreck, on the other hand, found off the coast of Tunisia near Mahdia, was in fact carrying a cargo of Attic works of art, some of them bearing reliefs and inscriptions helpful in dating

30. H. A. Thompson, *Hesperia* 6 (1937) 221; T. L. Shear Jr., *Hesperia* 39 (1970) 201; Thompson and R. E. Wycherley, *The Agora of Athens, Agora* XIV (Princeton 1972) 23.

31. Pausanias 10.21.5–6.

32. S. Aleshire, *The Athenion Asklepieion* (Amsterdam 1982) 16; H. A. Thompson, cited in D. M. Lewis, *Hesperia* 44 (1975) 384.

33. *IG* II^2.2990, where the dating is off by 2 years.

34. W. Hoepfner, *Das Pompeion und seine Nachfolgebauten* (Berlin 1976) 122, 129, and 139.

35. P. C. Bol, *AM Ergänzungsheft* 2 (1972); B. Barr-Sharrar, *The Hellenistic and Early Imperial Decorative Bust* (Mainz 1987) 22–23; G. D. Weinberg, *Glass Vessels in Ancient Greece* (Athens 1992) 28–33. I am indebted here and in the following paragraphs to Homer Thompson for comments and bibliographical suggestions.

the wreck. One inscription mentions Nicodemus, the Athenian archon of 122/1. For a while this cargo was also thought to be Roman booty, taken by Sulla's army during the sack of Athens or Piraeus; but a growing number of scholars now believe that the ship undertook its last voyage some time between 80 and 70, although earlier as well as later dates are also defended by some scholars.[36]

One of the best indicators of the intensity of fighting in Attica and Delos and the uncertain prospects of the war years 88–86 is the discovery of large number of caches of coins buried by their owners and never reclaimed. In a number of cases these hoards are reliably known to have been located in the same excavation levels as the war damage. Undoubtedly only a small fraction of such caches of hidden valuables has been uncovered. Apart from the archaeological evidence, the chronology is certain because the Athenian silver coins are dated, and the bronze coins of the corresponding years bear the same symbols. The bronze coins of 87/6, for instance, all bear the star between two half-moons used on the silver issues of that year, when Mithridates and Aristion were masters of the mint.

In eight of these hoards the latest bronze coins date from 88/7 and were certainly buried in 87/6; in three others the latest are those with the star and crescents just described, from 87/6, and must have been buried in the spring of 86.[37] The series of bronze coins from 87/6 was especially large, and the coins have a much higher lead content than normal, creating the impression that they were struck in haste.[38] The coins of one cache show clear signs of damage from fire,[39] and another hoard was found in the charred ruins of a house in Piraeus.[40] Just as clear a picture is offered by two finds of silver coins, one buried in Piraeus in 88/7[41] and one buried in 87/6 at the Dipylon, near the very spot where Sulla's troops broke through the walls.[42] Both hoards contain several coins of Mithridates in addition to Athenian ones. The

---

36. Some 90 papers from an international conference on the subject are published in G. Hellenkemper-Salies, ed., *Das Wrack. Der antike Schiffsfund von Mahdia,* 2 vols. (Cologne 1994).

37. F. Kleiner, *Hesperia* 45 (1976) 1–40; Kroll, *Coins* 67–80.

38. M. Oeconomides-Caramessini, *AAA* 9 (1976) 223; A. S. Walker, *Hesperia* 47 (1978) 44; 201 bronze coins from this year have been found in the Athenian Agora alone.

39. Walker, ibid., 44–45.

40. Oeconomides-Caramessini, *AAA* 9 (1976) 223.

41. *IGCH* 337.

42. *IGCH* 339.

distribution of coins from 87/6 in both city and harbor shows that a great deal of money had been put into circulation before Sulla sealed Athens and Piraeus off from each other that winter.

Six of the coin hoards found on Delos can be reliably assigned to the war years, and possibly a seventh.[43] Further caches from the period have been found on the island of Euboea off the coast of Attica, where the Pontic commander Archelaus set up his headquarters after losing the battles in Boeotia. They were discovered in Carystus, Chalcis, and Eretria.[44]

But the most spectacular find was made in Piraeus, very near the harbor, in 1959. In a warehouse burned by the Romans in 86, excavators came upon five bronze statues of exceptional quality from the archaic and classical periods, some of them larger than life size; and fragments of other bronze and marble sculptures. The works include two statues of Artemis, one of Apollo, and one of Athena, all between 192 and 235 centimeters high. The date of the warehouse's destruction was established precisely by the discovery of a coin from 87/6 in the ruins. It appears that because the building lay in ruins the Romans assumed it contained nothing of value and failed to discover the costly sculptures. The figure of Athena had been removed from its pedestal—wherever it may have stood—by force, in the process of which half of the left foot was broken off. According to one appealing theory, the statues are sacred images originally erected on Delos and brought to Athens by Aristion at the same time he carried off the temple treasure. Then, before they could be set somewhere else, the Romans arrived in Athens, and the statues were buried in the ruins of their storehouse.[45] This conjecture fits well with the older theory that the gold staters struck by Aristion in 87/6 were made from the gold he had taken from the temple treasure of Delos the previous year.[46]

Although they did considerable damage to the city and harbor, the Romans did not lay waste to Athens or reduce it to rubble. Certain

---

43. T. Hackens and E. Lévy, *BCH* 89 (1965) 503–566.

44. *IGCH* 344 and 345; *Antike Kunst* 17 (1974) 72.

45. This theory was proposed by E. B. Harrison in *Archaic and Archaistic Sculpture, Agora* XI (Princeton 1965) 127 n. 149; then by G. Dontas, *Antike Kunst* 25 (1982) 15–34. Much has been written on this find, including the initial report by E. Vanderpool, *AJA* 64 (1960) 265–267. Illustrations of the statues are in A. Stewart, *Greek Sculpture*, vol. 2 (New Haven 1990) plates 168–169 (Apollo), 511 (Athena), and 569–570 (Artemis).

46. J. N. Svoronos, *Journal international d'archéologie numismatique* 21 (1927) 168–169. Aristion's removal of the temple treasure is confirmed by Appian *Mithridateios* 109.

structures escaped harm altogether, even in areas where the fighting was heaviest, such as the Hephaestion to the west of the Agora, the Middle Stoa to the south, and a group of elaborate graves on the Cerameicus. Sulla allowed his soldiers to loot and plunder during their storming of the city, but he had ordered them not to destroy buildings. In his memoirs he took credit for saving Athens from annihilation, while some 250 years later Pausanias accused him of have shown excessive cruelty unworthy of a Roman. Both statements have some truth to them.[47]

After Sulla defeated the Greeks, he left Attica with a fleet assembled by his lieutenant Lucullus and moved the theater of the war against Mithridates to Asia Minor. It was not a permanent departure from Athens, however, for after defeating the king and forcing him to make peace, Sulla returned to the city in 84 and clearly remained there for some time. Plagued by gout, he sought relief in the warm sulfur springs of Aedepsus on Euboea. After the trial and execution of Aristion and his closest associates, political leadership had passed back into the hands of the men who had been in power before 89, all friends of Rome. Athenion and Aristion were now referred to only as "tyrants," and in 84/3, when Sulla had returned to Athens, the masters of the mint chose as the symbol for that year's coins a depiction of the famous tyrant slayers Harmodius and Aristogeiton, in an unmistakable allusion to the more recent tyrants' ends.[48] And just as the two tyrant-slayers of the past were venerated as heroes with an official cult, Sulla was also celebrated as a liberator and received corresponding honors; an inscription documents the existence of a state festival known as the Sylleia. The citizens erected a public statue to him out of gratitude.[49] And cruel as Sulla may have been during the storming of the city, he imposed no further penalties on it afterward. He even allowed Athens to keep Delos, which had been vacated by Mithridates' troops in the course of

---

47. Plut. *mor.* 202E; Pausanias 1.20.7. For the Cerameicus see R. Garland, *ABSA* 77 (1982) 128. Lucullus is said to have later complained that, unlike Sulla, he never had the opportunity to save a city he had conquered (Amisos) from destruction; Plut. *Lucullus* 19.5.

48. Habicht, *Chiron* 6 (1976) 135–142. However, Kroll assumes that an interruption in minting lasting approximately 5 years occurred at this time (*Coins* 81–82), which would place these coins in a later year. The question does not yet appear to have been fully resolved.

49. *IG* II².4103; for the festival, *SEG* 22.110.57 from 79/8 for the ephebes of the preceding year; A. E. Raubitschek, *Studies in Honor of A. C. Johnson* (Princeton 1950) 49–57. See Pélékidis, *Éphébie* 236–239. A list of victors from Aegium in Achaea, dating from about 80 B.C., notes a winner in the boys' sprint race at the Sylleia in Athens; *SEG* 13.279.

the war. But the island had been ravaged and its population decimated, and it never regained its former preeminence and prosperity. Sulla also demanded certain payments from Delos, not discontinued until about thirty years later.[50]

Athens is thought to have suffered one major loss as a result of the war, namely that of the island of Salamis. This has long been the opinion of most scholars, who disagree only on the cause of the loss. According to some, Sulla ordered the dispossession; according to others, Athens emerged from the war so poor that it was forced to sell Salamis. Nor can anyone say to whom ownership of the island passed, although there is general agreement that an Athenian named Nicanor eventually bought it back. This development emerges from a speech delivered by the philosopher Dio of Prusa in Rhodes at an unknown date, perhaps during the reign of the emperor Vespasian (69–79) or perhaps during that of Trajan (98–117). This Nicanor is identified as Julius Nicanor of Hieropolis in Syria, known as a benefactor of Athens from Athenian inscriptions containing references to him as a "new Themistocles" and "new Homer." The reasoning goes that the Athenians compared him with the famous victor of Salamis because he restored the site of their great victory to them; supposedly he was praised as a "new Homer" in recognition of his achievements as an epic poet.

This edifice of artful reasoning was assembled little by little, in several phases beginning in 1863; it culminates in the conclusions that Julius Nicanor was a contemporary of Augustus and that the loss of Salamis must have occurred earlier, either through Sulla's act or in Sulla's time, because in the interim some decrees honoring Athenian ephebes fail to mention the obligatory visit to Salamis by the ephebic corps, and because after Sulla's time these decrees refer to members of the corps from Salamis not as citizens but as "foreigners." In the meantime, however, it became known that a similar reference to "Salaminians" occurred in a decree from 123/2, long before Sulla's time and when the island was still in Athenian hands. The "Salaminians" in question, however, happen to be not inhabitants of the Attic island but citizens of the city of Salamis on Cyprus.

50. The Delians were released from this obligation by the *lex Gabinia Calpurnia* of 58 B.C.; see C. Nicolet's contribution in J. C. Dumont, J.-L. Ferrary, P. Moreau, and C. Nicolet, eds., *Insula sacra: La loi Gabinia Calpurnia de Délos (58 av. J.-C.)* (Paris 1980) 99–100.

Closer inspection reveals the theory to be unsound throughout.[51] No document or reliable indication of any kind exists showing that the Athenians lost possession of Salamis between the outbreak of the First Mithridatic War and the age of Augustus. If such an event ever did occur, as Dio of Prusa appears to attest, then it must have happened at a later time, for it is highly probable that Julius Nicanor was a contemporary not of Augustus but of a later emperor. When Sulla granted pardon to the citizens of Athens who had survived the taking of their city, he left their state territory unaltered, depriving them of neither Delos nor Salamis.[52]

During his sojourn in Athens in 84 Sulla took the opportunity to be initiated into the Eleusinian Mysteries, whose promise to initiates of a happy life in the afterworld must have had a particular appeal to a man as superstitious as he was.[53] He also paid the same high tribute to the quality of Attic art that earlier Roman victors had paid to Greek artworks in Syracuse, Ambracia, and Corinth, shipping a great many of them to Rome, including columns of the temple of Olympian Zeus for the Capitol. Not all these trophies reached Italy safely; one ship headed for Rome sank off Cape Malea south of the Peloponnese with a famous painting by the fifth-century artist Zeuxis.[54] Sulla also sent the library of Aristotle and Theophrastus to Italy. Their owner, Apellicon, leader of the failed expedition to Delos, had just died; and Sulla acquired the books, although he never really used them. Finally, at the time of Cicero, they fell at last into the right hands, becoming the property of the Greek grammarian Tyrannion from Amisos on the Black Sea. He devoted to them again the attention they deserved but had not received for centuries as the property of private collectors.[55]

In his history of Rome, written in the reign of the emperor Tiberius,

51. Serious doubts about the accuracy of the prevailing interpretation were expressed by E. Kapetanopoulos, first in *RFIC* 104 (1976) 375–377 and then more extensively in Ἑλληνικά 33 (1981) 217–237. At the time he convinced few scholars with his arguments. The subject is also discussed by C. Habicht, *ZPE* 111 (1996) 79–87.

52. Livy *Perioche* 82: "L. Sylla . . . urbi libertatem et quae habuerat reddidit."

53. Plut. *Sulla* 16; K. Clinton, however, doubts whether the Eleusinian Mysteries were involved; *ANRW* 18 (1989) 1503.

54. Pliny *Nat. hist.* 36.45; Plut. *Publicola* 15.4 (Temple of Zeus). Lucian describes the copy that remained in Athens (*Zeuxis* 3–7); M. Pape, *Griechische Kunstwerke aus Kriegsbeute und ihre öffentliche Aufstellung in Rom* (Diss. Hamburg 1975) 21–22. A map showing the cities, towns, and shrines in Greece plundered by Sulla in the First Mithridatic War is in G. Waurick, *Jahrbuch des Römisch-Germanischen Zentralmuseums* 22 (1975 [1977]) 44, fig. 4.

55. H. B. Gottschalk, *ANWR* II 36.2 (1987) 1083–88. Parts of the tradition are fable.

Gaius Velleius practically denied the defection of Athens in a truly startling manner, especially for a Roman. According to Velleius, Athens was such a reliable ally that Romans used to say the Athenians had distinguished themselves through their loyalty at all times and in every respect. They had fought against the Romans only because they were forced to by Mithridates' armies, and even during Sulla's siege of the city and harbor their friendship and sympathies had been with him.[56] This makes a nice story but does not correspond to the historical realities.

Appian reports that after taking Athens Sulla reinstituted the constitution that Rome had previously given the city, but all attempts to identify such an older law have failed.[57] The postwar political order in Athens—what the provisions of its constitution looked like after Sulla and how they came into being—is discussed in the next chapter.

---

56. Velleius 2.23.4–5.

57. Appian *Mithridateios* 152; Bernhardt, *Polis und römische Herrschaft* 41–42.

FOURTEEN

After the War

1. The Constitution

As we have seen, Appian reports that after condemning Aristion and his most highly compromised followers, Sulla pardoned the remaining citizens and reintroduced the constitution that Rome had previously given the city.[1] The second part of this statement is of doubtful authenticity, for no indication can be found that Rome ever interfered with the constitution of its independent ally Athens before the First Mithridatic War, and it is unlikely that Sulla would have done so after he had conquered it. The Athenian constitution in force after Sulla's defeat of the city need not necessarily have been imposed by Sulla.[2] More probably, he would have had no need to intervene, for his victory returned to power the old elite who had always been loyal to Rome and who had been only temporarily displaced by the rule of the tyrants Athenion and Aristion. However, Appian's account is probably correct to a certain extent, namely that the constitution in force after 86 was similar to that of the late second century and early part of the first century, up to the overthrow of Medeius in 89/8. The earlier constitution was characterized by the predominance of oligarchic over the remaining democratic elements, that is, a shift of power and decisionmaking away

---

1. Appian *Mithridateios* 152. For the following passage see Accame, *Dominio* 102–110 and 163–187; and D. J. Geagan, *Hesperia Suppl.* 12 (1967).

2. Geagan, however, speaks of "the new constitutional arrangements instituted by Sulla" (5) and "the abrupt change when Sulla imposed his new constitution on Athens"; *Hesperia Suppl.* 12 (1967) 17. Similarly, G. W. Bowersock: "repeated Roman tampering with their [the Athenians'] constitution" (with regard to the year 86); *Augustus and the Greek World* (Oxford 1965) 106.

from officials chosen by lot and from the popular Assembly, and into the hands of elected magistrates and the Areopagus, the council of former archons. The most powerful figures in this political order were the elected hoplite *strategos* and the president of the Areopagus, whose official title was "herald." This system had developed in the latter part of the second century, probably without direct Roman influence but with the tacit approval of ruling circles in Rome.[3]

After Sulla's storming of Athens the oligarchic elements of the constitution were given still more weight. The eponymous archon, for example, was no longer chosen by lot from a limited number of candidates, but by election, although there had been a precedent in Medeius' successive terms as archon in the 90s (never equaled later). The selection of the hierophant of Eleusis as the first eponymous archon after the fall of the city cannot have occurred by chance. It is clear, too, that the cycle according to which the secretaryship of the Council rotated annually among the different tribes had been suspended.[4] And although decrees of the Assembly are known until shortly before the outbreak of war, none are known after 86 until the 40s;[5] for this period the only surviving decrees emanated from the Council.[6]

The list of eponymous archons after Sulla begins in the year 86/5 with *hierophantes,* that is, with the officeholder's religious title rather than his name. The first archon of this era thus combined the lifelong

3. By the end of the second century, e.g., the hoplite general and the president of the Areopagus ranked second and third in importance after the eponymous archon, demoting the *archon basileus* to fourth place (Geagan, ibid., 10). The oligarchic character of the constitution is reflected especially clearly in the large inscriptions recording the events of the *Pythais* (see Chapter 11, Section 3) and in the catalogue *IG* II[2].2336 covering half a dozen years around the turn of the century, analyzed by S. V. Tracy in *HSCP* 83 (1979) 215–220 and *Contributors* 108–145.

4. S. Follet, *Athènes au IIe et au IIIe siècle* (Paris 1976) 301–303. The cycle remained in effect at least until 95/4.

5. P. J. Rhodes, *The Athenian Boule* (Oxford 1972) 86–87.

6. *Agora* XV.263–281; J. Pouilloux, *Rhamnonte* (Paris 1954) 139, no. 24, from 83/2; *IG* II[2].1039 (*SEG* 22.110), from 79/8, containing three decrees of the Council; *ASA,* n.s. 3–4 (1941–42) 83–84, no. 6, from 75/4; *IG* II[2].1046 from 52/1. See E. Rawson, *Athenaeum* 73 (1985) 59. A Council decree found recently in Rhamnus from the 80s at the earliest is itself dated in the archonship of Asclepides (otherwise unknown); *Ergon* (1992 [1993]) 3. The Council thereby authorized the coastal *strategos* to carry out repairs on the fortress of Rhamnus, which had suffered from attacks by pirates, presumably during the Mithridatic War.

office of high priest of the Eleusinian Mysteries (passed down in the clan of the Eumolpidae) with a one-year term of political office.[7] It is the first case of such a combination of profane and sacred offices, and probably for the obvious reason: in the year after the city's liberation from "tyranny" the Athenians wished to demonstrate that the holder of the highest office in the government, by virtue of his priestly calling, could neither have been connected with the previous regime nor have derived benefit from it.

A further demonstration that the tide of opinion had turned against the ousted regime is provided two years later, when the two masters of the mint for the year 84, Mentor and Moschion, depicted the earlier tyrant-slayers Harmodius and Aristogeiton on their silver coins. It was possible for the leaders of an oligarchic government to make use of democratic heroes in this fashion because the oligarchy understood itself also as having overthrown a tyrant. A variant of the same phenomenon occurred forty years later, when the Athenian government— still an oligarchy—honored the new "tyrant-slayers" Brutus and Cassius by placing statues of them next to those of Harmodius and Aristogeiton.[8]

For several decades after 86 we have not a single extant Assembly decree, and very few Council decrees, apart from routine measures honoring the *prytaneis* and their treasurer. Not one of these surviving decrees deals with political matters; the majority concern religious affairs. In 83/2 the Council had to deal with a new cult of the Phrygian goddess Agdistis being practiced in Rhamnus, far outside the city, apparently introduced there by foreign mercenary soldiers. Citizens residing in the surrounding areas had harassed the group attempting to worship her, which had then entered a protest with the Council; the decree was designed to put a stop to the harassment and interference.[9] In 81 the Senate awarded privileges to the city of Stratoniceia in southwest Asia Minor for its loyalty to Rome in the war against Mithri-

7. For the phenomenon known as "hieronymy" and the archon of 86/5, see Clinton, *Officials* 9 and 29 (no. 16) respectively. An instance of hieronymy alleged to date from the fourth century actually belongs to the second (see Tracy, *ALC* 155–156) and is the oldest known evidence of this practice along with the recently discovered document on the Panathenaea of 166, published in *Hesperia* 60 (1991) 180, col. II.37.53.

8. For the coins of 84/3 see C. Habicht, *Chiron* 6 (1976) 135–142; for Brutus and Cassius in 44/3 see Cassius Dio 47.20.4.

9. Pouilloux, *Rhamnonte* 139, no. 24.

dates, and Athens, like many other states, recognized the inviolability of the shrine of Hecate at that site.[10] It would be interesting to know if this guaranty was offered by the Council alone or if the citizenry was also consulted in the Assembly. Another Council decree from 75/4 found on Lemnos deals with the cult of the Cabiri (the "Great Gods" of Samothrace) on the island and with the officials elected by each tribe to supervise it.[11] A long Council decree from 52/1 mentions the initiative of a priest of Asclepius to repair dilapidated parts of the god's shrine, for which the Council had to give approval.[12] Various decrees passed by the Council honoring the ephebes of 80/79 are equally unpolitical in nature.[13] They show that the institution of *ephebia* continued actively, just like the philosophers' schools (see below). There is in fact a connection, for the ephebes are commended for attending lectures by rhetoricians, grammarians, and philosophers.

Several noted philosophers had left Athens either during the illegal regime of Medeius or in Athenion's time. The departure of the Epicurean Phaedrus (who went to Rome even before Athens joined Mithridates' cause) is documented, as is that of Philon of Larissa, the head of the Academy, who left the city after Athenion seized power. While Philon was still in Athens, his lectures were attended by the aristocratic Roman Gaius Aurelius Cotta, who had left Rome in 90 to avoid sentence. On Philon's advice Cotta also attended classes taught by Zeno, the Epicurean philosopher. The end of the war allowed Phaedrus and Philon to return to Athens, and Cotta to return to Rome.[14]

The first decree of the post-Sulla period that can be dated stems from 49/8, and since the Attic year ended in July, it probably predates Caesar's victory over Pompey, which took place at Pharsalus on 6 June 48. It almost certainly predates the time when Caesar could have taken control of the city's affairs. Since a considerable portion of the text has not survived, the subject of the decree is unclear, and the significance of the renewed involvement of the Assembly after such a long interval is also far from clear. It does not necessarily mean that at the time of

---

10. *OGI* 441.174.

11. *ASA*, n.s. 3–4 (1941–42) 83–84, no. 6.

12. *IG* II^2.1046 with 3174; S. Aleshire, *The Athenian Asklepieion* (Amsterdam 1989) 32–34. Cf. the new document from Rhamnus mentioned in note 6 above.

13. *SEG* 22.110.

14. J.-L. Ferrary, *Philhellénisme et impérialisme* (Rome 1988) 445–447; Dorandi, *Ricerche* 52–53.

its passage the oligarchy established after Sulla's conquest had acquired a more democratic face.[15] Another, slightly later inscription does create this impression, however. Dating from the late 40s, after Caesar's murder, it contains decrees honoring the ephebes in the year of the archon Nicandrus. In the oligarchy of the post-Sulla era, the main roles in awarding such honors had devolved to the hoplite general and the president of the Areopagus, but in the decree in question these roles fall once more to the board of *strategoi* and the army treasurer.[16] A few years later, in 38, when Mark Antony was master of Greece and Athens, a similar decree honoring a year-class of ephebes shows the oligarchic model prevailing once again.[17]

Scholars have debated the meaning of this shift between the two sets of magistrates; some have postulated that at various times the Romans intervened to alter the Athenian constitution. According to this theory, Caesar made the first change, and both Brutus and Mark Antony followed his example.[18] However, whether changes were actually made to the constitution, or whether the shifts merely represent minor administrative variations is far from certain, and no Roman intervention has been conclusively proven.[19] The popular hypothesis that Caesar restored a greater measure of democratic freedom to Athens in 48 is undermined by the fact that in 45/4 and 44/3 the Areopagus is still described as the dominant institution of government by no less a source than Cicero, whose son was studying in Athens and who thus had close contacts with the leading political figures of the city during these two years.[20] For this reason Accame, in contrast to earlier scholars, ascribes the first Roman intervention not to Caesar, but to his assassin Brutus,

15. *IG* II^2.1047.
16. *IG* II^2.1042; the above-mentioned magistrates appear in d.9–10. The same circumstances are reflected in two inscriptions for other year-classes of ephebes (*IG* II^2.1040.34 and 1041.36–37), but the two archons mentioned may have served about 20 years later, i.e., in the Augustan era.
17. *IG* II^2.1043.55. The magistrates named hold the same offices as in the decree from 79/8 (*IG* II^2.1039.63–64).
18. This view has been taken in recent years by Accame, *Dominio* 172–179; and Rawson, *Athenaeum* 73 (1985) 59–64.
19. J. Touloumakos takes a skeptical view of far-ranging assumptions in *Der Einfluss Roms auf die Staatsform der griechischen Stadtstaaten des Festlandes und der Inseln im ersten und zweiten Jahrhundert v. Chr.* (Diss. Göttingen 1977) 77.
20. Cicero *De natura deorum* 2.74; *De officiis* 1.75; Plut. *Cicero* 24.7; Accame, *Dominio* 174–175; Rawson, *Athenaeum* 73 (1985) 63. Rawson in particular sheds light on Cicero's contacts with the highest ranks of Athenian society in these years.

who visited Athens in 44/3. Accame then reasons that Brutus' successor Antony rescinded these reforms after 42, thereby restoring the Areopagus to its old powerful position.[21]

Rapid political shifts did in fact occur after 49, in the course of the Roman civil war. Athens fell under the sway first of Pompey, then of Caesar, then of Caesar's murderer Brutus, and finally of Antony, all in the space of less than ten years; only ten years after that Antony was himself defeated by Octavian. Thus the constitution may quite possibly have been altered more than once during this period, and power may have passed from one circle to another within the city. But it is by no means established that a change in the political constellation always involved a shift from oligarchy to democracy (or vice versa).

In the discussion about the constitution of Athens after Sulla a document published in 1971 plays a key role, despite its highly fragmentary state.[22] It is a decree carved in a style suggesting the first century B.C., but possibly from the late second century, passed by the Assembly or the Council on the motion of a man named Demeas.[23] It contains references to "democracy" (line 7), to the contrast between lots and elections (8), and to offices filled by drawing lots (10 and 20). The only provision of the decree that can be made out in its entirety states that laws previously passed by the Areopagus will remain in force.[24] The editor of the fragment, D. J. Geagan, argues that because the Areopagus plays such an important role in this decree, it must be connected with an oligarchic restoration. He proposes a connection with the post-Sulla constitution and in particular the year 84/3, when Sulla had returned to Athens. As a reaction to the previous "tyranny" of first Athenion and then Aristion, this constitution could be described as "democratic" (in the sense of "republican").[25]

However, J. H. Oliver understood the text to mean just the oppo-

---

21. Accame, *Dominio* 174–175.

22. D. J. Geagan, *Hesperia* 40 (1971) 101–108 and plate 16.

23. Demeas, son of Demeas [from Azenia], in Geagan's reconstruction. However, the only *documented* Demeas, son of Demeas, is a citizen of the deme Halai, *IG* II².2445.15 (ca. 140 B.C.); 5471. A Demeas, son of Demeas, appears without indication of his deme as an Athenian ephebe in Delphi in 138/7 (*FD* III.2.23, col. II.16). Geagan's identification of the deme is arbitrary and without foundation, as are his attempts to identify the Demeas who sponsored the decree with other men of the same name (for whom no deme is documented). Furthermore, the dates he suggests for the one or more masters of the mint named Demeas are off by one generation, since he follows Margaret Thompson's chronology.

24. Line 17.

25. Geagan, *Hesperia* 40 (1971) 107–108.

site, namely a return from oligarchy to democracy and the filling of offices by lots. In his view it reflects an abandonment—in 70/69—of Sulla's oligarchy as a result of events in Rome (particularly the renewal of the tribunes' political rights, formerly curtailed by Sulla).[26] Geagan later conceded that this view, though diametrically opposed to his original interpretation, is a possible alternative reading of the text.[27] Badian, on the other hand, categorically rejected Oliver's theory, calling it "a fanciful date, based on a 'correlation' with misinterpreted events at Rome."[28] He agreed with Oliver that the decree signals a return to democracy rather than a return to oligarchy, but read it as a democratic manifesto from the period of Athenion's "democracy" in 88.

This brief outline of the scholarly debate should make it clear that both the content and the dating of the inscription are uncertain in all respects. The attempts made by Geagan and Oliver (and criticized by Badian) to identify the year of the decree by means of the Council secretary's deme were unsuccessful: only the first three letters of the deme's name have been preserved; there are three different possible ways to complete it, and therefore three different tribes to which the recording secretary might have belonged. Furthermore, it is certain that although the rotation of the secretary's office was maintained at least until 95/4, it was abandoned not long thereafter. Thus the argument that the decree must date from either 84/3 (tribe IX) or 70/69 (tribe XI) is groundless.

As matters stand now, this inscription must be omitted from any discussion of the Athenian constitution after Sulla. It could just as well be from the pre-Sulla era, and what it actually means remains an unresolved question.

2. Ruling Circles

From the end of the second century on, the hierarchy of chief offices in Athens ran as follows: the eponymous archon at the top, followed by the hoplite general, the president of the Areopagus, and the *archon basileus*. The archons of earlier times, including the eponymous ar-

26. J. H. Oliver, *GRBS* 13 (1972) 101–102.
27. D. J. Geagan, *ANRW* II 7.1 (1979) 376.
28. E. Badian, *AJAH* 1 (1976) 105. Cf. Rawson, *Athenaeum* 73 (1985) 61 n. 79. M. C. Hoff agreed with Oliver; *Hesperia* 58 (1989) 272 n. 31.

chons, had been chosen by lot; they were frequently men of no special political standing, and rarely members of prominent families. But the selection of Sarapion of Melite (116/5) and repeated installments of Medeius of Piraeus in the office (101/0, 91/0, 90/89, and 89/8) show that even before Sulla's conquest the choice was no longer left to chance. As soon as the selection process came to be controlled in one form or another, the office—in addition to the great prestige it had always possessed—acquired political weight to the extent that its holders came from the city's leading families. As we shall see, this was usually the case in the post-Sulla era. Whether the other archons—the *archon basileus,* the polemarch, and the six *thesmothetai,* or lawgivers— were chosen in the same manner from that time on, and recruited from prominent families, is less certain. This should probably be assumed at least for the *basileus,* since his maintaining such a high position in the official hierarchy cannot otherwise be explained, and it is also probable for the polemarchs and thesmothetes.

The political weight of these officials was at least matched by the *epimeletes,* or "governor," of Delos, chosen annually. His standing is revealed first of all by the fact that only members of the Areopagus, or previous archons, held that office, and is confirmed by identification of many such governors as members of important families.[29] All the above-named offices had one-year terms and were not supposed to be filled by the same person twice (although we encounter two exceptions in the Delian *epimeletai* of 128/7 and 126/5, both of whom served two terms). The hoplite general was an exception: like all other generals, he could be reelected several times; this had been the practice for centuries, and even in periods of radical democracy generals were not chosen by lot. In the post-Sulla era the Athenians documented as having served as hoplite general more than once were most probably leading politicians.[30] Many others documented as serving only one term undoubtedly served more often. But even someone elected hoplite general only once in his life possessed both wealth and influence.[31]

29. For the *epimeletai* from 167 to 88 see C. Habicht, *Hermes* 119 (1991) 194–216; for those after Sulla to Augustus, see P. Roussel, *Délos, colonie athénienne* (Paris 1916; enl. ed. 1987) 114–117.

30. Up to the end of the century they were Herodes of Marathon, Antipater of Phlya, Epicrates of Leukonoe, and Xenocles of Rhamnus. Antipater served in this office 7 times, both Herodes and Xenocles at least 4 times, and Epicrates at least twice; T. Sarikakis, "The Hoplite General in Athens" (Diss. Princeton 1951) 25–27.

31. Leonides of Melite should be added to Sarikakis' list; he was eponymous archon of the year 12/1 and hoplite *strategos* in the late first century (*Agora* XV.300).

A prosopographic analysis of the mint magistrates (of whom there were two, often joined by a third for part of the annual term) has shown that in the documented cases the magistrates came from wealthy and politically active families; presumably this is true for all of them. Even Mithridates was not above having his name placed on the Athenian silver coins of 87/6 as one of the masters of the mint. Very often close relatives (father and son, or two brothers or cousins) served together for a year. Reelection was also possible for this office.[32] Many citizens documented as mint officials in the first century B.C. (down to about the year 40, when the manufacture of silver coins ceased) rose to the office of eponymous archon within a few years,[33] and a far higher number must have served in other archonships.[34]

The men who served as *agonothetai,* or sponsors of the great festivals, were recruited only from the wealthiest families, since the office required private expenditure of sums running to as much as several talents, especially every four years in the case of the Grand Panathenaea.[35] The known *agonothetai* of the larger festivals (Panathenaea, Eleusinian Mysteries, Theseia, and so on) from the middle of the second century on belong without exception to the most influential families of their day: Miltiades of Marathon,[36] Adeimantus of Icaria,[37] Leon of Aixone,[38] Apolexis of Piraeus,[39] Byttakus of Lamptrai,[40] Medeius of Piraeus,[41] Sarapion of Melite,[42] and, from the Augus-

---

32. C. Habicht, *Chiron* 21 (1991) 1–23, esp. 3–4 and 23.

33. The following eponymous archons (with their year of office) had previously served as masters of the mint at least once: Medeius (ca. 65/4), Herodes (60/59), Diocles (57/6), Diodorus (53/2), Lysander (52/1), Demochares (49/8), Philocrates (48/7), Polycharmus (ca. 43/2), and Diocles (39/8).

34. Since most of these archons are not known by name, there are few documented cases. Two *thesmothetai* of the year 56/5 had previously served as mint officials, namely Epigenes of Melite—master of the mint in 70/69 with his brother Xenon (*IG* II^2.1717.12 and Habicht, *Chiron* 21 [1991] 14)—and Architimus of Sphettos, in 62/1 (*IG* II^2.1717.11 and Habicht 16).

35. In the latter part of the third century Eurycleides of Kephisia spent 7 talents of his own money as *agonothetes* (*IG* II^2.834.4–5), and two sponsors of the Theseia in the middle of the second century each spent about half a talent, or 3,000 drachmas (*IG* II^2.956.18–19 and 958.15–16; cf. also 968.41–55).

36. Tracy, *ALC* 140 and 160–161; Gauthier, *Cités* 79 n. 7.

37. Habicht, *Hermes* 119 (1991) 197.

38. Habicht, *Studien* 194–197.

39. Habicht, *Chiron* 21 (1991) 17.

40. Tracy, *Contributors* 194.

41. Ibid., 210–211.

42. Ibid., 215.

tan era, Syndromus of Steiria.[43] Even monarchs such as Ariarathes V of Cappadocia (mid-second century) were willing to serve as sponsors of the Panathenaea when asked, and their names were inscribed for posterity on the amphorae awarded to victors of the competitions.[44]

In light of this evidence we may consider that all those citizens who served as eponymous archons, hoplite generals, presidents of the Areopagus, *epimeletai* of Delos, *agonothetai,* or mint magistrates, and presumably the lesser archons as well, came from Athens' first families. Of this group, those chosen hoplite general more than once or documented as having held several of the above-named offices must be considered leading political figures.[45] More information on leading families in Athens in Cicero's time can be found in a recent article by Elizabeth Rawson, "Cicero and the Areopagus," which discusses the families of Herodes of Marathon, Leonides of Melite, Epicrates of Leukonoe, Xenon of Melite, Polycharmus of Azenia, and Lysiades of Berenikidai.[46] They made up the circles frequented by young Roman aristocrats studying in Athens, such as Cicero's son Marcus. Cicero expected some of these men to send him reports on how his son was doing. As always, one must bear in mind that a large number of the leading politicians are unknown to us because most of the documents naming them happen to be lost. Thus it can never be said that a certain individual was not a political leader in his day; we can say only that another individual *was* a leading figure, because chance has preserved a sufficient number of inscriptions related to him.

Several high priestly offices brought more prestige to the holder than political power, particularly those of the *hierophantai* and *daduchoi,* the priesthoods associated with the cult of Eleusis and passed down in the noble families of the Eumolpidae and the Kerykes.[47] The first epony-

43. W. K. Pritchett, *Hesperia* 11 (1942) 247–249.

44. *Bulletin épigraphique* (1959) 79.

45. The combination of several of the highest offices is the rule for citizens who became eponymous archons. Epicrates, to whom the young Cicero referred during his stay in Athens in 44 as *princeps Atheniensium,* was a member of a family from Leukonoe that supplied several masters of the mint, archons, a president of the Areopagus, a commissar of Delos, and a hoplite general in this period (Tracy, *Contributors* 206–207; Rawson, *Athenaeum* 73 [1985] 51; Habicht, *Chiron* 21 [1991] 16). P. Graindor, *Chronologie des archontes athéniens sous l'empire* (Brussels 1922), contains a wealth of material, some of which requires updating on the basis of recent finds.

46. *Athenaeum* 73 (1985) 44–67.

47. The basic study is Clinton, *Officials* 8–68. In the post-Sulla period these two priesthoods were considered the most important and prestigious in the Athenian state.

mous archon after Sulla's storming of the city linked the two areas of cult and politics, however, for as we have seen, the hierophant took on the one-year political office from the summer of 86 to the summer of 85 in addition to his religious duties.[48] He may have been Theophemus of Kydathenaion, documented as hierophant around the turn of the century, whose father, Menecleides, was also hierophant.[49] The Theophemus who was eponymous archon in 61/0 and president of the Areopagus in 56/5 was either his son or his nephew.[50] Since the hierophants did not assume their high office until they had reached a considerable age, they may very likely have belonged to the political elite in their younger days; this was the rule in the imperial age and is well documented.[51]

The case of the *daduchoi* from the clan of the Kerykes is similar. From about 200 on two families shared this priesthood: that of Leontius, Sophocles, and Xenocles from Acharnai; and that of Philistides and Philoxenus from Hagnus. Soon after Sulla's conquest, another family from Hagnus succeeded them, that of Themistocles and Theophrastus, after the older Themistocles had married Acestion, a member of the family of *daduchoi* from Acharnai.[52] Thus for more than 200 years, from the beginning of the second century until past the time of Augustus, all the *daduchoi* were related by either blood or marriage. Acestion could boast that her great-grandfather, grandfather, father, brother, husband, and son (and his descendants) had all been *daduchoi,* a fact known to Pausanias 250 years afterward, and which he mentioned in his *Description of Greece.*[53] Even if the corrected chronology of Athenian New Style silver coinage requires some slight modification of the family trees,[54] it remains the case that members of this clan held the following offices: *hierope* (cult official) at the Athenaea of

48. See the beginning of this section.

49. Clinton, *Officials* 28–29, nos. 15 and 16.

50. For Theophemus the eponymous archon see Kastor, *FGrHist* 250 F 4–5; *IG* II^2.1716,15; *SEG* 36.267. For the president of the Areopagus Theophemus of Kydathenaion, see *IG* II^2.1717.15–16.

51. "It is characteristic of the hierophants of the Roman period to be politically very distinguished"; Clinton, *Officials* 45.

52. Ibid., 47–68, with the family tree on 58.

53. Pausanias 1.37.1.

54. The dates given by Clinton for the masters of the mint from the *daduchos* families (58) follow the original chronology established by M. Thompson in *The New Style Silver Coinage of Athens,* 2 vols. (New York 1961), which is off by 34 years.

156/5,[55] *agonothetes* at the Panathenaea of 108/7,[56] the priesthood "at the altar" in Eleusis,[57] and, in different generations and on repeated occasions, mint magistrates.[58] An earlier archon from the clan of the Kerykes, presumably a member of the family of *daduchoi*, was commander of the Athenian fleet in 103/2 and helped proconsul Marcus Antonius' campaign against the pirates operating off the southern coast of Asia Minor.

The rule that eponymous archons of the post-Sulla period uniformly came from wealthy and politically active families—and definitely did not attain their office by the chance dictates of a lottery—is clearly demonstrated by the fact that in many instances one family supplied several archons. Medeius, son of the Medeius of Piraeus who was four-term archon around the turn of the century, served as archon himself in about 65/4;[59] Herodes of Marathon, archon in 60/59, had a son Eucles who was archon in about 46/5,[60] later followed by Eucles' descendant Polycharmus.[61] Further eponymous archons included the brothers (or cousins) Diotimus (ca. 26/5) and Theophilus (11/10), sons of Diodorus of Halai,[62] and finally three successive generations in a family from Azenia, Demochares (49/8), Menander (38/7), and Demochares (after 9/8).[63]

For the fifty-four years between 84/3, when Sulla left Athens, and 31/0, the year of Octavian's defeat of Antony, forty-four eponymous archons are known by name. The year in which they served has thus far been established with a fair degree of certainty for only thirty-four. Of the remaining ten, six belong in the years between 74/3 and 65/4, and four in the years 46/5 to 43/2. It is not until the 60s, when the

---

55. *IG* II^2.1937.11.

56. *IG* II^2.1036.22–23.

57. Clinton, *Officials* 82, no. 8.

58. Xenocles (of Acharnai) 3 times with Harmoxenus, in 95/4, 92/1, and 90/89, i.e., during the rule of Medeius; Themistocles of Hagnus with Sotades in 78/7 and with his father Theophrastus in 75/4; see Habicht, *Chiron* 21 (1991) 6.

59. *IG* II^2.1340.1; 1095.12; and 2874.

60. *IG* II^2.1716.17; 2992 (Herodes); I *Délos* 2632.b.8; cf. *IG* II^2.1719 (Eucles).

61. *IG* II^2.1730; cf. 1728.5–6 and 3530.

62. *IG* II^2.2996 and 4465; I *Délos* 1840 (Diotimus); *IG* II^2.1713.31; *FD* III.2.62 (Theophilus).

63. *IG* II^2.1713, col. III.23; I *Délos* 2632.b.3; *IG* II^2.1047.6 (Demochares); *IG* II^2.1043.17 and frequently thereafter; 1343.24–25; 2994 (Menander); *IG* II^2.3176 (Demochares the younger). Cf. B. D. Meritt, *Hesperia* 36 (1967) 238.

surviving inscriptions become more numerous again, that the single name given in the list of archons can be connected with a deme and a father's name, and the archon in question assigned to a known family. Nearly all of them held other high posts at one time or another, and many must be considered members of the most important families of the time, such as the above-named Medeius of Piraeus, Herodes and Eucles of Marathon (whose descendant Herodes Atticus was the dominant figure in the city around the middle of the second century A.D.), Theophemus of Kydathenaion, Lysiades of Berenikidai, Lysander of Piraeus, and Diocles of Kephisia.

For the fifty-five-year period from 65/4 to 11/10, forty-five eponymous archons can be documented at the present time. Of this number, twenty-one can be assigned to known and politically active families. The others for whom there is (as yet) a lack of evidence probably came from similar backgrounds. Only a few of these eponymous archons belong to families that can be traced back for two centuries or more: the families of the archons Theophemus (61/0), Lysiades (51/0), Diotimus (ca. 26/5) and Theophilus (11/10), two related archons from Halai, and Polycharmus of Azenia, who was eponymous archon sometime between 9 B.C. and 14 A.D. In the early Augustan Age the *daduchos* Themistocles could trace his ancestry back to the Themistocles who defeated the Persians, and his wife Nicostrate traced hers back to the statesman Lycurgus. Other families, such as that of Medeius of Piraeus, did not rise to prominence until the second or even the first century, joining an elite circle from which many an earlier prominent family had disappeared.

After Sulla's time the number of families belonging to ruling circles and occupying all the important offices in Athens was in fact quite small, meaning that to the extent that Athens' own citizens controlled its fate, it was in the hands of an oligarchy. Nowhere is this more evident than in the long Assembly decree honoring Themistocles, the *daduchos* in 20/19.[64] In addition to Apolexis, the eponymous archon then in office, the text names six other eponymous archons of the time as cosponsors of the motion;[65] and it is highly probable that even more

---

64. Clinton, *Officials* 50–52, gives a revised edition of the text (*SEG* 30.93).

65. They are the Eleusinian altar priest Epicrates of Leukonoe (line 9) and the *hymnagogoi* Diotimus, Demochares, Diocles, Architimus, and Menander (lines 19–26).

of the sponsors, such as Cichesias of Aixone, also served as archons during the period, although documentation has not yet been discovered.[66]

3. A Difficult New Beginning

After the Roman general Sulla defeated Mithridates in Asia Minor, he returned to Athens in 84, where he enjoyed the company of a young Roman aristocrat named Titus Pomponius, who had taken up residence in the city during the war and was to make it his home for twenty years. Because of his fondness for the city Pomponius soon acquired the nickname "Atticus," and it is under this name that he became known as the lifelong friend and adviser of Cicero, from whom he received more than 400 letters. Atticus is far more than a marginal figure in Athenian history, for he came to the city's aid at a critical moment.[67]

Atticus arrived in Athens as a young man of twenty-four, soon after Sulla had stormed and taken the city. His friend and biographer Cornelius Nepos recounts that he had left Italy because of the civil war, not wanting to be forced to take sides. Another factor contributing to his departure was probably the turbulence of the Roman capital market, and the prospect of profitable business dealings undoubtedly played a role in his decision to go to Greece.[68] But the choice of Athens as a residence is more likely to have been determined by its favorable location and cultural attractions rather than any expectation of its being the best place to do business. Atticus had considerable business interests in other parts of Greece, such as Sicyon on the Peloponnese and Epirus; it would not have been chiefly commercial interests that drew him to Athens. There he assumed the role of a selfless benefactor, prompted by genuine admiration for the city and its unique heritage, which he shared with many educated Romans of his day.

Nepos reports that Atticus became a very popular figure in Athens, and with good reason, for he often used his fortune and connections to help the war-ravaged city. At least once in this period (and again in 50) when the price of grain soared, he bought up large amounts and

66. He is named in line 24 and belonged to a family that had been prominent for 200 years (Habicht, *Studien* 194–197, now in need of revision thanks to new discoveries).

67. O. Perlwitz, *Titus Pomponius Atticus* (Stuttgart 1992).

68. Nepos *Atticus* 2.2; Perlwitz, *Atticus* 35–39.

donated it to the citizens. Above all, however, he turned his abilities as a financier to the city's advantage. During those years, when the city often needed to borrow money, the conditions offered by moneylenders, usually Romans, were unacceptable. At this point Atticus would intervene, borrowing the sum needed in his own name at a more favorable rate and passing it on to the city without profit to himself.[69] In this way the impoverished city was able to save a great deal of money.

In gratitude for his frequent favors the Athenians voted Atticus many different honors, but as long as he continued to live in the city he would not allow them to erect a statue to him. He also refused an offer of Athenian citizenship (acceptance of which could have meant the loss of his Roman citizenship). He was well educated and spoke Greek like a native Athenian. He followed politics with a lively interest but from a distance, as he had no desire for a political career himself. He was just as concerned to maintain his independence and remain on good terms with politicians of all stripes in Greece as later on in Italy; for this reason Atticus declined Sulla's invitation to return home with him and join in the civil war against Sulla's domestic political opponents, who had seized power during his absence.[70]

Atticus' disinclination to become directly involved in politics probably resulted not only from the concentration of his main interests into business and finance but also from his devotion to the teachings of the Epicurean school. Atticus felt a lifelong attraction to this philosophy and established a friendship with Phaedrus and Zenon, the heads of the school in Athens at that time. He was far too independent in spirit, however, to become a genuine disciple of Epicurus, and in all important decisions he was guided by practical considerations rather than by a particular doctrine.[71]

His familiarity with the city, its society, and its intellectuals was of benefit to Cicero when, accompanied by several friends and relatives, he came to Athens for a six-month stay in 79, a few years after Atticus' arrival. Later Cicero began book 5 of his work *De finibus* with an

---

69. Nepos *Atticus* 2.6 (the donation of grain); 2.4–5 (the loans). See further L. Migeotte, who correctly interprets the odd role Atticus played as financial middleman in these transactions, particularly the phrase *semper se interposuit*, in *L'emprunt public dans les cités grecques* (Québec 1984) 34–35. This interpretation was offered in 1836 by J. Holtzmann but overlooked by Perlwitz.

70. Nepos *Atticus* 4.2. See also F. Millar, *G&R* 35 (1988) 42–43.

71. For more on his attitude toward Epicureanism see Perlwitz, *Atticus* 90–97.

emotional account, tinged by nostalgia, of a visit they paid to the Academy in which Atticus also plays a part. One afternoon in 79, not many years after the horrors of 86, they left the city by the Dipylon Gate to walk to the Academy grounds, twenty minutes away. The group consisted of Cicero, his brother Quintus, his younger cousin Lucius Cicero, Marcus Piso, and Pomponius Atticus. They wanted to pay their respects to Plato and his successors at the site where they had taught, and had chosen that hour of the afternoon because they thought it was likely to be deserted. They indeed found the stillness they had sought, and even signs of the devastation still evident (for Sulla had felled all the trees in the grove) failed to spoil the solemn mood in which they all—even those inclined to favor other philosophical schools—joined in a tribute to the great thinkers of the Academy: Plato, Speusippus, Xenocrates, Polemon, and the much younger Carneades.[72] The scene reflects the respect felt by educated Roman society for Greek culture, its leading thinkers, and Athens as their spiritual home, no matter where they may have been born. Cicero's description strikes the reader as a literary form of atonement for the barbarous acts committed by his fellow Romans not long before.

Probably in this same September of 79, Cicero was initiated into the Eleusinian Mysteries and had a religious experience that left him deeply affected.[73] Over the months Cicero remained in Athens he and his entourage also attended quite regularly the lectures of the philosophers. Cicero went most often to those of Antiochus of Ascalon, who had been trained at the Academy, while Atticus held the Epicurean Phaedrus in particularly high regard. Cicero considered Zeno to have the keenest mind of all the contemporary philosophers.[74] Clearly, instruction was carried on as usual in the philosophical schools of the city.

A decree passed by the *technitai* of Dionysus in honor of Philemon, their president *(epimeletes),* for the four years from 80 to 76, also confirms that that organization was pursuing its normal activities.[75] This fact is notable because the guild members, who owed so much to

---

72. Cicero *De finibus* 5.1–8; English translation by H. Rackham in the Loeb edition of 1914. Cicero mentions his visit to the Acropolis in *De natura deorum* 3.49.

73. Cicero *De leg.* 2.36; K. Clinton, *ANRW* II 18.2 (1989) 1500. Cf. 1504.

74. The numerous sources, including many from Cicero, are collected in M. Gelzer, "Tullius," *RE* (1939) 838. For Phaedrus see A. E. Raubitschek, *Hesperia* 18 (1949) 96–103.

75. *IG* II².1338. For the position of the *epimeletes* in the guild of the *technitai,* see F. Poland, *Geschichte des griechischen Vereinswesens* (Leipzig 1909) 368–369 and 405–408. The *technitai* in 88 B.C.: Poseidonius, *FGrHist* 87 F 36.49.

Rome, had played a large role in the ceremonies welcoming Athenion when he led Athens into the war against Rome.

But despite these signs of normality, there is eloquent evidence that all was not well in these postwar years; the city of Athens was forced to borrow money from private lenders, including foreigners; Romans such as Atticus had to intervene repeatedly to save it from bankruptcy. The city had grown poor as a result of destruction and looting that may have continued after the war. A year before Cicero's visit, Gaius Verres (later the notorious governor of Sicily, who would be prosecuted by Cicero) came through Athens on his way to the province of Cilicia; if we can believe the accusations Cicero raised at his trial (which in this case requires some effort), Gaius Verres stole all the gold of the goddess Athena in the Parthenon that Sulla had overlooked.[76]

It would be a long time before the city began to recover from the worst of the war damage and plundering, or envision the repair and reconstruction of ruined buildings. Some structures, such as the Pompeion, beyond saving, were left to decay. And only in a few cases did the money for rebuilding come from the city; most of the work was financed by foreign princes and members of the Roman nobility. Fully a quarter of a century passed before any sizable reconstruction occurred. From the late third century on, foreign rulers on good terms with Athens had contributed to the city's imposing appearance by financing large public buildings. These projects were not only gifts to the city but also a means of self-promotion, as if Athens were a form of world's fair at which a country or dynasty ought to be represented. The tradition seems to have originated around 224 with Ptolemy III Euergetes, the city's political patron at the time, who founded a gymnasium named in his honor.[77] Not long afterward Attalus I of Pergamum followed his example with the gift known as the "small Attalid dedication" on the Acropolis (if he really was the donor, and not his son of the same name). His sons Eumenes and Attalus, who followed him on the throne in succession, both had a stoa built in Athens and named after themselves; Eumenes' stoa stood at the foot of the Acropolis near the theater of Dionysus, and Attalus' stoa in the Agora. The "middle stoa," also in the marketplace, was built in the first half

76. Cicero *In Verrem* 2.1.44–45 and 2.4.71.
77. This passage contains a brief recapitulation of much that was reported in greater detail in Chapter 9, Section 1.

of the second century B.C. and may also have been the gift of a monarch, although there are no clues to his identity. In the second quarter of the same century the Seleucid ruler Antiochus IV Epiphanes generously repaid the city for the hospitality he had enjoyed for several years as a young man by financing further work on the temple of Olympian Zeus. Around the turn of the century Athens benefited from similar donations from Ptolemy IX Soter II, the Pontic kings Mithridates V Euergetes and Mithridates VI Eupator, and the Jewish ethnarch Hyrcanus, either in the city itself or for the gymnasium on Delos.

No largesse of this kind could be expected from their descendants in the post-Sulla era, since these dynasties had either vanished or were in decline. Their place was taken by Roman generals and the rulers of the smaller kingdoms on the periphery of the Roman Empire—on a smaller scale, of course, corresponding to their lesser means. Such benefactors included Ariobarzanes II and III of Cappadocia and, slightly later, Deiotarus of Galatia, Rhescuporis of Thrace, and Herod the Great of Judea.

Thus, the Athenians were accustomed to demonstrations of royal benevolence and public buildings financed by foreign monarchs. The Romans, by contrast, had not only destroyed a great deal of the city in 86 but had also plundered on a large scale and carried off many valuable works of art. It was therefore a turnabout when Roman aristocrats began making lavish gifts to the city, thereby replacing the kings of old as far as their means allowed. Their adoption of the custom of the great rulers of the past was certainly not accidental. The first such benefactor was none other than Pompey. On his departure from Brindisi in 67 to fight the pirates he was in such a hurry that he sailed past most Greek ports without visiting them. But he did take the time to land in Piraeus, go up to Athens, offer a sacrifice to the gods, and address the citizens. The Athenians, who hoped that he would put an end to the piracy plague, gave him a warm welcome.[78] Five years later, on his way back to Italy after defeating Mithridates and reorganizing the eastern provinces, Pompey stopped in Athens again to express his thanks. He had recently heard the great Posidonius speak in Rhodes, and in Athens he made the now obligatory gesture for upper-class Romans of visiting the lectures of several philosophers. He also donated fifty talents toward the city's restoration.[79]

78. Plut. *Pompeius* 27.3.
79. Ibid., 42.11: *eis episkeuen.*

Ten years later the city's main benefactors were two Romans from patrician families, Gaius Julius Caesar and Appius Claudius Pulcher. In his description of the former's years as governor of Gaul, Suetonius reports that Caesar, with an eye to the future and wishing to secure the gratitude and loyalty of kings and provincial rulers, donated grand buildings to the most important cities of the east and west (Suetonius names Italy, Gaul, Spain, Asia, and Greece).[80] It is quite certain that Athens numbered among them, as is confirmed explicitly in a letter Cicero wrote to Atticus in 50. At that time Cicero had heard that Herodes of Marathon, an Athenian citizen and eponymous archon of the year 60/59, had received fifty talents for his city from Caesar in Gaul, exactly the same sum donated earlier by Pompey. Pompey was supposed to have been greatly annoyed by the news.[81] More information is contained in the inscription on the architrave of the gateway to the Roman Agora in Athens. According to this inscription, the gate was dedicated during the archonship of Nicias (approximately 10/9), when Herodes' son Eucles was hoplite general. It was financed by the sums given by Caesar (to Herodes in 51) and Augustus (to Herodes' son Eucles). The father and son who had procured the money also oversaw the construction in succession; the gate itself was finally dedicated in the name of the people of Athens.[82] However, the real sponsors of the construction of the Roman Agora in Athens were Caesar and Augustus.

At the same time another Roman patrician financed a building in Eleusis, namely the lesser propylaea of the temple dedicated to the Eleusinian divinities. Appius Claudius Pulcher had made a vow to do so during his term as consul in 54, and began construction during or after his governorship in Cilicia (53–51). It was dedicated by his heirs after his death in 48.[83] The donor, a member of an impoverished patrician clan, had made a fortune as governor in Cilicia, where he

80. Suetonius *Caesar* 28.1: "nec minore studio reges atque provincias per terrarum orbem adliciebat . . . superque Italiae Galliarumque et Hispaniarum, Asiae quoque et Graeciae potentissimas urbes praecipuis operibus exornans."

81. Cicero *Ad Atticum* 6.1.25. All the questions connected with this donation, including the roles of Herodes and Eucles, are discussed by Rawson, *Athenaeum* 73 (1985) 44–49.

82. *IG* II^2.3175 (W. Ameling, *Herodes Atticus II* [Hildesheim 1983] 43, no. 20). Herodes Atticus was a descendant of the Herodes who visited Caesar in Gaul. For the Roman Agora, see also M. C. Hoff, *AA* (1994) 93–117.

83. *CIL* III.547 (A. Degrassi, *Inscriptiones Latinae Liberae Rei Publicae*^{2}, vol. 1 [Florence 1957] no. 401); K. Clinton, *ANRW* II 18.2 (1989) 1504–06 and plate 1. For literature on the monument see 1505 n. 28.

served as Cicero's immediate predecessor, and some of the funds for the construction at Eleusis undoubtedly stemmed from this source. The project reflects two of Pulcher's most prominent character traits: his greed and his piety. Cicero heard about the start of construction on this gateway in Cilicia in the winter of 51/0 at the same time he learned of Caesar's gift to Athens. The news caused him to consider donating a gate to be erected at the Academy, which he had visited with such emotion a generation earlier. But even as he toyed with the thought, which would occupy him for several months before he finally rejected it, he realized that many people would regard it as inappropriate—and so Cicero failed to become a benefactor of Athens.[84]

However, his friend Atticus, who had already helped Athens in cases of financial embarrassment, donated an unknown quantity of wheat to the city that same year, in 50. This gesture prompted Cicero to some mild criticism, not stronger only because Atticus was not Athenian himself and because his gift came under the heading of generosity in return for hospitality enjoyed rather than of a donation to one's own countrymen.[85]

On his way to his province in 51 Cicero, for the first time since his long visit in 79, had stopped in Athens from 25 June to 6 July and stayed with Ariston, brother of the late Academician Antiochus of Ascalon. He wrote to Atticus several times that he had a special fondness for Athens,[86] and this is why it occurred to him shortly after to erect a monument in the city, or rather at the Academy nearby. In his correspondence with Atticus he noted his plans for a return visit on his way back to Rome and his wish to participate in the Eleusinian Mysteries, if the time of year was right.[87] And although the threat of a civil war between Caesar and Pompey grew more and more acute during his governorship and ought to have hastened his return if he hoped to intervene in the cause of peace, Cicero nonetheless took the time to visit Athens again in the fall of the year 50. He arrived on 14 October, just in time to take part in the celebration of the Eleusinian Mysteries (between the twentieth and the twenty-eighth of the month) for the first time since his initiation many years before. He had, to be sure, already given up his idea of donating a monument to the Academy.

---

84. Cicero *Ad Atticum* 6.1.26 and 6.6.2.
85. Ibid., 6.6.2.
86. Ibid., 5.10.5 and 6.1.26.
87. John D. Morgan, "The Mystery of the Mysteries," *CQ* (forthcoming), provides the correct interpretation of Cicero *Ad Atticum* 5.21.14 and 6.1.26.

The plan of another Roman to erect a building in Athens at about this time is quite a different story. In this case, the planner was Gaius Memmius, a member of the Senate aristocracy and son-in-law of the dictator Sulla, and he intended to build a palace on the site where Epicurus' house had once stood. He did not aim this as a tribute to the founder of the school of philosophy, but wanted to erect a house for himself, since he was under a sentence of banishment from Rome and all Italy. Memmius had been praetor in 58 and a candidate for consul in 53, but his career had foundered over a scandal involving corruption on a scale startling even by Roman standards; he was found guilty and banished in 52. Nonetheless he still possessed enough money, influence, and connections to procure a vote from the Areopagus approving his plans for a palatial house. The disciples of the philosopher, who revered the site as sacred, were horrified and did their best to block the project. Under the circumstances it was particularly ironic that Lucretius had dedicated his epic poem glorifying Epicurus, *On the Nature of Things*, to none other than Memmius. Patron, then head of the Epicurean school, turned to his Roman acquaintances Atticus and Cicero for help, and both endeavored to save the philosopher's house, although Cicero had no hope that the Areopagus would reverse its decision without Memmius' consent. Cicero (who held a low opinion of Patron) wrote a very diplomatic letter to Memmius and sent it after him to Mytilene, for which he had departed the day before.[88] In the end Memmius dropped the project.

The architectural renewal begun by Pompey, Caesar, and Appius Claudius and continued by Augustus gradually changed the face of Athens from a Hellenistic to a Roman city. Magnificent donations could be no longer expected from the Hellenistic east, where Pompey brought about the permanent downfall of the once-powerful Seleucids, and where the Ptolemaic dynasty was in decline. The only monarch of the region to make a noteworthy contribution was a king installed by Pompey in the course of his reorganization of the Near East, who followed the example of his patron. Ariobarzanes II of Cappadocia sponsored the reconstruction of the Odeon, Pericles' concert hall at the foot of the Acropolis, which the tyrant Aristion had burned down shortly before the collapse of his regime as Sulla's troops were about to enter the city. The king himself, like so many other Hellenistic

88. Cicero *Fam.* 13.1. Cf. *Ad Atticum* 5.11.6; F. Münzer, "Memmius," *RE* (1931) 609–615, esp. 614–615.

princes, had received his education in Athens and is named in a list of Athenian ephebes from the year 80/79. The people of Athens showed their gratitude by dedicating a statue to him in the theater of Dionysus next to the Odeon; the three architects who worked on the rebuilding of the hall, two brothers from Rome named Gaius and Marcus Stallius and a Greek named Melanippus, also placed their own monument to the king in Athens.[89]

Around the middle of the first century repairs were made to the sanctuary of Asclepius at the foot of the Acropolis, as revealed by several inscriptions.[90] At about the same time—if the traditional but recently challenged dating is correct—the imposing new structure known as the "Tower of the Winds" was built in the center of the city. According to Vitruvius, the eight-sided tower near the eastern gate of the Roman Agora gave concrete expression to its builder's conviction that there were eight winds instead of four. However, the building's actual purpose was to serve as a public timekeeper, and Varro refers to it more accurately as a horologium. It had partial sundials on each of its walls, and inside there was a large water clock of complicated construction.[91] The master builder Andronicus, who is named as a citizen of the city of Cyrrhus, is the same Andronicus, son of Hermias from the Macedonian city of Cyrrhus, who built a marble sundial on the island of Tenos and was praised in an epigram as a "second Eudoxus."[92] Whether the Cyrrhus referred to is the city in Macedonia or the Macedonian colony named after it in northern Syria is a matter of controversy. Traditionally scholars favored Syria,[93] but recently the view that the Macedonian town is meant has gained ground.[94]

89. Vitruvius 5.9.1; IG II^2.3427 and 3426; H. A. Thompson, in *Roman Architecture in the Greek World*, ed. S. Macready and F. H. Thompson (London 1987) 4. The list of ephebes is IG II^2.1039, with a more complete reading of the names in *SEG* 22.110. Ariobarzanes is named in col. II.99–100.

90. IG II^2.1046, a Council decree from 52/1; IG II^2.3174, a dedication of the priests from 51/0. A dedication of the priest from 63/2, IG II^2.4464, may perhaps also be connected with the repairs; Aleshire, *Asklepieion* 16 and 32–34.

91. Vitruvius 1.6.4; Varro *De re rustica* 3.5.17.

92. IG XII.5.891; H. Diels, *Antike Technik*^{3} (Leipzig 1924) 172–173.

93. Diels, ibid., 172 n. 1; E. Fabricius, "Andronikos," *RE* (1894) 2167–68; F. Granger, ed., *Vitruvius* (Loeb Library 1931) 1: 57; R. E. Wycherley, *The Stones of Athens* (Princeton 1978) 103.

94. E. Honigmann, "Kyrrhos," *RE* (1924) 199; N. G. Hammond, *A History of Macedonia*, vol. 1 (Oxford 1972) 159; W. Zschietzschmann, "Athenai," *RE Suppl.* 13 (1973) 86–87; J. von Freeden, Οἰκία Κυρρήστου: *Studien zum sogenannten Turm der Winde in Athen* (Rome 1983) 7.

The tower, still standing in Athens in a remarkably good state of preservation, was recently the subject of a penetrating study by Joachim von Freeden, who among other things challenged the traditional dating and assigned it to the much earlier period between 150 and 125. Although this view has received some support, the evidence advanced is by no means conclusive, and several scholars have recommended retaining the traditional dating from the middle of the first century.[95]

95. Von Freeden's conclusions were endorsed by C. Bouras, *Akten des 13. Internationalen Kongresses für Archäologie* (Berlin 1990) 271; and by H. J. Kienast, *AA* (1993) 271–275. They have been rejected by H. S. Robinson, *AJA* 88 (1984) 423–425, who suggests that the 50 talents donated by Pompey in 62 may have been used toward construction of the tower. H. A. Thompson, in Macready and Thompson, *Roman Architecture in the Greek World* 6 and 16 n. 11; H. von Hesberg, *Gnomon* 57 (1985) 80–84. Cf. also R. R. R. Smith, *JHS* 105 (1985) 230–231.

FIFTEEN

Subjection

1. Clodius' Plebiscite

When Sulla pardoned those Athenians who had survived the storming of their city in the spring of 86 as well as the ensuing massacre, he showed unexpected clemency, for the city had taken part in the war against Rome. After the war the city resumed its old status as a state allied with Rome but legally independent. This remained the case for the next thirty years. True, in 74 a Roman official named Lucius Marcilius called upon Athens to act as arbitrator in a dispute between the town of Gytheion in Laconia and their Roman creditors, the Cloatii, and thus it might seem as if Athens had been required to follow instructions from this official, at that time a deputy of the praetor Marcus Antonius (away fighting the pirates). It is far more probable, however, that he requested the Athenians to take on this role after the parties appearing before him had either made or accepted such a proposal.[1] The Athenian Assembly presumably had little choice but to accede to Marcilius' request, but the diplomatic courtesies were observed and the sovereignty of the city upheld.

A further case should probably be judged along the same lines; in this instance a Roman official asked an Athenian court to stand in for him and pass judgment in a murder case:[2] in 68 the local authorities arrested a woman and brought her before Cornelius Dolabella, the

---

1. The inscription found in Gytheion has been edited with a commentary by L. Migeotte, *L'emprunt public dans les cités grecques* (Québec 1984) 90–96. See also C. Le Roy, *Ktema* 3 (1978) 261–266. The role of Athens is mentioned in line 12.

2. Valerius Maximus 8.1, *amb.* 2; Gellius 12.7; and Ammianus 29.19 (following Valerius Maximus) report the same thing with minor variations.

Roman governor in Smyrna in the province of Asia, for sentencing. She had confessed to murdering her husband and their son because they had killed her son from a previous marriage. The governor was faced with the dilemma of either acquitting the woman despite her confession, in view of the strong motives she had for committing the double murder, or ignoring the circumstance and condemning her anyway. Dolabella's step was as extraordinary as the circumstances of the crime itself; he chose neither to decide the case himself nor to hand it over to a court in the city (or another city in his province). Instead he hit on the ingenious solution of passing responsibility to a court in an allied state, the Areopagus in Athens, for centuries the institution in charge of trying cases of premeditated murder in the city. Confronted with the same dilemma as Dolabella, the Areopagus came up with an extraordinary solution: the members of the court ordered the defendant and the prosecutors to appear before them for the trial in 100 years. The case was widely known in ancient times[3] and clearly contributed to the fame of the Areopagus in the Roman era. All the evidence suggests that Dolabella respected Athenian sovereignty in making his request.

That sovereignty was flagrantly violated in 58, however, by a plebiscite of the tribune Publius Clodius, the *lex Clodia de provinciis consularibus*. To ensure the allegiance of the two consuls, Clodius allotted each a particularly large and profitable province, in defiance of existing laws. L. Calpurnius Piso (Caesar's father-in-law) was placed in charge of Macedonia, and Aulus Gabinius received Cilicia; later, through a second plebiscite, he was awarded Syria. A significant new feature of this law, sponsored by the tribune and voted on by the people, was the extension of the boundaries of the old province of Macedonia; this region, administered by a proconsul since 146, was enlarged to include sovereign Greek states.[4] Cicero, Piso's contemporary, explicitly states that his territory included Athens and Attica.[5]

---

3. Ammian. 29.18: "exemplum . . . illud antiquitati admodum notum."

4. The evidence is in G. Rotondi, *Leges publicae populi Romani* (Milan 1912) 393–394. A more detailed discussion will soon be published by J.-L. Ferrary, to whom I am indebted for suggestions and comments.

5. Speaking against Piso in the Senate after his return in 55 B.C. Cicero said, "Omnis erat tibi Achaia, Thessalia, Athenae, cuncta Graecia addicta" (37). He also accused Piso of having ruined the regions entrusted to him in the years of his governorship: "Achaia exhausta, Thessalia vexata, laceratae Athenae" (96). While these polemical utterances distorted by personal hatred should not be taken seriously, the statement that Piso was in fact in charge of these areas must be accurate. See also Cicero *De dom.* 23 and 60.

The step is noteworthy for several reasons: first, because Athens' sovereignty was violated or, more accurately, ignored; second, because it was taken not by the Senate, the institution normally responsible for such affairs, but by a tribune and the plebs. It is no less astounding that this extension of direct Roman rule resulted not from events on Greek soil, but from internal aspects of Roman politics. The aim was apparently to give Roman creditors a legal instrument for pursuing the cities that owed them money; it provided them with the possibility of suing these communities in the proconsul's courts, a step prohibited by the terms of a Senate decree of 60 and Caesar's *lex de repetundis* of 59.[6] Although the practical consequences of the plebiscite for Athens may have been relatively minor, there is no doubt that formally it placed the sovereign city under the jurisdiction of a Roman official. Further proof, in addition to Cicero's clear but prejudiced statements against Clodius, is offered by the dedication of a religious association on Delos devoted to the cult of Hermes; the inscription, in both Greek and Latin, is dated not by the name of the Athenian *epimeletes* or the eponymous archon, but by the name of the proconsul of Macedonia, the same Lucius Calpurnius Piso, who had acquired authority over Delos as part of the Athenian state.[7] Clodius' law of 58 turned Athens from a partner into a vassal of Rome. It is certain that the situation created by this *lex Clodia* came to an end when Piso ceased to be governor in 55, and that Athens regained its former status as an independent ally of Rome. But after all that had occurred, this amounted to little more than the conversion of formal dependency into de facto subjugation, however unofficial. Politically minded people in both Athens and Rome remained aware of what had transpired; if something had happened once, it could happen again, as long as one partner in the alliance was so much more powerful than the other. Officials of the *de jure* sovereign city had few means at their disposal to resist the directives of the Roman government and its representatives, and not many more when influential private citizens of Rome importuned them with personal demands. We cannot explain otherwise why the Areopagus gave its consent to the son-in-law of the once all-powerful dictator Sulla, Gaius Memmius, to tear down Epicurus' house to build his own palace on the site, or why even Cicero did not believe the Areopagus could be persuaded to

---

6. I am grateful to J.-L. Ferrary for this detailed information.

7. I *Délos* 1737, from 57/6 or 56/5. R. Etienne's attempt to place this text in the year 115/4 (*Ténos,* vol. 2 [Paris 1990] 255, no. 4) seems unconvincing.

reverse its decision.[8] Less than a decade was to pass before the outbreak of the civil war between Caesar and Pompey created conditions under which Roman leaders could no longer allow themselves to respect the privileged "independent" status of those Greek states that could still claim it.

In 58 a law of the consuls also freed Delos from certain taxes imposed by Sulla after Mithridates' troops had left the island.[9] Still an Athenian possession, Delos had suffered badly during the Third Mithridatic War in the previous decade. Athenodorus, a pirate allied with the Pontic king, had raided the island in 69, capturing many of its inhabitants to sell them into slavery, and damaging sacred images.[10] In the course of these depredations a fire occurred at a house recently excavated by French archaeologists and discovered to contain the remains of a private archive: 14,000 clay seals of the kind once attached to documents had been baked by the conflagration. The collection contained seals from at least a sixty-year period, for the oldest surviving one dates from 128/7.[11] Gaius Valerius Triarius, an officer serving under Lucullus, recaptured Delos in 69, supported by ships provided upon Roman demand by the Ionian cities Smyrna and Miletus. The island's inhabitants and ships' crews erected several monuments in Triarius' honor on Delos, and he employed the crews in building a wall with watchtowers at intervals, designed to offer better protection from invaders in the future.[12] Traces of this wall have been discovered, and its course can still be followed for a considerable stretch.[13] It is also mentioned in the much later chronicle of Phlegon of Tralles.[14]

The consuls' law of 58 mentioned the destruction wreaked upon Delos by Mithridates and the pirates, and represented an attempt, initiated by the Senate, to improve economic conditions on the island. There is some irony in the fact that Piso, one of the two consuls who presented the law to the people, was made ruler of Athens by the

8. Cicero *Ad Atticum* 5.11.6.

9. I *Délos* 1511, now with improved readings and commentary in C. Nicolet, ed., *Insula sacra: La loi Gabinia-Calpurnia de Délos (58 av. J.-C.)* (Paris 1980).

10. Phlegon, *FGrHist* 257 F 12 and 13.

11. M.-F. Boussac, *RA* (1988) II 307–340 and *Les sceaux de Délos*, vol. 1 (Athens 1992).

12. I *Délos* 1621 and 1855–58. See esp. J.-L. Ferrary, in Nicolet, *Insula sacra* 35–44. Triarius had bronze coins struck that year, perhaps to pay the workmen; 19 such coins have been found on the island and one in the Agora in Athens (Kroll, *Coins* 84 and 250, no. 830).

13. P. Bruneau and J. Ducat, *Guide de Délos*[3] (Paris 1983) 198–199, no. 69, with plan 2 facing 161 and plan 6 facing 247.

14. Phlegon, *FGrHist* 257 F 12.13. His chronicle dates from the reign of Hadrian.

plebiscite of Clodius at that time, and that in the law the consuls praised the "loyalty of Athens, this renowned city," at the very moment that its rights were being trampled underfoot.[15]

Delos must have experienced a considerable decline in trade as a result of the First Mithridatic War; however, the inscriptions found there create the impression that a return to prewar conditions took place within a few years. Several documents from 80/79 suggest quite normal activities: the decree awarding honors to the Roman proquaestor Manius Aemilius Lepidus in the name of "the Athenians, Romans, and other Greeks resident in Delos and the merchants and shipowners present";[16] the similar honors for another Roman, T. Manlius Torquatus;[17] and the honors voted by the ephebes to the gymnasiarch, who that year was none other than the son of the *epimeletes* then in office.[18] Nor are these the only indications of an at least outward normalization in the following years.[19]

After the catastrophe of 69 but before passage of the consuls' law of 58, the Athenians on the island and the private association for the cult of Pompey erected a monument to Pompeius Magnus.[20] "The Romans in Delos" appear in an inscription for the last time in 54/3, when they joined the resident Athenians, merchants, and shipowners in placing a statue to the *epimeletes* in office.[21] In 48 the Athenians alone honored Caesar with a statue immediately after his victory over Pompey at Pharsalus.[22]

2. Romans in Athens

According to tradition, the first Roman visitors to Athens were envoys from the Senate, who in 228 came to explain Rome's military intervention in Illyria. After 200, masses of Roman military personnel of high and low rank and many ordinary soldiers and sailors arrived for

---

15. Law quoted in n. 9, lines 6–7.

16. I *Délos* 1659. Lepidus received honors in the same year from Priene in Ionia; F. Hiller von Gaertringen, *Inschriften von Priene* (Berlin 1906) 244.

17. I *Délos* 1660. For Torquatus see T. R. S. Broughton, *The Magistrates of the Roman Republic*, vol. 3 (Atlanta 1986) 136–137.

18. I *Délos* 1935.

19. See Ferrary, in Nicolet, *Insula sacra* 35–44.

20. I *Délos* 1641.

21. I *Délos* 1662.

22. I *Délos* 1587, with the restoration of line 4 by A. E. Raubitschek, *JRS* 44 (1954) 65.

varying lengths of time. For a considerable period all the known civilian visitors were people of rank, some—mostly diplomats—on official missions, and others on their way to administrative posts in provinces further east. The "philosophers' embassy" of 155 had kindled in educated Romans an interest in Greek philosophy and rhetoric, and from that time on, members of this class whose travels led them to or through Athens made it a point to attend lectures by the teachers of these subjects. The next step was to send their sons to study there for longer periods.

In addition to these visitors, some Romans came and stayed. As in other parts of the Greek world, from the second century on we encounter a growing number of Roman names in lists of residents of Athens and Attica, or names with both Greek and Roman components.[23] Many of them are identified as *Romaioi*, namely Roman citizens or Italians, for the latter were also referred to as Romans in the second century, even before they officially became citizens of Rome in the aftermath of the Social War of 90–88. In any event, persons described as "Romans" were not citizens of Athens. But many others with wholly or partly Roman names are listed with an indication of the Attic community (demotic) or the name of the tribe to which they belonged, signalling that they were Athenian citizens. Almost without exception, inscriptions provide these data; before they can be evaluated it is necessary to investigate whether the members of the latter category were Athenian by birth or naturalization.

In some cases an unambiguous result cannot be obtained. For example, *Leukios* is an old Greek name, especially prevalent in Ionia and Attica; a man called *Leukios* may have been either a Greek, or a Roman with the name Lucius.[24] Only when it occurs in combination with Roman *gens* can we be certain that the family was of Roman origin, even if the bearer of the name may himself have possessed Athenian citizenship.[25] Further ambiguities are names with one Roman and

---

23. R. M. Errington covers the subject more broadly in *Alte Geschichte und schaftsgeschichte. Festschrift Karl Christ* (Darmstadt 1988) 140–157. I am indebted findings in much of what follows.

24. In the pre-Augustan era it is documented in at least 12 Attic demes. Nonethel scholars continue to treat it as of Roman origin in every case; see, e.g., E. Rawson, *A* 73 (1985) 64.

25. Thus, e.g., Λεύκιος Ποπίλλιος ἐξ Οἴου (*IG* II².2461.6) was of Ro but an Athenian citizen of the tribe of Leontis and the deme Oion Kerameikor Λευκίου Ῥωμαῖος (*IG* II².2460.5), on the other hand, was a Roman Λεύκιος Θεογείτονος Πειραιεύς (*IG* II².2463.9) a native-born Athenian

Greek component, if the Roman element is the given name and not the *nomen gentile,* as in the case of Seleucus, son of Marcus, of Marathon. He was a winner in a senior boys' event at the Theseia in 153/2, later serving as gymnasiarch on Delos in 129/8 and as a *strategos* in the second half of the century.[26] Nothing suggests that his father, Marcus, who must have been born about 200, was of Roman origin; it appears more likely that Marcus' father simply gave his son a Roman name, at about the time Athens and Rome first entered into close contact with one another. The same probably holds true for Marcus, son of Plutarch of Phalerum, a member of the Athenian Council shortly before 60;[27] and the athlete Menodorus, son of Gnaeus, an Athenian citizen of the late second century B.C.[28]

During the entire second century only one Roman is known to have served in an official capacity in the Athenian state, namely "Spurius the Roman" (Sporios Romaios), who acted as one of more than sixty *hieropoioi,* or cult officials, at the Ptolemaea in the year of the archon Lysiades, about 150.[29] From about 130 on, the corps of ephebes, previously open only to sons of Athenian citizens, became accessible to foreigners. The ephebes of foreign origin are listed for the first time for 123/2, separately from the citizens' sons; they number 14 (out of a total of at least 108), of whom 4 are identified as "Romans."[30] They acquired the full rights of citizens upon completion of their service and also became eligible for membership in the Council and service as magistrates when they reached the age of thirty. No evidence exists that a single Roman citizen received Athenian citizenship before this time.

---

26. As winner in a festival event: *IG* II².958.II.74; as *gymnasiarch: I Délos* 2589.48 and 1558; as *strategos: IG* II².2866.

27. *Agora* XV.267.11.

28. L. Moretti, *Iscrizioni agonistiche greche* (Rome 1953) no. 51.

29. *IG* II².1938.40. A man named Μάαρκος performed an official function not long afterward, but it is not possible to identify him conclusively as a Roman (*IG* II².1939.15). In contrast to the other 66 names on this list, no father's name or deme is given for him, but also no ethnic. The Γάιος Γαίου Ἀχαρνεύς who served in various priesthoods on Delos in 128/7, 115/4, and 97/6, possibly two people, a father and son (Tracy, *Contributors* 195), could very well have been born in Athens, despite the Roman given name in two generations.

30. *IG* II².1031.4, 5, 11, and 12. It was recognized as part of the decree *IG* II².1006 from 123/2 by O. Reinmuth, *Hesperia* 41 (1972) 185–191 (overlooked by Errington in *Alte Geschichte* 149). The citizens' sons named in the same decree, [Γ]άιος Γαίου Πειραιεύς and Γάιος Μαάρκου Μελ[ιτεύς] (IV.106 and III.122), are not necessarily of Roman descent.

It is known with certainty that during the second century growing numbers of Roman citizens settled in Athens for varying lengths of time but did not become naturalized citizens. Many may have had no desire to do so, for acceptance of Athenian citizenship could have meant loss of their status as citizens of Rome. However, an Assembly decree from the middle of the second century shows that they could receive other privileges normally limited to Athenians, such as *enktesis,* the right to own land in Attica.[31] This decree represents the last known case in which this right was granted, and the recipient was a Roman.

By the first century B.C. Romans who had become naturalized Athenian citizens were no longer a rarity, and by the second half of the century there were clearly large numbers of them. A certain Kointos (Quintus) served as mint magistrate in 89/8 and 86/5, but since only his given name is known, it is not possible to establish definitely that he was of Roman origin. Among the archons of 56/5 we find the eponymous archon Quintus, son of Quintus, from Rhamnus, and the thesmothete Leukios, son of Decimus, from Perithoidae,[32] and an Athenaeus, son of Marcus, from Stiria, as thesmothete in 14/3.[33] All three may have been of Roman origin, but it is quite possible that they were Athenian citizens and sons of Athenian citizens. In the case of another thesmothete from the Augustan era, Leukios Seppius from Kephisia, his Roman identity is established through the use of his Roman family name.[34] In 60/59 and 59/8 two Athenian officials of Roman origin are documented (although their function is unknown): Decimus Aufidius and Publius Ofrius. As magistrates they must have been Athenian citizens.[35] At about the same time we encounter the first Athenians of Roman descent as members of the Council.[36] In light of the foregoing one can say that the Romans who settled in Athens could not acquire citizenship until the last quarter of the second century;

31. *IG* II².907 for Λεύκιος Ο[. .] Ῥωμαῖος, with commentary by J. Pecírka, *The Formula for the Grant of Enktesis in Attic Inscriptions* (Prague 1966) 118–120. The decree was inscribed between 169 and 134; Tracy, *ALC* 148.

32. *IG* II².1717.1–2 and 13.

33. *IG* II².1721.10.

34. *IG* II².1922.9. For the dating see P. Graindor, *Chronologie des archontes athéniens sous l'empire* (Brussels 1922) 50 n. 16.

35. *IG* II².1716, col. II.18, 20; Errington, in *Alte Geschichte* 155.

36. *Agora* XV.272.2; 14; 273.53. Both inscriptions date from about 50 B.C. Of slightly later date are *Agora* XV.285.7, 286.28, 286.51, and *Hesperia* 14 (1978) 296, no. 21.19 and 26.

more often, we may assume, they acquired it not for themselves but for their sons, by sending them to the corps of ephebes. It is certainly no coincidence that from the latter part of the second century on, we know of = no more cases in which citizenship was awarded by decree of the *ekklesia*. Either they ceased to occur (or became very rare), or the Athenians ceased recording them in stone inscriptions.[37] It seems highly unlikely that such awards stopped altogether, but their numbers probably did drop, as the possibility of acquiring citizenship through *ephebia* reduced the need for them. This matches the observation that no cases of new Athenian citizens of Roman descent serving as magistrates or members of the Council are documented before the first century; they occur only occasionally in the first half and become relatively frequent by the second half of the first century.

Studies made of the increasing numbers of Romans and Italians active in the eastern Mediterranean during the last two centuries B.C. indicate that a high proportion of them were tax collectors, money-lenders, traders, and their employees, some of whom were unscrupulous in their practices.[38] Malcolm Errington deserves credit for demonstrating recently that many others were drawn to the east not by a desire for profits but by a fondness for Greek culture, such as Titus Albucius or Titus Pomponius Atticus. They came not to exploit but to study Greek life, and wished to live among Greeks. They participated actively in the life of their communities, donated money to civic causes, and frequently became citizens and paid taxes. When Cornelius Balbus, a Spanish-born aide to Julius Caesar, was accused in 56 of having unlawfully obtained Roman citizenship, Cicero successfully defended Balbus with the argument that he himself had encountered several Roman citizens in Athens who had taken Athenian citizenship and been admitted to a tribe and an Attic deme; they had served as judges and even as members of the Areopagus, unaware of the law that said a Roman lost his citizenship if he became the citizen of a foreign power.[39] It is immaterial in our context whether the view that acceptance of a second citizenship automatically meant loss of a Roman citizen's rights was still

---

37. M. J. Osborne finds that awards of citizenship ceased to be registered in inscriptions soon after 140; *Naturalization* 2: 191. Tracy dates the citizenship award inscribed in *IG* II^2.982 (= Osborne, D 113) to ca. 130; *ALC* 241.

38. J. Hatzfeld, *Les trafiquants italiens dans l'Orient hellénique* (Paris 1919); A. J. N. Wilson, *Emigration from Italy in the Republican Age of Rome* (Manchester 1966).

39. Cicero *Pro Balbo* 29–30 (cf. *Pro Caecina* 100).

generally held at the time of Cicero's speech.[40] What is important is his confirmation that a considerable number of Roman citizens were known to have become Athenian citizens and served not only as judges but even as archons, for Cicero refers to them as Areopagites.[41] In the very year of his speech in Balbus' defense, there were among the current archons two men with Roman names, who may have originally been Roman citizens.[42] Cicero mentions the reverse case in his *Philippics* of 43, where he notes that Mark Antony arranged for Lysiades, son of the Epicurean philosopher Phaedrus and a member of one of the foremost Athenian families, to be admitted to a Roman *decuria* of judges, thereby securing for him not only citizenship but also entry into the highest circles in Rome.[43]

Since Roman citizenship was a prerequisite for Lysiades' career in Rome, his case exemplifies the other side of the coin, namely the integration of Greeks into Roman society. Understandably, this process set in later than the integration of Romans into Greek communities, and did not occur to any great extent until the time of Caesar, Antony, and Octavian/Augustus. Within the context of Hellenistic Athenian history it thus plays a minimal role, although it has great significance for the history of the city at the time of the Roman empire. Presumably most city officials with Roman names encountered toward the end of the Hellenistic age were Romans who had taken Athenian citizenship. In the later period they are just as likely to have been Athenians who had been awarded Roman citizenship; in many cases such men are recognizable by the Greek cognomen following two Roman names.

Presumably a number of Romans chose to settle in Athens because Delos was in Athenian hands, for it is unlikely that the growing number of Roman traders on Delos would have failed to maintain agents in the city where all important administrative matters involving Delos were decided. It is also quite possible that wealthy Roman merchants preferred to reside in Athens instead of on the island, and that agents managed their business affairs on Delos. However, there is hardly any evidence of Romans residing in Athens before the early first century,

40. It is often assumed that Atticus refused an offer of Athenian citizenship (Nepos *Atticus* 3.1) only because he did not want to lose his Roman citizenship.

41. If one takes Cicero at his word that he had seen such men with his own eyes ("vidi egomet Athenis"), then this must also apply to the much earlier date of 79.

42. Those mentioned above in the text, with note 32; *IG* II^2.1717.1–2 and 13.

43. Cicero *Phil.* 5.14; *Phil.* 8.27; Rawson, *Athenaeum* 73 (1985) 55.

until Titus Pomponius Atticus arrived in the 80s and remained for twenty years. Jean Hatzfeld believed he had discovered proof of Roman residents in a decree he ascribed to the second or first century, but he overlooked Adolf Wilhelm's proof that the inscription actually refers to Pagai in Boeotia and to Romans residing there at the time of Pompey.[44] Among the thousands of surviving Athenian gravestones only two dating from the second century are for Roman citizens, along with one for a Roman lady.[45]

Finally, a third category of longtime Roman residents in Athens should be mentioned, namely persons of high rank forced to leave Rome as a result of banishment or to avoid banishment and who chose Athens as the place to spend their exile. The first Roman of whom this is reported is none other than Titus Albucius, who, as a young man, resided in Athens before the year 120, out of a love of Greece and its culture, and who was mocked for his Greek airs by a visiting Roman official. Albucius became praetor shortly before the turn of the century and governor of Sardinia the following year. After serving his year-long term he was accused of corruption and found guilty. It was only natural for him to spend his exile in a city he had previously sought out voluntarily. According to Cicero he spent a considerable period studying philosophy as a disciple of the Epicurean school.[46] In another case Gaius Aurelius Cotta was convicted in a political trial in the year 90, in the overheated atmosphere of the Social War, and moved to Athens. He returned to Rome when Sulla emerged as the victor of the civil war at the end of 82, and became consul in 75.[47] Gaius Memmius, one of the candidates for consul who became embroiled in a major scandal in 53 and was convicted in 52, was a gifted intellectual who wrote poetry and had an interest in philosophy. Athens may have struck him as the site where he could best endure his banishment.[48]

A few years earlier an incomparably greater man also briefly considered spending his exile in Athens: Marcus Tullius Cicero. On 29 April 58, just before leaving Italy on his way into exile, he wrote to Atticus

44. Hatzfeld, *Les trafiquants italiens* 41; A. Wilhelm, *JÖAI* 10 (1907) 17–32 (= *Abhandlungen und Beiträge zur griechischen Inschriftenkunde*, vol. 1 [Leipzig 1984] 261–276).

45. *IG* II².10153, 10155, and 10157.

46. Cicero *Tusc. disp.* 5.108.

47. E. Gruen, *Roman Politics and the Criminal Courts, 149–78 B.C.* (Cambridge 1968) 218–219. He notes, "The dictator evidently rescinded Cotta's banishment" (237).

48. F. Münzer, "Memmius," *RE* (1931) 609–616. For his role in the dispute over Epicurus' house see Chapter 14, Section 3.

from Brindisi and briefly mentioned that the thought had occurred to him; however, he had rejected it immediately out of a fear for his own safety, saying, "Now my enemies are there."[49] He decided instead in favor of Thessaloniki, where he spent the next six months. During the civil wars that soon followed Athens numbered among the cities where those on the losing side could find a refuge, as Aulus Manlius Torquatus did after the battle of Pharsalus; in 46 and 45 he was on friendly terms with Sulpicius Rufus, Caesar's governor, and corresponded with Cicero.[50]

Those Romans who settled in Athens in the second century or in the first half of the first century were considered guests of the city, resident aliens or metics in the terminology of earlier days.[51] Over time and as political conditions changed, Athenians came to see their Roman "guests" increasingly as representatives of the ruling power. The Romans who resided there must have viewed themselves more and more in this light, at no time more strongly than in 58–55, the years of Athens' official subjection under the law of Clodius.

In view of the long-standing close political ties between Athens and Rome it is somewhat surprising that no award of public honors to a Roman official is documented until relatively late. The first such official was Sextus Pompeius in 119 or 118, when he was killed by Celts while serving as proconsul of Macedonia.[52] This first documented case is of course not necessarily the first such honor awarded, but that it occurred fully eighty years after the creation of close ties betwee Athens and Rome is remarkable. The next award of this kind occurs fully a generation later, namely a statue for Gnaeus Pompeius, the son of Sextus holding the same office as governor of Macedonia in 92.[53] Next followed Sulla, who also received a statue in his honor, presumably in 86–84.[54] At the end of the 70s the Lucullus brothers received the same

---

49. Cicero *Ad Atticum* 3.7.1: "quod si auderem, Athenas peterem . . . nunc et nostri hostes ibi sunt et te non habemus."

50. Cicero *Fam.* 6.4.5; F. Münzer, "Manlius," *RE* (1928) 1194–99.

51. The concept of metic status was apparently abandoned in Athens around or soon after 300; D. Whitehead, *The Ideology of the Athenian Metic* (Cambridge 1977) 163–167. However, metics still appear in an unpublished inscription at Rhamnus from the middle of the third century (information kindly supplied by B. Petrakos).

52. *IG* II^2.4100; Broughton, *Magistrates* 3: 160. The honorand was the grandfather of Pompey the Great.

53. *IG* II^2.4101; Broughton, *Magistrates* 3: 165–166.

54. *IG* II^2.4103 and in more complete form in *Bulletin épigraphique* (1969) 163.

honor: Marcus Terentius Varro Lucullus, the consul of 73, as governor of Macedonia soon after his term as consul;[55] and Lucius Licinius Lucullus, consul in 74 and a commander in the Third Mithridatic War, who was honored with two statues.[56] Another proconsul of Macedonia, Gaius Cosconius, received a statue between 53 and 51.[57]

Inscriptions from the period of the civil war illustrate in a dramatic series of events the political vicissitudes to which Athens was subjected. At the beginning we have an inscription for Appius Claudius Pulcher, consul of 54, whom Pompey appointed governor of Greece in 48. The award of honors and the statue that went with them must have been voted in the first half of the year, for he died before the battle of Pharsalus was fought that summer.[58] The political shift following Pompey's defeat is reflected by the erection of a statue to Caesar that same year (48)[59] and a second monument the following year.[60] Only a few years later the Athenians paid their respects to his murderers by putting up statues to Brutus and Cassius.[61] After they were both killed at Philippi two years later, the victor in the battle, Mark Antony, became the new master of Greece and Athens, and honors were accordingly awarded to him and his chief lieutenants.

3. In the Civil Wars

The four-year-long war unleashed by Caesar when he crossed the Rubicon into Italy in January 49 ought to have remained a purely Roman affair, as it concerned Romans and Romans alone on both sides. In fact, however, in its first phase—up to Pompey's defeat at Pharsalus in August 48—the main theater of fighting was Greece. When Pompey fled Italy after Caesar's fierce attack on 17 March 49, he and his armies landed in Greece; from then on the Greek states could only watch helplessly as the war engulfed them. Pompey was able to build up a

---

55. *Hesperia* 23 (1954) 253, no 35.

56. *IG* II^2.4104 and 4105 (in more complete form in *SEG* 29.179). The inscription *IG* II^2.4233 concerns his daughter Licinia.

57. *IG* II^2.4106; Broughton, *Magistrates* 3: 77.

58. *IG* II^2.4109; Broughton, ibid. In the same year he was also honored by the city of Carystus on Euboea; *Hesperia* 23 (1954) 128–140.

59. Raubitschek, *JRS* 44 (1954) 65–66. Cf. Appian *Bell. civ.* 2.368; Cassius Dio 42.14.2–3.

60. *IG* II^2.3222 (*SEG* 14.122).

61. *SEG* 17.75 (Brutus); Cassius Dio 47.20.4 (Brutus and Cassius).

strong second front in Greece, thanks to the great prestige he commanded throughout the eastern Mediterranean and the personal contacts and numerous resources on which he could draw. Reinforcements joined him from all sides, many from great distances.

Most Greek states had no choice but to provide Pompey with the support he demanded from them, be it troops or supplies or both. Athens may have wanted to remain neutral,[62] but found itself in Pompey's camp within a short time. The city contributed a small number of ships (no more than three, according to the perhaps understated account of the poet Lucan) to Pompey's already vastly superior fleet operating in the Ionian Sea; the Athenians' primary task was to prevent Caesar's forces from crossing into Greece.[63] The contingent of Athenian infantry in Pompey's army appears to have been larger, for Lucan, now apparently exaggerating, reports that conscription took the lion's share of men of fighting age.[64] The Athenian contingent, in whom Pompey is said to have placed great hopes, occupied a position in the battle order near the Italian legions.[65]

Some time before the battle Caesar broadened his base of operations in Greece by sending his legate Quintus Fufius Calenus south from Illyria with fifteen cohorts. The chief aim of the operation was to reach the Peloponnese. On his march southward Calenus took Delphi and the cities of Thebes and Orchomenus in Boeotia without a fight and successfully stormed several others.[66] He also occupied Piraeus, which was no longer fortified. He was unable to take Athens, however, defended for Pompey, and had to be content with ravaging the coun-

---

62. This appears to be the import of a somewhat puzzling passage in Appian *Bell. civ.* 2.293. A few months before the decisive battle Caesar's legate Dolabella wrote from the camp near Durazzo to his father-in-law, Cicero, who was with Pompey, recommending that he withdraw from both parties and go to Athens or (another) quiet place (Cicero *Fam.* 9.9). However, Athens was then already firmly allied with Pompey.

63. Lucan *Pharsalia* 3.181–183: "exhausit totus quamvis dilectus Athenas, / exiguae Phoebea tenent navalia puppes / tresque petunt verum credi Salamina carinae," meaning that the number of ships was so small that one could hardly have believed that Athens really won the victory at Salamis. Livy (presumably Lucan's source) wrote: "nam Athenienses de tanta maritima gloria vix duas naves effecere" (109, fr. 36). Caesar also names Athens as one of the states that contributed ships to Pompey's fleet, suggesting that the number was perhaps not so small after all.

64. Lucan *Pharsalia* 3.181: "exhausit totus quamvis dilectus Athenas," paraphrased by Housman as "Athenae quamquam dilectu habito omnem eduxerunt iuventutem." The translations by W. Ehlers and J. D. Duff are similar.

65. Appian *Bell. civ.* 2.315.

66. Caesar *Bell. civ.* 3.56; Cassius Dio 42.14.1.

tryside.[67] Shortly before the battle of Pharsalus Calenus and his troops returned to the vicinity of Athens and Megara (the isthmus being blocked by Pompey's troops), and Caesar contemplated drawing them in as reinforcements before meeting Pompey's numerically far superior forces; but his army allegedly insisted on engaging the enemy at once.[68]

Athens surrendered to Caesar immediately after his victory. He pardoned the city, like Sulla before him, for the sake of its dead, meaning—as Cassius Dio explains—that he spared the living out of respect for the fame and courage of their ancestors.[69] Appian's account is more precise. He reports that Caesar issued his order to spare the inhabitants within two days after the battle, before leaving Pharsalus. This is quite possible, since it is likely that in anticipation of the outcome an Athenian delegation was waiting nearby, ready either to congratulate the victor and praise their own share in the victory or to throw themselves on his mercy, as the case might be. According to Appian, Caesar greeted the suppliants by asking, "How often do you expect to be rescued from the ruin you bring on yourselves by the fame of your forefathers?"[70] The verbal punishment, undeserved as it may have been, was still a tolerable outcome. Megara, unlike Athens, remained loyal to the defeated side after the battle, and was taken by Calenus partly by force, partly through treachery, and severely punished, before he had to relinquish one of his legions for Caesar's Egyptian campaign.[71]

The Athenians showed their gratitude to Caesar for having spared them with a statue and an inscription praising him as "savior and benefactor."[72] Another statue of Caesar with a similar inscription was dedicated at the same time by the community of Athenian citizens on Delos.[73]

It is widely assumed that after Caesar's victory over Pharnaces of Pontus and the end of the Alexandrine War he visited Athens the

---

67. Cassius Dio 42.14.1. The centurion in Pompey's 2nd Legion named N. Granonius from Luceria presumably was killed in this fighting (A. Degrassi, *Inscriptiones Latinae Liberae Rei Publicae*[2], vol. 1 [Florence 1957], no. 502).

68. Plut. *Caesar* 43.1.

69. Cassius Dio 42.14.2.

70. Appian *Bell. civ.* 2.368.

71. Cassius Dio 42.14.3; Plut. *Brutus* 8.2. Calenus was honored the same year with statues in various places, including Oropus (*IG* VII.380) and Olympia (W. Dittenberger and K. Purgold, *Inschriften von Olympia* [Berlin 1896] 330).

72. Raubitschek, *JRS* 44 (1954) 65–66; cf. also 68–69 on *IG* II[2].3222.

73. I *Délos* 1587, with Raubitschek's restoration, ibid., 65.

following year, on his way back to Rome. All that is known with certainty, however, is that Cicero, waiting for Caesar's return in Brindisi, wrote to Atticus in August 47 expressing doubts whether Caesar could arrive in Athens on 1 September, since he was clearly still detained in Asia Minor.[74] It is by no means established that he actually did visit Athens, and all discussion of details concerning his presumed stay, such as the possibility that he supervised the start of construction on the Roman Agora,[75] is groundless speculation.

The civil war continued for another year and a half, but in Africa and Spain, and Greece was spared further fighting. Nonetheless, most of the surviving reports of Athens in this period stem from a Roman source, namely Cicero, in his correspondence and late philosophical writings. One reason for this is his friendship with a former consul and jurist by the name of Servius Sulpicius Rufus, who served as Caesar's governor of the province of Achaea in 46–45 and appears to have spent a considerable amount of time in Athens. Another reason is the presence of Cicero's son Marcus in the city.

Two of Sulpicius Rufus' letters to Cicero from Athens are particularly noteworthy, the first from March 45 and the second from the end of May. The first is a letter of condolence to Cicero after the death of his daughter, Tullia, at a time when he was struggling to regain his equanimity. Rufus urged his friend to view his personal loss in relation to events in the outside world, such as the decline of great cities and the end of the Roman state. He described a recent trip he had taken through the Saronic Gulf, on which he had seen Aegina, Megara, Piraeus, and Corinth, all formerly flourishing cities now "laid low and in ruins". Tullia had been able to savor life almost to the fullest before she died, but had lived to see the death of the republic.[76] At the time Corinth, razed in 146, did in fact not exist, but was reestablished only a few months later by Caesar as a Roman colony. Megara, as mentioned, had recently suffered great damage from Calenus in punishment for its stubborn loyalty to Caesar's enemies. But as for the other two cities, it could truthfully be said only that they had seen better days and that their greatness lay in the past. Rufus' desire to give comfort led him greatly to overstate the case, and although his observation on

---

74. Cicero *Ad Atticum* 11.21.2. A visit to Athens by Caesar in 47 is presumed by M. Gelzer, among others; *Caesar, der Politiker und Staatsmann*[6] (Wiesbaden 1960) 241.

75. T. L. Shear Jr., *Hesperia* 50 (1981) 358.

76. Cicero *Fam.* 4.5.4–5.

the end of the Roman state may have agreed with Cicero's opinion, it sounds rather odd coming from someone quite willing to hold office under Caesar.

On 31 May Sulpicius Rufus wrote to Cicero to tell him of the death of a mutual friend:[77] Marcus Claudius Marcellus, who had been Rufus' colleague as consul in 51 but became one of Caesar's most outspoken and determined foes, attempting—unsuccessfully—to have him recalled from Gaul. Marcellus had taken part in the civil war against Caesar, but had given up the republican cause as hopeless after Pompey's defeat at Pharsalus. He had withdrawn for the remainder of the war to the island of Lesbos, and resisted the temptation to request a pardon from Caesar. Caesar harbored a particular grudge against Marcellus, and when, yielding to the urging of the entire Senate, he pardoned him in the fall of 46, it created a sensation. In the spring of 45 Marcellus set out for Rome. Sulpicius Rufus came from Epidaurus to meet him on 23 May in Piraeus, where Marcellus planned to spend a few days before continuing his journey. Rufus spent a day with him before returning, but was summoned back again almost immediately: during the night of 26 May he was notified that Marcellus and Magius Cilo, a friend from his days in exile, had quarreled, and Cilo, after gravely wounding Marcellus, had taken his own life. Rufus rushed to Piraeus with several physicians but was met outside the city and told that Marcellus had just died of his injuries. He ended his letter to Cicero with the following passage:

> I saw to his funeral, on as handsome a scale as the resources of Athens could provide. I could not induce the townspeople to grant him burial within the city precincts; they pleaded a religious bar, and it is a fact that they had never given such permission in the past. The next best thing they did allow, to bury him in a public hall, whichever I wished. So I chose a spot in the most celebrated hall in the world, the Academy. There we cremated him, and I later saw to it that the people of Athens should arrange for the erection of a monument to him in marble on the spot. So I have done all that in me lay for my colleague and kinsman, in life and in death.[78]

77. Cicero Fam. 4.12; the other sources are in F. Münzer, "Magius," RE (1928) 441–442.

78. Translation by D. R. Shackleton Bailey, Cicero's Letters to His Friends, vol. 2 (New York 1978) 24–25.

For a long time an inscription from the base of a statue found on the Acropolis was connected with this famous former consul Marcellus, erected in his honor and that of his wife during their lifetime, and from which his name, but not that of his wife, was later expunged (by Mark Antony, scholars assumed).[79] However, a plausible explanation for eradicating the name of the man pardoned by Caesar had been elusive until J. H. Oliver demonstrated that the Marcellus honored by the monument was in fact a different and later man found guilty of *lèse majesté* in the imperial age. He was probably Marcus Marcellus Aeserninus, praetor in 19 A.D. and almost certainly consul in a later year.[80]

During the years of Caesar's supremacy, 48–44, Athens retained its constitution, which granted the aristocracy favored status. One proof that the old system continued is Cicero's observation that in 45–44 the Areopagus remained the true governing body of the city.[81] It was therefore the Areopagus to which he appealed in 45/4 in connection with a political matter. He persuaded the Areopagites to pass a measure he hoped would induce Cratippus of Pergamum, a philosopher and teacher of Cicero's son Marcus, to remain in Athens and continue his teaching. The decree praises him in the highest terms, as an "ornament" to the city.[82] Cicero, on his way to his post in the province of Cilicia, had met Cratippus in Ephesus in 51. In the following years Cratippus—who had begun as a member of the Academy but then joined the Peripatetics—taught in Mytilene, where his lectures were attended by the exiled Marcus Marcellus and by Marcus Brutus when he visited Marcellus. Shortly afterward Cratippus moved to Athens and began lecturing there. Cicero undertook more on his behalf than just motivating the Areopagus to pass a decree in his honor; he also procured Roman citizenship for him from Caesar. In gratitude Cratippus took Cicero's first name and *nomen gentile* as his Roman names, and

79. *IG* II[2].4111 in the revised edition by O. Broneer with an accompanying photograph, *AJA* 36 (1932) 393–397; Accame, *Dominio* 175.

80. J. H. Oliver, *AJPh* 68 (1947) 150–155; cf. *PIR*[2], ed. E. Groag and A. Stein (Berlin 1936) C 928. Oliver confuses M. Marcellus, the consul of 51, with C. Marcellus, consul of 49 (152).

81. Cicero *De natura deorum* 2.74; *De officiis* 1.75; Accame, *Dominio* 172–176; Rawson, *Athenaeum* 73 (1985) 63–65. The older, contrasting view was argued by W. Kolbe, W. S. Ferguson, and J. Kirchner, among others.

82. Plut. *Cicero* 24.7–8, where the account makes it clear that in this matter Cicero used Herodes of Marathon as an intermediary, the same man who had procured the large donation of money for Athens from Caesar in Gaul.

called himself henceforth Marcus Tullius Cratippus.[83] Cicero considered him the outstanding philosopher of his day[84] and urged his son to study with him. Whether or not he did, the two men were at least acquaintances and encountered each other frequently on other occasions.[85]

In the same period many other sons of Roman *nobiles* were also studying in Athens; they included Marcus Valerius Messalla Corvinus; Lucius Calpurnius Bibulus, the son of Caesar's unfortunate co-consul; Manlius Acidinus; and Manlius Torquatus, who befriended a student of nonaristocratic origins, the later poet Horace (Quintus Horatius Flaccus).[86] In addition to philosophy, emphasis was placed on Latin and Greek rhetoric, and Horace later said that he had acquired the greater polish from his Athenian training.[87] As sons of Roman aristocrats these young men had access to the leading families in the city. Herodes of Marathon, Leonides of Melite, and Epicrates of Leukonoe are all named in connection with Cicero's son,[88] and they reported to his father on his conduct and progress in his studies. The young Marcus, however, was more devoted to pleasures such as drinking wine than to his books. His father intended to give him a talking-to in person in the summer of 44, and only accidental circumstances forced him to break off this long-planned journey, on which he had already embarked.

Although these young men may have differed in the degree of seriousness with which they approached their studies, they shared a conservative attitude toward Caesar, regarding him with reserve or even open hostility. When Marcus Brutus visited Athens a few months after Caesar's murder, he found them eager to back him in taking up arms to rescue the old order. The civil war begun by Caesar thus entered its second phase, in which Caesar's supporters opposed his

83. Basic information on Cratippus is in A. O'Brien-Moore, *YClS* 8 (1942) 25–49; further information derived from inscriptions from Pergamum, Cratippus' home, is in C. Habicht, *Altertümer von Pergamon* VIII.3: *Die Inschriften des Asklepieions* (Berlin 1969) 164–165.

84. Cicero *De officiis* 1.2. and 3.5; *De divinatione* 1.5.

85. Cicero *Fam.* 16.21.3.

86. R. Hanslik, "Valerius," *RE* (1955) 137; F. Münzer, "Calpurnius," *RE* (1897) 1367–68; "Manlius," *RE* (1928) 1163 (Acidinus) and 1193 (Torquatus); E. Stemplinger, "Horatius," *RE* (1913) 2339.

87. Horace *Epist.* 2.2.41 and 43: "Romae nutiriri mihi contigit atque doceri . . . adiecere bonae paulo plus artis Athenae."

88. Cicero *Ad Atticum* 14.16.3; 18.4; and 15.16; *Fam.* 16.21.5; Rawson, *Athenaeum* 73 (1985) 44–66.

assassins. Athens soon found itself allied with the latter group, once again without much real choice in the matter.

On 15 March 44, Caesar succumbed to a conspiracy headed by Marcus Brutus and Gaius Cassius with more than sixty members of high rank. For two and a half years afterward the enmity between his supporters and the group behind his assassins (also thought of as supporters of Pompey) was the real driving force behind political developments. At first the fragile compromise effected between the parties acted as a brake, with one side agreeing to grant amnesty to the murderers, and the other acquiescing to the measures through which Caesar had filled key posts for many years to come. Developments were further interrupted for a considerable time by a power struggle within the pro-Caesar camp between consul Mark Antony and Caesar's great-nephew Octavian. This gave the assassins' allies time to gather strength and prepare for the coming battle.

Six months after Caesar's death Brutus and Cassius left Italy, which was growing too hot for them, allegedly to take charge of their provinces, Crete and Cyrene. It soon became evident, however, that their real purpose was to build up military support in the eastern Mediterranean, just as Pompey had done on departing from Italy five years earlier. Both had unexpected successes, Cassius in Syria and Brutus on the Balkan peninsula. But during this same period Caesar's political heirs managed to bury their feud in Italy, making renewed civil war inevitable. It took place in the fall of 42 in Macedonia, where two great battles were fought at Philippi, and ended with the downfall of Caesar's assassins and of the Roman republic. The victors divided the empire among themselves.

As things were building up to the outbreak of war, Athens was assigned a key role, namely mobilization of the Greek mainland under Brutus' banner. Brutus himself had arrived there with Cassius in October 44. Their presence in Greece received great attention because of the deed they had committed on the Ides of March. Cassius Dio reports that they were voted honors almost everywhere, and in Athens they were awarded an exceptional honor: Bronze statues of them were placed next to those of the tyrant-slayers Harmodius and Aristogeiton,[89] despite the regulation reserving this place for the two past heroes

89. Cassius Dio 47.20.4. A fragment of the inscription on the base of Brutus' statue was found in the Agora; see A. E. Raubitschek, *Atti del terzo congresso internazionale di epigrafia Greca e Latina* (Rome 1959) 15–21.

alone. The Athenians had departed from this custom only once before, when they awarded statues to their "liberators" Antigonus and Demetrius in 307. It is clear that the citizens of Athens also celebrated Brutus and Cassius as tyrant-slayers and recognized them as national heroes. With these acts the city aligned itself politically long before armed conflict broke out. Other statues to Brutus were dedicated at that time by the city of Oropus and by the Athenian community on Delos.[90] The Delian inscription makes particular mention of the benefits Athens had received from him.[91]

Brutus was not the first of the assassins to visit Athens after the deed. He had been preceded by Gaius Trebonius, a longtime aide of Caesar recently appointed to serve as proconsul of Asia; Trebonius was on his way there when he arrived on 22 May. On the third day of his visit he wrote to Cicero to tell him that he had seen his son and received a very positive impression, but also to make a personal request: should Cicero be planning to write something on Caesar's end, he would be grateful to him for portraying his own role in the proper light![92]

In October Brutus and Cassius were welcomed to Athens with great ceremony; when Cassius departed after a short visit, Brutus stayed on as the guest of an Athenian or Roman friend. He attended some lectures by Theomnestus at the Academy and Cratippus at the Peripatetic school, creating the impression of a man of leisure with time to indulge his interest in philosophy. Secretly, however, he was putting out feelers in all directions, supported by the young Romans living in Athens. They idolized him and were willing to do whatever they could on his behalf.[93] His uncle Hortensius, the governor of Macedonia, placed his office at Brutus' disposal, thereby giving him control of the province and the troops stationed there. Next Brutus went to Carystus on Euboea to meet quaestor Marcus Appuleius, on his way back from Asia with a large sum of money; Brutus persuaded him to join his cause and divert to him the funds intended for the state treasury in Rome.

90. I *Délos* 1622 for the proconsul of Macedonia, Quintus Hortensius, was part of an *exhedra* with four statues, one of which must have represented Marcus Brutus, for the inscription on the base of Hortensius' statue mentions him.

91. I *Délos* 1622.

92. Cicero *Fam.* 12.16. Only a few months later Trebonius paid a terrible penalty for the deed of which he was boasting here.

93. Plut. *Brutus* 24–26, also for the passage that follows. For the larger context see R. Syme, *The Roman Revolution* (Oxford 1939) 97–206. For Athens' role in these events see A. E. Raubitschek, *Phoenix* 7 (1957) 1–11.

Quaestor Gaius Antistius Vetus, returning from Syria, also placed his services at Brutus' disposal. Veterans from Pompey's army who had remained in Thessaly in 48 came south in droves.

Once events began to move so rapidly, Brutus can hardly have remained in Athens for long. The first developments drew him north to Macedonia, Epirus, and Illyria. Gaius Antonius, brother of Mark Antony, supposed to succeed Hortensius in Macedonia, arrived at the head of a legion. Marcus Brutus forced him to capitulate at Apollonia, and did the same to Publius Vatinius, the governor in Illyria appointed by Caesar. Their troops, added to his own, increased the strength of his rapidly growing army, in which young Cicero served with particular distinction. In February 43, in a decree naming Brutus proconsul of Macedonia, Achaea, and Illyricum, introduced by the elder Cicero, the Senate retroactively sanctioned these thoroughly illegal acts of force. By then Brutus controlled almost all of the Balkan peninsula and had taken command of all the troops stationed there. He went on to seize Thrace and from there crossed to Asia Minor at the end of 43, to meet Cassius in Smyrna. This ended Athens' role as Brutus' initial headquarters.

When an Athenian inscription of 44/3 from Delos mentions Brutus as a benefactor of the city, the question naturally arises as to what form his generosity or favorable action took. Some scholars have surmised that the inscription refers to a more democratic form of government that Brutus installed, citing a decree in honor of the ephebes from about the same time that could be interpreted to reflect such a change. However, there is no solid evidence for such "democratic reform" in this period, whether at the prompting of Brutus or anyone else.[94] It is thus not yet possible to identify the ways in which Brutus may have aided Athens.

There is also no evidence indicating that Athenians fought among Brutus' troops at Philippi in October 42 who were defeated by Mark Antony and Octavian. It is possible, and indeed probable, that Brutus took no Athenian contingent with him on crossing to Asia Minor, and when he and Cassius returned to Europe in 42, their army, made up mostly of trained and battle-tested Roman legionaries, was so vast that they probably thought it unnecessary to add Greek reinforcements. Athens had solidly aligned itself behind Caesar's assassins, the losers at

94. See Chapter 14, Section 1.

Philippi, but the city suffered no harm; in fact it soon reaped benefits from the presence of Mark Antony, who developed a particular fondness for the city, after the victors had carved up the empire among themselves: Antony took charge of administering Greece and the entire eastern half, whereas Octavian governed the west.

Antony spent the rest of 42 in Greece, part of it in Athens. Wherever he went, he proved himself to be a lenient judge and a friend of Greece. He attended athletic contests, the philologists' disputations, and philosophers' lectures and also participated in religious mysteries, although it is not known where; it can hardly have been the most famous of them, for the Eleusinian Mysteries had already been celebrated. He showed special favor to Athens, and liked nothing better than to be called "a friend of Athens."[95] Many of his closest associates and friends were honored with statues in Athens in the following years: Lucius Marcius Censorinus, his proconsul for Macedonia and Greece from 42 to 40;[96] and his close associate Lucius Munatius Plancus, the consul of 42, in 40;[97] his legate Gaius Cocceius Balbus sometime around 39;[98] and Sempronia, daughter of his legate Lucius Sempronius Atratinus, who received at least three statues in Athens and Eleusis in 39–37.[99] Another honoree was Marcus Antonius Aristocrates, a rhetorician and friend of the triumvir, who procured Roman citizenship for him.[100]

In the spring of 41 Antony went to Asia Minor and took up temporary residence in Ephesus. An Athenian delegation came to him there or in another city he visited, and asked for the island of Tenos. However, Antony had just promised it to Rhodes, as a reward to the Rhodians for their loyalty and as reparation for the misfortune brought upon them by Caesar's assassins. Instead of this island he gave the Athenians Aegina, Ceus, and the three northern Sporades: Ikos, Skiathos, and Peparethos.[101]

95. Plut. *Antonius* 23. For Eleusis see K. Clinton, *ANRW* II 18.2 (1989) 1506.

96. *IG* II^2.4113.

97. *IG* II^2.4112.

98. *IG* II^2.4110.

99. *IG* II^2.4230, 4231, and 5179. Atratinus and his wife Censorina were honored at the time in Patras (*SEG* 30.433).

100. *IG* II^2.3889; cf. Plut. *Antonius* 69.1. He was also honored in Argos: *IG* IV.581.

101. Appian *Bell. civ.* 5.30; P. Graindor, *Athènes sous Auguste* (Brussels 1927) 5–8. The island of Thasos, which had served as a supply base for Brutus and Cassius during their final campaign, was thus punished. It had been awarded Skiathos and Peparethos by the dictator Sulla and the Senate in 80 B.C. as a reward for its role in the First Mithridatic War (C. Dunant

After spending the winter of 41/0 in Alexandria, Antony returned to Athens in the spring of 40, where he met with his wife Fulvia after a long separation and learned that a war against him was looming in Italy. His younger brother Lucius, as consul the previous year, had become involved in a serious conflict with Octavian, in which Fulvia had also taken part. The dispute erupted over the repatriation and settlement of veterans and the related necessity of seizing property from landowners in Italy. Hostilities had broken out without Antony's knowledge, in the course of which Octavian laid siege to Lucius Antonius in February 40. Lucius Antonius was forced to capitulate, while Fulvia departed for Greece. Their meeting in Athens was not auspicious. Fulvia knew of her husband's infidelities, but had to listen to his reproaches for the role she had played in Italy. Antony soon embarked on the apparently unavoidable military campaign against his former partner; Fulvia remained behind and died not long afterward in Sicyon. Her death, convenient in a certain sense, paved the way for a new settlement between the two rulers in Brindisi, sealed by the marriage of Antony to Octavian's sister, Octavia, at the end of the year.

After a long stay in Italy in the late summer of 39, the couple moved on to Athens, which, along with Alexandria, became Antony's principal residence for the next few years, until the start of the war against Octavian. He felt especially at home in Athens, where he lived without ceremony, more or less as a private citizen. He moved around the city without a large train or official pomp, again attended lectures by the philosophers, and shared Greek meals with Greek guests.[102] He appeared uninterested in serious matters at this point, even though a sizable military operation against the Parthians was planned for the coming spring (38). His informality and accessibility made him a very popular figure in the city; Athens and Octavia seem to have exercised a positive influence on him, in contrast to Alexandria and Cleopatra.

---

and J. Pouilloux, *Recherches sur l'histoire et les cultes de Thasos,* vol. 2 [Paris 1958] 53–54). Eretria and Oropus may have come to Athens through Antony, but it is by no means certain that this is the correct interpretation of the passage in Cassius Dio (54.7.2); D. Knoepfler, *Chiron* 22 (1992) 455. Cf. J. Day, *An Economic History of Athens under Roman Domination* (New York 1942) 134–135; and G. W. Bowersock, *Augustus and the Greek World* (Oxford 1965) 106.

102. Appian *Bell. civ.* 5.322–324.

Octavia captured the hearts of the city's inhabitants. As an inscription from the Agora shows, both were celebrated by the citizens as "benevolent divinities."[103]

Not until the beginning of the military campaign season did Antony return to business and his role as an active and competent leader. The campaign of 38 did not go well, however, and could have turned into a catastrophe such as Crassus had experienced in 53, had not Antony again risen to the occasion, as he could when things went against him. He spent the following winter in Athens, adopting more and more Greek ways and outlook. Just as Hellenistic monarchs and Nicanor, Cassander's Macedonian commander in Piraeus, had undertaken city offices pro forma, such as director of the games for a festival or mint magistrate, so now Antony accepted the post of gymnasiarch. In this role he may have actually visited the boys practicing at the gymnasium.[104] He wanted to be considered—and addressed as—the "new Dionysus"; he is referred to by this appellation in at least one Athenian inscription of the time, which reveals that the Great Panathenaea of 38 was celebrated as "the Antonian Panathenaea of the god Antonius, the new Dionysus."[105] On the other hand, there is probably not much truth to the story that the Athenians offered him their goddess Athena as a bride, and Antony, accepting the offer, demanded a dowry of a million drachmas (six million, according to another version) and actually pressured the city into paying it. This report is undoubtedly propaganda circulated somewhat later by the circles around Octavian, inspired by the temporary link between the new Dionysus and Athena at the festival and by Antony's polygamous nature.[106] In many respects the Roman ruler's residence in Athens is reminiscent of the Macedonian king Demetrius' stay there almost three centuries earlier. In

103. A. E. Raubitschek, *TAPhA* 77 (1946) 146–150.

104. Plut. *Antonius* 33.7.

105. *IG* II^2.1043.22–23, from 37/6, a decree for the ephebes of the preceding year; Socrates of Rhodes, *FGrHist* 192 F 2. In 39 Dionysus appears for the first time on Athenian coins, undoubtedly an allusion to Antony in his role of "new Dionysus"; Kroll, *Coins* 84–85 and 102–103, nos. 140–142.

106. Cassius Dio 48.39.2; Seneca Rhetor *Suasor.* 1.6. These claims are viewed skeptically by, e.g., W. W. Tarn, *CAH* 10 (1934) 54; and Day, *Economic History* 133. Others accept the report as accurate, including Raubitschek, *TAPhA* 77 (1946) 146–147; M. C. Hoff, *Hesperia* 58 (1989) 273 n. 36; and Kroll, *Coins* 85. Cf. also C. B. R. Pelling, ed., *Plutarch: Life of Antony* (Cambridge 1988) 209.

Athens Antony behaved more like a Hellenistic monarch than a Roman aristocrat.

A few years later the confrontation between Antony and Octavian that had been looming for so long finally came to a head. It became inevitable when Octavian grew dissatisfied with the half of the empire he had received and demanded sole dominion over the entire *imperium Romanum*. In the years since their victory at Philippi he had several times pursued his own interests in flagrant violation of the loyalty he owed his partner. For his part Antony had contributed to the growing breach in their personal relationship through his increasing attachment to the Egyptian queen Cleopatra. Thus when Octavia came from Rome to join him again in Athens in 35, he suggested that she go back home, and finally in the spring of 32, when the outbreak of war was no longer in doubt, he sent her a formal declaration of divorce. Octavian responded in late summer with a declaration of war—against Cleopatra, not Antony.

Antony was with Cleopatra in Athens at the time, preparing for the coming military confrontation, but characteristically not too busy to enjoy the queen's company and the entertainments Athens had to offer. Cleopatra could not help but notice that the Athenians were very attached to Octavia; she tried to win their favors with generous gifts. Having accepted them, the citizens had little choice but to offer her honors comparable to those Octavia had received. A decree in Cleopatra's honor was delivered to her in the city by a delegation of citizens that included Antony himself, acting as if he were an Athenian citizen or (less probably) in his capacity as an actual citizen.[107] As the outbreak of hostilities drew closer, several occurrences in Greece, and in Athens in particular, were interpreted as portents of a bad outcome; these were

---

107. Plut. *Antonius* 57.1–3. It does not necessarily follow from either Antony's participation in the delegation or Plutarch's wording in 57.3 and 33.7, in which he mentions Antony's service as *gymnasiarch,* that he had been granted and had accepted Athenian citizenship, as is often assumed (e.g., Rawson, *Athenaeum* 73 [1985] 58 and 62–63; Pelling: "he had presumably received the honor in 42–41"; *Plutarch: Life of Antony* 259). The reverse is far more likely, and the participation of foreigners in Athenian delegations was nothing exceptional. The same ambiguity of Plutarch's passage on Antony (57.3) is to be found in the oft-cited sentence in Arrian (*Anabasis* 7.23.2). There emissaries from Greece are described as paying tribute in Babylon to Alexander the Great "as if they were [*or* in their capacity as] festival delegates honoring a god." See E. Badian, *Ancient Macedonian Studies in Honor of C. Edson* (Saloniki 1981) 54–59.

recalled after Antony's defeat. During a violent storm the figure of Dionysus in the depiction of the Gigantomachy, a dedicatory gift from the Attalid monarchs, is said to have worked loose and plunged into the theater of Dionysus below, an evil omen for the "new Dionysus." And near the Propylaea the same storm toppled the colossal statues of Eumenes and Attalus, which had been rededicated to Antony.[108]

The two opponents assembled their fleets and armies in northwestern Greece, where they took up facing positions and waited months for one or the other to make a decisive move. The outcome was finally decided by the naval victory of Marcus Agrippa, Octavian's admiral, near Actium on 2 September 31. Antony and Cleopatra fled to Egypt, leaving Antony's large and fully intact land forces to negotiate a surrender with Octavian. Octavian thus acquired all of Greece in one stroke. It is not known whether any Athenian forces participated in these operations. The city had remained under Antony's control until the battle, and after his defeat one of his commanders, Cassius Parmensis, sought refuge there. The nightmare he experienced repeatedly was later interpreted as a premonition of his execution, ordered by Octavian soon afterward and presumably carried out in Athens. This Cassius was the next-to-last of Caesar's assassins to fall into Octavian's hands, and now paid with his life for the deed he had committed more than thirteen years earlier.[109] His arrest and execution constituted a violation of Athenian sovereignty, unless the city offered to cooperate in the matter. Nonetheless, Octavian had compelling reasons to insist: he was bound by his vow to avenge Caesar's murder, and required by the *lex Pedia* of 43 to punish the assassins by death.

Octavian went straight to Athens after his victory. Plutarch reports that "he became reconciled with the Greeks and distributed the army's remaining stores of grain to the cities, for they were in great need and had suffered heavy losses of money, slaves, and teams of horses."[110] It was the season for the celebration of the Mysteries in Eleusis, and Octavian, like so many Roman dignitaries before him, seized the opportunity to be initiated. Two pedestals found in Eleusis show that the

---

108. Plut. *Antonius* 60.4 and 6, with Pelling's commentary, 265–266. The two events are clearly conflated in Cassius Dio 50.15.2. See also T. Hölscher, *Antike Kunst* 28 (1985) 124–128; and C. Habicht, *Hesperia* 59 (1990) 572.

109. Val. Max. 1.7.7; Velleius 2.87.3.

110. Plut. *Antonius* 68.6. Tokens bearing Octavian's name found in Athens may perhaps stem from this distribution of grain; M. C. Hoff, *MH* 49 (1992) 232–233.

citizens of Athens placed statues there to honor him and his wife Livia, perhaps at this time but in any event before 27. Octavian is described as the city's "savior and benefactor" in the inscription, presumably because of his distribution of grain.[111]

One last report mentions Antony in connection with Athens. When Octavian was encamped in Asia Minor on his way to Egypt, emissaries from Antony in Alexandria appeared and sought permission for him to be allowed to live in Athens as a private citizen if he could not remain in Egypt.[112] The request was ignored, and the report may be an invention. But whether or not it is true, it reflects the close attachment of the last ruler of the Roman republic to the Hellenistic city. Both the republic and Hellenistic Athens came to an end at that time. A decade earlier, in 42/1, when Antony had assumed control of Greece, the Athenians had ceased to coin their "New Style" silver, which for a century had been the country's predominant currency. Athenian silver had been minted only sporadically for some time, as the Roman denarius was lighter and had become readily available.[113] After Actium the city would face harsh times under its new masters and new status as part of the *imperium Romanum,* until Roman philhellenism reached a new peak under Hadrian and Antoninus Pius a century and a half later, granting it one more era of late bloom.

111. Cassius Dio 51.4.1. For the statues see E. Vanderpool, *AD* 23 A (1968) 7–9, no. 3; Clinton, *ANRW* II 18.2 (1989) 507.

112. Plut. *Antonius* 72.1.

113. Kroll, *Coins* 16–17 and 85–87. Kroll speaks of the "quasi-Romanization of the city's currency which for the next 250 years was to be dominated by the denarius" (16).

Epilogue

An old and widespread view, still current among some scholars, holds that the outcome of the battle of Chaeronea in 338 spelled the end of "the Greek city." However, a large and constantly increasing body of unambiguous evidence from Hellenistic inscriptions has proved this erroneous without doubt. To be sure, Athens, Sparta, and Thebes lost their dominant role on the larger political stage as the power of the Macedonian monarchy grew, and Thebes was even wiped out of existence for two decades. Nonetheless, as leading experts on Hellenistic documents—Louis Robert foremost among them—have clearly shown, these cities as well as hundreds of smaller communities remained viable and vital political organisms.[1] For the majority of small and mid-sized towns the classical period, during which their more powerful neighbor states ruled them, was the saddest period of their history; with the coming of the Hellenistic age their position actually improved.[2] Even if afterward most cities had to shape their foreign policies to comply with monarchs' wishes and to rely on the same monarchs for protection, they were free to conduct their internal affairs as they saw fit. Their citizens were just as politically active and as

---

1. Of Robert's many publications on the subject see esp. *CRAI* (1969) 42 and *Xenion: Festschrift für P. I. Zepos* (Athens 1973) 778–779 (= *OMS* 2.150–151). See further, in *Akten des 8. Internationalen Kongresses für Griechische und Lateinische Epigraphik,* vol. 1 (Athens 1984), P. Herrmann 109–119 and P. Gauthier 82–87; Gauthier, *Cités* and *Opus* 6–8 (1987–1989 [1991]) 187–202; A. Giovannini, in *Images and Ideologies: Self-Definition in the Hellenistic World,* ed. A. Bulloch et al. (Berkeley 1993) 265–286; E. Gruen, in *Nomodeiktes: Greek Studies in Honor of M. Ostwald* (Ann Arbor 1993) 339–354; P. J. Rhodes, *CAH*[2] 6 (1994) 589–591.

2. P. Gauthier, *Opus* 6–8 (1987–1989 [1991]) 193–194.

patriotic as their forefathers had been, and they took it for granted that they would continue to perform the same tasks and functions for the defense of their city and its territory, the administration of the government, and the operation of the law courts.

Of the old Greek cities, Rhodes was perhaps the only one able to preserve its independence throughout the period; the island republic defended itself successfully from attacks by King Demetrius in 305/4 and by Mithridates VI in 88/7. Other cities gave up their sovereign rights to join leagues, thus managing to preserve their independence from foreign monarchs. For a long time Athens was almost the only city that alternated between periods of subjugation by a king and periods of freedom. With the appearance of the Romans on the scene came an era of independence for many communities, until the Romans themselves and their imperial ambitions put an end to it.

The alliance Athens forged with the Roman republic during the war against Antiochus was a treaty between sovereign states. Athens broke it in 88 B.C. by transferring its loyalty to Mithridates. The surviving sources do not refer to the new alliance as a treaty violation, but this may be because the immense difference in the real political power of the two parties had already rendered the treaty largely irrelevant in practical terms. After Sulla's defeat of Athens, the provisions of the treaty were clearly considered still to be in force—or to have been resumed—although once again this meant little for the conduct of political affairs.[3] The Romans violated it in their turn in 58 by passing the plebiscite of Clodius, which awarded control of the officially sovereign and independent city to the Roman governor of Macedonia for his term of office. This exceptional state of affairs did not last long, and officially the *status quo ante* was reinstated, but Athenian rights finally proved obsolete following Antony's defeat at Actium. When his supporter Cassius Parmensis fled to Athens, he should have been safe on the city's sovereign territory, but nonetheless he was killed by order of the victor.

The outcome of the Roman civil wars had given rise to new conditions no longer permitting Athens to offer asylum to the persecuted, thus ending a centuries-old tradition that had been one of the pillars of Athens' fame: its readiness to offer sanctuary to those seeking safety,

---

3. Germanicus treated the city as a community associated with Rome by treaty in his stay there in 18 A.D. (Tacitus *Ann.* 2.53.3).

particularly if they were victims of political change in their home towns. During the fifth century the Messenians fled there in 460/59, the Plataeans in 427, and the Samians in 405 and 404.[4] In the fourth century the city granted asylum to various groups of refugees large and small: the three hundred Thebans who fled after the citadel of Thebes was occupied by the Spartans in 382, the Plataeans after the Thebans had destroyed their city a decade later, and a group of eleven citizens from Delphi banned for harboring pro-Phocian sympathies.[5] In 348/7 they were followed by citizens of Olynthus after Philip had destroyed their city, and in 346 by Phocians escaping the Thessalians; groups of allies from Troizen and Acarnania, having fled their homes, came after the defeat at Chaeronea in 338,[6] and shortly afterward Thebans who had managed to escape the destruction of their city by Alexander. Athens took in these last refugees despite a royal order forbidding them to do so.[7] And after the defeat in the Hellenic War in 322 Athens took in fleeing citizens of allied states, Dolopians and about fifty Thessalians, who were personae non gratae in the new political order at home after its reorganization in line with Macedonian interests.[8] This is especially noteworthy because Athens itself had come under the control of the victors and was compelled to accept a Macedonian garrison in the fortress commanding the harbor in Piraeus.

Persons threatened or persecuted as individuals also sought and found refuge in Athens, such as Alexander's treasurer Harpalus in 324. The demand for his extradition, issued at once in the king's name on various sides, was not met by the Athenians, although they risked war if they rejected it. They solved this dilemma by placing Harpalus under arrest and allowing him to escape.[9] A similar case occurred a hundred

---

4. In a 1907 essay (still quite valuable) A. W. Verrall found in Euripides' plays the *Suppliants* and *Heracleidae*, both written between 431 and 421, the first literary expression of this particular role of Athens as "the guardian and champion of humanity"; *Oxford and Cambridge Review* (1907), cited here from the reprint: Verrall, *Collected Literary Essays, Classical and Modern* (Cambridge 1913) 219–235; quotation from 225–226.

5. Xenophon *Hellenica* 5.2.31 (Thebans); [Demosth.] 59.104–106 (Phocians); *IG* II^2.109 and *Corpus des inscriptions de Delphes*, vol. 2 (Paris 1989), nos. 67–73 (Delphians).

6. *IG* II^2.211; Harpocration s.v. ἰσοτελής (Olynthians); Demosthenes 5.19 (Phocians); Hypereides 5.31 (Troezenians); *IG* II^2.237 (Acarnanians).

7. The sources are collected in H. Berve, *Das Alexanderreich auf prosopographischer Grundlage,* vol. 1 (Munich 1926) 240 n. 2.

8. *IG* II^2.546 and Diodorus 18.11.1 (Dolopians); *IG* II^2.545 (Thessalians); see Chapter 2, Section 1.

9. See Chapter 1, Section 4.

years later, when Philip V demanded the extradition of his minister
Megaleas, taken into custody by an Athenian general upon entering
Attic territory and accused by his sovereign of having plotted against
him. Once again the consequence of an Athenian refusal would have
been war. Megaleas was not extradited, however, but merely deported
from Attica, whereupon he committed suicide in Thebes.[10] At the
beginning of the war against Antiochus in 192, Euthymidas of Chalcis
was living in exile in Athens. There he plotted a coup to give Antiochus
control of his home city. The plot failed, but even though Athens was
allied with the king's enemies, Euthymidas appears to have gone on
living in the city undisturbed.[11] When a decade later the descendants
of an executed Thessalian aristocrat found guilty of conspiring against
Philip sought safety from pursuit by the king's agents, Athens seemed
the natural refuge.[12] As late as the Roman civil wars high-ranking
Romans found a safe harbor in Athens,[13] although after Octavian's
victory at Actium the city was no longer able to protect one of them
from the victor's wrath.

From then on Athens, like all the other communities and peoples in
the Roman empire, were subject to the will of the new ruler. Augustus
and several of his successors may have requested and received initiation
into the Eleusinian Mysteries or assumed the office of eponymous
archon for a year, but the city had to bow to their decision. Augustus'
favor was variable, Hadrian's constant, yet Athens had to take what
came. The city was no longer the Athens that had challenged Alexander
the Great. It lived on as a self-administering community within the
Roman empire and remained a cultural center of the first rank. Its
legacy has survived to the present day and will outlast it.

10. Polybius 5.27. See Chapter 7, Section 3.
11. Livy 35.37.4–38.14.
12. Livy 40.4; F. W. Walbank, *Philip V of Macedon* (Cambridge 1940) 244–245.
13. F. Münzer, "Manlius," *RE* (1928) 1197.

ABBREVIATIONS AND SHORT TITLES

Periodicals are abbreviated as in *L'année philologique,* with the following exceptions:

AM	*Athenische Mitteilungen*
HSCP	*Harvard Studies in Classical Philology*

In addition, the following abbreviations and short titles are used for frequently cited works:

Accame, *Dominio*	S. Accame, *Il dominio Romano in Grecia* (Rome 1946)
Agora XV	B. D. Meritt and J. S. Traill, *The Athenian Agora,,* vol. XV: *Inscriptions: The Athenian Councillors* (Princeton 1974)
ANRW	*Aufstieg und Niedergang der römischen Welt,* ed. W. Haase and H. Temporini, 72 vols. to date (Berlin 1972–)
AP	*Anthologia Palatina*
Beloch, *GG*	K. J. Beloch, *Griechische Geschichte*², vol. 4.1–2 (Berlin 1925–1927)
Clinton, *Officials*	K. Clinton, *The Sacred Officials of the Eleusinian Mysteries* (Philadelphia 1974)
Daux, *Delphes*	G. Daux, *Delphes au II*ᵉ *et au I*ᵉʳ *siècle* (Paris 1936)
Davies, *APF*	J. K. Davies, *Athenian Propertied Families, 600–300 B.C.* (Oxford 1971)
Dorandi, *Ricerche*	T. Dorandi, *Ricerche sulla cronologia dei filosofi ellenistici* (Stuttgart 1991)
EAD	*Exploration archéologique de Délos,* ed. Ecole Française d'Athènes, 35 vols. to date (Athens 1909–)
FD	*Fouilles de Delphes,* vol. III: *Epigraphie,* ed. Ecole Française d'Athènes, 6 parts (Paris 1911–)

Ferguson, *HA*	W. S. Ferguson, *Hellenistic Athens* (London 1911)
FGrHist	F. Jacoby, *Die Fragmente der griechischen Historiker,* 3 parts in 18 vols. (Berlin 1923–1926, Leiden 1940–1958)
Gauthier, *Cités*	P. Gauthier, *Les cités grecques et leurs bienfaiteurs* (Paris 1985)
GHI	M. N. Tod, *Greek Historical Inscriptions,* vol. 2 (Oxford 1948)
GVI	W. Peek, *Griechische Vers-Inschriften,* vol. 1: *Die Grabepigramme* (Berlin 1955)
Habicht, *Gottmenschentum*	C. Habicht, *Gottmenschentum und griechische Städte* (Munich 1956; enl. ed. 1970)
Habicht, *Studien*	C. Habicht, *Studien zur Geschichte Athens in hellenistischer Zeit* (Göttingen 1982)
Habicht, *Untersuchungen*	C. Habicht, *Untersuchungen sur politischen Geschichte Athens im 3. Jahrhundert v. Chr.* (Munich 1979)
Hammond, *Macedonia*	N. Hammond, *A History of Macedonia,* vol. 3 (with F. Walbank) (Oxford 1988)
Holleaux, *Etudes*	M. Holleaux, *Etudes d'épigraphie et d'histoire grecques,* 6 vols. (Paris 1938–1968)
I Délos	*Inscriptions de Délos,* ed. Ecole Française d'Athènes, 7 vols. (Paris 1926–1972)
IG	*Inscriptiones Graecae,* many vols. and suppls. (Berlin 1873–1993)
IGCH	M. Thompson, O. Mørkholm, and C. Kraay, eds., *An Inventory of Greek Coin Hoards* (New York 1973)
ISE	L. Moretti, *Iscrizioni storiche ellenistiche,* 2 vols. (Florence 1967–1975)
Kroll, *Coins*	J. H. Kroll, *The Greek Coins: Athenian Bronze Coinage, 4th–1st Centuries B.C.* (*Agora* XXVI)(Princeton 1993)
OGI	W. Dittenberger, *Orientis Graeci Inscriptiones Selectae,* 2 vols. (Leipzig 1903–1905)
OMS	L. Robert, *Opera Minora Selecta,* 7 vols. (Amsterdam 1969–1990)
Osborne, *Naturalization*	M. J. Osborne, *Naturalization in Athens,* 4 vols. (Brussels: 1981–1983)

PA	J. Kirchner, *Prosopographia Attica*, 2 vols. (Berlin 1901–1903)
PCG	*Poetae Comici Graeci,*, ed. R. Kassel and C. Austin, 6 vols. to date (Berlin 1983–)
Pélékidis, *Ephébie*	C. Pélékidis, *Histoire de l'éphébie attique des origines à 31 av. J.-C.* (Paris 1962)
Rhodes, *Commentary*	P. J. Rhodes, *A Commentary on the Aristotelian Athenaion Politeia* (Oxford 1981)
SEG	*Supplementum Epigraphicum Graecum,* various editors, 42 vols. to date (Leiden 1923–1971, Alphen 1979–80, Leiden 1982–)
StV	*Die Staatsverträge der antiken Welt,* vol. 3, ed. H. Schmitt (Munich 1969)
Syll.	W. Dittenberger, *Sylloge Inscriptionum Graecarum*³, 4 vols. (Leipzig 1915–1924)
Tracy, *ALC*	S. V Tracy, *Attic Letter Cutters of 229 to 86 B.C.* (Berkeley 1990)
Tracy, *Contributors*	S. V. Tracy, IG II² 2336: *Contributors of First Fruits for the Pythais* (Meisenheim 1982)
Walbank, *Commentary*	F. W. Walbank, *A Historical Commentary on Polybius*, 3 vols. (Oxford 1957–1979)
Walbank, *Macedonia*	See Hammond
Wilhelm, *Akademieschriften*	A. Wilhelm, *Akademieschriften*, 3 vols. (Leipzig 1974)
Will, *Histoire*	E. Will, *Histoire politique du monde hellénistique,* 2 vols. (2d ed. Nancy 1979)

SELECT BIBLIOGRAPHY

General Studies
Hellenism

Beloch, K. J. *Griechische Geschichte²*. Vol. 4.1–2. Berlin 1925–1927.

Gauthier, P. *Les cités grecques et leurs bienfaiteurs (IVᵉ–1ᵉʳ siècle avant J.-C.)*. Paris 1985.

——— "Grandes et petites cités: Hégémonie et autarcie." *Opus* 6–8 (1987–1989 [1991]) 187–202.

Green, P. *Alexander to Actium: The Historical Evolution of the Hellenistic Age*. Berkeley 1990.

Hammond, N. G., and F. W. Walbank. *A History of Macedonia*. Vol. 3: *336–167 B.C.* Oxford 1988.

Niese, B. *Geschichte der griechischen und makedonischen Staaten seit der Schlacht bei Chaeronea*. 3 vols. Gotha 1893–1903.

Rostovtzeff, M. *The Social and Economic History of the Hellenistic World*. 3 vols. Oxford 1941.

Will, E. *Histoire politique du monde hellénistique (323–30 av. J.-C.)²*. 2 vols. Nancy 1979 and 1982.

Athens

Ferguson, W. S. *Hellenistic Athens: An Historical Essay*. London 1911.

Garland, R. *The Piraeus from the Fifth to the First Century B.C.* Ithaca, N.Y., 1987.

Habicht, C. *Athen in hellenistischer Zeit. Gesammelte Aufsätze*. Munich 1994.

——— *Studien zur Geschichte Athens in hellenistischer Zeit*. Göttingen 1982.

——— *Untersuchungen zur politischen Geschichte Athens im 3. Jahrhundert v. Chr.* Munich 1979.

Mossé, C. *Athens in Decline, 404–86 B.C.* Trans. J. Stewart. London 1973.

Athenian Constitution

Bleicken, J. *Die athenische Demokratie*. Paderborn 1986, ²1994.

Busolt, G. "Der Staat der Athener." In *Griechische Staatskunde³*. Ed. H. Swoboda. Vol. 2. Munich 1926. Pp. 758–1239.

Clinton, K. *The Sacred Officials of the Eleusinian Mysteries.* Philadelphia 1974.

Develin, R. "Age Qualifications for Athenian Magistrates." *ZPE* 61 (1985) 149–159.

Gauthier, P. "L'octroi du droit de cité à Athènes." *REG* 99 (1986) 119–133.

Hansen, M. H. *The Athenian Ecclesia: A Collection of Articles, 1976–1983.* Copenhagen 1983.

Harrison, A. R. W. *The Law of Athens.* 2 vols. Oxford 1968 and 1971.

Henry, A. S. "The One and the Many: Athenian Financial Officials in the Hellenistic Period." *ZPE* 72 (1988) 129–136.

—— *The Prescripts of Athenian Decrees.* Leiden 1977.

Mikalson, J. D. *The Sacred and Civil Calendar of the Athenian Year.* Princeton 1975.

Osborne, M. J. *Naturalization in Athens.* 4 vols. Brussels 1981–1983.

Pélékidis, C. *Histoire de l'éphébie attique des origines à 31 av. J.-C.* Paris 1962.

Piérart, M. "Les εὔθυνοι athéniens." *AC* 40 (1971) 526–573.

Rhodes, P. J. *The Athenian Boule.* Oxford 1972.

Traill, J. S. *The Political Organization of Attica: A Study of the Demes, Trittyes, and Phylai, and Their Representation in the Athenian Council.* Princeton 1975.

Wallace, R. W. *The Areopagus Council to 307 B.C.* Princeton 1989.

Whitehead, D. *The Demes of Attica, 508/7–ca. 250 B.C.: A Political and Social Study.* Princeton 1986.

Athenian Society

Cohen, D. *Law, Sexuality and Society* (Cambridge 1991).

Davies, J. K. *Athenian Propertied Families, 600–300 B.C.* Oxford 1971.

Drummond, G. "The Leisured Classes in Athens, 300–ca. A.D. 50." Diss. Oxford 1979. *(Non vidi.)*

Fisher, R. "From Polis to Province: An Analysis of the Athenian Governing Class from 167/6 B.C. to A.D. 13/14." Diss. McMaster 1986. *(Non vidi.)*

MacKendrick, P. *The Athenian Aristocracy, 399 to 31 B.C.* Cambridge 1969.

Grain Supply

Brun, P. "La stèle des céréales de Cyrène et le commerce du grain en Egée au IVe s. av. J.-C." *ZPE* 99 (1993) 185–196.

Garnsey, P. "Grain for Athens." In *Crux: Essays presented to G. E. M. de Ste. Croix on His 75th Birthday.* Ed. P. A. Cartledge and F. D. Harvey. Exeter 1985. Pp. 62–75.

Marasco, G. "Sui problemi dell'approvvigionamento di cereali in Atene nell'età dei Diadochi." *Athenaeum* 62 (1984) 286–294.

Migeotte, L. "Le pain quotidien dans les cités hellénistiques: À propos des fonds permanents pour l'approvisionnement en grain." *Cahiers Glotz* 2 (1991) 19–41.

Montgomery, H. "'Merchants Fond of Corn': Citizens and Foreigners in the Athenian Grain Trade." *SO* 61 (1986) 43–61.

Chapter 1

Ampolo, C. "Un politico 'evergete' del IV secolo a. C.: Xenokles figlio di Xeinis del demo di Sphettos." *PP* 34 (1979) 167–178.

Atkinson, J. E. "Macedon and Athenian Politics in the Period 338 to 323 B.C." *Acta Classica* 24 (1981) 37–48.

Badian, E. "Agis III: Revisions and Reflections." In *Ventures into Greek History.* Ed. I. Worthington. Oxford 1994. Pp. 258–292.

Bosworth, A. B. *Conquest and Empire: The Reign of Alexander the Great.* Cambridge 1988.

Burke, E. M. "*Contra Leocratem* and *De corona:* Political Collaboration?" *Phoenix* 31 (1977) 330–340.

——— "Lycurgan Finances." *GRBS* 26 (1985) 251–264.

Clinton, K. "The Ephebes of Kekropis of 333/2 at Eleusis." *AE* 127 (1988 [1991]) 19–30.

Dreizehnter, A. "Die Bevölkerungszahl in Attika am Ende des 4. Jahrhunderts v. u. Z." *Klio* 54 (1972) 147–151.

Engels, J. "Das Eukratesgesetz und der Prozess der Kompetenzerweiterung des Areopages in der Eubulos- und Lykurgära." *ZPE* 74 (1988) 181–209.

——— *Studien zur politischen Biographie des Hypereides. Athen in der Epoche der lykurgischen Reformen und des makedonischen Universalreiches.* Munich 1989.

——— "Zur Entwicklung der attischen Demokratie in der Ära des Eubulos und des Lykurg (355–322 v. Chr.) und zu Auswirkungen der Binnenwanderung von Bürgern innerhalb Attikas." *Hermes* 120 (1992) 425–451.

Faraguna, M. *Atene nell'età di Alessandro: Problemi politici, economici, finanziari.* Rome 1992.

Hansen, M. H. "The Athenian 'Politicians,' 403–322 B.C." *GRBS* 24 (1983) 33–55.

——— *Demography and Democracy: The Number of Athenian Citizens in the Fourth Century B.C.* Herning 1986.

——— "Rhetores and Strategoi in Fourth-Century Athens." *GRBS* 24 (1983) 151–180.

Heckel, W. "The Flight of Harpalus and Tauriskos." *CP* 72 (1977) 133–135.

Humphreys, S. "Lycurgus of Butadae: An Athenian Aristocrat." In *Essays in Honor of C. G. Starr.* Ed. J. W. Eadie and J. Ober. N.p. 1985. Pp. 199–252.

Jaschinski, S. *Alexander und Griechenland unter dem Eindruck der Flucht des Harpalos.* Bonn 1981.

Keaney, J. J. "The Date of Aristotle's *Athenaion Politeia.*" *Historia* 19 (1970) 323–336.

Levi, M. A. "Filippo, Alessandro e l'opinione pubblica attica." *Contributi dell'Istituto di storia antica* 5 (Milan 1978) 59–67.

Lingua, A. "Nota di cronologia arpalica." *RFIC* 107 (1979) 35–39.

Matthaiou, A. P. Ἡρίον Λυκούργου Λυκόφρονος Βουτάδου. *Horos* 5 (1987) 31–44.

Mitchel, F. "Athens in the Age of Alexander." *G&R* 12 (1965) 189–204.

—— *Lykourgan Athens, 338–322.* Cincinnati 1970.

Mossé, C., "Lycurgus l'Athénien, homme du passé ou précurseur de l'avenir?" *Quaderni di storia* 30 (1989) 25–36.

Ostwald, M. "The Athenian Legislation against Tyranny and Subversion." *TAPhA* 86 (1955) 103–128.

Palagia, O., and D. M. Lewis. "The Ephebes of Erechtheis 333/2 and Their Dedication." *ABSA* 84 (1989) 333–344.

Reinmuth, O. W. *The Ephebic Inscriptions of the Fourth Century B.C.* Leiden 1971.

—— "The Spirit of Athens after Chaeronea." In *Acta of the Vth International Congress of Greek and Latin Epigraphy, Cambridge 1967.* Oxford 1971. Pp. 47–51.

Rhodes, P. J. "Ephebi, Bouleutae and the Population of Athens." *ZPE* 38 (1980) 191–201.

Ruschenbusch, E. "Die soziale Herkunft der Epheben um 330." *ZPE* 35 (1979) 173–176.

—— "Zum letzten Mal. Die Bürgerzahl Athens im 4. Jh. v. Chr." *ZPE* 54 (1984) 253–269.

Schaefer, A. *Demosthenes und seine Zeit*[2]. Vol. 3. Leipzig 1887.

Schröder, S. F. "Der Apollon Lykeios und die attische Ephebie des 4. Jh." *AM* 101 (1986) 167–184.

Sealey, R. "The Athenians Defeated." In *Demosthenes and His Time: A Study in Defeat.* New York 1993. Pp. 194–219.

Sekunda, N. V. "Athenian Demography and Military Strength 338–322 B.C." *ABSA* 87 (1992) 311–355.

Will, W. *Athen und Alexander. Untersuchungen zur Geschichte der Stadt von 338 bis 322 v. Chr.* Munich 1983.

Worthington, I. "The Chronology of the Harpalus Affair." *SO* 61 (1986) 63–76.

Chapter 2

Ashton, N. G. "The Lamian War: A False Start?" *Antichthon* 17 (1983) 47–63.

———— "The Naumachia near Amorgos in 322 B.C." *ABSA* 72 (1977) 1–11.

Bosworth, A. B. "Philip III Arrhidaeus and the Chronology of the Successors." *Chiron* 22 (1992) 55–81.

Chroust, A. "Aristotle's Flight from Athens in the Year 323 B.C." *Historia* 15 (1966) 185–192.

Dow, S., and A. H. Travis. "Demetrios of Phaleron and His Lawgiving." *Hesperia* 12 (1943) 144–165.

Dusanic, S. "The Year of the Athenian Archon Archippus II (318–317)." *BCH* 89 (1965) 128–141.

Eckstein, F. "Die attischen Grabmälergesetze (Cicero, *de legibus* II, 59 ff.)." *JDAI* 73 (1958) 18–29.

Errington, M. R. "Diodorus Siculus and the Chronology of the Early Diadochoi 320–311 B.C." *Hermes* 105 (1977) 478–504.

———— "From Babylon to Triparadeisos, 323–320 B.C." *JHS* 90 (1970) 49–77.

Fortina, M. *Cassandro, re di Macedonia.* Turin 1965.

Gehrke, H.-J. *Phokion. Studien zur Erfassung seiner historischen Gestalt.* Munich 1976.

———— "Das Verhältnis von Politik und Philosophie im Wirken des Demetrios von Phaleron." *Chiron* 8 (1978) 149–193.

Gullath, B. *Untersuchungen zur Geschichte Boiotiens in der Zeit Alexanders und der Diadochen.* Frankfurt 1982.

Gullath, B., and L. Schober. "Zur Chronologie der frühen Diadochenzeit. Die Jahre 320 bis 315 v. Chr." In *Festschrift S. Lauffer.* Ed. H. Kalcyk, B. Gullath, and A. Graeber. N.p. 1986. Pp. 329–378.

Hackl, U. "Die Aufhebung der attischen Demokratie nach dem Lamischen Krieg 322 v. Chr." *Klio* 69 (1987) 58–71.

Heckel, W. "Honours for Philip and Iolaos (*IG* II^2 561)." *ZPE* 44 (1981) 75–77.

———— "*IG* II^2 561 and the Status of Alexander IV." *ZPE* 40 (1980) 249–250.

Lehmann, G. A. "Der 'Lamische Krieg' und die 'Freiheit der Hellenen': Überlegungen zur hieronymianischen Tradition." *ZPE* 73 (1988) 121–149.

Lock, R. A. "The Date of Agis III's War in Greece." *Antichthon* 6 (1972) 10–27.

Marzi, M. "Demàde, politico e oratore." *A&R* 36 (1991) 70–83.

Mitchel, F. W. "Demades of Paeania and *IG* II^2 1493, 1494 and 1495." *TAPhA* 93 (1962) 213–229.

——— "Derkylos of Hagnous and the Date of *IG* II² 1187." *Hesperia* 33 (1964) 337–351.

Morrison, J. S. "Athenian Sea-Power in 323/2: Dream and Reality." *JHS* 107 (1987) 88–97.

Potter, D. "Telesphoros, cousin de Demetrius: A Note on the Trial of Menander." *Historia* 36 (1987) 491–495.

Roesch, P. *Etudes béotiennes.* Paris 1982.

Schmitt, O. *Der Lamische Krieg.* Diss. Bonn 1992. *(Non vidi.)*

Stein, M. "Drei Bemerkungen zur Diadochengeschichte." *Prometheus* 19 (1993) 143–153.

Stichel, R. H. "Columella-mensa-labellum. Zur Form der attischen Grabmäler im Luxusgesetz des Demetrios von Phaleron." *AA* 107 (1992) 433–440.

Tritle, L. A. *Phocion the Good.* London 1988.

Wehrli, C. *Antigone et Démétrios.* Geneva 1968.

Will, E. "Ophellas, Ptolémée, Cassandre et la chronologie." *REA* 66 (1964) 320–333.

Williams, J. M. *Athens without Democracy: The Oligarchy of Phocion and the Tyranny of Demetrius of Phalerum, 322–307 B.C.* Ann Arbor 1985.

——— "A Note on Athenian Chronology, 319/8–318/7 B.C." *Hermes* 112 (1984) 300–305.

Chapter 3

Badian, E., and T. R. Martin. "Athenians, Other Allies, and the Hellenes in the Athenian Honorary Decree for Adeimantos of Lampsakos." *ZPE* 61 (1985) 167–172.

De Sanctis, G. "Atene dopo Ipso e un papiro fiorentino." *RFIC* 64 (1936) 134–152 and 253–273.

Ferguson, W. S. "Lachares and Demetrius Poliorcetes." *CP* 24 (1929) 1–31.

Franco, C. "Lisimaco e Atene." In *Studi ellenistici.* Ed. B. Virgilio. Vol. 3. Pisa 1990. Pp. 113–134.

——— *Il regno di Lisimaco. Strutture amministrative e rapporti con le città.* Pisa 1993.

Hauben, H. "*IG* II² 492 and the Siege of Athens in 304 B.C." *ZPE* 14 (1974) 10.

Henry, A. S. "Athenian Financial Officials after 303 B.C." *Chiron* 14 (1984) 49–92.

——— "Bithys, Son of Kleon, of Lysimacheia: Formal Dating Criteria and *IG* II² 808." In *"Owls to Athens": Essays on Classical Culture Presented to Sir Kenneth Dover.* Ed. E. M. Craik. New York 1990. Pp. 179–189.

Lanciers, E. "Het eredecreet voor Kallias van Sphettos en de Grieks-Egyptische relaties in de vroege Ptolemaeëntijd." *RBPh* 65 (1987) 52–86.

Landucci Gattinoni, F. "Demetrio Poliorcete e il santuario di Eleusi." *CISA* 9 (1983) 117–124.

Lund, H. S. *Lysimachus: A Study in Early Hellenistic Kingship.* New York 1992.

Marasco, G. *Democare di Leuconoe. Politica e cultura a Atene fra IV e III sec. a. C.* Florence 1984.

Osborne, M. J. "Kallias, Phaidros and the Revolt of Athens in 287 B.C." *ZPE* 35 (1979) 181–194.

Seibert, J. *Untersuchungen zur Geschichte Ptolemaios' I.* Munich 1969.

Shear, T. L., Jr. *Kallias of Sphettos and the Revolt of Athens in 286 B.C.* Princeton 1978.

Chapter 4

Drama

Buchanan, J. *Theorika: A Study of Monetary Distributions to the Athenian Citizenry during the Fifth and Fourth Centuries B.C.* Locust Valley, N.Y., 1962.

Casson, L. "The Athenian Upper Class and New Comedy." *TAPhA* 106 (1976) 29–59.

Fantham, R. "Sex, Status, and Survival in Hellenistic Athens: A Study of Women in New Comedy." *Phoenix* 29 (1975) 44–74.

Ghiron-Bistagne, P. *Recherches sur les acteurs dans la Grèce antique.* Paris 1976.

Gomme, A. W., and F. H. Sandbach. *Menander: A Commentary.* Oxford 1973.

Habicht, C. "The Comic Poet Archedikos." *Hesperia* 63 (1993) 253–256.

Handley, E. W., ed. *The Dyskolos of Menander.* London 1965.

Henderson, J. "Women and the Athenian Dramatic Festivals." *TAPhA* 121 (1991) 133–147.

Le Guen, B. "Théâtre et cités à l'époque hellénistique." *REG* 108 (1995) 59–90.

Mette, H.-J., ed. *Urkunden dramatischer Aufführungen in Griechenland.* Berlin 1977.

Nesselrath, H.-G. *Die attische Mittlere Komödie. Ihre Stellung in der antiken Literaturkritik und Literaturgeschichte.* Berlin 1990.

Philipp, G. B. "Philippides, ein politischer Komiker in hellenistischer Zeit." *Gymnasium* 80 (1973) 493–509.

Pickard-Cambridge, A. W. *The Dramatic Festivals at Athens*[2]. Rev. J. Gould and D. M. Lewis. Oxford 1968.

Poland, F. "Technitai." *RE* 5 A (1934), cols. 2473–2558.

Préaux, C. "Ménandre et la société athénienne." *CE* 32 (1957) 84–100.

Sifakis, G. M. *Studies in the History of Hellenistic Drama.* London 1967.

Stefanis, I. E. Διονυσιακοὶ τεχνῖται. Συμβολὲς στὴν προσωπογραφία τοῦ θεάτρου καὶ τῆς μουσικῆς τῶν ἀρχαίων. Heraklion 1988.

Turner, E. G. "Menander and the New Society of His Time." *CE* 54 (1979) 106–126.

Wilhelm, A. *Urkunden dramatischer Aufführungen in Athen.* Vienna 1906.

Zucker, F., et al. *Menanders Dyskolos als Zeugnis seiner Epoche.* Berlin 1965.

The Schools of Philosophy

Dorandi, T. *Filodemo. Storia dei filosofi. Platone e l'academia (PHerc. 1021 e 164).* Naples 1991.

—— *Filodemo. Storia dei filosofi. La stoa da Zenone a Panezio.* Leiden 1994.

—— *Ricerche sulla cronologia dei filosofi ellenistici.* Stuttgart 1991.

Erskine, A. *The Hellenistic Stoa: Political Thought and Action.* London 1990.

Glucker, J. *Antiochus and the Late Academy.* Göttingen 1978.

Gottschalk, H. B. "Notes on the Wills of the Peripatetic Scholarchs." *Hermes* 100 (1972) 314–342.

Habicht, C. *Hellenistic Athens and Her Philosophers.* Princeton 1988 (= *Athen in hellenistischer Zeit. Gesammelte Aufsätze.* Munich 1994. Pp. 231–247).

Isnardi Parente, M. "Per la biografia di Senocrate." *RFIC* 109 (1981) 129–162.

Kristeller, P. O. *Greek Philosophers of the Hellenistic Age.* New York 1993.

Long, A. A. "Diogenes Laertius, Life of Arcesilaus." *Elenchos* 7 (1986) 429–449.

Long, A. A., and D. N. Sedley. *The Hellenistic Philosophers.* 2 vols. Cambridge 1987.

Lynch, J. P. *Aristotle's School: A Study of a Greek Educational Institution.* Berkeley 1972.

Steinmetz, P. "Die Krise der Philosophie in der Zeit der Hochhellenismus." *Antike und Abendland* 15 (1969) 122–134.

Wehrli, F., ed. *Die Schule des Aristoteles.* 10 vols. plus 2 suppl. vols. Basle 1944–1978.

Weiher, A. *Philosophen und Philosophenspott in der attischen Komödie.* Diss. Munich 1913.

Whitehead, D. "Aristotle the Metic." *Proceedings of the Cambridge Philological Society* 21 (1975) 94–99.

Art

Andreae, B., ed. "Phyromachos-Probleme. Mit einem Anhang zur Datierung des Großen Altares von Pergamon." *DAI (R)*, Ergänzungsheft 31, 1990.

Corso, A. *Prassitele: Fonti epigrafiche e letterarie, vita e opere.* Rome 1988.

Marcadé, J. *Recueil des signatures de sculpteurs grecs.* 2 vols. Paris 1953 and 1957.

Richter, G. M. A. *The Portraits of the Greeks.* Rev. R. R. R. Smith. Ithaca, N.Y., 1984.

Ridgway, B. S. *Hellenistic Sculpture.* Vol. 1: *The Styles of ca. 331–200 B.C.* Madison 1990.

Smith, R. R. R. *Hellenistic Royal Portraits.* Oxford 1988.

Stewart, A. *Attika: Studies in Athenian Sculpture of the Hellenistic Age.* London 1979.

Prose

Dalby, A. "The Curriculum Vitae of Duris of Samos." *CQ* 41 (1991) 539–541.

Jacoby, F. *Apollodors Chronik. Eine Sammlung der Fragmente.* Berlin 1902.

———— *Atthis: The Local Chronicles of Ancient Athens.* Oxford 1949.

Kebric, R. B. *In the Shadow of Macedon: Duris of Samos.* Wiesbaden 1977.

Lane Fox, R. "Theophrastus' *Characters* and the Historian." *PCPS* 42 (1996) 127–170.

Momigliano, A. "Atene nel III secolo a. C. e la scoperta di Roma nelle Storie di Timeo di Tauromenio." *Rivista storica italiana* 71 (1959) 529–556. Reprinted in Momigliano, *Terzo Contributo alla Storia degli Studi Classici e del Mondo Antico.* Rome 1966. Pp. 23–53.

Regenbogen, O. "Theophrastos." *RE Suppl.* 7 (1940) 1354–1562.

Rhodes, P. J. "The Atthidographers." *Studia Hellenistica* 30 (1990) 73–81.

Chapter 5

Bultrighini, U. "Pausania 1, 26, 3 e la liberazione del Pireo." *RFIC* 112 (1984) 54–72.

Burstein, S. M. "Arsinoe II Philadelphos: A Revisionist View." In *Philip II, Alexander the Great, and the Macedonian Heritage.* Ed. W. L. Adams and E. N. Borza. Washington, D.C., 1982. Pp. 197–212.

De Sanctis, G. "Il dominio macedonico nel Pireo." *RFIC* 5 (1927) 480–500.

Dreyer, B. "Der Beginn der Freiheitsphase Athens 287 v. Chr. und das Datum der Panathenäen und Ptolemaia im Kalliasdekret." *ZPE* 111 (1996) 45–67.

Flacelière, R. *Les Aitoliens à Delphes.* Paris 1937.

Gauthier, P. "La réunification d'Athènes en 281 et les deux archontes Nicias." *REG* 92 (1979) 348–399.

Grzybek, E. *Du calendrier macédonien au calendrier ptolémaïque: Problèmes de chronologie hellénistique.* Basle 1990.

Hatzopoulos, M. *Une donation du roi Lysimaque.* Athens and Paris 1988.

Hauben, H. "Philocles, King of the Sidonians and General of the Ptolemies." *Orientalia Lovaniensia Analecta* 22 (1987) 413–427.

Heinen, H. *Untersuchungen zur hellenistischen Geschichte des 3. Jahrhunderts v. Chr. Zur Geschichte der Zeit des Ptolemaios Keraunos und zum Chremonideischen Krieg.* Wiesbaden 1972.

Kirchner, J. "Attische Grabstelen des dritten und zweiten Jahrhunderts v. Chr." *AE* 100 (1937) 338–340.

Knoepfler, D. "Les *kryptoi* du stratège Épicharès à Rhamnonte et le début de la guerre de Chrémonidès." *BCH* 117 (1993) 327–341.

——— "Les relations des cités eubéennes avec Antigone Gonatas et la chronologie delphique au début de l'époque étolienne." *BCH* 119 (1995) 137–159.

Launey, M. "Etudes d'histoire hellénistiques. II: L'exécution de Sotadès et l'expédition de Patroklos dans la mer Egée (266 av. J.-C.)." *REA* 47 (1945) 33–45.

Lauter, H. "Das Teichos von Sunion." *Marburger Winckelmannsprogramm* (1988) 11–33.

Lauter-Bufe, H. "Die Festung Koroni und die Bucht von Porto Raphti." *Marburger Winckelmannsprogramm* (1988) 67–102.

Marasco, G. *Sparta agli inizi dell'età ellenistica: Il regno di Areo I (309/8–265/4 a. C.).* Florence 1980.

McCredie, J. *Fortified Military Camps in Attica.* Princeton 1966.

Nachtergael, G. *Les Galates en Grèce et les Sôtéria de Delphes: Recherches d'histoire et d'épigraphie hellénistiques.* Brussels 1977.

Pouilloux, J. "Glaucon, fils d'Etéoclès d'Athènes." In *Le monde grec. Pensée, littérature, histoire, documents. Hommages à Claire Préaux.* Ed. J. Bingen et al. Brussels 1975. Pp. 376–382.

Reger, G. "Athens and Tenos in the Early Hellenistic Age." *CQ* 42 (1992) 365–383.

——— "The Date of the Battle of Kos," *AJAH* 10 (1985 [1993]) 155–177.

Siewert, P. "Poseidon Hippios am Kolonos und die athenischen Hippeis." In *Arktouros: Hellenic Studies Presented to Bernard M. W. Knox.* Berlin 1979. Pp. 280–289.

Tarn, W. W. *Antigonos Gonatas.* Oxford 1913.

Vanderpool, E., J. R. McCredie, and A. Steinberg. "Koroni, a Ptolemaic Camp on the East Coast of Attica." *Hesperia* 31 (1962) 26–61.

——— "Koroni. The Date of the Camp and the Pottery." *Hesperia* 33 (1964) 69–75.

Chapter 6

Braun, K. "Der Dipylon. Brunnen B1. Die Funde," *AM* 85 (1970) 129–269.

Bugh, G. R. *The Horsemen of Athens.* Princeton 1988.

Buraselis, K. *Das hellenistische Makedonien und die Ägäis. Forschungen zur Politik des Kassandros und der drei ersten Antigoniden (Antigonos Mono- phthalmos, Demetrios Poliorketes und Antigonos Gonatas) im Ägäischen Meer und in Westkleinasien.* Munich 1982.

Dorandi, T. "Arrenide." *ZPE* 81 (1990) 36.

Etienne, R., and M. Piérart. "Un décret du Koinon des Hellènes à Platées en l'honneur de Glaucon, fils d'Étéoclès, d'Athènes." *BCH* 99 (1975) 51– 75.

Henry, A. S. "Lyandros of Anaphlystos and the Decree for Phaidros of Sphet- tos." *Chiron* 22 (1992) 25–33.

Kroll, J. H. "An Archive of the Athenian Cavalry." *Hesperia* 46 (1977) 83– 140.

Lewis, D. M. "The Archonship of Lysiades." *ZPE* 58 (1985) 271–274.

Osborne, M. J. "The Chronology of Athens in the Mid Third Century B.C." *ZPE* 78 (1989) 209–242.

Pouilloux, J. "Antigonos Gonatas et Athènes après la guerre de Chrémonidès." *BCH* 70 (1946) 488–496.

Roussel, P. "Un nouveau document relatif à la guerre démétriaque." *BCH* 54 (1930) 268–282.

Urban, R. *Wachstum und Krise des Achäischen Bundes. Quellenstudien zur Entwicklung des Bundes von 280 bis 222 v. Chr.* Wiesbaden 1979.

Chapter 7

Badian, E. "Notes on Roman Policy in Illyria (230–201 B.C.)." *PBSR* 20 (1952) 72–93.

Brulé, P. *La piraterie crétoise hellénistique.* Paris 1978.

Derow, P. S. "Pharos and Rome." *ZPE* 88 (1991) 261–270.

Errington, R. M. "Philip V, Aratus and the 'Conspiracy of Apelles.'" *Historia* 16 (1967) 19–36.

Fine, J. V. A. "The Problem of Macedonian Holdings in Epirus and Thessaly in 221 B.C." *TAPhA* 63 (1932) 126–155.

Gruen, E. S. *The Hellenistic World and the Coming of Rome.* 2 vols. Berkeley 1984.

——— *Studies in Greek Culture and Roman Policy.* New York 1990.

Harris, W. V. *War and Imperialism in Republican Rome, 327–70 B.C.* Oxford 1979.

Holleaux, M. *Rome, la Grèce et les monarchies hellénistiques au IIIe siècle av. J.-C.* Paris 1921.

Le Bohec, S. *Antigone Dôsôn roi de Macédoine.* Nancy 1993.

Migeotte, L. "L'aide béotienne à la libération d'Athènes en 229 a. C." In *Boiotika.* Ed. H. Beister and J. Buckler. Munich 1989. Pp. 193–201.

Oikonomides, A. N. "The Cult of Diogenes 'Euergetes' in Ancient Athens." *ZPE* 45 (1982) 118–120.

Rich, J. W. "Roman Aims in the First Macedonian War." *Proceedings of the Cambridge Philological Society* 210 (1984) 126–180.

Robert, L. "Inscriptions hellénistiques de Dalmatie." *Hellenica* 11–12 (1960) 505–541.

Thompson, H. A. "Athens Faces Adversity." *Hesperia* 50 (1981) 343–355.

Tracy, S. V. *Attic Letter-Cutters of 229 to 86 B.C.* Berkeley 1990.

Walbank, F. W. *A Historical Commentary on Polybius.* 3 vols. Oxford 1957–1979.

———— *Philip V of Macedon.* Cambridge 1940.

Chapter 8

Astin, A. E. *Cato the Censor.* Oxford 1978.

Aymard, A. *Les premiers rapports de Rome et de la confédération achaïenne (198–189 av. J.-C.).* Bordeaux 1938.

Bernhardt, R. *Imperium und Eleutheria. Die römische Politik gegenüber den freien Städten des griechischen Ostens.* Diss. Hamburg 1971.

Bousquet, J. "Le roi Persée et les Romains." *BCH* 105 (1981) 407–416.

Daux, G. *Delphes au IIe et au Ier siècle, 191–31 av. J.-C.* Paris 1936.

Deininger, J. *Der politische Widerstand gegen Rom in Griechenland 217–86 v. Chr.* Berlin 1971.

Derow, P. S. "Rome, the Fall of Macedon and the Sack of Corinth." In *CAH*^{2}. Vol. 8. Cambridge 1989. Pp. 290–323.

Errington, R. M. "Rome against Philip and Antiochus." In *CAH*^{2}. Vol. 8. Cambridge 1989. Pp. 244–289

Erskine, A. "The Romans as Common Benefactors." *Historia* 43 (1994) 70–87.

Ferrary, J.-L. *Philhellénisme et impérialisme: Aspects idéologiques de la conquête romaine du monde hellénistique, de la seconde guerre de Macédoine à la guerre contre Mithridate.* Rome 1988.

Giovannini, A. "Roman Eastern Policy in the Late Republic." *AJAH* 9 (1984 [1988]) 33–42.

Holleaux, M. "Les conférences de Lokride et la politique de T. Quinctius Flamininus (198 av. J.-C.)." *REG* 36 (1923) 115–171 (= *Etudes* 5: 29–79).

———— "Notes sur Tite Live. I: Les additions annalistiques au traité de 196 (33, 30, 6–11)." *RPh* 57 (1931) 5–19 (= *Etudes* 5: 104–120).

Meloni, P. *Perseo e la fine della monarchia macedone.* Rome 1953.

Pantos, P. A. "Echedemos, the Second Attic Phoibos." *Hesperia* 58 (1989) 277–288.

Chapter 9

Andreae, B. *Laokoon und die Gründung Roms*. Mainz 1988.

———— "Il messaggio politico di gruppi scultorei ellenistici." In *Studi ellenistici*. Ed. B. Virgilio. Vol. 4. Pisa 1994. Pp. 119–135.

Bugh, G. R. "The Theseia in Late Hellenistic Athens." *ZPE* 83 (1990) 20–37.

Deubner, L. *Attische Feste*. Berlin 1932.

Edwards, G. R. "Panathenaics of Hellenistic and Roman Times." *Hesperia* 26 (1957) 320–349.

Errington, R. M. "The Peace Treaty between Miletus and Magnesia (I. Milet 148)." *Chiron* 19 (1989) 279–288.

———— *Philopoemen*. Oxford 1969.

Giovannini, A. "Philipp V, Perseus und die delphische Amphiktyonie." In *Ancient Macedonia*. Vol. 1. Thessaloniki 1970. Pp. 147–154.

Grace, V. "The Middle Stoa Dated by Amphora Stamps." *Hesperia* 54 (1985) 1–54.

Habicht, C. "Athens and the Attalids in the Second Century B.C." *Hesperia* 59 (1990) 561–577.

———— "Athens and the Ptolemies." *CA* 11 (1992) 68–90.

———— "Athen und die Seleukiden." *Chiron* 19 (1989) 7–26.

———— "Milesische Theoren in Athen." *Chiron* 21 (1991) 325–327.

———— "The Role of Athens in the Reorganization of the Delphic Amphictiony." *Hesperia* 56 (1987) 59–71.

———— "Royal Documents in Maccabees II." *HSCP* 80 (1976) 1–18.

———— "The Seleucids and Their Rivals." In *CAH²*. Vol. 8. Cambridge 1989. Pp. 324–387.

———— "Zu den Münzmeistern der Silberprägung des Neuen Stils." *Chiron* 21 (1991) 1–23.

Holleaux, M. "Un prétendu décret d'Antioche sur l'Oronte." *REG* 13 (1900) 258–280 (= *Etudes* 2: 127–147).

Lauffer, S. *Die Bergwerkssklaven von Laureion²*. Wiesbaden 1979.

Lewis, D. M. "The Chronology of the Athenian New Style Coinage." *NC* 2 (1962) 275–300.

Mommsen, A. *Feste der Stadt Athen im Altertum*. Leipzig 1898.

Nikitsky, A. Ἀνεπιβασία. *Hermes* 38 (1903) 406–413.

Queyrel, F. "Art pergaménien, histoire, collections: Le Perse du Musée d'Aix et le petit ex-voto attalide." *RA* (1989) 253–296.

Rocchi, G. Daverio. *Frontiera e confini nella Grecia antica*. Rome 1988.

Schalles, H.-J. *Untersuchungen zur Kulturpolitik der pergamenischen Herrscher im dritten Jahrhundert vor Christus*. Tübingen 1985.

Simon, E. *Festivals of Attica: An Archaeological Commentary*. Madison 1983.

Thompson, M. *The New Style Silver Coinage of Athens*. 2 vols. New York 1961.

Tracy, S. V., and C. Habicht, "New and Old Panathenaic Victor Lists." *Hesperia* 60 (1991) 187–236.

Virgilio, B. "Gli Attalidi di Pergamo, fama, eredità, memoria," In *Studi ellenistici.* Ed. B. Virgilio. vol. 5. Pisa 1993.

Wilhelm, A. "Urkunde aus dem Jahre des Archon Nikosthenes 164/3 v. Chr." *SAWW* 180 (1916) 23–30.

Chapter 10

Baslez, M.-F., and C. Vial. "La diplomatie de Délos dans le premier tiers du IIe s." *BCH* 111 (1987) 281–312.

Boussac, M.-F. "Sceaux déliens." *RA* (1988) 307–340.

Bruneau, P. *Recherches sur les cultes de Délos à l'époque hellénistique et à l'époque impériale.* Paris 1970.

Bruneau, P., and J. Ducat. *Guide de Délos*^{3}. Paris 1983.

Chapouthier, F. "Le sanctuaire des dieux de Samothrace." *EAD* 16 (1935).

Engelmann, H. *The Delian Aretalogy of Sarapis.* Leiden 1975.

Gross, W. H. "Die Mithradates-Kapelle auf Delos." *Antike und Abendland* 4 (1954) 105–117.

Habicht, C. "Zu den Epimeleten von Delos 167–88 v. Chr." *Hermes* 119 (1991) 194–216.

Kreeb, M. "Zur Basis der Kleopatra auf Delos." *Horos* 3 (1985) 41–61.

Laidlaw, W. A. *A History of Delos.* Oxford 1933.

Meyer, H. "Zur Chronologie des Poseidoniastenhauses in Delos." *AM* 103 (1988) 203–220.

Müller, H. "Königin Stratonike, Tochter des Königs Ariarathes." *Chiron* 21 (1991) 393–424.

Rauh, N. K. *The Sacred Bonds of Commerce: Religion, Economy, and Trade Society at Hellenistic Roman Delos.* Amsterdam 1993.

Robert, L. "Monnaies et textes grecs, II: Deux tétradrachmes de Mithridate V Evergète, roi du Pont." *JS* (1978) 151–163 (*OMS* 7.283–295).

Roussel, P. *Les cultes égyptiens à Délos du IIIe au Ier siècle av. J.-C.* Nancy 1916.

——— *Délos, colonie athénienne*^{2}. Paris 1987.

Vial, C. *Délos indépendante.* Paris 1984.

Chapter 11

Baronowski, D. W. "The Provincial Status of Mainland Greece after 146 B.C.: A Criticism of Erich Gruen's Views." *Klio* 70 (1988) 448–460.

Bélis, A. "Les Hymnes à Apollon." In *Corpus des inscriptions de Delphes.* Vol. 3. Paris 1992.

Boëthius, A. *Die Pythais. Studien zur Geschichte der Verbindungen zwischen Athen und Delphi.* Uppsala 1918.

Franke, P. R. *Die antiken Münzen von Epirus.* 2 vols. Wiesbaden 1961.

Garbarino, G., ed. *Roma e la filosofia greca dalle origini alla fine del II secolo a. C.* 2 vols. Turin 1973.

Kirchhoff, A. "Zur Geschichte der attischen Kleruchie auf Lemnos." *Hermes* 1 (1866) 217–228.

Klaffenbach, G. "Zur Geschichte von Ost-Lokris." *Klio* 20 (1926) 68–88.

Lehmann, G. A. *Untersuchungen zur historischen Glaubwürdigkeit des Polybios.* Münster 1967.

Pöhlmann, E. *Denkmäler altgriechischer Musik.* Nuremberg 1970.

———— *Griechische Musikfragmente.* Nuremberg 1960.

van Effenterre, H. *La Crète et le monde grec de Platon à Polybe.* Paris 1948.

Chapter 12

Audiat, J. "Le gymnase." *EAD* 28 (1970).

Candiloro, E. "Politica e cultura in Atene da Pidna alla guerra mitridatica." *Studi classici e orientali* 14 (1965) 134–176.

Daly, L. W. "Roman Study Abroad." *AJPh* 71 (1950) 40–58.

Day, J. *An Economic History of Athens under Roman Domination.* New York 1942.

Doria, L. Breglia Pulci. "Per la storia di Atene alla fine del II sec. a.C. Il decreto sui pesi e misure, *IG* II² 1013." *MEFRA, Antiquité* 97 (1985) 411–430.

Dow, S. "A Leader of the Anti-Roman Party in Athens in 88 B.C." *CP* 37 (1942) 311–314.

Giovannini, A. *Rome et la circulation monétaire en Grèce au II* siècle avant Jésus-Christ.* Basle 1978.

Habicht, C. "Ehrung eines thessalischen Politikers in Athen." *ZPE* 20 (1976) 193–199.

Herrmann, P. "Milesier am Seleukidenhof. Prosopographische Beiträge zur Geschichte Milets im 2. Jhdt. v. Chr." *Chiron* 17 (1987) 171–192.

Tracy, S. V. "*IG* II² 937: Athens and the Seleucids." *GRBS* 29 (1988) 383–388.

———— *IG II² 2336: Contributors of First Fruits for the Pythais.* Meisenheim 1982.

———— "Inscriptiones Deliacae: *IG* XI 713 and *IG* XI 1056." *AM* 107 (1992) 303–314.

Vanderpool, E. "An Athenian Decree in Phocian Stiris." *AAA* 4 (1971) 439–443.

Viedebantt, O. "Der athenische Volksbeschluss über Mass und Gewicht." *Hermes* 51 (1916) 120–144.

Chapter 13

Badian, E. "Rome, Athens and Mithridates." *AJAH* 1 (1976) 105–128.

Barr-Sharrar, B. *The Hellenistic and Early Imperial Decorative Bust.* Mainz 1987.

Bernhardt, R. *Polis und römische Herrschaft in der späten Republik (149–31 v. Chr.).* Berlin 1985.

Boffo, L. "Grecità di frontiera: Chersonasos Taurica e i signori del Ponto Eusino (*SIG vol.* 3, 709)." *Athenaeum* 67 (1989) 211–259. 369–405.

Bol, P. C. "Die Skulpturen des Schiffsfundes von Antikythera." *AM Ergänzungsheft* 2 (1972).

Bugh, R. "Athenion and Aristion of Athens." *Phoenix* 46 (1992) 108–123.

Desideri, P. "Posidonio e la guerra mitridatica." *Athenaeum* 51 (1973) 3–29, 237–269.

Dontas, G. "La grande Artémis du Pirée: Une oeuvre d'Euphranor." *Antike Kunst* 25 (1982) 15–34.

Dumont, J. C., J.-L. Ferrary, P. Moreau, and C. Nicolet, eds. *Insula sacra: La loi Gabinia Calpurnia de Délos (58 av. J.-C.).* Paris 1980.

Fuchs, W. *Der Schiffsfund von Mahdia im Musée Alaoui zu Tunis.* Tübingen 1963.

Geagan, D. J. "Roman Athens. Some Aspects of Life and Culture, I, 86 B.C.–A.D. 267." *ANRW* II 7.1 (Berlin 1979) 371–437.

Glew, D. G. "Mithridates Eupator and Rome: A Study of the Background of the First Mithridatic War." *Athenaeum,* n.s. 55 (1977) 380–405.

Gottschalk, H. B. "Aristotelian Philosophy in the Roman World: The Revival of Aristotelianism." *ANRW* II 36.2 (Berlin 1987) 1083–88.

Habicht, C. "Zur Geschichte Athens in der Zeit Mithridates' VI." *Chiron* 6 (1976) 127–142.

Hellenkemper-Salies, G., ed. *Das Wrack. Der antike Schiffsfund von Mahdia.* 2 vols. Cologne 1994.

Hind, J. G. F. "Mithridates." In *CAH²*. Vol. 9. Cambridge 1994. Pp. 129–165.

Hoepfner, W. *Das Pompeion und seine Nachfolgerbauten.* Berlin 1976.

Kapetanopoulos, E. "Salamis and Julius Nikanor." Ἑλληνικά 33 (1981) 217–237.

Kidd, I. G. *Posidonius,* II *The Commentary.* 2 vols. Cambridge 1988.

Kleiner, F. "The Agora Excavations and Athenian Bronze Coins, 200–88 B.C." *Hesperia* 45 (1976) 1–40.

Kroll, J. H. *The Greek Coins: Athenian Bronze Coinage, 4th–1st Centuries B.C. Agora.* Vol. XXVI. Princeton 1993.

Malitz, J. *Die Historien des Poseidonios.* Munich 1983.

McGing, B. C. *The Foreign Policy of Mithridates VI Eupator, King of Pontus.* Leiden 1986.

Pape, M. *Griechische Kunstwerke aus Kriegsbeute und ihre öffentliche Aufstellung in Rom. Von der Eroberung von Syrakus bis in augusteische Zeit.* Diss. Hamburg 1975.

Reinach, T. *Mithridates Eupator, König von Pontos.* German edition by A. Goetz. Leipzig 1895.

Rostovtzeff, M., and H. A. Ormerod. "Pontus and Its Neighbours: The First Mithridatic War." In *CAH.* Vol. 9. Cambridge 1932. Pp. 211–260.

Waurick, G. "Kunstraub der Römer. Untersuchungen zu seinen Anfängen anhand der Inschriften." *Jahrbuch des Römisch-Germanischen Zentralmuseums* 22 (1975 [1977]) 1–46.

Weinberg, G. D. *Glass Vessels in Ancient Greece.* Athens 1992.

Chapter 14

Geagan, D. J. *The Athenian Constitution after Sulla. Hesperia Suppl.* 12 (1967).

——— "A Family of Marathon and Social Mobility in Athens of the First Century B.C." *Phoenix* 46 (1992) 29–44.

——— "Greek Inscriptions: A Law Code of the First Century B.C." *Hesperia* 40 (1971) 101–108.

Graindor, P. *Chronologie des archontes athéniens sous l'empire.* Brussels 1922.

Hoff, M. C. "Civil Disobedience and Unrest in Augustan Athens." *Hesperia* 58 (1989) 267–276.

Kienast, H. J. "Untersuchungen am Turm der Winde." *AA* (1993) 271–275.

Migeotte, L. *L'emprunt public dans les cités grecques.* Québec 1984.

Millar, F. "Cornelius Nepos, 'Atticus' and the Roman Revolution." *G&R* 35 (1988) 40–55.

Münzer, F. "Memmius." *RE* 10 (1931) 609–615.

Perlwitz, O. *Titus Pomponius Atticus.* Stuttgart 1992.

Raubitschek, A. E. "Phaidros and His Roman Pupils." *Hesperia* 18 (1949) 96–103.

Rawson, E. "Cicero and the Areopagus." *Athenaeum* 73 (1985) 44–67.

Sarikakis, T. "The Hoplite General in Athens." Diss. Princeton 1951.

Steinhauer, G. "Inscription agoranomique du Pirée." *BCH* 118 (1994) 51–68.

Thompson, H. A. "The Impact of Roman Architects and Architecture on Athens, 170 B.C.–A.D. 170." In *Roman Architecture in the Greek World.* Ed. S. Macready and F. H. Thompson. London 1987. Pp. 1–17.

Touloumakos, J. *Der Einfluss Roms auf die Staatsform der griechischen Stadtstaaten des Festlandes und der Inseln im ersten und zweiten Jahrhundert v. Chr.* Diss. Göttingen 1977.

von Freeden, J. Οἰκία Κυρρήστου. *Studien zum sogenannten Turm der Winde in Athen.* Rome 1983.

Chapter 15

Bowersock, G. W. *Augustus and the Greek World*. Oxford 1965.

Broneer, O. "Some Greek Inscriptions of Roman Date from Attica, I." *AJA* 36 (1932) 393–397.

Broughton, T. R. S. *The Magistrates of the Roman Republic*. 3 vols. New York 1951–1986.

Errington, R. M. "Aspects of Roman Acculturation in the East under the Republic." In *Alte Geschichte und Wissenschaftsgeschichte. Festschrift Karl Christ*. Ed. P. Kneissl and V. Losemann. Darmstadt 1988. Pp. 140–157.

Gelzer, M. *Caesar, der Politiker und Staatsmann*[6]. Wiesbaden 1960.

Graindor, P. *Athènes sous Auguste*. Brussels 1927.

Gruen, E. S. *Roman Politics and the Criminal Courts, 149–78 B.C.* Cambridge 1968.

Hatzfeld, J. *Les trafiquants italiens dans l'Orient hellénique*. Paris 1919.

Hölscher, T. "Die Geschlagenen und Ausgelieferten in der Kunst des Hellenismus." *Antike Kunst* 28 (1985) 120–136.

Hoff, M. C. "Augustus, Apollo, and Athens." *MH* 49 (1992) 223–232.

——— "The So-called Agoranomion and the Imperial Cult in Julio-Claudian Athens." *AA* (1994) 93–117.

Le Roy, H. "Richesse et exploitation en Laconie au Ier siècle av. J.-C." *Ktema* 3 (1978) 261–266.

O'Brien-Moore, A. "Tullius Cratippus, Priest of Rome: *CIL* III 399." *YClS* 8 (1942) 25–49.

Oliver, J. H. "The Descendants of Asinius Pollio." *AJPh* 68 (1947) 147–160.

Pecírka, J. *The Formula for the Grant of Enktesis in Attic Inscriptions*. Prague 1966.

Pelling, C. B. R., ed. *Plutarch: Life of Antony*. Cambridge 1988.

Raubitschek, A. E. "Brutus in Athens." *Phoenix* 11 (1957) 1–11.

——— "The Brutus Statue in Athens." In *Atti del terzo congresso internazionale di epigrafia Greca e Latina*. Rome 1959. Pp. 15–21.

——— "Epigraphical Notes on Julius Caesar." *JRS* 44 (1954) 65–75.

——— "Octavia's Deification at Athens." *TAPhA* 77 (1946) 146–150.

Reinmuth, O. W. "*IG* II[2], 1006 and 1031." *Hesperia* 41 (1972) 185–191.

Shear, T. L., Jr. "Athens: From City-state to Provincial Town." *Hesperia* 50 (1981) 356–377.

Syme, R. *The Roman Revolution*. Oxford 1939.

Wilson, A. J. N. *Emigration from Italy in the Republican Age of Rome*. Manchester 1966.

INDEX